FRAUDS, MYTHS, AND MYSTERIES

Science and Pseudoscience in Archaeology

FIFTH EDITION

KENNETH L. FEDER

Central Connecticut State University

Boston   Burr Ridge, IL   Dubuque, IA   Madison, WI   New York
San Francisco   St. Louis   Bangkok   Bogotá   Caracas   Kuala Lumpur
Lisbon   London   Madrid   Mexico City   Milan   Montreal   New Delhi
Santiago   Seoul   Singapore   Sydney   Taipei   Toronto

Higher Education

Published by McGraw-Hill, an imprint of The McGraw-Hill Companies, Inc.,
1221 Avenue of the Americas, New York, NY 10020.

This book is printed on acid-free paper.

1 2 3 4 5 6 7 8 9 0 DOC/DOC 0 9 8 7 6 5

ISBN 0-07-286948-8

Editor in Chief: Emily Barrosse
Publisher: Phillip Butcher
Sponsoring Editor: Kevin Witt
Marketing Manager: Dan Loch
Production Editor: Holly Paulsen
Manuscript Editor: Joan Pendleton
Design Manager: Cassandra Chu
Text Designers: Donna Davis,
   Glenda King
Cover Designer: Cassandra Chu
Art Editor: Ayelet Arbel

Illustrators: Carto-graphics, Joan Carol,
   John and Judy Waller, and
   Ayelet Arbel
Photo Research Manager: Brian Pecko
Production Supervisor: Tandra
   Jorgensen
Composition: 10/12.5 Palatino by
   Thompson Type
Printing: 45# Pub Matte, R. R. Donnelley
   & Sons/Crawfordsville, IN
Cover: © Royalty-Free/Corbis

Library of Congress Cataloging-in-Pubication Data has been applied for.

The Internet addresses listed in the text were accurate at the time of publication.
The inclusion of a Web site does not indicate an endorsement by the authors
or McGraw-Hill, and McGraw-Hill does not guarantee the accuracy of the
information presented at these sites.

www.mhhe.com

For Lissa

◈◈◈◈◈◈◈◈◈◈◈ ◈◈◈◈◈◈◈◈◈◈◈

Preface

Frauds, myths, and supposed mysteries about humanity's past are moving targets for those of us committed to the scientific investigation of human antiquity. Clearly, it is important for anyone interested in the human past to know, for example, that there is no evidence for a race of giant human beings in antiquity, no broken shards of laser guns under Egyptian pyramids, and no proof that thousands of years ago ancient Polynesian explorers were racking up frequent flyer miles rocketing from island to island on spacecraft left behind by globe-trotting extraterrestrial aliens. Debunking such nonsense is fun and useful in its own way, but of much greater importance is the process we employ to determine that such claims *are* nonsense. The utility of *Frauds, Myths, and Mysteries* rests in its use of interesting and often hilarious archaeological hoaxes, myths, and mysteries to show how we can *truly* know things about the past through science.

Frauds, Myths, and Mysteries:
The Book That Almost Never Was

When I first began circulating the manuscript for this book back in 1986, I was hopeful that *Frauds* had at least the potential to make a meaningful contribution to the teaching of archaeology. I was confident that it would be a valuable resource for my colleagues, and, most important, I was convinced that it would be a book students would enjoy. Apparently I was the only one who thought so. I no longer remember the precise number of rejection letters my unsolicited manuscript produced; I think I stopped counting at sixteen. Those letters were dreary in their sameness—metaphorical pats on the head for producing an "unusual manuscript" that seemed very interesting, but not one that might lead to a book that archaeologists would be willing to consider for adoption in their courses. After all, the rejection letters maintained, a semester is already too short a period of time to cover all the methodology that should be covered in an introductory archaeology course. That same semester framework, I was told, hardly allows sufficient time in a world prehistory survey course to cover the breadth of human antiquity. There just wouldn't be enough time in standard archaeology and prehistory courses to include a deconstruction of preexisting misapprehensions students might harbor about the archaeological record and its study. And while the book seemed well suited to a course dedicated to the discussion of popular misconceptions about antiquity—the discussion, in fact, of "frauds, myths, and mysteries" about the human past—there couldn't be very many such courses in the first place.

I think the low point in my quest to find a home for *Frauds* came when one particular book representative seemed, at first, quite interested, in fact even excited about the manuscript, and took a copy to pass along to his publisher's anthropology editor. At last, I thought, someone who might actually see the value in publishing my book. When I hadn't heard from the rep in about six months I called, only to be told by him that, well, actually, he hadn't passed it along to the anthropology editor because he had lost the manuscript in a hotel room a couple of days after I had handed it to him. Brilliant.

Finally, along came Jan Beatty, then of Mayfield Publishing. I knew Jan from another book of mine and I passed the manuscript along to her, just for her wise counsel, hoping for a suggestion or two, never really thinking that Mayfield would be interested. Jan read through it, called, and suggested that before I sent it to anyone else she would send it out for review. At the time, I thought that she and the Mayfield crew did this merely as a favor to me. I was wrong. Jan is a terrific editor with a great track record for signing successful anthropology texts and saw potential in the *Frauds* book where others didn't. The fact that this book is going into its fifth edition is a direct reflection of its success, a success made possible by Jan's vision. I am forever grateful for her support.

What's New in the Fifth Edition?

Though there is nothing magical about the number five, it seemed that the fifth edition of *Frauds* presented an opportunity to assess more deeply what worked and what didn't work as well in the book. As a result, this new edition marks the most substantial revision of *Frauds* to date, with a merging of two chapters into one and the addition of a brand new chapter.

Specifically, I have made the following revisions.

Chapter 1: Science and Pseudoscience
New surveys of levels of student acceptance of extreme claims about the human past are included in this chapter.

Chapter 2: Epistemology: How You Know What You Know

An entirely rewritten discussion of the science behind the solution of the childbed fever mystery is presented.

Chapter 3: Anatomy of an Archaeological Hoax

The title of this chapter has been changed to reflect a change in its focus. Though the Cardiff Giant remains a lynchpin in my discussion of archaeological fakery, the chapter is now much more firmly grounded in a consideration of archaeological fraud in general. The first part of the chapter deals with the Fujimura debacle in Japan, and the Current Perspectives section details the ways in which Connecticut archaeologists exposed the Pachaug Forest archaeological fakes.

Chapter 4: Dawson's Dawn Man: The Hoax at Piltdown

Charles Dawson's background is more fully explored, revealing a long history of involvement with questionable discoveries.

Chapter 5: Who Discovered America?

Those familiar with previous editions of *Frauds* will notice a major change here. The discussion of the historical and archaeological investigation of the initial human settlement of the New World (previously Chapter 5) and evidence of the exploration and settlement of the New World by people from the Old (previously Chapter 6) has been entirely reorganized, combined into a single chapter, and made more succinct. New material in this chapter includes a detailed discussion of the Piri Reis map and the claim made in a recent popular book by author Gavin Menzies that the Chinese discovered and settled the New World in the early fifteenth century, some seventy years before the first Columbus expedition.

Chapter 6: The Myth of the Moundbuilders

A more thorough and detailed discussion of the Newark Holy Stones is provided.

Chapter 7: Lost: One Continent—Reward

A new discussion and map are presented here, detailing the many places where Atlantis has been claimed to have been found.

Chapter 8: Prehistoric E.T.: The Fantasy of Ancient Astronauts

Now that Erich von Däniken's ancient astronaut theme park has opened, it was only fair to add a discussion of what appears to be the silliest place on Earth. The discussion of the archaeology of Mars has been expanded.

Chapter 9: Mysterious Egypt

This is a new chapter, focusing on the archaeology of ancient Egypt. I present archaeological evidence for the evolutionary development of the Egyptian pyramid—without invoking globe-trotting Atlanteans, ancient astronauts, or a spectacularly advanced civilization based at the South Pole. Another section of the chapter addresses the reign of the pharaoh Tutankhamun, and the evidence, or lack thereof, for a curse on his tomb.

Chapter 10: Good Vibrations: Psychics and Dowsers

Did Nostradamus predict the destruction of the World Trade Center in New York City? Read this chapter and find out.

Chapter 11: Old Time Religion—New Age Visions

Intelligent design and the hypothesis that the flood story told in the Bible is based on an early Holocene, catastrophic in-filling of the Black Sea are addressed here.

Chapter 12: Real Mysteries of a Veritable Past

The section on the "mystery" of the Maya has been rewritten and expanded.

Special Features of *Frauds*

- Each chapter continues to have an associated **Frequently Asked Questions** section. These questions represent a sample of queries from my students over the years that relate specifically to the issues and controversies addressed in the chapter.

- The informal, uncontrolled, unfiltered, and freewheeling context of the Web continues to have exciting implications for disseminating information about the human past. These same qualities of the Internet, however, also mean that more misinformation about the past can be spread to a far greater number of people far more quickly. Rumors about the discovery of Noah's Ark or the excavation of extraterrestrial alien bodies beneath an Egyptian pyramid can appear on anyone's computer anywhere in the world virtually the instant such stories are fabricated. Tall tales about the human past no longer need rely on word of mouth to be spread; anyone with a computer, a modem, and an Internet provider can shout such nonsense to the world. The good news here is that archaeologists can shout back. There are many fine Web sites presenting genuine archaeological discoveries and some that respond explicitly to the folderol that dogs our discipline. Each chapter includes an annotated list under the title **Best of the Web** with a selection of Web sites (and their Internet addresses) put up by museums, individual archaeologists (amateur and professional), anthropology departments, and others. A brief description of what each of these sites presents is a new feature to this edition. Don't look for the bizarre, absurd, extreme, or nonsensical on my lists. These sites are produced by people who conduct field research, analyze artifacts and sites, and are committed to the scientific interpretation of the human past.

- To make it easier to locate and scan the Best of the Web sites, the *Frauds* **home page** is available at www.mhhe.com/frauds5. Every Web site listed in the Best of the Web sections of *Frauds* is linked to and accessible through the *Frauds* page. Instead of typing in the URLs, you need only to get onto the *Frauds* page. From there, click on any of the *Frauds* chapters and you will call up the addresses for the Best of the Web sites for that chapter. Then simply click on any of the URLs and you will be taken to that site.

- Each chapter continues to provide **Critical Thinking Exercises.** In these I attempt to challenge the reader to apply the scientific method and scientific reasoning to the general issues raised in the specific archaeological examples that are at the core of each chapter. In answering the questions posed or in carrying out the specific exercise, the reader must be able to synthesize and apply the most important messages of the chapter.

- The *Reality Check* that appeared on the inside front and back covers in the fourth edition has been moved to immediately after the contents and renamed the **Quick Start Guide.** It made more sense to put the whole thing together in one place where readers would be more certain to read it. The renaming more accurately reflects its purpose.

- The **Video Companion Guide,** of use primarily to professors using videos in a course, has been removed from the printed book and placed on the *Frauds* Web site. The purpose of this guide is twofold: (1) to direct readers to helpful video documentaries of the topics covered in each of the chapters of this book, and (2) to assist the professor who is looking for audiovisual material to accompany this book in a university course.

Acknowledgments

I have the terrific folks at McGraw-Hill to thank for making this edition of *Frauds* such a pleasant undertaking. Thanks especially to Cassandra Chu and freelance designer Glenda King for the absolutely gorgeous design of the book; I think it's the best yet. Brian Pecko at McGraw-Hill is a magician, though his official title is Photo Research Manager. His ability to find often obscure images for use in my books is nothing short of remarkable. Holly Paulsen has been the production editor for the fourth and fifth editions of *Frauds.* Not only has she made my job much easier, *Frauds* is a much better book because of her work behind the scenes. Freelance copyeditor Joan Pendleton is a joy to work with. I told the folks at McGraw-Hill that I would hold my breath until I turned blue if they couldn't convince Joan to copyedit the fifth edition. My threat worked and I have been breathing comfortably ever since. Finally, my senior sponsoring editor at McGraw-Hill, Kevin Witt, is just plain fun to work with. When you look up the term "unflappable" in the dictionary, you'll find Kevin's photograph. Kevin just makes it all work, no problem.

Friends both old and new and many colleagues contributed in various ways to the successful completion of this edition of *Frauds*. For their always gentle corrections, for the role some served as a sounding board, for their generosity with their photographs and reprints, and for their assistance in tracking down artwork, I would like to thank Nick Bellantoni, Lawrence B. Conyers, Garrett Fagan, Jeff Gill, Nathalie Guenette, Colin Harty, Charles A. Hoffman, Kevin Ihrig, Brad Lepper, Frédéric Paradis, Frank Roy, Patricia Sutherland, and John Wall.

Reviewers make a crucial contribution to a new edition of a book. Usually, these folks are using the current version in the classroom and are acutely aware of what works and what doesn't and, especially in the case of *Frauds*, what misconceptions are currently bedeviling those who teach archaeology. Many grateful thanks to the reviewers of this edition:

Mark J. Hartmann
University of Arkansas

Susan Johnston
George Washington University

Dr. Marie Selvaggio
Southern Connecticut State University

Robert Simpkins
San Jose State University

Alexia Smith
Harvard University

LuAnn Wandasnider
University of Nebraska, Lincoln

Thanks as always to my father, Dr. Murray H. Feder, for his historical insights, splendid photographs, and late-night phone calls. And thanks as well to my mother, who complained that she didn't get appropriate acknowledgment in some previous editions of this book. It was an oversight, Mom.

This book has grown up with my now eighteen-year-old son. In fact, one of Josh's first intelligible sequences of words referred to my writing the first edition: "Dada work, book." More than a decade later it's nice to know that he still finds its content interesting enough to want to occasionally chat with his old man about it. My younger guy, Jacob, isn't sure what all the fuss is about but seems at least amused when he sees his dad on the television being interviewed about Atlantis, the Cardiff Giant, or King Tut's curse.

Finally, an author's acknowledgment of the contribution of a spouse often seems a dispassionate formality. My "thank you" to my wife, Melissa, is anything but. This book is dedicated to her; it always has been and always will be. Truly, her love and support, as well as a degree of emotional stability far surpassing my own, are what make the whole enterprise—our lives together as well as working on books—not a fraud or a myth, but a lovely mystery.

Contents

◈◈◈◈◈◈◈◈◈◈ ◈◈◈◈◈◈◈◈◈◈

Quick Start Guide

I have just purchased a digital camera. Scattered across its sides, back, and top are more buttons than I could have possibly imagined when I opened the box. Some of them are labeled with arcane and, to be honest, incomprehensible icons, things like lightning bolts, tulips, and mountains. Others are marked with mysterious names printed in tiny letters, things like QUICK (is the camera commanding me to hurry up?), FUNC (I beg your pardon), and MF (I don't want to even consider what the camera is telling me here).

Okay, it's all very confusing and complicated to me. There is a thick manual that I understand I will need to read to be able to use the camera to its fullest capability, but I want to get started—I want to jump ahead a bit and take the thing out for a spin. Fortunately, the camera came with a highly condensed version of the key information contained in the manual. It's called the *Quick Start Guide,* and it provides a very brief, succinct summary of the information needed to begin using the camera.

It occurs to me that this book is, in fact, a thick manual focusing on how to think about the human past. Certainly, you need to read the entire "manual" to understand what you need to know to assess claims made about human antiquity, but the equivalent of a Quick Start Guide would be a useful prelude to the book. My version of a Quick Start Guide follows.

During the time it takes you to read this book, you will likely encounter—in newspapers and magazines, on television shows, in books, and on Web sites—assertions about the human past that contradict views widely accepted by archaeologists. Some of these claims can easily be proven false, but some may be accurate. How can you assess the validity of an extraordinary claim or revolutionary interpretation about the human past that appears in popular media? Though there is no simple way to determine accuracy absolutely, you can make a good start in your assessment by answering the following questions.

◈ Where is the particular claim or discovery presented? Is it in an article in a peer-reviewed journal, where other scientists in the same field have had an opportunity to appraise its validity? Does the story appear in a widely respected magazine with science advisors on its staff, in a newspaper article written by an experienced science writer, or in a television news report or special series produced by a national network or a science-based organization? These are all sources that we can feel confident in. Of course, they are not perfect, but they usually check their facts and apply the scientific method (see Chapter 2). On the other hand, is the report about the human past found on an anonymous Web site with no attributed source, in the informal discussions of an Internet chat group, or in an audiovisual presentation prepared by an individual affiliated with a political or religious organization with a particular axe to grind? In these cases, it is wise to be skeptical about the objectivity of the source and the accuracy of the claim.

◈ Who is making the claim? Is it a trained scientist? Just as important, is it a researcher trained in archaeology, anthropology, or history? Remember, a scientist skilled in an unrelated field may be no better prepared than a nonscientist to assess an archaeological discovery or interpretation. Certainly, researchers with Ph.D.'s in archaeology, anthropology, or history make mistakes in their chosen fields, but they are less likely to make mistakes on issues related to the human past than are people with little experience or study in those fields.

◈ In assessing the validity of any assertion about the human past that appears in popular media, you need to ask yourself this question: How does the person announcing the discovery, making the claim, or interpreting the results of a study "know"? Does the discussion or claim seem to follow standard scientific thinking as presented in this and other books that explain how science works (see Table 2.1)? Are hypotheses based on observations? Are hypotheses tested with independent data? Among a series of explanations offered for some phenomenon, is the simplest one (with no other unsupported assumptions) presented as the most probable? Or does the claimant instead assert that his or her knowledge is simply the result of revelation or intuition and that no proof is needed?

◈ Are other experts consulted, and how do they respond to the claims being made? Are other scientists convinced? Are other scientists uncertain, skeptical, but intrigued? Are other scientists quite certain the claims are unfounded, and on what basis are they so skeptical? Are alternate points of view offered; are other interpretations presented? Accepting the authority of scientists just because they have diplomas or teach at prestigious universities is a mistake, but when experienced researchers working in the same field are universally skeptical, it's a pretty good idea for you to be skeptical too—unless and until supporting data are forthcoming.

◈ Are confirming data presented? Are the "petrified giant," the humanlike cranium with the apelike jaw, the Hebrew tablet in the ancient archaeological site in Ohio, and other archaeological "mysteries" unique, one-of-a-kind objects, or are scientists able to confirm the validity of these by finding additional examples?

◈ Is enough information presented for you to make an informed decision concerning the legitimacy of what is being asserted? Or, instead, are you left with important questions that the report simply does not address?

Analyze new ideas about the human past with the same careful approach you would apply when purchasing a used car. Have an open mind but be skeptical of unwarranted claims.

◈◈◈◈◈◈◈ **1** ◈◈◈◈◈◈◈

Science and Pseudoscience

Extrasensory perception. Astrology. Faith healing. Alien abductions. Palmistry. Reincarnation. Pyramid power. Ancient astronauts. Crop circles. Feng shui. If all of the claims related to these and other supposed phenomena were true, this world would be an extraordinarily strange place, far different from what orthodox science would suppose.

Cats would be psychic. Children could bend spoons with the power of their minds. Aliens from outer space would regularly fly over the earth, kidnap people, and perform medical exams on them, with a particular emphasis on bodily orifices. Along with their medical research, the aliens would flatten farmers' wheat crops, leaving monumentally scaled, perplexing, but beautiful designs in their fields.

People could read minds, and your future could be predicted by shuffling and dealing a special deck of playing cards (called Tarot). A sixteenth-century physician could have predicted the September 11 attack on the United States with chilling accuracy. Sleeping under a pyramid-shaped bedframe would be conducive to good health, and wearing a quartz crystal suspended on a chain around your neck would make you more energetic. The exact location and positioning of your furniture and the orientation of the stairway leading to the second floor of your house would play a substantial role in determining your health as well as your economic and psychological well-being.

Furthermore, the precise locations of enormously distant celestial bodies at the instant of your birth would determine your personality as well as your future. People could find water, treasure, and even archaeological sites with forked sticks or bent coat hangers. In the strange world we are pondering here, Elvis would still be alive, visiting shopping malls and making regular midnight runs to convenience stores for Slim Jims and MoonPies.

Beyond this, if all of the claims were true, people living today would actually have lived many times in the past and could remember when they were kings or artists (few would remember being ordinary). And hundreds of boats and planes and thousands of people would have disappeared under mysterious circumstances in the dreaded "Bermuda Triangle."

And there's more. Plants would think and have feelings, dolphins would write poetry, and cockroaches would be clairvoyant. Autism could be cured through exorcism (though, to be honest, in the one cited case, the cure was worse than the condition and the child died during the procedure). Some people would spontaneously burst into flames for no apparent reason; and tiny ridges on your hands, bumps on your head, and even the shape of your behind could be used to understand your personality.

In this extraordinary version of the world, it might not be a bad idea to insure yourself against the possibility of being abducted by extraterrestrials. I personally am covered for $10 million (for the low, low price of $19.95, as offered by an insurance agency in Florida). My heirs can double this payment to $20 million if they are able to prove that the aliens ate me!

In this world of infinite possibilities, all your problems could be solved by a stranger at the other end of a 1-900 psychic hotline or by your feng shui consultant, and your health would improve dramatically simply by putting magnetic inserts into your shoes. Finally, in this most peculiar world, human prehistory could best be understood as the result of supernatural occurrences, enormous cataclysms, and the interference of extraterrestrial space aliens.

It would be a strange world indeed, and the list of extreme, mysterious, and occult claims goes on and on (Figure 1.1). For many of you, some of these claims—all of which have actually been published—might seem to be interesting to think about. Maybe you are a fan of one of the many television shows that tend to blur the distinction between fact and fiction (*The X-Files* is the most obvious of these). Perhaps you have dialed a 1-900 phone number, looking for psychic insights into your future. Maybe you believe that it's good to have an open mind and that some of the remarkable claims listed here are plausible.

Belief in the Unbelievable

If you find yourself in agreement with at least some of these claims, rest assured, you are not alone. Not long ago, an entertainment/news television show conducted a survey among watchers concerning their opinions on some controversial claims. More than a quarter of those responding believed in the accuracy of dreams in foretelling the future, 12 percent believed in the utility of astrological forecasts, and 22 percent accepted the reality of clairvoyance in predicting the future. In the same sample, 3 percent of those re-

HUMANS EVOLVED FROM PIGS

BELGIUM DESTROYED BY ROGUE ASTEROID!
AND NO ONE NOTICES!

APE GIVES BIRTH TO HUMAN BABY

Space Alien Skull Found

MYSTERIOUS CROP CIRCLES WERE MADE BY SUPER-SMART ANTS

ARCHAEOLOGIST DISCOVERS LOST ARMS OF VENUS DE MILO

FORGET ABOUT THE FACE ON MARS.... NASA PROBE HAS SPOTTED THE BUTT ON MARS

Bush's Secret Plan... Invade Atlantis!

3000-YEAR-OLD PRIESTESS REVIVED IN TOP-SECRET LIBYA LAB!

Figure 1.1 Actual headlines as they appeared in issues of tabloid, or "supermarket," newspapers.

sponding also expressed confidence in the accuracy of predictions contained in fortune cookies!

In a Gallup poll conducted in 1996 among a representative sample likely reflecting the opinions of the American public, 45 percent believed that extraterrestrial aliens have visited the earth and that UFOs are their spacecraft; 12 percent of that same sample reported having actually seen one of those craft (Newport 1997). Another polling agency, Yankelovich Partners, obtained comparable results in 1997 on these and similar issues; 37 percent of its sample of 1,000 people accepted the validity of astrology, 45 percent believed faith healing to be effective, and 25 percent believed in reincarnation (Nisbet 1999). More recently, the Harris Poll found that 31 percent of a sample of more than 2,000 American adults accept the validity of astrology and 51 percent believe in ghosts (Taylor 2003).

Perhaps people who watch "infotainment" TV are naive and those members of the American public included in polls are generally gullible. One might hope, however, that bright, highly educated college students are probably a lot less likely to fall for such claims. But I have taken several surveys of college students at various institutions (Feder 1984, 1987, 1995b, 1998, 2004), and there is a depressingly high level of belief in unsubstantiated claims about the human past even among university students.

For example, 27 percent of my 1983 student sample agreed (either strongly or mildly) with the claim that extraterrestrial aliens visited our planet in the distant past and were responsible for teaching our ancestors to build things like the pyramids (Figure 1.2a; see Chapter 9). The percentage of believers grew to a peak in 1994 (about 32 percent), dropped to 15 percent in 1998, rose back up to 21 percent in 2000, and then, thankfully, dropped to a low of only about 6 percent in 2003 (Figure 1.2a). Belief that the Lost Continent of Atlantis was a real place and not just the literary invention of the Greek philosopher Plato (see Chapter 7) has been remarkably stable during the last two decades, measuring at about 29% in 1983, 1994, and 1998, rising to an astonishingly high 43 percent in 2000, and then dropping to the still extremely high level of 33 percent in the 2003 sample (Figure 1.2b). Acceptance of the claim that an ancient curse on the tomb of the Egyptian pharaoh Tutankhamun killed archaeologists involved in excavating the tomb and analyzing its contents (see Chapter 9) has alternately risen and fallen during the last twenty years (Figure 1.2c). In 1983, 12 percent of my student sample expressed some level of belief in Tut's curse. The percentage of believers doubled to 24 percent in 1994, dropped to 15 percent in 1998, jumped back up to a whopping 34 percent in 2000, and dropped to a still high 22 percent in 2003.

Throughout the years and for each of these and other archaeological topics, high percentages of students opted for the don't know/no opinion response. Some might argue that this is a good sign. After all, isn't it reasonable for students to recognize their own ignorance and admit that they don't know enough to react either positively or negatively to such claims? Perhaps. However, as researcher Susan Richardson (1999:36) has pointed out, "Given that most of the cult archaeologies have been more than adequately discredited, the 'undecided' option seems far from satisfactory." I would have to agree with her assessment.

Maybe it's just American students who are simply gullible or ill-informed. What about students in other countries? How do they respond

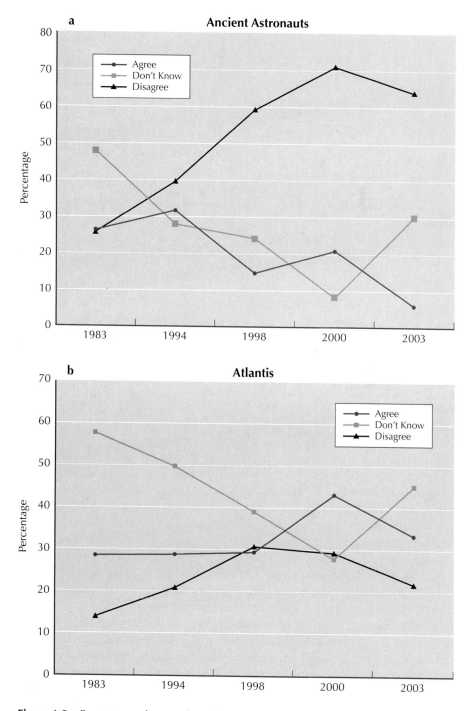

Figure 1.2 Percentage of my students in 1983, 1994, 1998, 2000, and 2003 who agreed with, were not sure about (didn't know), or disagreed with these statements: "Aliens from other worlds visited the earth in the prehistoric past" **(a)**, "There is good evidence for the existence of the Lost Continent of Atlantis" **(b)**,   *(continued)*

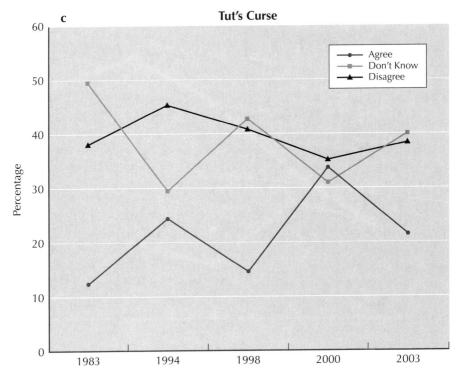

Figure 1.2 (continued) "An ancient curse placed on the tomb of the Egyptian Pharaoh, King Tut, actually killed people" **(c)**.

when faced with these same claims about the human past? In 1996, Dirk Spennemann at Charles Stuart University in New South Wales, Australia, distributed a questionnaire similar to mine to 142 of his university students. His results were quite similar to those we derived from the American sample (Spennemann 1996). More recently, Susan C. Richardson conducted a similar survey as part of her master's thesis in archaeology at the University of Southampton in England (1999). Using many of the questions from my original study, she found students at her university to be a bit more skeptical than those in my American sample. For example, only about 10 percent of her students expressed some level of belief in the ancient astronaut hypothesis, 16 percent similarly expressed belief in the Lost Continent of Atlantis, and 10 percent accepted the notion that there was an effective, deadly curse on the tomb of King Tut. One cannot conclude from this, however, that British students are better informed than their American counterparts. Few of the British students actually rejected such claims; the largest percentages held the opinion that the evidence on these issues was inconclusive (Richardson 1999:37).

But wait. You might reasonably ask if the kinds of beliefs or claims mentioned in the surveys discussed here can be dismissed so easily. "Science," after all, is merely a process of understanding the world around us through the application of logical thought (see Chapter 2). Most of us like to think of ourselves as scientific-minded, but is science perfect? Do scientists know everything? Are they always right? Of course not. Science has scoffed at things in the past that eventually turned out to be true (see the discussion of meteors in Chapter 2). Maybe scientists are wrong to dismiss a lot of other interesting claims. Maybe there is more to some of these claims than closed-minded scientists are willing to admit. There could be something to UFOs, ESP, astrology, reincarnation, palmistry, biorhythms, fortune telling, dowsing, feng shui, ancient astronauts, faith healing, and so on; magazines, television, and movies flaunt these topics frequently. They can't all be fake, can they?

I have a confession to make. I used to read books on flying saucers and psychic power. I owned a Ouija board and a pendulum, and I analyzed handwriting and conducted ESP tests. I felt that there had to be some truth to these interesting ideas.

But it bothered me that the results of my ESP tests never really deviated from chance expectations, and my Ouija board didn't work at all. I owned a small telescope and spent a lot of time looking at the nighttime sky, but I never saw anything that did not have some natural or ordinary explanation (an airplane, helicopter, blimp, bird, satellite, star, planet, or whatever). Yet I kept searching. Like most people, I was fascinated by these possibilities rejected by orthodox science. In truth, I wanted to believe.

In the late 1960s, lured by the promise of four books for a dollar in the introductory offer, I signed up for a book club catering to occult tastes. In return, I received *The Complete, Illustrated Book of the Psychic Sciences; Yoga, Youth, and Reincarnation; The Black Arts;* and *The Morning of the Magicians.* The first three contained interesting little tidbits that seemed perfectly reasonable to me at the time: evidence of "real" hauntings and prophetic dreams, the usefulness of astrology, testimony about people's subconscious memories of past lives, and so on. The yoga book, along with some strange claims about reincarnation, actually taught some healthy exercises.

It was the fourth book, though, that really opened my eyes. Without their knowing it, the authors of this marvelous collection of outrageous claims, Louis Pauwels and Jacques Bergier (1960), played an important role in converting me from a completely credulous individual, open to all sorts of absolutely absurd ideas, to a scientific rationalist, still open to the possibility of all sorts of absolutely absurd ideas, but demanding substantial evidence that, unfortunately, their claims all seemed to lack.

The Morning of the Magicians

Remarkable claims about things scientists were trying to hide from the public filled *The Morning of the Magicians*—evidence for reincarnation, levitation, ghosts, and so on. As always when I read most of these books, the first claim left me excited and fascinated. The second claim provided almost the same sense of intellectual exhilaration. But the third, fourth, fifth, and sixth were just more of the same. I slowly began to lose the ability to be surprised by the authors' claims of effective magical incantations, telepathy, the mystically engineered transformation of lead to gold, and the like. As exciting as any one of these claims might have been, the cumulative effect was simply a buildup of an intellectual resistance to surprise. I became immune to the claims. I was bored.

In skimming through the book, I found a section on remarkable discoveries in prehistoric archaeology related to the occult. It surprised me that there was any archaeology in the book at all; I had never considered connections between the occult and archaeology. Fascinated by the possibilities, I immediately began to read that section.

I was absolutely appalled by what I read. I knew quite a bit about the archaeological topics they discussed, and what they said was incredible. Their claims about Egyptian pyramids; the massive, carved stone heads of Easter Island; the ancient culture of Peru; and other archaeological artifacts, sites, and cultures were based on misinformation, twisted facts, and misrepresentation of archaeological data and the study of the past.

At their very best, the authors' claims showed extreme ignorance. For example, their assertions about the super-sophistication of prehistoric metallurgy in South America were misleading. Their insistence that this industry was somehow mysterious ignored very well documented sixteenth-century eyewitness accounts by Spanish explorers of the native metal-making process.

Their claims about advanced information exhibited in the dimensions of the Egyptian pyramids—the distance from the earth to the sun, for example, and the precise value of pi—had been made years before. Such claims were invariably based on incorrect measurements, miscalculation, and not just a little wishful thinking.

The authors' extraordinarily strange view of the past is best summed up in their own words:

> It is possible that our civilization is the result of a long struggle to obtain from machines the powers that primitive man possessed, enabling him to communicate from a distance, to rise into the air, to liberate the energy of matter, abolish gravitation, etc. (Pauwels and Bergier 1960:109)

In other words, according to the authors of *The Morning of the Magicians*, today we are simply rediscovering abilities that prehistoric people had—the ability to fly, to harness the energy of the atom, and to communicate electronically, for example. Although today we do so with machines, prehistoric people apparently could do it with their minds. Pauwels and Bergier were honest enough; they had entirely, openly, and unabashedly abandoned a skeptical approach: "No hypothesis is excluded: an atomic civilization long before what we call the prehistoric era; enlightenment received from the inhabitants of Another World, etc." (p. 105).

On simple facts, they were consistently wrong. These were things that might not be noticed by a nonarchaeologist. For example, they stated that the Toltecs built the Pyramid of the Sun at the Mexican site of Teotihuacán (p. 115). That's like saying that billionaire real estate developer Donald Trump built the White House. Teotihuacán was at its peak more than 700 years before the Toltecs rose to power.

In South America, the authors noted with amazement, archaeologists have found statues of camels, "which are unknown in South America" (p. 114), implying some sort of ancient mystery. Yet camels originated in South America, where four separate camel-like species still exist (llama, alpaca, vicuña, and guanaco). The authors of *The Morning of the Magicians* also stated that there were prehistoric statues of dinosaurs in South America, though science tells us that the last of the dinosaurs became extinct some 60 million years ago (see Chapter 11 in this book).

They stated that the Maya civilization of Mesoamerica is "far older than that of Greece" (p. 115). Yet classical Greece dates to well over 2,500 years ago, whereas the Maya civilization was at its peak more than a thousand years later, barely 1,500 years ago.

How, I wondered, could authors who seemed so well informed about physics, psychology, chemistry, biology, and history be so confused when it came to my own field of archaeology? How could they so eloquently "prove" the existence of all sorts of occult things related to these other fields of science and be so lacking in their knowledge of the human past?

Then it struck me. Of all of the disciplines discussed in *The Morning of the Magicians,* archaeology was the only one with which I had more than just a passing familiarity. The more I thought about it, the clearer it became. The often bizarre claims in *The Morning of the Magicians* that were related to physics, chemistry, biology, psychology, and history seemed reasonable to me primarily because I did not have the knowledge necessary to assess them intelligently.

It was a valuable lesson indeed. The authors had not mysteriously abandoned scholarly research and the scientific method (see Chapter 2 of this book) only in the one field in which I was well versed. As I looked further into their claims, it became obvious that they had ignored the truth in just about every phenomenon they had described.

I began to read a number of books written by scientists in various fields who had been similarly appalled by the extreme claims made by occultists like Pauwels and Bergier. Again and again, I saw reactions and arguments that mirrored mine after reading the prehistory section of *The Morning of the Magicians.* When astronomers analyzed claims about extraterrestrial life, astrology, and UFOs; when psychologists examined telepathy and clairvoyance; when physicists and chemists investigated alleged evidence for perpetual motion machines or alchemy, they were nearly unanimous in their skepticism. In other words, claims that may have sounded good to me could easily be discounted, disproven, and disposed of by people who knew more than just a little bit about them. All those interesting occult claims that had fascinated me could be shown to be, at best, highly speculative and unproven or, at worst, complete nonsense.

Pseudoscience and Archaeology

I then began to search out more of the unsubstantiated, occult, and speculative claims that were being made about the prehistoric past by people who, it seemed, were wholly ignorant of modern archaeology. I have been doing this ever since, and it has been a surprisingly fruitful, sometimes hilarious, often depressing search. Little did I realize when I began to read *The Morning of the Magicians* how popular archaeological occultism and fraud are.

No one can deny that archaeology generates a great deal of public interest. People are fascinated by subjects like pyramids, cave paintings, human evolution, Stonehenge, and the Maya. Archaeology survives because people are interested enough in it to take courses, go to museums, visit sites, and buy books about it—including this book.

Sadly, some attempt to exploit this interest by making unsubstantiated claims about the discoveries made in this fascinating field. *The Morning of the Magicians* was not the first, and it certainly will not be the last, of the published, printed, spoken, filmed, or televised attempts to twist and pervert the discoveries made in archaeology.

Because professional archaeologists spend the bulk of their time writing and talking to each other about their discoveries, the public often learns about archaeology from mass-market paperbacks written by those whose major motivation may be not to educate people but rather to prove some pet theory or make a lot of money. The result is a public interested in the human past but often grossly misinformed about it.

In other words, archaeology is a fascinating field that has, ironically, suffered because of its popularity. There are lots of interesting, often quite funny, examples of the misuse of archaeology. Book publishers, movie makers, magazines, and tabloid newspapers have fed us a steady diet of ancient astronauts, psychic archaeology, Bigfoot, Atlantisology, and so on. And there is nothing new about it.

An important question to ask is, Why? From the tales related in this book, six basic motives or explanations are revealed:

1. Money, undeniably, can be a major motivating factor. The public's interest in archaeology is so great that many people willingly pay to see

artifacts or read about sites. The opportunities for charlatans to take advantage of an interested audience through book deals, lecture tours, T-shirts, commemorative mugs, and assorted other bric-a-brac are virtually limitless. Quite a bit of money has been and will continue to be made from people's great curiosity about human antiquity (see Chapter 3, for instance).

2. Fame is another consideration. The desire to find the oldest site or the one that shows everybody else to be wrong has motivated many, including some professional archaeologists. This desire for fame and notoriety has unfortunately led more than a few to alter or exaggerate their data.

3. Nationalism is a broader sort of fame that has also served as a motive for extreme or unsubstantiated archaeological claims. The desire to prove some sort of nationalistic or racial claim through archaeology has been common. Wanting to show that "we" were here first or that "we" were civilized before "you" has led some to play fast and loose with the archaeological facts. The Nazis provide a particularly odious example of this. In the 1930s and 1940s many artifacts discovered outside of Germany proper were interpreted by Nazi archaeologists as belonging to ancient Germanic people. The presence of these ostensible "Germanic" artifacts was viewed as evidence of previous German ownership of these other territories, providing at least part of the rationale for evicting or even slaughtering the non-Germans living there. An article by Bettina Arnold (1992) provides a chilling account of this kind of misuse of archaeology to support racism and nationalism.

4. Unfortunately, religion has also played a significant role in archaeological fraud. Many religions have their roots in remote antiquity. Some of their adherents dabble in archaeology, trying to prove the validity of their religious beliefs or claims through the discovery of archaeological evidence. Martin Luther, leader of the Protestant Reformation in the sixteenth century, asked, "What harm would it do if a man told a good strong lie for the sake of the good and for the Christian Church . . . a useful lie, a helpful lie, such lies would not be against God; he would accept them" (cited in Arthur 1996:88). Perhaps for some, an archaeological fraud that led people to the Church might be just such a "useful lie."

5. The desire for a more "romantic" past also plays a role. For some, lost continents, ancient astronauts, and psychic archaeologists seem more interesting than the discoveries of genuine archaeology. The quest for a more romantic past is the cause of at least some of the public's desire and willingness to believe claims that, if given some thought, could be easily disposed of.

6. Finally, and put bluntly, some of the extreme, unproven, bizarre, silly, and crazy claims made about the human past can be traced to the mental instability of their proponents. In other words, crazy claims may sometimes originate in crazy minds.

Why I Wrote This Book

My purpose is simple. I am passionately curious about human antiquity, and I enjoy few things as much as sharing that passion with people. I find the misrepresentation of what we actually know about that past to be troubling and attempt in these pages to respond to some of the more egregious examples. Simply stated, my purpose here is to provide the perspective of a professional archaeologist on unsubstantiated claims made about the human past, as well as on extreme claims made concerning how we can learn about that past.

The nonarchaeological topics I mentioned earlier in this chapter (UFOs, ESP, etc.) have been discussed at length by experts in the relevant scientific fields. They will not be the focus here. However, I hope that through reading this book you will come to understand that ancient astronauts, psychic archaeology, extreme diffusionism (the view that most important ideas were developed by one great culture and were "borrowed" by others), and the other claims to be discussed are the archaeological equivalents of these. Two excellent journals present articles where paranormal or extreme claims made in the name of science are skeptically assessed (*The Skeptical Inquirer* and *Skeptic*). In addition, I have provided a brief list of books focusing on these nonarchaeological topics (Table 1.1).

In this book, I present a discussion of the scientific method (Chapter 2) and then go on to detail popular frauds in the field of prehistoric archaeology—the Cardiff Giant (Chapter 3) and Piltdown Man (Chapter 4). Next, I explore the controversy concerning the origin of the American Indians and the debate over who discovered the Americas after the Indians (Chapter 5), and the historical argument over the source of the so-called Moundbuilder culture of North America (Chapter 6). Next, I delve into some unsubstantiated claims about the prehistoric archaeological record—the Lost Continent of Atlantis (Chapter 7), the ancient astronaut hypothesis (Chapter 8), the mysteries swirling around the civilization of ancient Egypt (Chapter 9), the efficacy of psychic archaeology (Chapter 10), and alleged archaeological evidence for particular religious beliefs (Chapter 11). Finally, some genuine archaeological mysteries are assessed in Chapter 12. Throughout, the theme will be how the methodology of science allows us to assess claims made in the name of the science of archaeology.

There is a reason for focusing on the history of the misuse and misinterpretation of the archaeological record as well as on individual misadventures.

Table 1.1   *Skeptical Publications on Extreme Claims Not Directly Related to Archaeology*

Topic	Author	Book Title	Year	Publisher
Astrology	Roger B. Culver and Philip A. Ianna	*Astrology: True or False?*	1988	Prometheus Books
	J. V. Stewart	*Astrology: What's Really in the Stars*	1997	Prometheus Books
Astronomy	Philip Plait	*Bad Astronomy*	2002	John Wiley
Bermuda Triangle	Larry Kusche	*The Bermuda Triangle Mystery Solved*	1995	Prometheus Books
Bigfoot	Daniel Taylor-Ide	*Something Hidden Behind the Range: A Himalayan Quest*	1995	Mercury House
	Greg Long	*The Making of Bigfoot: The Inside Story*	2004	Prometheus Books
	David J. Daegling	*Bigfoot Exposed: An Anthropologist Examines America's Enduring Legend*	2004	AltaMira Press
Crystal Power	Lawrence Jerome	*Crystal Power: The Ultimate Placebo Effect*	1989	Prometheus Books
ESP	Joe Nickell	*Psychic Sleuths*	1994	Prometheus Books
	James Randi	*The Magic of Uri Geller*	1975	Ballantine Books
	C. E. M. Hansel	*The Search for Psychic Power*	1989	Prometheus Books
	Richard Wiseman	*Deception and Self-Deception: Investigating Psychics*	1997	Prometheus Books
	Georges Charpak and Henri Broch	*Debunked: ESP, Telekenesis and Other Pseudoscience*	2004	Johns Hopkins
Faith Healing and Miracles	James Randi	*The Faith Healers*	1989	Prometheus Books
	Joe Nickell	*Looking for a Miracle*	1993	Prometheus Books
General	Gordon Stein (editor)	*The Encyclopedia of the Paranormal*	1996	Prometheus Books
	Simon Hoggart and Mike Hutchinson	*Bizarre Beliefs*	1995	Richard Cohen Books

(continued)

Table 1.1   *(continued)*

Topic	Author	Book Title	Year	Publisher
General	Christopher Toumey	*Conjuring Science*	1996	Rutgers University Press
	Michael Shermer	*How We Believe*	2000	W. H. Freeman and Co.
	Robert Todd	*The Skeptic's Dictionary*	2003	John Wiley
	Wendy Kaminer	*Sleeping with Extra-Terrestrials*	1999	Pantheon
Holocaust Denial	Michael Sheremer and Alex Grobman	*Denying History: Who Says the Holocaust Never Happened and Why Do They Say It?*	2000	University of California Press
Loch Ness Monster	Steuart Campbell	*The Loch Ness Monster: The Evidence*	1991	Aberdeen University Press
	Ronald Binns	*The Loch Ness Mystery Solved*	1984	Prometheus Books
Medical Quackery	James Harvey Young	*American Health Quackery*	1992	Princeton University Press
Satanic Cults	Mike Hertenstein and Jon Trott	*Selling Satan: The Tragic History of Mike Warnke*	1993	Cornerstone Press
	Robert Hicks	*In Pursuit of Satan: The Police and the Occult*	1991	Prometheus Books
UFOs	Joel Achenbach	*Captured by Aliens*	1999	Simon and Schuster
	Philip J. Klass	*UFO Abductions: A Dangerous Game*	1989	Prometheus Books
	Kal K. Korff	*The Roswell UFO Crash*	1997	Prometheus Books
	Curtis Peebles	*Watch the Skies: A Chronicle of the Flying Saucer Myth*	1994	Smithsonian Institution Press
Urban Legends	Jan Harold Brunvand	*The Truth Never Stands in the Way of a Good Story*	2000	University of Illinois Press

Only, for example, by seeing the contemporary claims of the Swiss author Erich von Däniken (see Chapter 8) as what amounts to our modern version of the Cardiff Giant (Chapter 3), only by realizing that the claims of the "scientific" creationists (Chapter 11) have been around for close to two hundred years and discredited for almost that long, and only by seeing that the public has been pretty gullible about archaeology almost from its inception can we hope to understand the entire phenomenon in its proper context. And only by understanding it can those of us dedicated to the study of the human past hope to deal with it.

FREQUENTLY ASKED QUESTIONS

1. What's the harm in believing pseudoscientific or nonscientific claims about the world?

It must be admitted that the impact of belief in at least some unsubstantiated claims may be minor. For example, you might buy a new weight-loss product based on the manufacturer's claim that the all-natural elixir was discovered while studying a colony of wild gorillas living in "Surinam" (Selling It 2000). The company's brochure offered the claim that after ingesting the material now incorporated into their product, the gorillas became eerily skinny. Interestingly, Suriname is a country in South America, and there are no colonies of wild gorillas there, chubby or slim. Gorillas live in Africa, not South America! You certainly should feel foolish if you purchased this product based on such a claim—but what's the harm?

There is great harm when people do not obtain appropriate medical intervention for serious illnesses—opting for unproven remedies and dying prematurely as a result. In extreme cases, charismatic leaders have led their gullible followers—some of whom believed in the psychic powers of the leader (the Reverend Jim Jones of the People's Temple) or the extraterrestrial connections of the leader (Marshall Applewhite of Heaven's Gate)—to their deaths. Belief in nonsense often is just foolish, but it sometimes is tragic.

2. Will science ever eliminate superstition and pseudoscience?

No, it likely never will. We human beings have an enormous capacity to understand the world around us, but that understanding brings with it a heavy burden. Comfortable fables may not reflect the way things actually work, but they may help us all—even the scientists among us—to deal with the more terrible and frightening things that afflict our lives. In Stephen Sondheim's play *Into the Woods*, Little Red Riding Hood sings, "Maybe it's nice to know a lot. . . . And a little bit not." Or, as writer Joel Achenbach

(1999:78) puts it in his terrific book, *Captured by Aliens,* "The nightmare of science is that sometimes you learn things that you do not want to know." Science can only show what works and what does not. Ultimately, it is up to each of us to accept or ignore what science reveals.

BEST OF THE WEB

http://www.csicop.org/
Web site for the Committee for the Scientific Investigation of Claims of the Paranormal (CSICOP) and its journal, the *Skeptical Inquirer.* Online articles from the magazine, a newsletter, and an annotated bibliography are all useful elements of this site.

http://www.skeptic.com/
Web site for the Skeptic Society and *Skeptic* magazine.

http://skepdic.com/
Voluminous dictionary of terms, concepts, and claims defined and explained with a skeptical perspective, from acupuncture to zombies. Includes many of the claims discussed in this book.

http://www.skepticfriends.org/
The Web site for the aptly named Skeptic Friends Network. A series of fun one-liners about various pseudoscientific claims and, even better, a concise description of the scientific method.

CRITICAL THINKING EXERCISES

1. What are the differences between a supermarket weekly and a regular newspaper? Are they always different?
2. Which of the topics listed in Table 1.1 (UFOs, ESP, and the rest) do you accept as genuine phenomena? On what basis do you accept those claims?

2

Epistemology:
How You Know What You Know

Knowing Things

The word *epistemology* means the study of knowledge—how you know what you know. Think about it. How does anybody know anything to be actual, truthful, or real? How do we differentiate fact from fantasy, the reasonable from the unreasonable, the meaningful from the meaningless—in archaeology or in any other field of knowledge? Everybody knows things, but how do we really know these things?

I know, for example, that there is a mountain in a place called Tibet. I know that the mountain is called by Westerners Everest and by Tibetans *Chomolungma* (Goddess of the Universe). I know that it is the tallest land mountain in the world (there are some a bit taller under the ocean). I'm even pretty sure how tall it is: 29,028 feet. But I have never measured it; I've never even been to Tibet. Beyond this, I have not measured all of the other mountains in the world to compare them to Everest. Yet I am quite confident that Everest is the world's tallest peak. But how do I know that?

On the subject of mountains, there is a run-down stone monument on the top of Bear Mountain in the northwestern corner of Connecticut. The monument was built toward the end of the nineteenth century and marks the "highest ground" in Connecticut (Figure 2.1). When the monument was built to memorialize this most lofty and auspicious of peaks—the mountain is all of 2,316 feet high—people knew that it was the highest point in the state and wanted to recognize this fact with the monument.

There is only one problem. In recent times, with more accurate, sophisticated measuring equipment, it has been determined that Bear Mountain is not the highest point in Connecticut. The slope of Frissell Mountain, which actually peaks in Massachusetts, reaches a height of 2,380 feet on the Connecticut side of the border, eclipsing Bear Mountain by about 64 feet.

Figure 2.1   Plaque adorning a stone monument perched atop Bear Mountain in the northwestern corner of Connecticut. Note that the height of the mountain is given as 2,354 feet (it actually is only 2,316 feet) and, in either case, though memorialized as "the highest ground" in the state, it is not. (K. L. Feder)

So, people in the late 1800s and early 1900s "knew" that Bear Mountain was the highest point in Connecticut. Today we *know* that they really did not "know" that, because it was not true—even though they thought it was and built a monument saying so.

Now, suppose that I read in a newspaper, hear on the radio, or see on television a claim that another mountain has been found that is actually 10 (or 50, or 10,000) feet higher than Mount Everest. Indeed, just a few years ago, new satellite data convinced a few, just for a while, that a peak neighboring Everest was, in actuality, slightly higher. That measurement turned out to be in error. But what about the precise height of Everest itself?

Remember my statement that I am "pretty sure" that the height of Everest is 29,028 feet? You will find that number in virtually every book on world geography or geology, in every encyclopedia, and, in fact, in almost every published reference to the great peak—at least before November 1999. That number, 29,028 feet, was, until recently, part of our common knowledge about the world. And it turns out to be wrong, albeit by only a little bit. The quoted figure was determined in 1954 using the best technology available at the time. Our technology for doing such things as measuring elevations has improved radically in the intervening years. In a project sponsored by the National Geographic Society, a team of climbers ascended Everest in March 1999 to remeasure the "roof of the world." Using information gleaned from Global Positioning System satellites, it was determined that Everest is actually 7 feet higher, 29,035 feet high, and may be growing, if only by a small fraction of an inch each year, as a result of geological forces (Roach 1999).

One of the defining characteristics of science is its pursuit of modification and refinement of what we know and how we explain things. Scientists realize they have to be ever vigilant and, contrary to what some people seem to think, ever open to new information that enables us to tweak, polish, overhaul, or even overturn what we think we know. Science does not grudgingly admit the need for such refinement or reassessment but rather embraces it as a fundamental part of the scientific method.

But now back to Everest. You and I have likely never been to Tibet to personally assess or verify any measurement of the mountain. So what criteria can we use to determine if any of it is true or accurate? It all comes back to epistemology. How, indeed, do we know what we think we know?

Collecting Information:
Seeing Isn't Necessarily Believing

In general, people collect information in two ways:

1. Directly through their own experiences

2. Indirectly through specific information sources such as friends, teachers, parents, books, TV, the Internet, and so forth

People tend to think that obtaining firsthand information—what they see or experience themselves—is always the best way. Unfortunately this is a false assumption because most people are poor observers.

For example, the list of animals that people claim to have observed—and that turn out to be figments of their imagination—is staggering. It is fascinating to read Pliny, a first-century thinker, or Topsell, who wrote in the seventeenth century, and see detailed accounts of the nature and habits of dragons, griffins, unicorns, mermaids, and so on (Byrne 1979). People claimed to have seen these animals, gave detailed descriptions, and even drew pictures of them (Figure 2.2). Many folks read their books and believed them.

Nor are untrained observers very good at identifying known, living animals. A red or "lesser" panda escaped from the zoo in Rotterdam, Holland, in December 1978. Red pandas are very rare animals indigenous to China, Tibet, Nepal, and Burma, not Holland. They are distinctive in appearance and cannot be readily mistaken for any other sort of animal. The zoo informed the press that the panda was missing, hoping the publicity would alert people in the area of the zoo and aid in the panda's return. Just when the newspapers came out with the panda story, it was found, quite dead, along some railroad tracks adjacent to the zoo. Nevertheless, over one hundred sightings of the panda *alive* were reported to the zoo from all over the Netherlands *after* the animal was obviously already dead. These reports did not stop until several days after the newspapers announced the discovery of the dead panda (van Kampen 1979). So much for the absolute reliability of firsthand observation.

Figure 2.2   A seventeenth-century rendition of a clearly mythological beast—a *Mantichora*. The creature was considered to be real and was described as being the size of a wild ass, as having quills on its tail that it could hurl at adversaries, and as having a fondness for human flesh.

Collecting Information: Relying on Others

In exploring the problems of secondhand information, we run into even more complications. When we are not in place to observe something first-hand, we are forced to rely on the quality of someone else's observations, interpretations, and reports—as with the reported height of Mount Everest.

In assessing a report made by others, you need to ask yourself several questions: How did they obtain the information in the first place—revelation, intuition, science? What are their motives for providing this information? What agenda—religious, philosophical, nationalistic, or otherwise—do they have? What is their source of information, and how expert are they in the topic?

Most people obtain information about the world and current events from established sources such as television news, books, or newspapers. Let's look at the last of these.

Not all newspapers are equally accurate and believable. The *New York Times* has a reputation for factual reporting and carries the following promise in its masthead: "All the News That's Fit to Print." No one, not even their publishers, would characterize tabloid papers like the *Enquirer,* the *Star,* the *Examiner,* the *Weekly World News,* or the *Sun* in those same terms (Bird 1992). When asked about the accuracy of some of the more bizarre stories that appear in his paper, the editor of the *Weekly World News* has been quoted as responding, "For heaven's sake, we entertain people. We make people feel better" (Johnson 1994:27). Notice there is nothing in that response that defends or maintains the accuracy of the stories.

The *Sun* is even more revealing in the disclaimer published in every edition: "*Sun* stories seek to entertain and are about the fantastic, bizarre, and paranormal. The reader should suspend belief for the sake of enjoyment." I presume this means "The reader should suspend *dis*belief for the sake of enjoyment." In other words, leave your skepticism behind because this isn't serious stuff; even we don't believe most of it. Just read these weird and improbable stories for the entertainment value in them.

In fact, most people follow that advice. In her wonderful anthropological study of the tabloids, S. Elizabeth Bird (1992) shows that most people who read the tabloids regularly do so for the celebrity gossip (which occasionally turns out to be true) and for the uplifting human interest stories that are ignored by the popular press, as well as for the more bizarre material that adorns the pages of these publications. In terms of the latter, regular readers believe some (usually the stuff that reinforces previously held beliefs), but discard most of the rest, viewing it with a combination of interest and humor.

Anthropological topics do attract quite a bit of attention from the tabloids (see Figure 1.1). Mark Allen Peterson (1991), a writer with backgrounds in anthropology and journalism, classifies tabloid stories about anthropology into four categories:

1. *Aliens and ape men*—These stories usually assert some alleged connection between an isolated group of people and extraterrestrial aliens or Bigfoot.

2. *Whacky savages*—These stories focus on the "bizarre" (that term shows up a lot) antics of a tribal or "primitive" people. Sexual and marriage practices are closely scrutinized in these articles.

3. *Whacky anthropologists*—These are usually upbeat stories about anthropologists who are viewed as peculiar and eccentric intellectuals who travel to awful places to study odd, but nevertheless interesting, things.

4. *Silly studies*—These stories are somewhat similar in terms of topic to those included in category 3, but the perspective is quite different, being highly critical of the tax money "wasted" in supporting the frivolous studies conducted by those "whacky anthropologists."

Tabloid stories often are absurd, and few of the writers or even the readers believe them. This still leaves us with the broader question: How do we know what to believe? This is a crucial question that all rational people must ask themselves, whether talking about medicine, religion, archaeology, or anything else. Again, it comes back around to epistemology; how do we know what we think we know, and how do we know what or whom to believe?

Science: Playing by the Rules

There are ways to knowledge that are both dependable and reliable. We might not be able to get to absolute truths about the meaning of existence, but we can figure out quite a bit about our world—about chemistry and biology, psychology and sociology, physics and history, and even prehistory. The techniques used to get at knowledge we can feel confident in—knowledge that is reliable, truthful, and factual—are referred to as *science.*

In large part, science is a series of techniques used to maximize the probability that what we think we know really reflects the way things are, were, or will be. Science makes no claim to have all the answers or even to be right all the time. On the contrary, during the process of the growth of knowledge and understanding, science is often wrong. Remember that even as seemingly fundamental a fact as the height of the tallest mountain on earth is subject to reassessment and correction. The only claim that we do make in science is that if we honestly, consistently, and vigorously pursue knowledge using some basic techniques and principles, the truth will eventually surface and we can truly know things about the nature of the world in which we find ourselves.

The question then is, What exactly is science? Hollywood has a number of different stereotypes of scientists. Though there is the occasional female—typically bookish, shy, with thick eyeglasses and hair in a permanent bun—most movie scientist archetypes are white men: the wild-eyed and even wilder-haired eccentric who mixes assorted chemicals in a dark, mysterious laboratory; the brilliant but egotistical young man who misuses the power of his remarkable discovery; the unkempt, nerdy, antisocial genius who is oblivious to the impact his work has on the world. The classic Doctor Frankenstein (Figure 2.3) comes immediately to mind.

So much for Hollywood. Scientists are not misfits or megalomaniacs without practical concerns or interests beyond their specialties. We are just people trying to arrive at some truths about how the world and the universe work. Although the application of science can be a slow, frustrating, all-consuming enterprise, the basic assumptions we scientists hold are very simple. Whether we are physicists, biologists, or archaeologists, we all work from four underlying principles. These principles are quite straightforward, but equally quite crucial.

1. There is a real and knowable universe.
2. The universe (which includes stars, planets, animals, and rocks, as well as people, their cultures, and their histories) operates according to certain understandable rules or laws.

Figure 2.3   Gene Wilder depicted a stereotypical—and quite hilarious—mad scientist in the movie *Young Frankenstein*. As funny as his character was, it reflects a common, though quite mistaken, view of what real scientists are like and how they go about their research. (© Motion Picture & TV Photo Archive)

3. These laws are immutable—that means they do not, in general, change depending on where you are or "when" you are.

4. These laws can be discerned, studied, and understood by people through careful observation, experimentation, and research.

Let's look at these assumptions one at a time.

There Is a Real and Knowable Universe

In science we have to agree that there is a real universe out there for us to study—a universe full of stars, animals, human history, and prehistory that exists whether we are happy with that reality or not.

Recently, it has become fashionable to deny this fundamental underpinning of science. A group of thinkers called *deconstructionists*, for example, believe that all science and history are merely artificial constructs, devoid of any objective reality or truth. For some deconstructionists, "history exists only in the minds of historians" (Shermer and Grobman 2000:26); the actual past, if there is one, can never be known. As scientists Kurt Gottfried and Kenneth Wilson (1997:545) state, the deconstructionists claim that "scientific knowledge is only a communal belief system with a dubious grip on reality."

Deconstructionists try to take apart common beliefs in an attempt to show that much of what we think we know is purely subjective and culturally based.

To some deconstructionists, there is no absolute reality for science to observe or explain; there are only cultural constructs of the universe that are different among people in different societies and even different between men and women within the same culture. There is not one reality but many, and all are equally valid.

Deconstructionists describe science as a purely Western mode of thought, a mechanistic, antinature pattern based on inequality, capitalist exploitation, and patriarchy. The objective observation and understanding at the heart of the scientific approach are impossibilities; the things we see and the explanations we come up with are informed by who we are. (See Paul R. Gross and Norman Levitt's [1994] disturbing book *Higher Superstition: The Academic Left and Its Quarrel with Science* for a detailed criticism of the deconstructionists.) Science, to the deconstructionists, is merely the Western "myth"; it is no more objective and no more "real" than nonscientific myths.

As Theodore Schick and Lewis Vaughn (1999) point out, however, if there is no such thing as objective truth, then no statements, including this one—or any of those made by the deconstructionists themselves—are objectively true. We could know nothing because there would be nothing to know. This is not a useful approach for human beings. Science simply is not the same as myth or oral tradition. Science demands rigorous testing and retesting, and it commonly rejects and discards previous conclusions about the world as a result of such testing. The same cannot be said for nonscientific explanations about how things work.

I suppose one could attempt to demonstrate the culturally subjective nature of the physical principle that two things cannot occupy the same place at the same time by, say, standing in front of a moving train. You probably will not see any deconstructionist attempting this anytime soon.

The Universe Operates According to Understandable Laws

In essence, what this means is that there are rules by which the universe works: Stars produce heat and light according to the laws of nuclear physics; nothing can go faster than the speed of light; all matter in the universe is attracted to all other matter (the law of gravity).

Though human societies are extremely complex systems and people may not operate according to rigid or unchanging rules of behavior, social scientists can nevertheless construct lawlike generalizations that accurately predict how human groups react to changes in their environment and how their cultures evolve through time. For example, development of complex civilizations in Egypt, China, India/Pakistan, Mesopotamia, Mexico, and

Peru was not based on random processes (Haas 1982; Lamberg-Karlovsky and Sabloff 1995). Their evolution seems to reflect similar general patterns. This is not to say that all of these civilizations were identical, any more than we would say that all stars are identical. On the contrary, they existed in different physical and cultural environments, and so we should expect that they would be different. However, in each case the rise to civilization was preceded by development of an agricultural economy and socially stratified societies. In each case, civilization was also preceded by some degree of overall population increase as well as increased population density in some areas (in other words, the development of cities). Again, in each case we find monumental works (pyramids, temples), evidence of long-distance trade, and development of mathematics, astronomy, and methods of record keeping (usually, but not always, in the form of writing). The cultures in which civilization developed, though some were unrelated and independent, shared these factors because of the nonrandom patterns of cultural evolution.

The point is that everything operates according to rules. In science we believe that by understanding these rules or laws we can understand stars, organisms, and even ourselves.

The Laws Are Immutable

That the laws do not change under ordinary conditions is a crucial concept in science. A law that works here works there. A law that worked in the past will work today and will work in the future.

For example, if I go to the top of the Leaning Tower of Pisa today and simultaneously drop two balls of unequal mass, they will fall at the same rate and reach the ground at the same time, just as they did when Galileo performed a similar experiment in the seventeenth century. If I perform the same experiment countless times, the same thing will occur because the laws of the universe (in this case, the law of gravity) do not change through time. They also do not change depending on where you are. Go anywhere on the earth and perform the same experiment—you will get the same results (try not to hit any pedestrians or you will see some other "laws" in operation). This experiment was even performed by U.S. astronauts on the moon during the Apollo 15 mission. A hammer and a feather were dropped from the same height, and they hit the surface at precisely the same instant (the only reason this will not work on earth is because the feather is caught by the air and the hammer, obviously, is not). We have no reason to believe that the results would be different anywhere or "anywhen" else.

If this assumption of science, that the laws do not change through time, were false, many of the so-called historical sciences, including prehistoric archaeology, could not exist.

For example, historical geologists are interested in knowing how the various landforms we see today came into being. They recognize that they cannot go back in time to see how the Grand Canyon was formed. However, because the laws of geology that governed the development of the Grand Canyon have not changed through time and because these laws are still in operation, historical geologists can study the formation of geological features today and apply what they learn to the past. The same laws they can directly study operating in the present were operating in the past when geological features that interest them first formed.

In the words of nineteenth-century geologist Charles Lyell, the "present" we can observe is the "key" to understanding the past that we cannot. This is true because the laws, or rules, that govern the universe are constant—those that operate today operated in the past. This is why science does not limit itself to the present but makes inferences about the past and even predictions about the future (listen to the weather report for an example of this). We can do so because we can study modern, ongoing phenomena that work under the same laws that existed in the past and will exist in the future.

This is where science and theology are often forced to part company and respectfully disagree. Remember, science depends on the constancy of the laws that we can discern. In contrast, advocates of many religions, though they might believe that there are laws that govern things (and which, according to them, were established by a Creator), usually (but not always) believe that these laws can be changed at any time by their God. In other words, if God does not want the apple to fall to the ground but instead wants it to hover, violating the law of gravity, that is precisely what will happen. As a more concrete example, scientists know that the heat and light given off by a fire result from the transformation of mass (of the wood) to energy. Physical laws control this process. A theologian, however, might agree with this ordinarily but feel that if God wants to create a fire that does not consume any mass (like the "burning bush" seen by Moses in the Old Testament), then this is exactly what will occur. Most scientists simply do not accept this assertion. The rules are the rules. They do not change, even though we might sometimes wish that they would.

The Laws Can Be Understood

This may be the single most important principle in science. The universe is, theoretically at least, knowable. It may be complicated, and it may take years and years to understand even apparently simple phenomena. Each attempt at understanding leads us to collect more data and to test, reevaluate, and refine our proposed explanations—for how planets formed, why a group of animals became extinct while another thrived, or how a group of ancient people responded to a change in their natural environment, contact with an alien group of people, or adoption of a new technology. We rarely get it right the first time and are continually collecting new information, abandoning some interpretations while refining others. We constantly rethink our explanations. In this way, little by little, bit by bit, we expand our knowledge and understanding. Through this kind of careful observation and objective research and experimentation, we can indeed know things.

So, our assumptions are simple enough. We accept the existence of a reality independent of our own minds, and we accept that this reality works according to a series of unchanging laws or rules. We also claim that we can recognize and understand these laws, or at least recognize the patterns that result from these universal rules. The question remains then: How do we do science—how do we explore the nature of the universe, whether our interest is planets, stars, atoms, or human prehistory?

The Workings of Science

We can know things by employing the rules of logic and rational thought. Scientists—archaeologists or otherwise—usually work through a combination of the logical processes known as *induction* and *deduction*. The dictionary definition of induction is "arguing from specifics to generalities," whereas deduction is defined as the reverse, arguing from generalities to specifics.

What is essential to good science is objective, unbiased observations—of planets, molecules, rock formations, archaeological sites, and so on. Often, on the basis of these specific observations, we induce explanations called *hypotheses* for how these things work.

For example, we may study the planets Mercury, Venus, Earth, and Mars (each one presents specific bits of information). We then induce general rules about how we think these inner planets in our solar system were formed. Or we might study a whole series of different kinds of molecules and then induce general rules about how all molecules interact chemically. We may study different rock formations and make general conclusions about their origin. We can study a number of specific prehistoric sites and make generalizations about how cultures evolved.

Notice that we cannot directly observe planets forming, the rules of molecular interaction, rocks being made, or prehistoric cultures evolving. Instead, we are inducing general conclusions and principles concerning our data that seem to follow logically from what we have been able to observe.

This process of induction, though crucial to science, is not enough. We need to go beyond our induced hypotheses by testing them. If our induced hypotheses are indeed valid—that is, if they really represent the actual rules according to which some aspect of the universe (planets, molecules, rocks, ancient societies) works—they should be able to hold up under the rigors of scientific hypothesis testing.

Observation and the suggestion of hypotheses, therefore, are only the first steps in a scientific investigation. In science we always need to go beyond observation and hypothesizing. We need to set up a series of "if . . . then" statements; "if" our hypothesis is true, "then" the following deduced "facts" will also be true. Our results are not always precise and clear-cut, especially in a science like archaeology, but this much should be clear—scientists are not just out there collecting a bunch of interesting facts. Facts are always collected within the context of trying to explain something or of trying to test a hypothesis.

As an example of this logical process, consider the health effects of smoking. How can scientists be sure that smoking is bad for you? After all, it's pretty rare that someone takes a puff on a cigarette and immediately drops dead. The certainty comes from a combination of induction and deduction. Observers have noticed for about 300 years that people who smoked seemed to be more likely to get certain diseases than people who did not smoke. As long ago as the seventeenth century, people noticed that habitual pipe smokers were subject to tumor growths on their lips and in their mouths. From such observations we can reasonably, though tentatively, induce a hypothesis of the unhealthfulness of smoking, but we still need to test such a hypothesis. We need to set up "if . . . then" statements. If, in fact, smoking is a hazard to your health (the hypothesis we have induced based on our observations), then we should be able to deduce some predictions that must also be true. Sure enough, when we test specific, deduced predictions such as

1. Smokers will have a higher incidence of lung cancer than nonsmokers
2. Smokers will have a higher incidence of emphysema
3. Smokers will take more sick days from work
4. Smokers will get more upper-respiratory infections
5. Smokers will have diminished lung capacity
6. Smokers will have a shorter life expectancy

we see that our original, induced hypothesis—cigarette smoking is hazardous to your health—is upheld.

That was easy, but also obvious. How about an example with more mystery to it, one in which scientists—acting like detectives—had to solve a puzzle to save lives?

The Case of Childbed Fever

In nineteenth-century Europe, the hospital could be a very dangerous place for a woman about to give birth. Death rates in some so-called lying-in wards were horrifically high, the result of what became known as "childbed fever." A seemingly healthy young woman would arrive at the hospital with an unremarkable pregnancy, experience a normal labor, and give birth to a healthy baby. Over the course of the hours and days following birth, however, she might exhibit a rapid pulse, high fever, distended and painful abdomen, foul discharge, and delirium—and then would die.

Oddly, while childbed fever took a horrible toll in hospital deliveries, it was rare or absent in home births. In fact, as Sherwin Nuland (2003:97), physician and author of a fascinating book on childbed fever points out, a woman was generally much safer if she gave birth on the street or in an alley on her way to the hospital than if she actually arrived there. For example, carefully maintained mortality statistics show that between 1831 and 1843 in London, approximately 10 out of 10,000 home births resulted in the death of the mother, while in the hospital the death rate was 60 times higher; 600 out of 10,000 died (Nuland 2003:41). In France, similar statistics show that, between 1833 and 1842, the death rate for mothers giving birth in hospitals in Paris was as high as 880 per 10,000 (Nuland 2003:41). By way of comparison, in the United States today, on average, for every 10,000 births there is only about a single maternal death (Chang et al. 2003).

In the nineteenth century, there were two wards, or divisions, at the Vienna General Hospital in Austria. Each year between 6,000 and 7,000 women arrived at the gates of the hospital to give birth, and an equal number ended up in each of the two divisions. In Division 2, in a given year, on average, about 60 women died soon after giving birth, a death rate of about 2 percent. Astonishingly, in Division 1, in the same hospital, the number of yearly deaths was more than ten times higher, with more than 600 and as many as 800 dying in a given year, a terrifying death rate as high as 27 percent (Nuland 2003:97).

Physicians were, needless to say, appalled by such statistics. Performing autopsies on patients who had died in the hospital had become a regular practice in the nineteenth century in Europe. Many doctors carefully examined the bodies of the women who had died of childbed fever and found them ravaged by an aggressive infection and filled with an intensely foul smelling whitish fluid. Many of these physicians were more than willing to propose hypotheses suggesting possible causes of the condition. Perhaps, it was suggested, tight petticoats worn early in pregnancy were involved, leading to a woman's inability to expel fluids after giving birth. Or perhaps it was the foul air in hospitals with their closed-in spaces. Magnetic fields and atmospheric disturbances were blamed. Perhaps some women simply were predisposed to having their milk ducts get blocked and then dying when milk deteriorated inside of them; the whiteness of the infection seen in autopsy was assumed by some to indicate its source as soured mother's milk. Others, aware that home births with their very low rates of childbed fever were attended to by midwives, all of whom were themselves women, suggested that the condition was the result of female modesty.

In other words, childbed fever afflicted women who were particularly embarrassed by being examined by male doctors and medical students. Some even proposed the wonderfully circular explanation that childbed fever had a psychological origin, the result of the great fear many women had of the hospital because of the possibility of contracting childbed fever!

Back in Vienna at the General Hospital, Ignaz Semmelweis, a young Hungarian doctor who had been turned down for a couple of plum assignments, ended up, by default, in obstetrics. Determined to solve the childbed fever riddle, Semmelweis realized that the General Hospital, with its two divisions having very different mortality rates, presented a unique opportunity to experimentally test the various hypotheses proposed to explain childbed fever.

Semmelweis immediately rejected those proposed explanations that didn't differentiate the two divisions. For example, one doctor suggested that childbed fever was caused by badly maintained hospital walls, but the walls were in equal disrepair in both divisions, and the mortality rates were entirely different, so it was pointless to pursue this explanation. While outright rejecting hypotheses related to atmospheric conditions, earth energies, and dirty walls, Semmelweis and some of his colleagues at the hospital recognized a handful of genuine and potentially important differences between the two obstetrical divisions in the hospital and induced a series of possible explanations for the drastic difference in their mortality rates. They suggested:

1. Division 1 tended to be more crowded than Division 2. The overcrowding in Division 1 was a possible cause of the higher mortality rate there.

2. Women in Division 2 were assisted by midwives who directed the women to deliver on their sides, while those in Division 1 were attended to by physicians and medical students who kept women on their backs during delivery. Birth position was a possible cause of the higher mortality rate.

3. There was a psychological factor involved; the hospital priest had to walk through Division 1 to administer the last rites to dying patients in other wards. Perhaps this sight so upset some women already weakened by the ordeal of childbirth that it contributed to their deaths.

4. Unlike the women in Division 2, who were assisted by experienced midwives using far less invasive techniques, the women in Division 1 were attended to by medical students being trained in obstetrics. Perhaps all of the additional poking and prodding conducted during this training was harmful and contributed to the higher death rate of women in Division 1.

These induced hypotheses all sounded good. Each marked a genuine difference between Divisions 1 and 2 that might have caused the difference in the death rate. Semmelweis was doing what most scientists do in such a situation; he was relying on creativity and imagination in seeking out an explanation.

Creativity and imagination are just as important to science as good observation. But being creative and imaginative was not enough. It did not help the women who were still dying at an alarming rate. Semmelweis had to go beyond producing possible explanations; he had to test each one of them. So, he deduced the necessary implications of each:

1. If hypothesis 1 were correct, then alleviating the crowding in Division 1 should reduce the mortality rate. The result: no change. So the first hypothesis was rejected. It had failed the scientific test; it simply could not be correct.

2. Semmelweis went on to test hypothesis 2 by changing the birth positions of the women in Division 1 to match those of the women in Division 2. Again, there was no change, and another hypothesis was rejected.

3. Next, to test hypothesis 3, the priest was rerouted. Women in Division 1 continued to die of childbed fever at about five times the rate of those in Division 2.

4. To test hypothesis 4, it was decided to limit the number of invasive procedures used on the women to train the students in their examination techniques. This was accomplished by limiting the number of students who actually examined the women. Specifically, the many non-Austrian students in the obstetrics program were restricted from examining these patients, while the native Austrians continued to be trained in the ward. The statistics showed that this had no impact on the death rate in Division 1; 10 or 11 percent of the women continued to die even when fewer students were allowed to examine them internally.

Then, as so often happens in science, Semmelweis had a stroke of luck. An acquaintance—also a doctor—died, and the manner of his death provided Semmelweis with another possible explanation for the problem in Division 1. Though Semmelweis's friend was not a woman who had recently given birth, he did have precisely the same symptoms as did the women who were dying of childbed fever. Most important, this doctor had died of a disease similar to childbed fever soon after accidentally cutting himself during an autopsy.

Viruses and bacteria were unknown in the 1840s. Surgical instruments were not sterilized, no special effort was made to clean the hands, and doctors did not wear gloves during operations and autopsies. Supposing that there was something bad in dead bodies and this something had entered Semmelweis's friend's system through his wound—could the same bad "stuff" (Semmelweis called it "cadaveric material") get onto the hands of the physicians and medical students, who then might, without washing, go on to help a woman give birth? Then, if this "cadaveric material" were transmitted into the woman's body during the birth of her baby, it might lead to her death.

This possibility inspired Semmelweis's final hypothesis: The presence of physicians and medical students in Division 1 was at the root of the mystery. Students who attended the women in Division 1 regularly conducted autopsies as part of their training and so would be in contact with dead bodies on the same days they were assisting women giving birth. Furthermore, physicians would frequently perform autopsies on the bodies of women who had already died of childbed fever, often going directly from the autopsy room to the birthing rooms to assist other women giving birth. Herein was a grimly ironic twist to this new hypothesis; the attempt by physicians to solve the mystery of childbed fever by performing autopsies on its victims was one of the most important factors in transmitting the disease to additional women.

To test this hypothesis, Semmelweis instituted new policies in Division 1, including the requirement that all attending physicians and students cleanse their hands with chlorine before entering. The result: The death rate among women birthing in Division 1 dropped to between 1 and 2 percent, exactly the rate in Division 2. Semmelweis had both solved the mystery and halted an epidemic.

Science and Nonscience: The Essential Differences

Through objective observation and analysis, a scientist, whether a physicist, chemist, biologist, psychologist, or archaeologist, sees things that need explaining. Through creativity and imagination, the scientist suggests possible hypotheses to explain these "mysteries." The scientist then sets up a rigorous method through experimentation or subsequent research to deductively test the validity of a given hypothesis. If the implications of a hypothesis are shown not to be true, the hypothesis must be rejected and then it's back to the drawing board. If the implications are found to be true, we can uphold or support our hypothesis.

A number of other points should be made here. The first is that for a hypothesis, whether it turns out to be upheld or not, to be scientific, it must be testable. In other words, there must be clear, deduced implications that can be drawn from the hypothesis and then tested. Remember the hypotheses of "magnetic fields" and "atmospheric disturbances"? How can you test these? What are the necessary implications that can be deduced from the hypothesis "More women died in Division 1 because of atmospheric disturbances"? There really aren't any, and therefore such a hypothesis is not scientific—it cannot be tested. Remember, in the methodology of science, we ordinarily need to

1. Observe
2. Induce general hypotheses or possible explanations for what we have observed
3. Deduce specific things that must also be true if our hypothesis is true
4. Test the hypothesis by checking out the deduced implications

As Michael Shermer (1997:19) points out, "Science, of course, is not this rigid, and no scientist consciously goes through 'steps.' The process is a constant interaction of making observations, drawing conclusions, making predictions, and checking them against evidence."

Testing a hypothesis is crucial. If there are no specific implications of a hypothesis that can then be analyzed as a test of the validity or usefulness of that hypothesis, then you simply are not doing and cannot do "science."

For example, suppose you observe a person who appears to be able to "guess" the value of a playing card picked from a deck. Next, assume that someone hypothesizes that "psychic" ability is involved. Finally, suppose the claim is made that the "psychic" ability goes away as soon as you try to test it (actually named the "shyness effect" by some researchers of the paranormal). Such a claim is not itself testable and therefore not scientific.

Beyond the issue of testability, another lesson is involved in determining whether an approach to a problem is scientific. Semmelweis induced four different hypotheses to explain the difference in mortality rates between Divisions 1 and 2. These "competing" explanations are called *multiple working hypotheses*. Notice that Semmelweis did not simply proceed by a process of elimination. He did not, for example, test the first three hypotheses and—after finding them invalid—declare that the fourth was necessarily correct because it was the only one left that he had thought of.

Some people try to work that way. A light is seen in the sky. Someone hypothesizes it was a meteor. We find out that it was not. Someone else hypothesizes that it was a military rocket. Again this turns out to be incorrect. Someone else suggests that it was the Goodyear blimp, but that turns out to have been somewhere else. Finally, someone suggests that it was the spacecraft of people from another planet. Some will say that this must be correct because none of the other explanations panned out. This is nonsense. There are plenty of other possible explanations. Eliminating all of the explanations *we* have been able to think of except one (which, perhaps, has no testable implications) in no way allows us to uphold that final hypothesis. You will see just such an error in logic with regard to the Shroud of Turin artifact discussed in Chapter 11.

A Rule in Assessing Explanations

Finally, there is another rule to hypothesis making and testing. It is called *Occam's razor* or *Occam's rule*. In thinking, in trying to solve a problem, or in attempting to explain some phenomenon, "Entities are not to be multiplied beyond necessity." In other words, the explanation or hypothesis that explains a series of observations with the fewest other assumptions or leaps—the hypothesis that does not multiply these entities beyond necessity—is the best explanation.

Here's an example. My archaeology class was to begin in about ten minutes, and the previous class was just dispersing from what had obviously been a raucous session. As I entered the room, I noticed the three-dimensional, geometric shapes made of heavy stock paper suspended by string from the seminar room ceiling. I caught the attention of the professor, a truly gentle soul and one of the nicest people I had met in my first year of teaching, and I asked the obvious question: "What's the deal with the shapes?" She smiled and launched into a passionate discourse about the exercise just conducted by the class—an experiment in "psychokinesis," the ostensible ability to move or otherwise affect objects simply by the power of thought. Perhaps my jaw dropped a little too obviously, and my colleague asked, "Would you like to see me do it?" Without waiting for a response, she gazed up at the shape directly above her head and closed her eyes; when she opened them we both looked up to see the suspended object swaying back and forth. "See?" she said.

Before you get too terribly excited about this demonstration, perhaps I should add that it was a rather breezy day and the windows in the seminar room were wide open. The object toward which my colleague had directed her ostensibly paranormal talents indeed was moving, but so were all of the other suspended objects, as were papers on the desk at the front of the class and just about anything else that wasn't nailed down. I pointed out that, just perhaps, the suspended object was moving simply because of the wind. My colleague just smiled broadly, patted me on the shoulder, and said, "Oh Kenny, you're such a skeptic." Indeed I am, and in this story rests the essence of Occam's razor. Could the object have been moving as the result of my colleague's psychokinetic prowess? Well, yes. But it also could have been moving as a result of open windows and wind. Which explanation—psychokinesis or wind—requires the least violence to our understanding of reality? Which requires the fewest logical leaps or as yet unsupported assumptions about how the universe operates? Occam's razor directs the

Figure 2.4   An 1827 lithograph of a fossil quarry in the Tilgate Forest, Sussex, England. Workers are extracting a dinosaur bone from a large rock fragment. (From Mantell's Geology of Sussex)

gambler in reality's casino to bet on the sure thing or, at least, the surer thing, until a preponderance of evidence convinces one otherwise. In this particular case, I'm betting on the wind.

Here's another example. During the eighteenth and nineteenth centuries, huge buried, fossilized bones were found throughout North America and Europe (Figure 2.4). One hypothesis, the simplest, was that the bones were the remains of animals that no longer existed. This hypothesis simply relied on the assumption that bones do not come into existence by themselves but always serve as the skeletons of animals. Therefore, when you find bones, there must have been animals who used those bones. However, another hypothesis was suggested: The bones were deposited by the Devil to fool us into thinking that such animals existed (Howard 1975). This hypothesis "multiplied" those "entities" Occam warned us about. This explanation demanded many more assumptions about the universe than did the first: There is a Devil, that Devil is interested in human affairs, he wants to fool us, he has the ability to make bones of animals that never existed, and he has the ability to hide them under the ground and inside solid rock. That is quite a number of unproven (and largely untestable) claims to swallow.

Thus, Occam's razor says the simpler hypothesis, that these great bones are evidence of the existence of animals that no longer exist—in other words, dinosaurs—is better. The other explanation raises more questions than it answers.

The Art of Science

Don't get the impression that science is a mechanical enterprise. Science is at least partially an art. It is much more than just observing the results of experiments.

It takes great creativity to recognize a "mystery" in the first place. In the apocryphal story, countless apples had fallen from countless trees and undoubtedly conked the noggins of multitudes of stunned individuals who never thought much about it. It took a fabulously creative individual, Isaac Newton, to even recognize that herein lay a mystery. Why did the apple fall? It could have hovered in midair. It could have moved off in any of the cardinal directions. It could have gone straight up and out of sight. But it did not. It fell to the ground as it always had, in all places, and as it always would. It took great imagination to recognize that in this simple observation (and in a bump on the head) rested the eloquence of a fundamental law of the universe.

Where Do Hypotheses Come From?

Coming up with hypotheses is not a simple or mechanical procedure. The scientific process requires creativity. Hypotheses arrive as often in flashes of insight as through plodding, methodical observation. Consider this example.

My field crew and I had just finished excavating the 2,000-year-old Loomis II archaeological site in Connecticut where a broad array of different kinds of stones had been used for making tools. Some of the "lithics" came from sources close to the site. Other sources were located at quite a distance, as much as a few hundred miles away. These nonnative "exotic" lithics were universally superior; tools could be made more easily from the nonlocal materials, and the edges produced were much sharper.

At the time the site was being excavated, I noticed that there seemed to be a pattern in terms of the size of the individual tools we were recovering. Tools made from the locally available and generally inferior materials of quartz and basalt were relatively large, and the pieces of rock that showed no evidence of use—archaeologists call these discarded pieces *debitage*— were also relatively large. In contrast, the tools made from the superior materials—a black flint and two kinds of jasper—that originated at a great distance from the site were much smaller. Even inconsequential flakes of exotic stone—pieces you could barely hold between two fingers—showed evidence of use, and only the tiniest of flakes was discarded without either further modification for use or evidence of use, such as for scraping, cutting, or piercing.

I thought it was an interesting pattern but didn't think much of it until about a year later when I was cleaning up the floor of my lab after a class in experimental archaeology where students were replicating stone tools. We used a number of different raw materials in the class, and just as was the case for the site, stone of inferior quality was readily available a few miles away, whereas more desirable material was from more distant sources.

As I cleaned up, I noticed that the discarded stone chips left by the students included perfectly serviceable pieces of the locally available, easy-to-obtain stone, and only the tiniest fragments of flint and obsidian. We obtained flint in New York State from a source about 80 miles from campus, and we received obsidian from Wyoming. Suddenly it was clear to me that the pattern apparent at the archaeological site was repeating itself nearly two thousand years later among my students. More "valuable" stone—functionally superior and difficult to obtain—was used more efficiently, and there was far less waste than in stone that was easy to obtain and more difficult to work. I could now phrase this insight as a hypothesis and test it using the site data: More valuable lithic materials were used more efficiently at the Loomis II archaeological site (Feder 1981). In fact, by a number of measurements, this turned out to be precisely the case. The hypothesis itself came to me when I wasn't thinking of anything in particular; I was simply sweeping the floor.

It may take great skill and imagination to invent a hypothesis in the attempt to understand why things seem to work the way they do. Remember, Division 1 at the Vienna General Hospital did not have written over its doors, "Overcrowded Division" or "Division with Student Doctors Who Don't Wash Their Hands After Autopsies." It took imagination, first, to recognize that there were differences between the divisions and, second, to hypothesize that some of the differences might logically be at the root of the mystery. After all, there were in all likelihood many differences between the divisions: their compass orientations, the names of the nurses, the precise alignment of the windows, the astrological signs of the doctors who worked in the divisions, and so on. If a scientist were to attempt to test all of these differences as hypothetical causes of a mystery, nothing would ever be solved. Occam's razor must be applied. We need to focus our intellectual energies on those possible explanations that require few other assumptions. Only after all of these have been eliminated can we legitimately consider others. As summarized by that great fictional detective, Sherlock Holmes:

> It is of the highest importance in the art of detection to be able to recognize, out of a number of facts, which are incidental and which are vital. Otherwise, your energy and attention must be dissipated instead of being concentrated. (Doyle 1891–1902:275)

Semmelweis concentrated his attention on first four, then a fifth possible explanation. Like all good scientists he had to use some amount of what we can call "intuition" to sort out the potentially vital from the probably incidental. Even in the initial sorting we may be wrong. Overcrowding, birth position, and psychological trauma seemed like very plausible explanations to Semmelweis, but they were wrong nonetheless.

Testing Hypotheses

Finally, it takes skill and inventiveness to suggest ways for testing the hypothesis in question. We must, out of our own heads, be able to invent the "then" part of our "if . . . then" statements. We need to be able to suggest those things that must be true if our hypothesis is to be supported. There really is an art to that. Anyone can claim there was a Lost Continent of Atlantis (Chapter 7), but often it takes a truly inventive mind to suggest precisely what archaeologists must find if the hypothesis of its existence is indeed to be validated.

Semmelweis tested his hypotheses and solved the mystery of childbed fever by changing conditions in Division 1 to see if the death rate would change. In essence, testing each hypothesis was an experiment.

It might seem obvious that medical researchers, physicists, or chemists working in labs can perform experiments, observe the results, and come to reasonable conclusions about what transpired. But how about the historical disciplines, including historical geology, history, and prehistoric archaeology? Researchers in these fields cannot go back in time to be there when the events they are attempting to describe and explain took place. Can they really know what happened in the past?

Yes, they can, by what historians Michael Shermer and Alex Grobman (2000:32) call a "convergence of evidence." For example, in their book *Denying History: Who Says the Holocaust Never Happened and Why Do They Say It?* they respond to those who deny that the Germans attempted to exterminate the Jewish population of Europe in the 1930s and 1940s. After all, even though that era isn't ancient history, we still can't return to observe it for ourselves, so how do we know what really happened? Shermer and Grobman marshal multiple sources of evidence, including documents like letters, speeches, blueprints, and articles where Germans discussed their plans; eyewitness accounts of individual atrocities; photographs showing the horror of the camps; the physical remains of the camps themselves; inferential evidence like demographic data showing that approximately 6 million European Jews disappeared during this period. Though we cannot travel back in time to the 1940s, these different and independent lines of evidence converge, allowing us to conclude with absolute certainty that a particular historical event—in this case, the Holocaust—actually happened. Indeed, we can know what happened in history—and prehistory.

Ultimately, whether a science is experimentally based or not makes little logical difference in testing hypotheses. Instead of predicting what the results of a given experiment must be if our induced hypothesis is useful or valid, we predict what new data we must be able to find if a given hypothesis is correct.

For instance, we may hypothesize that long-distance trade is a key element in the development of civilization based on our analysis of the ancient Maya. We deduce that if this is correct—if this is, in fact, a general rule of cultural evolution—then we must find large quantities of trade items in other parts of the world where civilization also developed. We might further deduce that these items should be found in contexts that denote their value and importance to the society (for example, in the burials of leaders). We must then determine the validity of our predictions and, indirectly, our hypothesis by going out and conducting more research. We need to excavate sites belonging to other ancient civilizations and see if they followed the same pattern as seen for the Maya relative to the importance of trade.

Testing of hypotheses takes a great deal of thought, and we can make mistakes. We must remember: We have a hypothesis, we have the deduced implications, and we have the test. We can make errors at any place within this process—the hypothesis may be incorrect, the implications may be wrong, or the way we test them may be incorrect. Scientists are not perfect, and biases and preconceptions can interfere with this process. Certainty in science is a scarce commodity. There are always new hypotheses, alternative explanations, and more deductive implications to test. Nothing is ever finished, nothing is set in concrete, nothing is ever defined or raised to the level of religious truth.

The Human Enterprise of Science

Science is a very human endeavor practiced by imperfect human beings. Scientists are not isolated from the cultures and times in which they live. They share many of the same prejudices and biases of other members of their societies. Scientists learn from mentors at universities and inherit their perspectives. It often is quite difficult to go against the scientific grain, to question accumulated wisdom, and to suggest a new approach or perspective.

Consider the case of meteors. Today we take it for granted that sometimes quite large, extraterrestrial, natural objects go streaking across the sky and sometimes even strike the ground (then they are called meteorites). You may even be aware that major meteor showers can be seen twice a year: the Perseid shower in August and the Leonid shower in November. Perhaps you have been lucky enough to see a major meteor or "bolide," an awesome example of nature's fireworks. But until about two hundred years ago the notion that solid stone or metallic objects originating in space regularly enter the earth's atmosphere and sometimes strike the ground was controversial and, in fact, rejected by most scientists. In 1704 Sir Isaac Newton categorically rejected the notion that there could be meteors because he did not believe there could be any cosmological source for them.

The quality of an argument and the evidence marshalled in its support should be all that matters in science. The authority or reputation of the scientist should not matter. Nevertheless, not many scientists were willing to go against the considered opinion of as bright a scientific luminary as Isaac Newton. Even so, a few brave thinkers risked their reputations by concluding that meteors really did originate in outer space. Their work was roundly criticized, at least for a time. But science is "self-corrective." Hypotheses are constantly being refined and retested as new data are collected.

In 1794, over the skies of Siena, Italy, there was a spectacular shower of about three thousand meteors, seen by tens of thousands of people (Cowen 1995). Even then, a nonmeteoric explanation was suggested. By coincidence, Mount Vesuvius had erupted just eighteen hours before the shower, and some tried to blame the volcano for being the source of the objects flaming in the skies over Italy.

Critics did what they could to dispel the "myth" of an extraterrestrial source for the streaks of light over Siena, but they could not succeed. Further investigation of subsequent major meteor falls in the late 1700s and early 1800s, as well as examination of the chemical makeup of some of the objects that had actually fallen from the sky (an iron and nickel alloy not found on earth), convinced most by the early nineteenth century that meteors are what we now know them to be—extraterrestrial chunks of stone or metal that flame brightly when they enter our planet's atmosphere.

Philosopher of science Thomas Kuhn (1970) has suggested that the growth of scientific knowledge is not neatly linear, with knowledge simply building on knowledge. He maintains that science remains relatively static for periods and that most thinkers work under the same set of assumptions—the same *paradigm*. New ideas or perspectives, like those of Semmelweis or Einstein, that challenge the existing orthodoxy are usually initially rejected. Only once scientists get over the shock of the new ideas and start testing the new frameworks suggested by these new paradigms are great jumps in knowledge made.

That is why in science we propose, test, tentatively accept, but never prove a hypothesis. We keep only those hypotheses that cannot be disproved. As long as a hypothesis holds up under the scrutiny of additional testing through experiment and is not contradicted by new data, we accept it as the best explanation so far. Some hypotheses sound good, pass the rigors of initial testing, but are later shown to be inadequate or invalid. Others—for example, the hypothesis of biological evolution—have held up so well (all new data either were or could have been deduced from it) that they will probably always be upheld. We usually call these very well supported hypotheses *theories*. However, it is in the nature of science that no matter how well an explanation of some aspect of reality has held up, we must always be prepared to consider new tests and better explanations.

Table 2.1 *Books That Explain the Scientific Method*

Author	Book Title	Year	Publisher
Stephen Carey	*A Beginner's Guide to Scientific Method*	1998	Wadsworth
Thomas Gilovich	*How We Know What Isn't So*	1991	Free Press
Howard Kahane	*Logic and Contemporary Rhetoric: The Use of Reason in Everyday Life*	1998	Wadsworth
Robert Park	*Voodoo Science: The Road from Foolishness to Fraud*	2000	Oxford University Press
Daisie Radner and Michael Radner	*Science and Unreason*	1982	Wadsworth
Milton Rothman	*The Science Gap: Dispelling Myths and Understanding the Reality of Science*	1992	Prometheus Books
Carl Sagan	*The Demon-Haunted World*	1996	Random House
Michael Shermer	*Why People Believe Weird Things*	1997	W. H. Freeman
Theodore Schick and Lewis Vaughn	*Thinking About Weird Things: Critical Thinking for a New Age*	1999	Mayfield
Lewis Wolpert	*The Unnatural Nature of Science*	1993	Harvard University Press
Charles Wynn and Arthur Wiggins	*Quantum Leaps in the Wrong Direction*	2001	Joseph Henry Press

We are interested in knowledge and explanations of the universe that work. As long as these explanations work, we keep them. As soon as they cease being effective because new data and tests show them to be incomplete or misguided, we discard them and seek new ones. In one sense, Semmelweis was wrong after all, though his explanation worked at the time—he did save lives through its application. We now know that there is nothing inherently bad in "cadaveric material." Dead bodies are not the cause of childbed fever. Today we realize that it is bacteria that can grow in the flesh of a dead body that can get on a doctor's hands, infect a pregnant woman, and cause her death. Semmelweis worked in a time before the existence of such things was known. Science in this way always grows, expands, and evolves. See Table 2.1 for a number of works that discuss the method of science.

Science and Archaeology

The study of the human past is a science and relies on the same general logical processes that all sciences do. Unfortunately, perhaps as a result of its popularity, the data of archaeology have often been used by people to attempt to prove some idea or claim. Too often, these attempts have been bereft of science.

Archaeology has attracted frauds and fakes. Myths about the human past have been created and popularized. Misunderstandings of how archaeologists go about their tasks and what we have discovered about the human story have too often been promulgated. As I stated in Chapter 1, my purpose is to describe the misuse of archaeology and the nonscientific application of the data from this field. In the chapters that follow, the perspective of science will be applied to frauds, myths, and mysteries concerning the human past.

FREQUENTLY ASKED QUESTIONS

1. Can science answer all of our questions?

No, but it never promised to. Science is a process, a way to approach questions about the physical world (including people and their cultures), not the metaphysical world. Scientists endeavor to understand how the universe works. The search for meaning is valuable and we all do it: Why are we here in this universe? What is the point of our existence? How should we behave toward one another? How should we treat the planet on which we live? Though science can provide the framework for a worldview or philosophy, the answers to these philosophical questions are not discovered through science.

2. Doesn't scientific truth change in every generation?

In a sense, this is true. But our understanding of the world is not simply cyclical. We do not build an edifice of knowledge today only to tear it down tomorrow. The knowledge accumulated by each generation of scientists is refined and built upon by each subsequent generation. We really do know more today about how the solar system formed, the constituents of atoms, earth history, the etiology of disease, and the evolution of our species than we knew a century, a decade, or even a year ago.

BEST OF THE WEB

http://www.research-nurses.com/retrospective_semmelweis.html
A brief presentation about childbed fever, with a series of statements taken directly from *The Etiology, Concept and Prophylaxis of Childbed Fever,* written by Ignaz Semmelweis, the Hungarian doctor who solved the mystery.

http://www.csicop.org/bibliography/home.cgi
Extensive bibliography and reviews by skeptics of numerous topics related to the occult and the paranormal, as well as examination of fringe claims, including those made about the field of archaeology.

http://www.skepticfriends.org/
Click on the links for The Scientific Method and A Field Guide to Critical Thinking. Wonderfully concise discussions to supplement Chapter 2.

CRITICAL THINKING EXERCISES

1. A televised "documentary" called "The Alien Autopsy" purported to depict the genuine autopsy of an extraterrestrial alien killed in a crash, presumably at Roswell, New Mexico, more than forty years ago. Using Occam's razor, how would you explain such a film? What kind of evidence would be needed before you would accept the claim that the alien autopsy shown in the film represents the genuine examination of the corpse of an extraterrestrial alien? After answering these questions, visit the Web site http://www.trudang.com/autopsy.html for the perspective of a group of Hollywood special effects experts.

2. How do we know that the Holocaust really happened? What is meant by the assertion that we know it happened as the result of a "convergence of evidence"?

3. Now go back and look at the topics listed in Table 1.1 in Chapter 1. How would you test each of these topics scientifically—in other words, how would you test the validity of UFOs as extraterrestrial spacecraft, the reality of ESP, and the rest?

◆◆◆◆◆◆◆◆ *3* ◆◆◆◆◆◆◆◆

Anatomy of an Archaeological Hoax

It is not certain which was the best part for Shinichi Fujimura before he was found out and relegated to a psychiatric hospital. Perhaps it was being a well-respected, internationally known archaeologist, even though he had no degree or even training in the subject. Maybe it was when the newspapers called him "God's Hand" for his remarkable ability to regularly find archaeological sites more than ten times older than any previously discovered in Japan. It might have been seeing artifacts he had personally unearthed gracing the glass exhibit cases of the National Museum of his home nation. Or perhaps the most gratifying aspect of the entire affair was having his colleagues joyfully exclaim that his work would lead to rewriting the textbooks of Japanese history—and then their rewriting of those textbooks, gratefully acknowledging Fujimura for his inestimable contribution to the discipline of archaeology.

Well, they are rewriting the textbooks again in response to the accomplishments of Shinichi Fujimura, but this time it is a result of the revelation—and admission—that he was a fraud. Before Fujimura, an amateur prehistorian with little scientific training, Japanese prehistory was chronologically shallow compared to that of China or Korea, a mere 35,000-year tip on the more than 600,000-year iceberg that is northeast Asian prehistory. But beginning in 1981, first alone and later with the naïve assistance of dozens of scholars from all over the world, Fujimura expanded Japanese prehistory deep into the Asian Stone Age, easily matching the antiquity of its continental neighbors. A grateful nation proud of its past and an admiring cohort of colleagues lauded Fujimura, making him the most famous archaeologist in Japan—the man they called God's Hand.

God's Hand, indeed. Fujimura, ultimately, was as much a fool as a fabricator, never learning one of the cardinal rules of the archaeological hoaxer: Don't appear too lucky. Whether fueled by jealousy, resentment, or scientific

Figure 3.1   Caught in the act. Japanese archaeologist Shinichi Fujimura, whose incredible luck at finding astonishingly ancient artifacts in Japan earned him the nickname "God's Hand," is here caught by a hidden camera showing that neither luck nor God had anything to do with it. Fujimura is planting genuine artifacts from the Asian mainland at a Japanese site that, in reality, is not nearly as old as the artifacts. (© Mainichi Newspapers)

skepticism over his seemingly uncanny ability to find extraordinarily ancient sites, a few archaeologists had quietly felt that Fujimura must have had something more than mere luck going for him. Whatever luck he did have ran out when on October 22, 2000, a team of investigative reporters from one of Japan's national daily newspapers, *Mainichi Shimbun*, took the extraordinary step of positioning a hidden video camera at the site Fujimura was excavating (Holden 2000; Normille 2001a, 2001b). Blissfully unaware that he had been caught on tape, Fujimura sprung the trap on himself the very next day when he announced at a press conference his discovery of yet another astoundingly ancient site, with clusters of stone tools found under, and therefore older than, a volcanic deposit dated to 570,000 years ago. *Mainichi Shimbun* held its fire until November 5, when it printed still images from the video clearly showing Fujimura on the night before the discovery and press conference, carefully placing artifacts that obviously came from somewhere else into the excavation where he was to "find" them on the following day (Figure 3.1).

In a word: busted. Within hours of the revelation of fraud, a contrite and emotionally decimated Fujimura held a press conference where he confessed, explaining his behavior as the result of the enormous pressure placed on him by his colleagues, his countrymen, and himself to find ever older and more impressive evidence of ancient Japanese culture. He maintained at the time that he had planted artifacts at only two sites and had never before fabricated data. It was only the result of bad luck, it seemed, that in one of the two instances where he committed an archaeological fraud, a hidden camera was watching and recording his actions.

Fujimura's colleagues in Japanese archaeology were aghast, certainly, at their own unintentional complicity in the affair: by not asking enough questions, by not being skeptical enough, by not more carefully monitoring Fujimura's fieldwork. At the same time, Fujimura's colleagues understood that whatever damage had been done to their own professional reputations, the damage to Japanese prehistory was far more significant (Lepper 2001). When did Fujimura's lies begin—and had they really stopped? Was he being honest in maintaining that he had falsified only two sites? What about all the other sites he had worked on? Could archaeologists accept any as legitimate? Were there, in fact, any Japanese sites older than 35,000 years that could be trusted? Were all the textbooks—the ones rewritten to accommodate a far deeper Japanese prehistory as a result of Fujimura's discoveries—wrong and in need of serious *re*-revision? Or was Fujimura just a pitiable figure, once an important researcher, whose work should not be dismissed simply because he had made a significant, but understandable, mistake?

Additional investigation, very regrettably, proved that Fujimura's insistence that he had faked just two sites was yet another falsification in a fabric of deceit. It was far worse than two sites. By October 2001, the *Mainichi Shimbun* reporters (Dirty-Digger Scandal 2001) had documented not two, but *forty-two* sites where Fujimura had obtained older artifacts, often from China or Korea, where sites of greater age are well known, and planted them in deep and ancient soil layers at Japanese sites. Indeed, the textbooks would have to be rewritten by a contrite, deeply saddened, and, to be honest, humbled archaeological community.

Was it fame, wealth, the respect of his colleagues, a desire to provide his nation with a depth of antiquity the equal of its neighbors, or, more likely, some complex combination or permutation of all of these that led to Shinichi Fujimura's descent into, first, deceit and, then, disgrace? There doesn't seem to be any evidence of another rationale for archaeological hoaxes listed in Chapter 1—the desire for wealth. Fujimura does not appear to have been in it for the money.

The same cannot be said for George Hull or Stub Newell in New York State, in 1869. Unlike Fujimura, the rationale for their hoax cannot be explained as the result of a genuine love for and interest in archaeology, their nation, or even a desire for fame. Their singular archaeological hoax was done for a singular reason: money.

The Cardiff Giant: The Goliath of New York

Hull and Newell's hoax succeeded, if only briefly, for the rather peculiar reason that many people in the nineteenth century believed in the past existence of a race of giant human beings, 8, 9, or even 10 feet tall. They believed this because the Bible clearly stated that giant people inhabited the earth in ancient times. The Book of Genesis in the Old Testament makes it clear: "There were giants in the earth in those days" (Genesis 6:4). A computer search of the Bible produces eighteen specific references to giant people, including the entire Kingdom of Og in a place called Bashan (part of modern Syria). There are several other biblical references to "the valley of the giants" and a few allusions to the "remnants of the giants"—it seems that even in biblical times the feeling was that the giants' tenure on earth had already passed, and there were only a few of them left.

There is an explicit description of one of these remaining "giants" in the Bible's Book of Samuel. In relating the famous story of David and Goliath, the writers provide this very detailed description of Goliath's truly mammoth proportions:

> And there went out a champion out of the camp of the Philistines named Goliath of Gotha whose height was six cubits and a span. And he had a helmet of brass upon his head, and he was armed with a coat of mail, and the weight of the coat was five thousand shekels of brass . . . his spear's head weighed six hundred shekels of iron. (1 Samuel 17:4–7)

We do not measure things in *cubits, spans,* or *shekels,* so you'll need some help here. A cubit, the distance from the tip of the middle finger to the elbow, has had a number of slightly varying definitions in different cultures and times. The range has been between 17 and 21 inches. The nearest guess for biblical times is about 18 inches. A span is defined as the distance between your thumb and pinky with your palm spread, which should be half a cubit or about 9 inches. A shekel, an ancient Hebrew measure of weight, was about one-half of one of our ounces.

If we translate Goliath's measurements into our modern system, we can calculate that, according to the authors of the Old Testament, Goliath stood 9 feet 9 inches in height, his armor weighed over 150 pounds, and his spearhead alone tipped the scales at close to 19 pounds.

Remember, in the nineteenth century the literal truth of everything in the Bible was believed by more than just a small minority of zealous fundamentalists. For many, claims made in the Bible were not considered hypotheses to be tested against data. They were not seen as legends, myths, or allegorical tales. They were instead viewed as revelations simply to accept and believe as historical truths. For many, there was no question about it; Adam and Eve really were the first human beings, Jonah really was swallowed by a whale, and a nearly 10-foot-tall giant named Goliath actually existed. Although most of us today would be highly skeptical of the existence of a race of 10-foot-tall giants, many God-fearing people in Europe and North America before the twentieth century probably did believe in giants.

Not surprisingly, during this time rumors circulated concerning the discovery of evidence of ancient giant men (along with tales of the discovery of Noah's Ark, pieces of the true cross, and so on). In New York State there was a rumor that the skeletons of five enormous human beings had been found during the building of a railroad grade (Silverberg 1989). In the early 1700s Cotton Mather, who previously had helped inspire the Salem witch trials, claimed that some huge bones sent to him by the governor of Massachusetts were the remains of "sinful giants" drowned in Noah's Flood (Howard 1975).

So, it was clear. The Bible said there had been a race of giants in the old days, and there could be no question about it—there really had been giants. Any artifacts or finds that would help support such a biblical claim were accepted unquestioningly by many.

The Discovery

On Saturday, October 16, 1869, a local farmer by the name of Stub Newell hired some men to dig a well behind the barn on his farm in Cardiff, New York, just south of Syracuse. While digging, the workmen came across something very hard and large at a depth of about 3 feet. Though curious, Newell was said to be "annoyed and perplexed" by the discovery—it was reported in the *Syracuse Daily Journal* of Wednesday, October 20, 1869, that he had even suggested filling up the pit and keeping the whole thing quiet. Nevertheless, Newell had the workers expand their excavations. When they were done, the group of men looked down with amazement on their thoroughly remarkable discovery. Lying at their feet in the pit was a man of enormous size and proportions whose body, it seemed, had turned to stone (Figure 3.2). He indeed appeared to be a man over 10 feet in height, with 21-inch-long feet and 3-foot-wide shoulders. He seemed to be "petrified" like the trees in Petrified Forest National Park in eastern Arizona (Figure 3.3).

More than 200 million years ago, trees growing in Arizona in what was then a marshland were buried by sediment rich in minerals—silica in particular. The silica leached into the trees, filling in the spaces both between and within the individual cells of wood, solidifying and replacing the wood as it decayed away. In some cases the silica faithfully reproduced the appearance of the original tree rings and even the actual cells of the ancient trees. If it could happen to trees, so the argument went, perhaps it could have hap-

Figure 3.2   An 1869 photograph of the Cardiff Giant in its place of discovery on the Stub Newell farm. An unidentified digger stands to the right of the Giant, and curious onlookers gaze down on the remarkable discovery. (Courtesy of the New York State Historical Association, Cooperstown)

pened to a person. Thus was the "discovery" of the Cardiff Giant made and the legend of a petrified giant man born.

The potential value of the discovery was an immediate topic of conversation among the discoverers and a growing group of curious neighbors. One neighbor proffered Newell $50 for a one-quarter share of the Giant. Another offered to do all the work in removing the Giant and preparing it for exhibition for a one-half share. According to a *Syracuse Daily Journal* article (The Lafayette Wonder, October 20, 1869), a couple of local farmers were so certain of the potential profits to be made that they offered to give Newell their farms in exchange for the Giant! In that same article, a bid of $10,000 is mentioned. Yet Newell, ostensibly just a simple country farmer, turned down these remarkable offers.

Word quickly spread in the sleepy little town of a few hundred, and soon, that very afternoon and the next day in fact, local people were gazing with astonishment at the spectacular find in the bottom of the pit behind Stub Newell's barn. As a reporter for the *Syracuse Daily Journal* put it, "Men

Figure 3.3   Petrified wood, like these remarkably preserved specimens of fossilized trees from Arizona, were seen as models for what might have happened to the Cardiff Giant. If wood could turn to stone, the argument went, so might the body of a giant man from before Noah's Flood. (K. L. Feder)

left their work, women caught up their babies, and children in numbers all hurried to the scene where the interest of that little community centered" (The Lafayette Wonder, 1869).

Newell then exhibited a remarkable degree of business acumen as well as surprising intuition concerning the marketability of the unique discovery on his property. No more than two days passed before Newell obtained a license to exhibit the Giant and purchased and erected a tent over the slumbering, petrified man. He then began to charge twenty-five cents, soon upping the fee to fifty cents for a peek, and the paying public came in droves (Figure 3.4).

From all over New York State, the Northeast, and even beyond, 300 to 500 people daily flocked to the Newell farm. On the first few weekends after its discovery, thousands showed up, all more than ready to wait in line and pay their half-dollar to get a brief glimpse of the petrified "Goliath" of Cardiff (it was actually called that in advertisements). All thoughts of farming on the Newell homestead were abandoned as the crowd of carriages carrying the curious from the train station in Syracuse to the Newell farm increased. The entire farm was transformed virtually overnight into a highly profitable tourist enterprise, with a food tent, carriage service, cider stand, and, of course, the center of attraction—the awe-inspiring Giant himself

Figure 3.4   Just days after his "discovery," Stub Newell forgot about farming, erected a tent over the giant petrified man, and began charging people fifty cents to view its remains. (Courtesy of the Onondaga Historical Association, Syracuse)

(Figure 3.5). One of Newell's relatives, George Hull, estimated in a later report that appeared in the *Ithaca Daily Journal* (The Cardiff Giant, January 4, 1898) that by not quite three weeks after the discovery Newell had collected approximately $7,000 in admission fees—a remarkable sum even by today's standards.

Stub Newell was not the only one profiting from this lucky discovery on his property. Although the two small hotels in town were benefiting from a great influx of business, Cardiff was simply too small to accommodate the incredible surge of tourists who were making the trek to see the Giant. These people needed to be fed and housed, and that job fell to the businessmen of nearby Syracuse. In a very short time, the Cardiff Giant became a major factor in the economy of that city. Pilgrims streamed into town to pay homage to the Giant and, at the same time, to pay their dollars for the services such a tourist attraction demanded.

The economic impact of the Giant on Syracuse cannot be underestimated and was enough to convince a consortium of Syracuse businessmen and professional people to make Stub an offer he couldn't refuse. Although a number of attempts to purchase shares in the Giant previously had been rebuffed, on October 23, just one week after its discovery, these astute people paid Newell $37,000 for a three-fourths interest in the Giant. Although

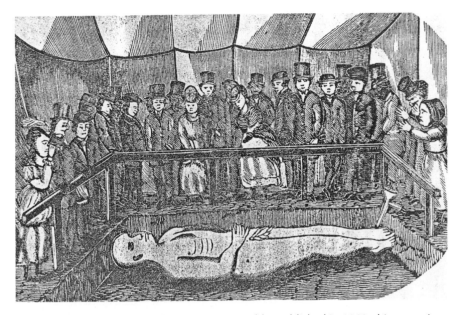

Figure 3.5   From *The Onondaga Giant,* a pamphlet published in 1869, this engraving shows a crowd of people viewing the Giant in the tent on the Newell farm. Note the strategically placed fig leaf.

difficult to calculate, a colleague (John Coyle) estimates that in modern currency this would translate to about half a million dollars. Amazing. By purchasing a controlling share in the Giant, these businessmen were ensuring that it would stay near Syracuse, where it could continue to boost the local economy. At the same time they were assuring themselves a part of the enormous profits the Giant seemed certain to produce.

They were almost right. Between October 23 and November 5, the Syracuse investors had already made back $12,000 of their investment exhibiting the Giant at the Newell farm (Franco 1969:431). I'll save you the math—at fifty cents admission and three-fourths ownership of the Giant and its profits, in that short period about 32,000 people paid for the privilege of seeing the Cardiff Giant.

With no sign of "Giant mania" abating and with visions of dollar signs dancing in their heads, the Syracuse businessmen decided to move the Giant to Syracuse itself, where it would be easier for even greater numbers of people to see it. With great pomp and ceremony, not to mention free publicity through local newspaper coverage, the Giant was disinterred and transported to an exhibition hall in Syracuse. Among its admirers was the circus entrepreneur P. T. Barnum, who made an attempt to buy the Giant but was turned down. According to the *Ithaca Daily Journal* article mentioned earlier, Barnum then offered the syndicate of owners $60,000 (about $750,000 in modern dollars) merely for the use of the Giant for three months. Again he was rebuffed. Barnum was not to give up trying to make a circus attraction out of the Giant, however. His unique solution to the problem will be discussed later.

The Beginning of the End

Everything seemed to be going well. Newspapers were printing feature articles about the Giant. The local railroad even made a regular, 10-minute stop across the street from where it was being exhibited in Syracuse to enable people just passing through to run in to see the giant petrified man. People continued to come in great numbers to see the miraculously preserved, petrified giant man from before Noah's Flood.

But all was not well. Slowly at first, but then at an accelerating rate, rumors began to surface that the Giant was a fake. A local resident, Daniel Luce, provided a detailed report, recounted in the *Syracuse Standard* (The Stone Giant, November 1, 1869), of an extremely large wagon, carrying a sizable and obviously heavy load, that he remembered traveling toward Cardiff the previous year. Some wondered out loud whether the very large wagon had been carrying a giant statue of a man.

There is also some testimony, as indicated in the *Ithaca Daily Journal* article already cited, that Stub Newell had begun bragging to relatives about the profitable fraud he had perpetrated on the American public.

Beyond this—and this is very important—professional scientists, including geologists and paleontologists, and even artists who had traveled to Cardiff or Syracuse to examine the Giant in detail, almost without exception immediately declared it to be at best a statue and at worst a fraud. J. F. Boynton, a geologist at the University of Pennsylvania, stated after carefully examining the Giant:

> It is positively absurd to consider this a fossil man. It has none of the indications that would designate it as such, when examined by a practical chemist, geologist, or naturalist. (The Lafayette Wonder, 1869)

At first Boynton thought the Cardiff Giant might have been an actual historical artifact of some antiquity, a statue produced by a community of Jesuits who had lived in the area between 1520 and 1760. Boynton was suspicious, however, after noting the presence of fresh plant material mixed in with the soil from above the Giant, indicating a probable recent burial.

Following a more detailed analysis of the Giant, Boynton declared to a reporter for *Harper's Weekly* magazine (The Cardiff Giant, December 4, 1869) that it was carved of a soft stone called gypsum. He went on to say in that same article that the soft nature of the stone and the amount of weathering on its surface suggested that the Giant had been buried *not more than three years* previous to its disinterment. He even went on to calculate more precisely that the Giant had most likely been in the ground only a little more than one year (approximately 370 days), based on his precise analysis of the rate of weathering of the gypsum from which it was made. As we will see, Boynton's calculation was amazingly accurate.

Othniel C. Marsh, a professor at Yale University and one of the best-known paleontologists of his time, probably was the most important of the scientific skeptics. Marsh examined the Giant and declared it to be "very remarkable." When asked by one of the Giant's owners if they could quote Marsh on that, Marsh is supposed to have said, "No. You may quote me on this though: a very remarkable fake!" (Howard 1975:208).

Like Boynton, Marsh correctly noted that the Giant was made of gypsum, a soft stone that would not last long in the wet soil of the Newell farm. (Gypsum is a sedimentary rock and exhibits layering, unlike petrified wood.) Previous to Marsh's investigation, a well-known sculptor, Eratus Dow Palmer, had examined the Giant, identifying the marks of a sculptor's tools on its surface. Marsh confirmed the existence of tool marks on the alleged petrified man.

The skepticism of so highly respected a scientist as Marsh had some impact, and a number of the New York City newspapers (in particular, the *New York Herald*) that had previously praised the Giant now changed their opinions. But the statements of Marsh and other, less well known scientists could not alone dissuade the public from the notion that the Cardiff Giant was a real, petrified man whose existence supported biblical stories of human giants before Noah's Flood.

Hull's Confession

The meteoric rise to fame of the Cardiff Giant was cut short, and his fall from grace was just as quick. A previously shadowy figure involved with promoting the Giant confessed in December 1869 to perpetrating a fraud on the American public. George Hull, a distant relation of Stub Newell, unburdened his soul, and the Giant's value dropped from that of a spectacular archaeological find to that of one slightly worn chunk of gypsum.

George Hull was a cigar manufacturer in Binghamton, New York. Ironically, he also was a devout atheist. He revealed the entire story toward the end of his life in an interview he gave to the *Ithaca Daily Journal* (The Cardiff Giant, 1898).

During a visit to his sister's house in Iowa in 1866, Hull had a long and heated conversation with a Methodist minister traveling through the area. Apparently, the conversation focused on extraordinary biblical stories, like those mentioned at the beginning of this chapter concerning the existence of an ancient race of giant men. Hull suggested to the minister that the Bible was filled with such tall tales, impossibilities that only the gullible would believe. The minister took strong exception to this characterization, maintaining the literal truth of every Bible story. At midnight Hull retired to bed and, in his own words, "I lay wide awake wondering why people would believe those remarkable stories in the Bible about giants, when I suddenly thought of making a stone giant, and passing it off as a petrified man" (The Cardiff Giant, 1898).

In a subsequent visit to the Midwest in June 1868, Hull purchased an acre of land in Fort Dodge, Iowa, from which he quarried a 5-ton block of gypsum. He then had the block shipped to Chicago, where, swearing them to secrecy, he hired sculptors to produce a statue of a giant, slumbering man.

After work had gone on for a couple of months, the Giant was almost complete. On viewing it, however, Hull was unhappy. Initially, the face of the giant statue looked just like George Hull's own! The sculptors had even given the Giant hair and a beard to match Hull's. The stoneworkers could not be blamed. After all, this rather strange, secretive man had requested that they create a statue of a giant, naked, recumbent man—not the usual kind of request.

Obviously, it would not satisfy Hull's plan to have the Giant bear any resemblance whatsoever to its creator. It would not have been very convenient if any of the Giant's investigators had noticed the rather astonishing similarity between the face of the petrified man and that of Stub Newell's mysterious cousin.

But all was not lost. Hull first had the sculptors remove the hair on the head and face. However, he still was unsatisfied. He next got some blocks of wood into which he hammered a bunch of knitting needles so that their points stuck out of the faces of the blocks. Hull proceeded to pound on the Giant with these blocks. You can imagine the expression on the faces of the sculptors, seeing this madman attack the artistic creation he had just paid them to produce. Hull liked the effect though; it gave the surface of the statue the porelike appearance of skin. As if this weren't enough, Hull next rubbed acid all over the sculpture, which further reinforced its ancient appearance.

After all this, Hull finally was satisfied. The Giant now looked nothing like him. Better still, it looked very old. The scene at last was set for the great archaeological fraud.

Hull had the Giant shipped in a wooden box by railroad to Union, New York. In November 1868 it was finally brought by wagon to his cousin Stub Newell's farm and secretly buried behind the barn (with Newell's knowledge and cooperation). To make certain that no one would connect the shipment with the discovery of the Giant, it was left to lie in the ground for about a year—nearly the exact length of time geologist J. F. Boynton had suggested. Then, according to plan, nearly twelve months later, Hull instructed Newell to hire a crew of men to dig a well where they were both very much aware the Giant would be discovered. The rest is embarrassing history. It should finally be pointed out that it was apparently Newell's bragging to friends and relatives about the fraud that induced Hull to come clean before the whole thing blew up in their faces.

The other owners of the Giant, the businessmen of Syracuse who were benefiting from the Giant's presence, and the ministers who had included reference to the Giant's discovery in their Sunday sermons were not pleased by Hull's revelations. It did not seem likely that people were going to go out of their way and pay to see a gypsum statue that was 1½ years old. Beyond this, religious support for a fraud could damage the credibility of the religious leaders involved.

The syndicate of owners initially tried to quash the confession or at least discredit it. They claimed that Hull had been put up to it by the people of the surrounding towns because they were jealous of the discovery in Cardiff and the successful exploitation of it by Syracuse. But Hull's story was too detailed and reasonable to ignore. When the sculptors in Chicago came forward to verify Hull's confession, the Giant's days as a major tourist attraction were at an end.

The End of the Giant

The Giant's demise was not without its ironies. After P. T. Barnum had been turned down in his initial attempt to purchase the Giant, he simply went out and had a plaster duplicate made. He even billed the statue as the "real" Cardiff Giant, claiming that the owners had sold him the original and that they were exhibiting the copy. In truth, however, Barnum was charging people to see the Cardiff Giant, but his Cardiff Giant was the fake; it was, put bluntly, a fake of a fake! Needless to say, lawsuits were filed. After revenues dropped as a result of the Hull confession, the owners of the "real" fake took the Giant on the road, hoping to drum up some business and maybe even turn the whole fiasco of the confession to their advantage (Figure 3.6). Coincidentally, the real fake and Barnum's fake of the fake were both displayed at the same time in New York City—and Barnum's copy outdrew the real Cardiff Giant.

Mark Twain was so amused by the whole mess that he wrote a short story about it. "A Ghost Story" concerns a man who takes a room at a hotel in New York City and is then terrorized by the ghost of a poor, tormented, giant man. The ghost turns out to be, in fact, the spirit of the Cardiff Giant. The Giant's soul has been condemned to wander the earth until his physical remains are once again laid to rest. He nightly wanders the corridors of the hotel as his fossilized body is cruelly displayed in the exhibit hall across the street. But, as luck would have it, the poor tormented soul of the Giant has made a grievous error. As the hotel resident informed him, "Why you poor blundering old fossil, you have had all your trouble for nothing—you have

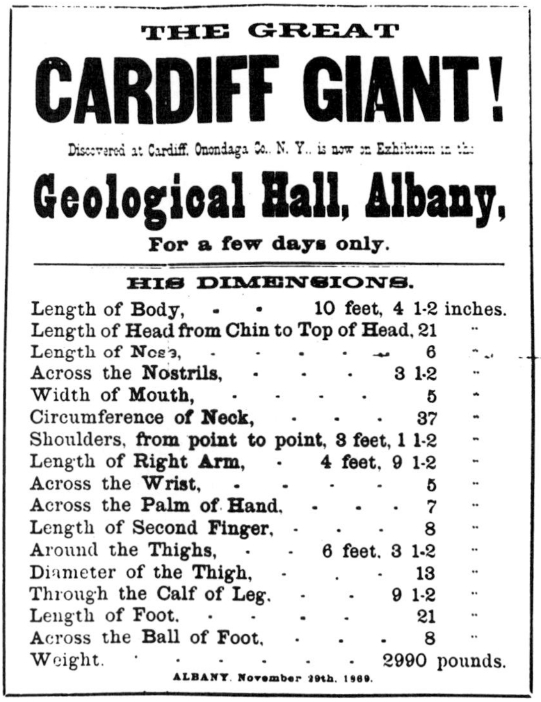

THE GREAT

CARDIFF GIANT!

Discovered at Cardiff, Onondaga Co., N. Y., is now on Exhibition in the

Geological Hall, Albany,

For a few days only.

HIS DIMENSIONS.

Length of Body,	10 feet, 4 1-2 inches.
Length of Head from Chin to Top of Head, 21	"
Length of Nose,	6 "
Across the Nostrils,	3 1-2 "
Width of Mouth,	5 "
Circumference of Neck,	37 "
Shoulders, from point to point, 3 feet, 1 1-2	"
Length of Right Arm,	4 feet, 9 1-2 "
Across the Wrist,	5 "
Across the Palm of Hand,	7 "
Length of Second Finger,	8 "
Around the Thighs,	6 feet, 3 1-2 "
Diameter of the Thigh,	13 "
Through the Calf of Leg,	9 1-2 "
Length of Foot,	21 "
Across the Ball of Foot,	8 "
Weight,	2990 pounds.

ALBANY, November 29th, 1869.

Figure 3.6 The Giant on tour. After serious questions were raised regarding the Giant's authenticity, the consortium of owners decided to take their show on the road. This handout advertised the Giant's appearance in Albany, New York, on November 29, 1869. (Courtesy of the New York State Historical Association, Cooperstown)

been haunting a plaster cast of yourself." The ghost of the poor Giant was haunting Barnum's fake. Even he was fooled.

Needless to say, once the hoax had been revealed, the lawsuits settled, and much fun poked, interest in the Giant waned. Though, thankfully, it was not broken up for road fill or some other use, the Giant faded into near oblivion, for decades stored in a barn and sadly awaiting, we can only imagine, his terrible fate. The Giant was not forgotten entirely, however, and on occasion he was trotted out for state fairs in New York, where he had achieved his initial fame, and Iowa, the place of his birth. Gardner Cowles, Jr., a newspaper publisher in Des Moines, Iowa, saw the Giant on one of its midwestern excursions and felt strongly that as a great American archaeological humbug it deserved a better fate. Cowles managed to purchase the Giant and brought it to Des Moines, where for a time it rested in repose in the recreation room of his house as what has to be one of the most peculiar conversation pieces that has ever graced an American domicile. It regained enough of its fame there as a local curiosity that a photograph of the Cowles rec room showing the Cardiff Giant appeared in the August 1939 issue of *National Geographic* magazine in an article about Iowa (coincidentally, a retired dean at my university, James Fox, grew up in the Des Moines area, was a frequent visitor to the Cowles house, being friends with Gardner

Cowles's young son, and clearly remembers the odd stone giant in the basement). The New York State Historical Association acquired the Giant from Cowles in 1947, returning it, so to speak, to the scene of the crime. It was installed as an exhibit at the Farmers' Museum in Cooperstown, New York, not far from the location of its greatest, though short-lived, triumph—in fooling people.

Why Did They Do It?

The motive for the perpetration of the Cardiff Giant fraud was, of course, money. George Hull and Stub Newell made far more money displaying the Giant than they ever could have through selling cigars or farming—their usual professions. Money continued to motivate those who benefited from the Giant but who played no part in perpetrating the fraud in the first place. The businessmen of Syracuse grew rich as a result of the Giant, and a small town in rural New York was put on the map.

There also is an explanation for why people with no monetary investment wished to believe that the Cardiff Giant was genuine. Certainly, the religious element behind the public's desire to believe in the validity of the Giant cannot be overestimated. When publications in 1869 referred to the discovery as a "Goliath," they were not making a simple analogy; they were making a serious comparison between the Cardiff discovery and the biblical story of Goliath of Gotha.

Moreover, I would also include the love of a mystery as an explanation for why people chose to accept the Giant even though scientists who studied it declared it to be, at best, a statue and, at worst, a fraud. Whether the Giant lent proof to a biblical claim or not, perhaps it was the simple romance of such an amazing discovery that played at least a secondary role in convincing people to part with their hard-earned money to see what was clearly a gypsum statue.

The lesson of the Cardiff Giant is one that you will see repeated in this book. Trained observers, professional scientists, had viewed the Giant and pronounced it to be an impossibility, a statue, a clumsy fraud, and just plain silly. Such objective, rational, logical, and scientific conclusions, however, had little impact. A chord had been struck in the hearts and minds of many otherwise levelheaded people, and little could dissuade them from believing in the truth of the Giant. Their acceptance of the validity of the Giant was based on their desire, religious or not, to believe it.

Even today, many creationists (see Chapter 11) claim that every word in the Bible is literally true. Just as many in previous centuries believed the literal, historical accuracy of biblical stories (including those of Adam and Eve, the Flood, and even giants), so do the modern creationists. Their belief in biblical giants has led some to claim that they have discovered enormous "mantracks"—the alleged footprints of human giants from "before the Flood." Some go even further, claiming, for example, that the ancient skeleton of a man 11 feet 6 inches tall was found in Italy in 1856 (Baugh 1987). Of course, when the so-called footprints are examined scientifically (see Chapter 11), they turn out not to be human footprints at all. The evidence exists, apparently, only in the minds of the claimants; not a single bone has been provided as evidence for this claim.

Though one might have hoped for their rehabilitation after the Cardiff Giant debacle, neither Hull nor Barnum was finished with giant hoaxes. Despite being competitors and even enemies in the case of the Cardiff Giant, they apparently called a truce, joined forces, and together produced yet another supposed petrified giant. Hull was the idea man; Barnum supplied the financial backing. Called the "Solid Muldoon," it was planted in Beulah, Colorado, in 1877 and "discovered" by a co-conspirator in the hoax in that same year. It looked a bit more authentic than that other member of its species, but its career was equally short-lived. One of Hull's associates revealed the Solid Muldoon's fraudulent origins when, perhaps not coincidentally, it was being shown in New York, the home state of its predecessor.

Finally, after laughing at all those silly people who in 1869 paid fifty cents to see the Giant, you can now all laugh at me; I recently paid several dollars to see him at the Farmers' Museum in Cooperstown—actually a wonderful place, well worth the price of admission. The poor, tortured Giant has at last found a final resting place in a recently refurbished exhibit there. Do I detect a hint of a smile on his face? I guess the Cardiff Giant has the last laugh after all (Figure 3.7).

Current Perspectives: Frauds

A clumsy fraud like the Cardiff Giant didn't fool scientists in the nineteenth century and certainly would fool no one today, but the hoaxers keep on trying. Consider this example. The artifacts that Connecticut State Archaeologist Nick Bellantoni and his crew recovered in their excavation of one corner of an otherwise unremarkable 3,000-year-old site in Pachaug State Forest in Voluntown, Connecticut, were unlike anything he had ever encountered in the state (Bellantoni 2002). To be frank, the objects Nick had excavated were equally perplexing to the other archaeologists he called in for counsel (Stowe 2001). Nothing like the twenty oddly carved stone effigies of birds, snakes, sperm whales, and people had ever been found by any of us at any native or colonial site in the state (Figure 3.8).

Nick had been directed to the site by a local hunter in 1997. While most of the 1997 excavation was uneventful, revealing stone spearpoints and ancient pottery, a handful of objects including a clay pipe, stone pendant, and copper beads didn't match the age of the site. Intrigued, Nick and his crew

Figure 3.7   In silent repose, the Giant has at last found his eternal rest at the Farmers' Museum in Cooperstown, New York. (K. L. Feder)

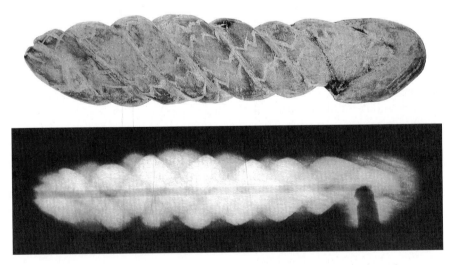

Figure 3.8   One of the Pachaug Forest fake artifacts. The top photograph is of a supposed smoking pipe; the bottom is an x ray of the artifact. The x-ray image shows a single, continuous drill hole running across the length of the pipe. This hole almost certainly was made with a mechanical, metal drill bit, applying technology unknown to the ancient inhabitants of Connecticut. (Courtesy Connecticut Archaeology Center)

returned in 2000 and discovered twenty strange stone carvings in a series of soil-filled pits in a location somewhat removed from the 1997 excavation.

Nick is a careful, methodical, meticulous, and experienced excavator. None of those adjectives could be applied to whoever clearly had buried the objects found in the 2000 dig. Nick's careful examination of the soil convinced him that the exotic artifacts they found that year had been planted only very recently. The soil in the general area where the objects were found was compact and hard, but the specific locations where the artifacts were recovered were much looser and softer, clearly having been dug up in the not-too-distant past.

Something else about the places where the objects were excavated betrayed the ineptitude of the hoaxer. The forest soil of Connecticut is universally rooty. Anybody digging through that soil, today or a thousand years ago, will, as a matter of course, cut through roots. For a period of a year or so after infilling, the interior surfaces of soil-filled pits will be dotted by the roots of trees and bushes incidentally cut through by whatever tool was used to dig the pit in the first place. After a time, however, some of the cut roots will die and disintegrate, some will regrow, and, over the years, new root growth will cut through the soil in the filled hole. But the soil-filled holes in which the Pachaug Forest artifacts were found showed little or no regrowth of roots and no new roots cutting through the surfaces of the now soil-filled pits. In fact, cut roots, still relatively fresh, were visible when Nick excavated the pits, and there even were a couple of fairly fresh oak leaves mixed in the soil matrix. It was Fujimura (with planted artifacts) and the Cardiff Giant (with fresh plant material underlying the statue) all over again. There was no way the pits into which the artifacts had been placed could have been dug more than a year or two before Nick excavated the site. Microscopic evidence of the use of metal power tools to carve some of the stone artifacts clinched it; the Pachaug Forest artifacts were a modern, very recent archaeological hoax.

The only remaining mysteries underlying the Pachaug Forest artifacts concern the identity and motive of the hoaxer. It might be nice to solve those mysteries, but the far more important issue is resolved. We need not rewrite the history books; the Pachaug Forest artifacts were made by neither ancient Indians nor colonial settlers of New England, but by a modern prankster with far too much time on his or her hands, in an attempt, apparently, to waste the time of our state archaeologist.

In later chapters a number of other famous, and some not so famous, archaeological and historical hoaxes will be discussed. Piltdown Man (Chapter 4), the Vinland Map (Chapter 5), the Newark Holy Stones (Chapter 6), and the giant "man-tracks" of the Paluxey River and the Shroud of Turin (Chapter 11) all have in common the fact that they were frauds perpetrated to fool people about some aspect of the past. They also have in common the fact that they were exposed by the careful application of the analytical tools of the archaeologist.

FREQUENTLY ASKED QUESTIONS

1. The Cardiff Giant was a hoax, but can a human body turn to stone?

No, not really. Wood cells are resilient enough, under the right circumstances, to preserve long enough for minerals to penetrate them, solidify, and take on their appearance. Bones, including human bones, can become mineralized in much the same way. Soft tissue—skin and muscle—simply is too soft for this process to work on it.

2. Can human bodies be preserved for long periods of time?

Yes, under the right, very rare circumstances, they can be preserved for thousands of years. Found in 1991, the so-called Ice Man, a remarkably well preserved body frozen in glacial ice near the border between Austria and Italy, was approximately 5,300 years old. The bodies of the so-called Bog People of Denmark were preserved for more than three thousand years by moisture and a combination of natural chemicals in the peat in which they were buried. Also, natural mummification under very dry conditions (in either warm or very cold climates) has preserved bodies for millennia. Ancient bodies have been found in Greenland and in the higher elevations of the Andes in South America. Waterlogged human brain tissue was preserved for more than seven thousand years at the Windover site in Florida. The key to the preservation of animal (including human) bodies rests in keeping away those organisms that ordinarily would recycle them. Bacteria that eat dead flesh do not do well under very cold, very wet (waterlogged), or very dry conditions. Keep bacteria away, and human bodies can be preserved for millennia.

3. Whatever happened to Barnum's fake of the Cardiff Giant?

Barnum's copy has turned up and can be seen at Marvin's Marvelous Mechanical Museum in Farmington Hills, Michigan. Further, it turns out that there is a replica of Barnum's copy (making it a fake of a fake of a fake) at Circus World Museum in Baraboo, Wisconsin. I thought you might like to know.

BEST OF THE WEB

http://www.lhup.edu/~dsimanek/cardiff.htm
Chapter from Andrew White's autobiography detailing the author's experiences in upstate New York when the Cardiff Giant was discovered.

http://www.roadsideamerica.com/attract/NYCOOgiant.html
Very cool site dealing with offbeat tourist sites, here discussing the Cardiff Giant.

http://www.stribble.com/cardiffgiant/
Senior thesis in history at Harvard by Scott Tribble devoted to a detailed discussion of the Cardiff Giant.

http://www.marvin3m.com/cardiff.htm
Marvin's Marvelous Mechanical Museum's home page. Visit to see P. T. Barnum's fake of the Cardiff Giant.

http://www.farmersmuseum.org/exhibitions/cardiff.htm
Web site of the Farmers' Museum, home to the Cardiff Giant.

◈ ◈ ◈ CRITICAL THINKING EXERCISE ◈ ◈ ◈

Which groups of people were immediate believers in the Cardiff Giant? On what did they base their acceptance of the "petrified man"? Which groups of people were immediately skeptical? On what did they base their skepticism? How can we explain the Giant's acceptance by the former groups and its rejection by the latter? What lessons in this story are applicable to other instances of frauds or hoaxes in science?

◈◈◈◈◈◈◈◈ 4 ◈◈◈◈◈◈◈◈

Dawson's Dawn Man:
The Hoax at Piltdown

Today, when you visit the Web site of the British Museum of Natural History, you can explore some of the details of the case of "Piltdown Man," certainly the most significant paleoanthropological hoax ever perpetrated and one in which the museum's scientists played an important, though likely unintentional, role (http://www.nhm.ac.uk/interactive/science-casebooks/piltdown/). The museum, however, has not always been so open about the hoax and its connection to it.

I visited the museum in the summer of 1996, hoping to see the actual remains of Piltdown Man. I knew the fossil was in the museum's possession, so, rather naturally, I assumed that this most famous of frauds would be prominently displayed.

When I had trouble finding the fossil in a museum case, I approached a woman at the front desk, asking where I might see the Piltdown remains. "Oh, that is not on display sir," she said, and went on to inform me, rather condescendingly, "It was all rubbish, you know." Well, I guess I knew that. It seems that the Piltdown Man fossil has been a literal skeleton in the closet of prehistoric archaeology and human paleontology.

This single specimen seemed to turn our understanding of human evolution on its head and certainly did turn the heads of not just a few of the world's most talented scientists. The story of Piltdown has been presented in detail by Ronald Millar in his 1972 book *The Piltdown Men*, by J. S. Weiner in his 1955 work *The Piltdown Forgery*, in 1986 by Charles Blinderman in *The Piltdown Inquest*, in 1990 by Frank Spencer in *Piltdown: A Scientific Forgery*, and most recently by John E. Walsh in 1996 in *Unraveling Piltdown: The Science Fraud of the Century and Its Solution*. The story is useful in its telling if only to show that, as seen in the Fujimura case, even scientific observers can be fooled. This is particularly the case when trained scientists are faced with something they are not trained to detect—intellectual criminality. But let us begin before the beginning, before the discovery of the Piltdown fossil.

The Evolutionary Context

We need to turn the clock back to Europe of the late nineteenth and early twentieth centuries. The concept of evolution—the notion that all animal and plant forms seen in the modern world had descended or evolved from earlier, ancestral forms—had been debated by scientists for quite some time (Greene 1959). It was not until Charles Darwin's *On the Origin of Species* was published in 1859, however, that a viable mechanism for evolution was proposed and supported with an enormous body of data. Darwin had meticulously studied his subject, collecting evidence from all over the world for more than thirty years in support of his evolutionary mechanism called *natural selection*. Darwin's arguments were so well reasoned that most scientists soon became convinced of the explanatory power of his theory. Darwin went on to apply his general theory to humanity in *The Descent of Man*, published in 1871. This book was also enormously successful, and more thinkers came to accept the notion of human evolution.

Around the same time that Darwin was theorizing about the biological origin of humanity, discoveries were being made in Europe and Asia that seemed to provide concrete evidence supporting the concept of human evolution from ancestral forms. In 1856 workmen building a roadway in the Neander Valley of Germany came upon a piece of a remarkable-looking fossil bone. Though just a "skull cap"—technically a *calvarium*, lacking the face and lower jaw—it clearly was no ape, but it was no modern human either. Though no smaller than a modern human's, the top of the skull was much flatter, the bone was thicker and heavier, and there was a massive ridge of bone across the eyebrows of a size unseen in modern populations. Around the same time, other, similar-looking but more complete fossils were found in Belgium and Spain. As well as being flat and massive and bearing thick brow ridges, these skulls exhibited sloping foreheads and jutting, snoutlike faces, quite distinct from those of modern human beings. However, the postcranial bones (all the bones below the skull) of these fossils were similar to those of modern humans.

There was some initial confusion about how to label these specimens. Some scientists concluded that they simply represented pathological freaks. Rudolf Virchow, the world's preeminent anatomist, explained the curious bony ridges above the eyes as the result of "stupendous blows" to the foreheads of the creatures (Kennedy 1975). Eventually, however, scientists realized that these creatures, then and now called *Neandertals* after the Neander Valley, represented an ancient form of humanity.

The growing acceptance of Darwin's theory of evolution and the discovery of primitive-looking, though humanlike, fossils combined to radically shift people's opinions about human origins. In fact, the initial abhorrence many felt concerning the entire notion of human evolution from lower, more primitive forms was remarkably changed in just a few decades (Greene 1959). By the turn of the twentieth century, not only were many people comfortable with the general concept of human evolution but there actually also developed a feeling of national pride concerning the discovery of a human ancestor within one's borders.

The Germans could point to their Neandertal skeletons and claim that the first primitive human being was a German. The French could counter that their own Cro-Magnon—ancient, though not as old as the German Neandertals—was a more modern-looking and advanced ancestor; therefore, the first true human was a Frenchman. Fossils had also been found in Belgium and Spain, so Belgians and Spaniards could claim for themselves a place within the story of human origin and development. Even so small a nation as Holland could lay claim to a place in human evolutionary history; in 1891 a Dutchman, Eugene Dubois, had discovered the fossilized remains of a primitive human ancestor in Java, an island in the Dutch colony of Dutch East India (now Indonesia).

However, one great European nation did not and could not materially contribute to the debate over the ultimate origins of humanity. That nation was England. Very simply, by the beginning of the second decade of the twentieth century, no fossils of human evolutionary significance had been located in England. This lack of fossils led French scientists to label English human paleontology mere "pebble-collecting" (Blinderman 1986). The conclusion reached by most was completely unpalatable to the proud English—no one had evolved in England. The English must have originally arrived from somewhere else.

The Brain-Centered Paradigm

At the same time that the English were feeling like a people with no evolutionary roots of their own, many other Europeans were still uncomfortable with the fossil record as it stood in the first decade of the twentieth century. Although most were happy to have human fossils in their countries, they generally were not happy with what those fossils looked like and what their appearance implied about the course of human evolution.

Java Man seemed quite apelike, with its large eyebrow ridges and small cranium—a volume of about 900 cubic centimeters (cc) compared with an average of 1,450 cc for modern humans (Figure 4.1). Neandertal Man, with his sloping forehead and thick, heavy brow ridges appeared to many to be quite ugly, stupid, and brutish. The skulls of these fossil types were clearly not those of apes, but they were equally clearly not fully human. In

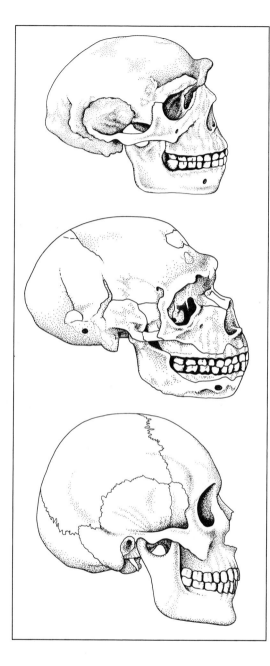

Figure 4.1 Drawings showing the general differences in skull size and form among *top, Homo erectus* (Peking Man, 500,000 years ago); *center,* Neandertal Man (100,000 years ago); and *bottom,* a modern human being. Note the large brow ridges and forward-thrusting faces of *Homo erectus* and Neandertal, the rounded outline of the modern skull, and the absence of a projecting chin in earlier forms.

contrast, the femur (thigh bone) of Java Man seemed identical to the modern form. Although some emphasized what they perceived to be primitive characteristics of the postcranial skeleton of the Neandertals, this species clearly had walked on two feet; and apes do not.

All this evidence suggested that ancient human ancestors had primitive heads and, by implication, primitive brains, seated atop rather modern-looking bodies. This further implied that the human body evolved first, followed only later by the development of the brain and associated human intelligence.

Such a picture was precisely the opposite of what many people had expected and hoped for (Feder 1990). After all, it was argued, it is intelligence that most clearly and absolutely differentiates humanity from the rest of the animal kingdom. It is in our ability to think, to communicate, and to invent that we are most distant from our animal cousins. This being the case, it was assumed that such abilities must have been evolving the longest; in other words, the human brain and the ability to think must have evolved first. Thus, the argument went, the fossil evidence for evolution should show that the brain had expanded first, followed by the modernization of the body.

Such a view is exemplified in the writings of anatomist Grafton Elliot Smith. Smith said that what most characterized human evolution must have been the "steady and uniform development of the brain along a well-defined course" (as quoted in Blinderman 1986:36). Arthur Smith Woodward, ichthyologist and paleontologist at the British Museum of Natural History, tellingly characterized the human brain as "the most complex mechanism in existence. The growth of the brain preceded the refinement of the features and of the somatic characters in general" (Dawson and Woodward 1913).

Put most simply, many researchers in evolution were looking for fossil evidence of a creature with the body of an ape and a brain near that of a human being. This, in simplest terms, represents the brain-centered paradigm. What was being discovered, however, was the reverse; both Java and Neandertal Man seemed more to represent creatures with skulls that enclosed apelike, or certainly not humanlike, brains perched atop quite humanlike bodies. Many were uncomfortable with such a picture.

A Remarkable Discovery in Sussex

Thus was the stage set for the initially rather innocuous announcement that appeared in the British science journal *Nature* (News, December 5, 1912) concerning a fossil find in the Piltdown section of Sussex in southern England. The notice read, in part:

> Remains of a human skull and mandible, considered to belong to the early Pleistocene period, have been discovered by Mr. Charles Dawson in a gravel-deposit in the basin of the River Ouse, north of Lewes, Sussex. Much interest has been aroused in the specimen owing to the exactitude with which its geological age is said to have been fixed. (p. 390)

In *Nature* two weeks later (Paleolithic Man, December 19, 1912), further details were provided concerning the important find:

The fossil human skull and mandible to be described by Mr. Charles Dawson and Dr. Arthur Smith Woodward at the Geological Society as we go to press is the most important discovery of its kind hitherto made in England. The specimen was found in circumstances which seem to leave no doubt of its geological age, and the characters it shows are themselves sufficient to denote its extreme antiquity. (p. 438)

According to the story later told by those principally involved, in February 1912 Arthur Smith Woodward at the British Museum received a letter from Charles Dawson, a Sussex lawyer and an amateur scientist. Woodward had previously worked with Dawson and knew him to be an extremely intelligent man with a keen interest in natural history. Dawson informed Woodward in the letter that he had in his possession several fragments of a remarkable and ancient fossil human skull. The first piece had been discovered in 1908 by workers near the Barcombe Manor in the Piltdown region of Sussex, England. In 1911, four more pieces of the skull came to light in the same pit, along with a fossil animal bone and tooth.

In the letter to Woodward, Dawson expressed some excitement over the discovery and claimed to Woodward that the find was quite important and might even surpass the significance of Heidelberg Man, an important specimen found in Germany just the previous year.

Because of bad weather, Woodward was not immediately able to visit Piltdown. Dawson, undaunted, continued to work in the pit, finding fossil hippo and elephant teeth. Unable to contain his excitement and anxious for Woodward's reaction, he brought the fossil to Woodward at the museum in May 1912. What Woodward saw was a skull that matched his own expectations and those of many others concerning what a human ancestor should look like. The skull, stained a dark brown from apparent age, seemed to be modern in many of its characteristics. The thickness of the bones of the skull, however, argued for a certain primitiveness. The association of the skull fragments with the bones of extinct animals implied that an ancient human ancestor indeed had inhabited England. By itself this was enormous news; at long last England had a human fossil (Figure 4.2).

Things were to get even more exciting for English paleontologists. On June 2, 1912, Woodward arrived at Piltdown together with Dawson and Pierre Teilhard de Chardin, a priest at the local Jesuit seminary whom Dawson had befriended in 1909 after finding him collecting fossils in the same pit where the skull fragments had been found the previous year. Along with a workman, the three excavated in the same location unsuccessfully for several hours when, at last, Dawson found another fragment of the skull. Very soon thereafter, Teilhard recovered an elephant tooth.

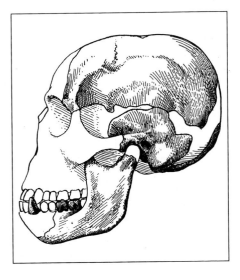

Figure 4.2 Drawn reconstruction of the Piltdown skull. The portion of the skull actually recovered is shaded. As reconstructed, the cranium shows hominid (human) traits and the mandible shows pongid (ape) traits. Compare this drawing to those in Figure 4.1. With its humanlike head and apelike jaw, the overall appearance of the Piltdown fossil is far different from *Homo erectus,* Neandertal, or modern humans.

Woodward was so impressed by their success that he decided to spend the remainder of his summer weekends at Piltdown, excavating alongside Dawson (Figure 4.3). Though work went slowly, in the ensuing weeks the pair found four additional large pieces of the cranium, along with some possible stone tools, animal teeth, and a fossilized deer antler. The apparent age of the fossils based on comparisons to other sites indicated not only that Piltdown was the earliest human fossil in England but also that, at an estimated age of 500,000 years, the Piltdown fossil represented potentially the oldest known human ancestor in the world.

Then, to add to the excitement, when Dawson and Woodward returned later in the summer, Dawson discovered half of the mandible. Though two key areas—the chin and the condyle, where the jaw connects to the skull—were missing, the preserved part did not look anything like a human jaw. The upright portion, or *ramus*, was too wide, and the bone was too thick. In fact, the jaw looked remarkably like that of an ape (Figure 4.4). Nonetheless, and quite significantly, the two intact molar teeth exhibited humanlike wear. The human jaw, lacking the large canines of apes, is free to move from side to side while chewing. The molars can grind in a sideways motion in a manner impossible in monkeys or apes. The wear on human molars is, therefore, quite distinct from that of other primates. The Piltdown molars exhibited humanlike wear in a jaw that was otherwise entirely apelike.

That the skull and the jaw had been found close together in the same geologically ancient deposit seemed to argue for the obvious conclusion that they belonged to the same ancient creature. But what kind of creature could it have been? There were no large brow ridges like those of Java or Neandertal Man. The face was interpreted as having been flat as in modern humans and not snoutlike as in the Neandertals. The profile of the cranium was

Figure 4.3 Paleontological excavations proceed at Piltdown. From left to right: Robert Kenward, Jr., a tenant of Barcombe Manor; Charles Dawson; workman Venus Hargreaves; the goose "Chipper"; and Arthur Smith Woodward. (© The British Museum)

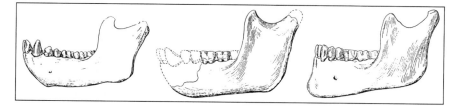

Figure 4.4 Comparison of the mandibles (lower jaws) of a young chimpanzee (left), a modern human (right), and Piltdown (center). Note how much more similar the Piltdown mandible is to that of the chimp, particularly in the form of the reconstructed chin. The presence of a projecting chin is a uniquely human trait.

round as it is in modern humans, not flattened as it appeared to be in the Java and Neandertal specimens (see Figures 4.1 and 4.2). According to Woodward, the size of the skull indicated a cranial capacity, or brain size, of about 1,070 cc (Dawson and Woodward 1913), larger than Java Man's and within the lower range for modern humanity. Anatomist Arthur Keith (1913) suggested that the capacity of the skull was actually much larger, as much as 1,500 cc, placing it almost exactly at the modern mean. But the jaw, as described above, was entirely apelike. Therefore, although only two molar teeth were recovered initially, Woodward reconstructed the Piltdown jaw with large, projecting canine teeth, similar to those of the apes.

The conclusion drawn first by Dawson, the discoverer, and then by Woodward, the professional scientist, was that the Piltdown fossil—named for its discoverer *Eoanthropus dawsoni*, meaning Dawson's Dawn Man—was the single most important fossil find yet made anywhere in the world. Concerning the Piltdown discovery, the *New York Times* headline of December 19, 1912, proclaimed "Paleolithic Skull Is a Missing Link." Three days later the *Times* headline read "Darwin Theory Is Proved True."

The implications were clear. Piltdown Man, with its modern skull, primitive jaw, and great age, was the evidence many human paleontologists had been searching for: an ancient man with a large brain, a modern-looking head, and primitive characteristics below the important brain. As anatomist G. E. Smith summarized it:

> The brain attained what may be termed the human rank when the jaws and face, and no doubt the body also, still retained much of the uncouthness of Man's simian ancestors. In other words, Man at first, so far as his general appearance and "build" are concerned, was merely an Ape with an overgrown brain. The importance of the Piltdown skull lies in the fact that it affords tangible confirmation of these inferences. (Smith 1927:105–6)

If Piltdown were the evolutionary "missing link" between apes and people, then neither Neandertal nor Java Man could be. Because Piltdown and Java Man lived at approximately the same time, Java might have been a more primitive offshoot of humanity that had become extinct. As Neandertal was much more recent than Piltdown, yet looked more primitive where it really counted (that is, the head), Neandertal must have represented some sort of primitive throwback, a slip down the evolutionary ladder (Figure 4.5).

By paleontological standards the implications were breathtaking. In one sweeping blow Piltdown had presented England with its first ancestral human fossil, it had shown that human fossils found elsewhere in the world were either primitive evolutionary offshoots or later throwbacks to a more primitive type, and it had forced the rewriting of the entire story of human evolution. Many paleontologists, especially those in England, were enthralled by the discovery in Sussex. An artist's conception of "the first Englishman" was published in a popular weekly magazine, *The Illustrated London News* (Figure 4.6).

In March 1913, Dawson and Woodward published the first detailed account of the characteristics and evolutionary implications of the Piltdown fossil. In their discussion they repeatedly pointed out the modern characteristics of the skull and the simian appearance of the mandible. Their comments regarding the modernity of the skull and the apelike characteristics of the jaw, as you will see, turned out to be accurate in a way that few suspected at the time.

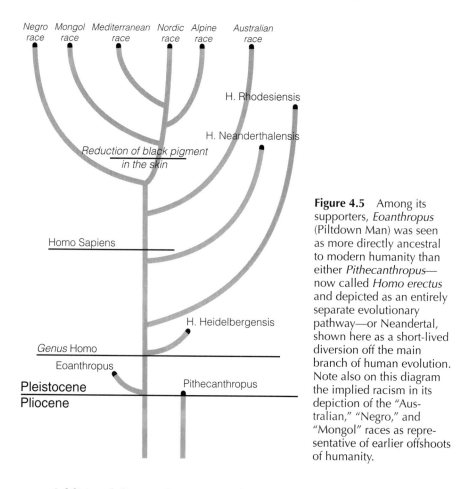

Negro race, Mongol race, Mediterranean race, Nordic race, Alpine race, Australian race

H. Rhodesiensis

H. Neanderthalensis

Reduction of black pigment in the skin

Homo Sapiens

H. Heidelbergensis

Genus Homo

Eoanthropus

Pleistocene

Pliocene

Pithecanthropus

Figure 4.5 Among its supporters, *Eoanthropus* (Piltdown Man) was seen as more directly ancestral to modern humanity than either *Pithecanthropus*—now called *Homo erectus* and depicted as an entirely separate evolutionary pathway—or Neandertal, shown here as a short-lived diversion off the main branch of human evolution. Note also on this diagram the implied racism in its depiction of the "Australian," "Negro," and "Mongol" races as representative of earlier offshoots of humanity.

Additional discoveries were made at Piltdown. In 1913 a right canine tooth apparently belonging to the jaw was discovered by Teilhard de Chardin. It matched almost exactly the canine that had previously been proposed by Woodward for the Piltdown skull and that appeared in the reconstruction produced at the British Museum of Natural History. Its apelike form and wear were precisely what had been expected: "If a comparative anatomist were fitting out *Eoanthropus* with a set of canines, he could not ask for anything more suitable than the tooth in question," stated Yale University professor George Grant MacCurdy (1914:159).

Additional artifacts were found in the Piltdown pit in 1914, the most astonishing of which was almost immediately called the "cricket bat" (Figure 4.7). It was a flat piece of carved bone that, indeed, looked a bit like the bat used to strike the ball in the British game of cricket. It seemed that at Piltdown, not only had the British found the missing link and not only could they assert that he was British, but he had played the British national sport as well! It could have been no more peculiar had the diggers at Piltdown found a set of teacups and fossilized crumpets at the site.

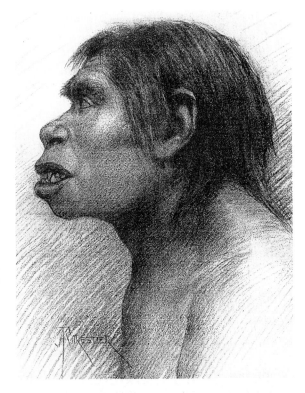

Figure 4.6   Artist's conception of Piltdown Man. Note how the illustrator has depicted the lower part of the face, with jaw thrust forward, just like an ape. (From *The Illustrated London News,* January 11, 1913, New York Edition)

Figure 4.7   This bone artifact found at Piltdown is viewed by some scientists today as an obvious joke—after all, it is shaped like a British cricket bat and was found in a gravel deposit more than one-half million years old. (© The Natural History Museum, London)

Certainly, Dawson's discovery at Piltdown inspired a vigorous search for confirming evidence, especially in the form of other fossils that looked like *Eoanthropus* and that dated to a similar time period. For a while, no one could find any such evidence. Then, in what appeared to be a spectacular stroke of luck, in January 1915 none other than Charles Dawson found that evidence in the form of fragments of another fossil human skull located on Netherhall Farm, about 2 miles from Piltdown. This skull, dubbed Piltdown II, looked just like the first with a rounded profile and thick cranial bones. Though no jaw was discovered, a molar recovered at the site bore a pattern of wear similar to that seen in the first specimen.

Dawson died in 1916 and, in part due to a serious illness suffered by his own son, Woodward held back announcement of the second discovery until the following year. When the existence of a second specimen became known, many of those skeptical after the discovery of the first Piltdown fossil became supporters. As Henry Fairfield Osborn, president of the American Museum of Natural History, suggested:

> If there is a Providence hanging over the affairs of prehistoric man, it certainly manifested itself in this case, because the three minute fragments of this second Piltdown man found by Dawson are exactly those which we should have selected to confirm the comparison with the original type. (1921:581)

The Piltdown Enigma

There was no unanimity of opinion, however, concerning the significance of the Piltdown discoveries. The cranium was so humanlike and the jaw so apelike that some scientists maintained that they simply were the fossils of two different creatures; the skeptics suggested that the association of the human cranium and the ape jaw was entirely coincidental. Gerrit S. Miller, Jr. (1915), of the Smithsonian Institution conducted a detailed analysis of casts of Piltdown I and concluded that the jaw was certainly that of an ape (see Figure 4.4). Many other scientists in the United States and Europe agreed. Anatomy professor David Waterston (1913) at the University of London, King's College, thought the mandible was that of a chimpanzee. The very well known German scientist Franz Weidenreich concluded that Piltdown I was "the artificial combination of fragments of a modern-human braincase with an orangutan-like mandible and teeth" (1943:273).

Though some viewed the combination of a humanlike cranium and an apelike jaw as "an improbable monster" (Spencer 1990:113), the only other possibility being considered seemed even more improbable. As anatomist Grafton Elliot Smith put it:

> This [other possibility] would involve the supposition that a hitherto unknown and extremely primitive ape-man, and an equally unknown manlike ape, died on the same spot, and that one of them left his skull without the jaw and the other his jaw without the skull. (In Spencer 1990:101)

This seemed a strong argument against the hypothesis that Piltdown represented the accidental and coincidental discovery in precisely the same place of the remains of more than one creature.

Coincidentally or not, after Dawson's death no further discoveries were made in either the Piltdown I or II localities. Elsewhere in the world, however, human paleontology became an increasingly exciting and fruitful endeavor. Beginning in the late 1920s as many as forty individuals of a species now called *Homo erectus* were unearthed at Zhoukoudian, a cave near Beijing in China (see Figure 4.1). Ironically, Davidson Black, anatomist at the Peking Union Medical College, who was instrumental in obtaining financial support for the excavation, had visited Grafton Elliot Smith's laboratory in 1914 and had become fascinated by the Piltdown find (Shapiro 1974). Further, the Jesuit priest who had dug at Piltdown, Teilhard de Chardin, participated in the excavation at the cave. The Zhoukoudian fossils were estimated to be one-half million years old. Also, on Java, another large group of fossils (close to twenty) was found at Sangiran; these were similar to those from Zhoukoudian.

Also in the 1920s, in Africa, a fossil given the name *Australopithecus africanus* was discovered. It was initially estimated to be more than one million years old and, therefore, older than Piltdown. In the 1930s and 1940s additional finds of this and other varieties of *Australopithecus* were made. In Europe the number of Neandertal specimens kept increasing; and even in England, in 1935, a fossil human ancestor was discovered at a place called Swanscombe.

Though *Eoanthropus* had inspired much of this research, all of these discoveries seemed to contradict its validity and the validity of the brain-centered paradigm. The Chinese and Sangiran *Homo erectus* evidence pointed to a fossil ancestor with a humanlike body and a primitive head; these specimens were similar to Java Man in appearance (Java Man is also now considered to belong to the species *Homo erectus*), possessing large brow ridges, a flat skull, and a thrust-forward face while being quite modern from the neck down. Even the much older australopithecines showed clear evidence of walking on two feet; their skeletons were remarkably humanlike from the neck down, though their heads were quite apelike. Together, both of these species seemed to confirm the notion that human beings began their evolutionary history as upright apes, not as apelike people. *Eoanthropus* seemed more and more to be the evolutionary "odd man out."

How could Piltdown be explained in light of the new fossil evidence from China, Java, Europe, and Africa? Either Piltdown was the one, true human ancestor, rendering all the manifold other discoveries members of extinct offshoots of the main line of human evolution, or else Piltdown was the remarkable coincidental find of the only known ape fossil in England within a few feet of a rather modern human skull that seemed to date back 500,000 years. Neither explanation sat well with many people.

Unmasking the Hoax

This sort of confusion characterized the status of Piltdown until 1949, when a newly rediscovered dating procedure was applied to the fossil. A measurement was made of the amount of the element fluorine in the bones. This was known to be a relative measure of the amount of time bone had been in the ground. Bones pick up fluorine in groundwater; the longer they have been buried, the more fluorine they have. Interestingly, Woodward knew of such a technique and, in fact, championed its use in a number of other cases. Woodward would not allow its use in this instance, however, and it was not applied until after his death in 1944.

Kenneth Oakley of the British Museum of Natural History conducted the test. The fossil animal bones from the site showed varying amounts of fluorine, but they exhibited as much as ten times more than did either the cranium or the jaw of the fossil human. Piltdown Man, Oakley concluded, based on comparison to fluorine concentrations in bones at other sites in England, was no more than 50,000 years old (Oakley and Weiner 1955).

Although this cast Piltdown in a new light, the implications were just as mysterious; what was a fossil human doing with an entirely apelike jaw at a date as recent as 50,000 years ago? Then, in 1953, a more precise test was applied to larger samples of the cranium and the jaw. The results were conclusive; the skull and jaw were of entirely different ages. The cranium possessed 0.10 percent fluorine, the mandible less than 0.03 percent (Oakley 1976). The inevitable conclusion was reached that the skull and the jaw must have belonged to two different creatures.

As a result of this determination, a detailed reexamination of the fossil was conducted, and the sad truth was finally revealed. The entire thing had been a hoax. The skull was that of a modern human being. Its appearance of age was due, at least in part, to its having been artificially chemically stained. It has been suggested that the thickness of the bone may have been due to a pathological condition (Spencer 1984) or the result of a chemical treatment that had been applied, perhaps to make it appear older than it was (Montague 1960).

Those scientific supporters of *Eoanthropus* who previously had pointed out the apelike character of the jaw were more right than they could have imagined; it was, indeed, an ape jaw, probably that of an orangutan. When Gerrit Miller of the Smithsonian Institution had commented on the broken condyle of the mandible by saying, "Deliberate malice could hardly have been more successful than the hazards of deposition in so breaking the fossils as to give free scope to individual judgement in fitting the parts together" (1915:1), he was using a literary device and not suggesting that anyone had purposely broken the jaw. But that is likely precisely what happened. An ape's jaw could never articulate with the base of a human skull, and so the area of connection had to be removed to give "free scope" to researchers to hypothesize how the cranium and the jaw went together. Otherwise the hoax would never have succeeded. Beyond this, the molars had been filed down to artificially create the humanlike wear pattern. The canine tooth had been stained with an artist's pigment and filed down to simulate human wear; the pulp cavity had been filled with a substance not unlike chewing gum.

It was further determined that at least one of the fragments of the Piltdown II skull was simply another piece of the first one. Oakley (1976) further concluded that all the other paleontological specimens had been planted at the site; some were probably found in England, but others had likely originated as far away as Malta and Tunisia. Some of the ostensible bone artifacts—including the cricket bat—had been carved with a metal knife.

The verdict was clear; as Weidenreich (1943) put it, Piltdown was like the chimera of Greek mythology—a monstrous combination of different creatures. The question of Piltdown's place in human evolution had been answered; it had no place. That left still open two important questions: Who did it, and why?

Whodunnit?

The most succinct and honest answer to the question "Whodunnit?" is, No one knows. Many of those directly involved with the discoveries made at Piltdown or the analysis of the fossils—and even some who were very indirectly connected to the site—have been accused as perpetrators or co-conspirators in the hoax (Figure 4.8). Tobias (1992) lists twenty-one possible suspects. We can assess the cases against some of the more likely of them.

Suspect: Charles Dawson

Charles Dawson was a well-known and highly respected amateur scientist whose great diligence and luck at finding rare or unique specimens was both admired and envied (Russell 2003). Though he had no university degree or specialized training, even before his discovery at Piltdown he had been named a "fellow" of two very prestigious scientific societies: the Geological Society and the Society of Antiquaries of London. Dawson donated much of his geological, paleontological, and archaeological collection to the British Museum (Natural History) and was given the title "honorary collector" by that institution. Further, *Eoanthropus dawsoni* was not the first fossil named for him; one fossil plant, one dinosaur, and a fossil mammal species all bore the species name *dawsoni*, each having been brought to light by Dawson (Russell 2003:28). Certainly not "God's hand" (like Shinichi Fujimura; see Chapter 3) but Dawson's great luck at finding significant specimens earned him, in archaeological circles, the nickname "the Wizard of Sussex" (Russell 2003:10).

Figure 4.8   Portrait of scientists examining a number of specimens, including *Eoanthropus*, in 1915. From left to right, standing: F. O. Barlowe, G. E. Smith, Charles Dawson, and A. S. Woodward; from left to right, seated: A. S. Underwood, A. Keith, W. P. Pycraft, and E. R. Lankester. Charles Darwin peers over their shoulders in the portrait hanging on the wall behind them. (© The British Museum)

Dawson's recent biographer, Miles Russell (2003), however, is highly suspect of much of Dawson's apparent wizardry. Russell finds inadequacies and inconsistencies in many of Dawson's own records of his pre-Piltdown discoveries, some of which are viewed by modern researchers as unlikely and, in a few cases, even fraudulent. In one particularly egregious case, Russell (2003:30) points out that a careful reexamination of the unique abrasion on the mammalian tooth that Dawson reported and that contributed significantly to the decision on the part of paleontologists to name a new mammal species, *Plagiaulax dawsoni*, showed it had been fabricated, either by Dawson or by someone else. Russell's meticulous investigation of Dawson's work reveals a clear pattern of, at best, sloppy research and, in a few instances, something far worse: deception.

It should come as no surprise, therefore, that Dawson is a prime suspect in the case of Piltdown. He is the only person who was present at every discovery, including Piltdown II. In fact, his apparently spectacular luck in being the only researcher able to find any confirming evidence for the original discovery, also made by him, raises a red flag. Being considered "God's hand" (Fujimura) or a "wizard" may be gratifying, but being too lucky in paleoanthropology or archaeology should arouse suspicion. Also, it should be mentioned that Dawson served as steward on both Barcombe Manor, where Piltdown I was discovered, and Netherhall Farm, the site of Piltdown II, so he had access to and familiarity with both locations of "discovery." This circumstantial evidence alone strongly implicates Dawson in the hoax. It would have required incredible luck for someone else to have planted the bones and, both times, to have Dawson find them. Dawson's motive may have been rooted in his desire for acceptance within the scientific community. He certainly gained notoriety; even the species name is *dawsoni*.

Beyond this, Dawson did indeed stain the bones with potassium bichromate. This gave the bones a more antique appearance. This is not a "smoking gun," however, because such staining was widespread in the early twentieth century. It was thought that this chemical helped preserve fossil bone, and Dawson was quite open about having stained the Piltdown specimens. Nevertheless, Dawson claimed that the bones were already iron-stained when he found them, indicating either that someone else had already stained the bones to make them look old and then planted them for Dawson to find or that Dawson was lying, hoping to convince skeptics that the bones were really very old.

There is an additional, intriguing piece of circumstantial evidence regarding the Piltdown skull fragments that seems to implicate Dawson. He apparently obtained an unusual human skull in 1906, by his own testimony, two years before the first of the Piltdown cranial fragments came into his possession. We know further that the 1906 skull came from the area around Piltdown; Dawson told friends that a local individual had given it to him, but he admitted that he could not determine precisely where the skull originated.

L. Harrison Matthews (1981a, 1981b) has speculated that the 1906 skull and Piltdown may have been one and the same. Perhaps Dawson was frustrated that a skull he thought was enormously important would not attract much attention unless its geological stratum and, by implication, its age could be specified. Dawson already knew about the old gravel beds at Barcombe Manor and may have concluded that it was the most likely place for the skull to have been found. Perhaps, truly believing in the antiquity and great significance of the specimen, Dawson exaggerated his certainty concerning its place of discovery. In this scenario, Dawson did not set out to hoax anyone, but, at least initially, merely stretched the truth to get scientists to pay attention. Matthews believes that fraudulent specimens like the jaw were added later to prove to skeptics that the skull, which Dawson believed to be ancient and significant, really was.

With all of this in mind, it is difficult to dispute Russell's (2003:208) conclusion: " In short, Dawson *cannot* have been innocent of the Piltdown hoax. From the start to the finish, he is implicated at every single stage."

Suspect: Arthur Smith Woodward

Arthur Smith Woodward possessed the opportunity and the expertise to pull off the fraud. Certainly he was the scientist most intimately involved with Piltdown, co-announcing its discovery, co-authoring the first scientific publication describing the find, and participating in the discovery of additional materials in later excavations at the site. His association with Dawson can be traced for thirty years before Piltdown. Nevertheless, the likelihood that Woodward was a co-conspirator in the hoax has been downplayed by most of those who have written about it.

On the other hand, a circumstantial case against Woodward has been presented by biological anthropologist Gerrell Drawhorn (1994). He points out that Woodward may be directly connected to at least some of the fraudulent specimens recovered at the site, including several of the animal bones that were salted there. Drawhorn goes on to suggest a possible source for the cranial fragments that also implicates Woodward. Woodward had obtained, for the British Museum of Natural History, skulls of Ona Indians of Patagonia, located in South America. Remember that one presumably primitive trait displayed by the Piltdown skull was the extreme thickness of the bone. This bone thickening is a very rare trait in almost all recent human populations. But there is an exception; it is fairly common among the Ona Indians.

Why might Woodward have done it? It may have been done for notoriety. Woodward was an ichthyologist, well respected among his peers as an expert in fossil fish. He hoped to become director of the British Museum of Natural History and may have felt that public as well as professional recognition was necessary to obtain the post. His involvement in the discovery and analysis of an extremely significant human fossil certainly provided a boost to his career and gave him the public recognition he may have felt he needed.

There are, as yet, no smoking guns proving that Woodward was involved. Nevertheless, Drawhorn's case seems at least as strong as—and perhaps quite a bit stronger than—the cases presented against some of the other suspects.

Suspect: Pierre Teilhard de Chardin

Pierre Teilhard de Chardin has come under scrutiny as well, most recently by Harvard paleontologist and chronicler of science Stephen Jay Gould (1980). Teilhard is a reasonable suspect because he was present during many of the key discoveries at Piltdown. It is also the case, as Gould points out, that Teilhard's later reconstruction of the chronology of his involvement with Piltdown was suspicious; at one point he asserted that he had seen the remains of Piltdown II and had been taken to the site in 1913, which was two years before Dawson supposedly found them. It is also somewhat perplexing that, after the hoax was unmasked toward the end of his life, Teilhard became increasingly reluctant to comment on the entire affair or to clarify his role in it.

But the evidence implicating Teilhard is weak. When, late in life, he maintained that Dawson had taken him to the Piltdown II site, he may have been confusing it with another site with fossil material Dawson did take him to in 1913. Furthermore, he steadfastly defended Dawson and Woodward when they were accused of being the hoaxers; he wrote world-renowned paleoanthropologist Louis Leakey, "I know who was responsible for the Piltdown hoax and it was not Charles Dawson" (cited in Tobias 1992:247). If he were guilty, he might be eager to see someone else take the blame for the fraud.

The mere facts that an embarrassed Teilhard mentioned Piltdown but little in his later writings on evolution and was confused about the precise chronology of discoveries in the pit do not add up to a convincing case.

Suspect: Sir Grafton Elliot Smith

The evidence for involvement by G. E. Smith in the hoax is slim, and all of it is circumstantial. Smith was born in Australia, and his arrival in England was followed relatively quickly by the appearance of the Piltdown skull; thus, a connection has been suggested. In Australia, he was involved in the debate over a controversial skull found there. Smith emphasized the primitive features of the so-called Talgai skull and viewed it as an extremely ancient and primitive representative of the human race. He was a supporter of Woodward's interpretation of Piltdown and, in fact, cited the Talgai skull in the debate. But Smith did not visit the Piltdown location until 1915–16 and would have had no opportunity to have planted the fossils. Similarly, he would have had no motive for doing so, save to support his fundamental perspective of human evolution. His view of the temporal priority of brain expansion in human evolution was similar to that of many of his colleagues, so this in no way distinguishes Smith from a multitude of scientists who welcomed the implications of Piltdown, but who had nothing to do with the hoax itself.

Suspect: Sir Arthur Keith

Anatomist Arthur Keith has been accused of participation in the hoax (Spencer 1990; Tobias 1992). According to Keith's own diary, on December 16, 1912, he had written an anonymous article describing events at Piltdown for the *British Medical Journal*. Curiously, this was two days *before* some of the events discussed took place (Spencer 1990:189). Also, the article contained information that, ostensibly, no one but Woodward, Dawson, and the hoaxer could have known. Further, Keith knew or at least had met Dawson before he told people he had, and later he destroyed his correspondence with Dawson.

This may show that Keith was guilty of obtaining additional information about the discovery from someone else (perhaps one of the workers at the excavation) and then of publishing it, but it is not convincing evidence of participation in the hoax. The rest seems attributable to a faulty memory and an innocent mistake in recording a date in a personal log. Again, there is no direct evidence of involvement.

Further, Keith's subsequent criticism of Woodward's reconstruction of the skull and his advocacy of a change in the fossil's designation from *Eoanthropus dawsoni* to *Homo piltdownensis* seem odd because the hoaxer would logically wish to distance himself from the entire affair, not thrust himself into the middle of it. Finally, Keith insistently disputed the apelike nature of the jaw, which makes no sense if he was the hoaxer, because it was, after all, an ape's jaw that was planted. The evidence implicating Keith is weak.

Suspect: Martin A. C. Hinton

Martin A. C. Hinton was a curator of zoology at the Natural History Museum in London. Hinton had worked under Arthur Smith Woodward at the time of the hoax, and some have claimed that before the Piltdown affair they had a falling out about payment for some work Hinton had done at the museum. So, conceivably, Hinton may have had a motive for embarrassing Woodward.

More important, some have pointed to what they consider to be a smoking gun with Hinton's fingerprints—a trunk found at the museum in the mid-1970s bearing Hinton's initials (Gee 1996). The trunk contained an assemblage of fossil hippopotamus and elephant teeth stained and carved in a fashion similar to the fake animal fossils found with Piltdown Man. In fact, the proportions of chemicals that had been used in staining the bones found in Hinton's trunk were the same as those used to make the Piltdown specimens look old.

However, there is no evidence that Hinton had been to Piltdown before Dawson's discovery, so there is no direct evidence of his having any opportunity to plant the bones. Beyond this, if Hinton played this trick to get back at some perceived slight on the part of Arthur Smith Woodward, (1) why would he plant bones at Piltdown, (2) how would he know that anyone would find them, (3) how would he know that the person who found them would know they were significant, and (4) how would he know that this person would take them to Woodward? Hinton certainly is a viable suspect, but there does not appear to be definitive proof of his guilt.

L. Harrison Matthews came to know Hinton quite well toward the end of his life. In an intriguing bit of sleuthing (Matthews 1981a, 1981b), he concluded that Hinton may have played an important role, not as one of the hoaxers, but as an attempted "hoaxer of the hoaxers." Specifically, Matthews hypothesizes that Hinton figured out that Dawson, possibly along with Lewis Abbott (our next suspect), had faked the Piltdown fossil cranium and jaw in the first place. Amused that his enemy Woodward had fallen for the hoax, Matthews suggested, Hinton began adding more fakes to the Piltdown pit, specimens like the cricket bat that were transparently absurd. Of course, with somebody else planting fake artifacts, the original culprits would realize that someone was on to them. More gratifying to Hinton, the new fakes would lead his nemesis Woodward to the inevitable and agonizing conclusion that he had been duped and had wasted a significant part of his career and not just a little of his professional currency on a clumsy fraud. It is an intriguing, if complicated, scenario; like every other proposal in the Piltdown whodunnit, there is no compelling evidence to support this version.

Suspect: Lewis Abbott

Blinderman (1986) argues that Lewis Abbott, another amateur scientist and artifact collector, is the most likely perpetrator. He had an enormous ego and felt slighted by professional scientists. He claimed to have been the one who directed Dawson to the pit at Piltdown and may even have been with Dawson when Piltdown II was discovered (Dawson said only that he had been with a friend when the bones were found). Abbott knew how to make stone tools and so was capable of forging those found at Piltdown. Again, however, the evidence, though tantalizing, includes no smoking gun.

Another possibility is that Abbott was a co-conspirator with Dawson, again not in an elaborately planned hoax, but only in crafting specific fraudulent objects and planting these at Piltdown in order to convince skeptical scientists of the significance of the skull Dawson obtained in 1906 (Matthews 1981a, 1981b). Abbott was an ardent believer that crudely broken flints found in very ancient gravels were actually human-made tools. We know these so-called eoliths are merely naturally fractured rocks, but Abbott may truly have believed that the 1906 skull supported his perspective that the eoliths were the product of human manufacture; he may have surmised that the bearer of the skull could have been the maker of eoliths.

Suspect: W. J. Sollas

W. J. Sollas, a geology professor at Oxford and a strong supporter of Piltdown, has been accused from beyond the grave. In 1978, a tape-recorded statement made just before his death by J. A. Douglass, who had worked in Sollas's lab for some thirty years, was made public. The only evidence provided is Douglass's testimony that on one occasion he came across a package containing the fossil-staining agent potassium bichromate in the lab—certainly not the kind of evidence needed to convince a jury to convict.

Suspect: Sir Arthur Conan Doyle

Even Sir Arthur Conan Doyle has come under the scrutiny of would-be Piltdown detectives. Doyle lived near Piltdown and is known to have visited the site at least once. This provides him with the opportunity, but what would have been his motive to perpetrate the hoax?

Ironically, though Doyle was the creator of Sherlock Holmes, possessor of the most logical, rational mind in literature, Doyle himself was quite credulous when it came to spiritualism. He became an ardent supporter of two young English girls who claimed that fairies regularly visited their garden. They even concocted some outrageously bad photographs to prove their point, and Doyle accepted these obvious fakes without reservation. The 1997 movie *Fairy Tale: A True Story* is a fanciful version of this.

One of Doyle's chief critics in this arena was British anatomist and zoologist Ray Lankester. Lankester had been for some time publicly contemptuous of Doyle's belief in spirits and fairies. If Doyle were truly involved in the Piltdown hoax, Lankester would have been one obvious target. In this scenario, Doyle crafted the hoax hoping that Lankester would fall for it and then be humiliated when Doyle revealed that it was all a fraud.

But this is all quite a stretch; after all, how would Doyle know that Lankester would become deeply involved in Piltdown? In fact, Lankester was not one of the key researchers; he was a follower, not a leader, at Piltdown, becoming a supporter of Woodward's interpretation of *Eoanthropus*. Finally, there is no direct evidence to implicate Doyle. In the final analysis, he is an unlikely suspect.

The Lesson of Piltdown

Certainly, in the case of the Piltdown hoax, there is no shortage of suspects, and there is plenty of circumstantial evidence implicating many of them. Unfortunately, there is nothing that has yet surfaced that definitively eliminates any of them or that would lead us confidently to a guilty verdict for any one of them either. But does that matter now, nearly a century after the first of the bones came into Charles Dawson's possession? If the Piltdown tale were a detective mystery, the question of "whodunnit" would be at the core of the story. However, in his review of Frank Spencer's book accusing Sir Arthur Keith, British prehistorian Christopher Chippindale (1990) has expressed the opinion of many anthropologists in his title: "Piltdown: Who Dunit? Who Cares?" Chippindale doubts that definitive evidence of anyone's guilt exists and suggests that this is beside the point anyway.

Of far greater significance is the reason for Piltdown's acceptance by such a broad group of scientists. Piltdown provided validation for a preferred view of human evolution, one in which the development of the brain preceded all other aspects of human evolution. The hoaxer may never be known, but we do know that he or they almost certainly crafted the fraud to conform to this "brain-centered" perspective of human evolution. He or they gave people a fossil they would want to accept, and many fell into their trap.

A definitive answer to the question "Whodunnit?" may never be forthcoming. The lesson of Piltdown, though, is clear. Unlike the case of the

Cardiff Giant, where scientists were not fooled, but just as was the case in the Fujimura hoaxes, here many were convinced by what appears to be, in hindsight, an inelegant fake. It shows quite clearly that scientists, though striving to be objective observers and explainers of the world around them, are, in the end, human. Many accepted the Piltdown evidence because they wished to—it supported a more comfortable view of human evolution. The perpetrator provided the British with an ancient ancestor and also a prehistory with a time depth at least the equal to and perhaps even greater than that of other nations. In his archaeological hoaxes, Fujimura provided much the same to the people of Japan. In fact, the widespread acceptance of Piltdown and, more recently, of Fujimura's planted sites may be attributable, in part, to the desire on the part of the British and the Japanese for a national connection to a more ancient period of time. Furthermore, perhaps out of naivete, scientists could not even conceive that a fellow thinker about human origins would wish to trick them; the possibility that Piltdown was a fraud probably occurred to few, if any, of them.

Nevertheless, the Piltdown story, rather than being a black mark against science, instead shows how well it ultimately works. Even before its unmasking, Piltdown had been consigned by most to a netherworld of doubt. There was simply too much evidence supporting a different human pedigree than that implied by Piltdown. Proving it a hoax was just the final nail in the coffin lid for this fallacious fossil. As a result, though we may never know the hoaxer's name, at least we know this: If the goal was to forever confuse our understanding of the human evolutionary story, the hoax ultimately was a failure.

Current Perspectives: Human Evolution

With little more than a handful of cranial fragments, scientists defined an entire species, *Eoanthropus*, and recast the story of human evolution. Later, in 1922, on the basis of a single fossil tooth found in Nebraska, an ancient species of man, *Hesperopithecus*, was defined. It was presumed to be as old as any hominid species found in the Old World and convinced some that then-current evolutionary models needed to be overhauled. The tooth turned out to belong to an ancient pig. Even in the case of Peking Man, the species was defined and initially named *Sinanthropus pekinensis* on the basis of only two teeth.

Today, the situation in human paleontology is quite different (Tattersall and Schwartz 2000). The tapestry of our human evolutionary history is no longer woven with the filaments of a small handful of gauzy threads. We can now base our evolutionary scenarios (Figure 4.9) on enormous quantities of data supplied by several fields of science (see Feder and Park 2001 for a detailed summary of current thinking on human evolution).

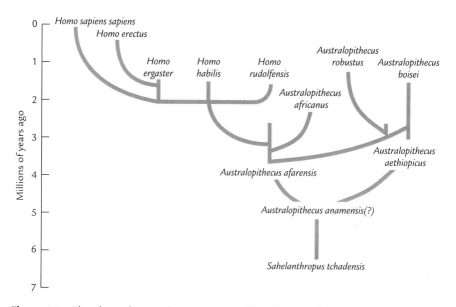

Figure 4.9   The chronology and connections of fossil hominids over the past 6.5 million years are depicted here. Each of the named species is represented by a number of fossil specimens. As can be seen, though many hominids existed in the past—and some lived at the same time—there currently is only a single species, *Homo sapiens sapiens.* All living people are members of this group.

Australopithecus afarensis, for example, dating to about 4 million years ago, is represented by more than a dozen fossil individuals from East Africa. The most famous specimen, known as "Lucy," is more than 40 percent complete. Its discovery by a team led by paleoanthropologist Donald Johanson was far more exciting than any hoax possibly could have been (Johanson and Edey 1982). Lucy's pelvis is remarkably modern and provides clear evidence of its upright, and therefore humanlike, posture. Mary Leakey, Tim White, and their team in Tanzania (White and Suwa 1987) found further evidence of upright locomotion dating to nearly 4 million years ago. At a place called Laetoli, they discovered a pathway of fossilized *Australopithecus* footprints preserved in hardened volcanic ash. At least two individuals, walking in an entirely human pattern, crossed the soft ash, leaving an unmistakably human trail. The chemical makeup of the ash caused it to harden and preserve the footprints. The ash itself has been directly dated to more than 3.5 million years ago. By the way, though *Australopithecus* walked in a humanlike fashion, its skull was quite apelike and contained a brain the size of a chimpanzee's. The fossil evidence, contrary to Piltdown and the brain-centered view of evolution, shows quite clearly that human evolution proceeded from the feet up, not the head down.

Alan Walker and Richard Leakey (1993) excavated the 80-percent-complete skeleton of a 9- or 10-year-old boy who died on the shore of a lake more than 1.5 million years ago. He clearly walked upright and possessed a brain far larger than that of *Australopithecus* and about two-thirds the modern human size. That the so-called Nariokotome boy exhibits evidence of physical immaturity at the age of 9 or 10 reflects how human he was. Compared to most other animals, human beings have an extended period of maturation during which we master the skills we need as creatures who rely on learned behavior to a far greater degree than physical characteristics or instinct. The Nariokotome boy is placed in the taxonomic category *Homo ergaster*. *Homo ergaster*'s Asian descendant, *Homo erectus*, is known from dozens of individuals—forty from Zhoukoudian alone, nearly twenty from Java, and more than a dozen from Africa.

Excavators of the Sima de los Huesos site in the Atapuerca Mountains of northern Spain have, at that single locale, recovered more than 1,600 hominid bones representing the remains of more than thirty and perhaps as many as fifty ancient people (Bermúdez de Castro et al. 1997). These ancient people lived 300,000 years ago, and their physical characteristics suggest that they were the ancestors of the Neandertals who flourished in Europe between 120,000 and 30,000 years ago.

Recovered Neandertal skeletons number in the hundreds, allowing detailed comparisons between this extinct form of human being and us (Arsuaga 2002; Jordan 2001). In one of the most exciting advances in paleoanthropological research in this century, in three separate studies actual segments of DNA have been extracted from Neandertal bone fragments, allowing scientists for the first time to compare the genetic instructions for an extinct form of humanity with the DNA of our own species (Krings et al. 1997; Ovchinnikov et al. 2000; Scholz et al. 2000). Now, in our comparisons between Neandertals and modern humans, we can look at more than just bone; we can see the very genes. This "molecular archaeology" of the Neandertals shows that they were genetically quite distinct from modern humans. The degree of difference seen in the DNA suggests that the Neandertals were not our immediate ancestors but evolutionary cousins, plying their own separate course through ancient history.

The human fossil record is rich and growing. Our evolutionary scenarios are based not on a handful of fragmentary bones but on the remains of hundreds of individuals. Grafton Elliot Smith, Arthur Smith Woodward, and the others were quite wrong. The abundant evidence shows very clearly that human evolutionary history is characterized by the precedence of upright posture and the tardy development of the brain. It now appears that although our ancestors developed upright posture and humanlike bodies more than 6 million years ago, the modern human brain size and shape were not attained until as recently as 195,000 years ago (McDougall et al. 2005).

It is to be expected that ideas will change as new data are collected and new analytical techniques are developed. Certainly our current views will be fine-tuned, and perhaps even drastic changes of opinion will take place. This is the nature of science. It is fair to suggest, however, that no longer could a handful of enigmatic bones that contradicted our mutually supportive paleontological, cultural, and genetic databases cause us to unravel and reweave our evolutionary tapestry. Today, the discovery of a Piltdown Man likely would fool few.

FREQUENTLY ASKED QUESTIONS

1. Why didn't they just radiocarbon-date the Piltdown cranium and jaw to show how old they were?

Radiocarbon dating was not developed until the 1950s, nearly forty years after Piltdown's discovery. If the Piltdown skull had been a genuine million-year-old fossil, carbon dating would have been useless anyway. Carbon dating works only on organic material (all the organic material in fossilized bone has been replaced with minerals) and can be applied to specimens no more than about 50,000 years old. After scientists realized that Piltdown had been a hoax, they did radiocarbon-date the cranium; it was about six hundred years old. The jaw was only ninety years old (Spencer and Stringer 1989).

2. Isn't the theory of human evolution based on the discovery of just a handful of tiny bone fragments that could mean just about anything?

Not at all. Paleoanthropologists have recovered thousands upon thousands of bones of our human ancestors. There are more than a dozen partial skeletons of *Australopithecus* and more than three hundred partial skeletons of Neandertals. Beyond this, some ancient skeletons—the Nariokotome boy from Africa and Jinniushan Man from China are two examples—are nearly complete, giving us a very detailed picture of what some of our extinct ancestors looked like. Modern scenarios of human evolution are based on a solid, large, and expanding database that includes DNA, ancient tools, and geology as well as bones—another reason why today a Piltdown hoax would be unlikely to fool anyone.

BEST OF THE WEB

http://www.talkorigins.org/faqs/piltdown.html
Timeline and detailed discussion; assessment of most of the possible perpetrators.

http://home.tiac.net/~cri_a/piltdown/piltdown.html
Detailed discussion of the hoax; enormous bibliography is linked.

http://home.tiac.net/~cri_a/piltdown/bibliog.html
Piltdown bibliography with an extensive section on possible perpetrators.

http://home.tiac.net/~cri_a/piltdown/winslow.html
Presents the argument that Conan Doyle was the Piltdown "perp."

http://home.tiac.net/~cri_a/piltdown/drawhorn.html
Gerrell Drawhorn's paper presenting the argument that Arthur Smith Woodward was the perpetrator of the Piltdown hoax.

http://www.lhup.edu/~dsimanek/piltdown.htm
Web site arguing that Martin Hinton was the perpetrator of the Piltdown hoax.

❖ ❖ ❖ CRITICAL THINKING EXERCISE ❖ ❖ ❖

The Cardiff Giant and Piltdown Man hoaxes were similar in that both related to archaeology and the study of human prehistory. However, they were quite different in terms of motives, the reasons for their success, and their impacts. Compare the motives for these two hoaxes. What were the goals of the hoaxers? Compare the reasons each was successful. Why did people want to believe them? Compare the impacts of the Cardiff Giant and Piltdown hoaxes on the *scientific* understanding of the human past. Do you think archaeologists would be fooled by these hoaxes today? Can modern archaeologists be fooled by any hoaxes considering the modern technology we now have available to assess the legitimacy of artifacts and skeletons?

Which of these two implications drawn from the Piltdown hoax do you agree with and why?

- Piltdown shows that even "objective" scientists cannot be trusted to apply a skeptical eye to data when those data fulfill their expectations and desires.
- Piltdown exemplifies the self-corrective nature of science.

◈◈◈◈◈◈◈◈ 5 ◈◈◈◈◈◈◈◈

Who Discovered America?

America's First People

Each October, on Columbus Day, pundits ponder the significance of the voyages of Christopher Columbus to the New World and debate whether, in fact, Columbus "discovered" America. Heated arguments ensue, and ink, if not blood, is spilled. But the issue of who discovered America is and should be a simple question of scientific fact. Did Columbus "discover" America? The only reasonable answer is, No, certainly not.

The scientific facts are so clear it is perplexing that the point is argued at all. When Columbus arrived in the Caribbean in 1492, he found people already there. In fact, it is estimated that at the time of Columbus's voyages the New World was home to tens of millions of people exhibiting a broad spectrum of cultural diversity. There were hunters and gatherers in the Alaskan Arctic, pyramid-building farmers in the midwestern United States, mobile hunter-gatherers in the desert West, and corn-farming town dwellers in the Southwest. The New World also was home to a number of full-blown civilizations including the Aztec, Inka, and Maya. These cultures were, in the view of the conquering Spaniards themselves, the equal to any in the Old World. What the Aztec, Inka, Maya, and others were lacking, however, was gunpowder (a Chinese, not European, invention) and, even more significantly, immunity to European diseases, which killed more of them than did any conquistadors with swords or guns.

The unanswered question, then, is not, Who discovered America? but, Where did the Indians, who clearly were the first people to enter and settle America, come from? This very question was, in fact, asked by European scholars soon after they became aware of the inhabitants of the New World.

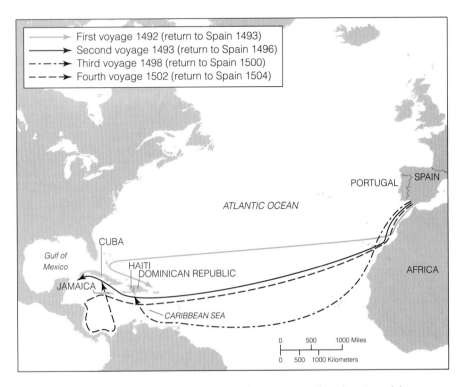

Figure 5.1   Routes taken by Columbus in his four voyages of exploration of the New World in 1492, 1493, 1498, and 1502. Columbus never gave up hope that he had discovered the coast of either Japan or China or lands immediately adjacent to the Orient.

A New World—To Europeans

Between 1492 and 1502, Christopher Columbus made four separate voyages to the New World searching for a shortcut to the riches of China and Japan (Figure 5.1). On the first and second of these he made landfalls on "San Salvador" (today identified as Watling Island or, possibly, Samana Cay), Cuba, and Haiti (Marden 1986). On the third and fourth voyages, a landfall was made on the coast of South America, and a large section of the coast of Middle America (Panama, Costa Rica, and Honduras) was explored (Fernandez-Armesto 1974).

Columbus never fully understood that he had accidentally discovered the Western Hemisphere, but he did come to realize that he had not successfully reached his hoped-for destination of Cathay (China) or Cipangu (Japan). For a short time during the first voyage, he thought Cuba was part of mainland Asia (Fuson 1987), but he soon concluded that it was, in fact, an island. Nevertheless, Columbus remained convinced that Cuba and the other islands he explored lay in proximity to the Asian mainland. As a result, he thought that the people he encountered during his voyages were Asians.

Others in Europe, however, believed that Columbus had discovered something far more intriguing than a handful of inhabited islands off the Chinese coast. It seemed clear to many that Columbus had discovered, as Amerigo Vespucci called it for the first time in print in 1503, "*a new world*, because none of these countries were known to our ancestors" (Vespucci 1904). When Magellan circumnavigated the globe in 1519–22, any lingering doubts that Columbus had indeed discovered a "new world" were erased.

Biblical Exegesis and American Indians

If the lands explored by Columbus were not part of Asia, then the people he encountered were not actual Asians, but some heretofore unknown group. This idea was problematical to sixteenth-century scholars and clerics. In their worldview, all people could be traced to Adam and Eve. Beyond this, all people could be more recently traced to Noah and his family (his wife, sons, and daughters-in-law), for all other descendants of the first couple had been wiped out in a great flood (see Chapter 11).

According to the Book of Genesis in the Old Testament, Noah had three sons, Shem, Ham, and Japheth. Biblical scholars had long since decided that each of the three sons represented the source for the three "races" of humanity recognized by Europeans: European, Oriental, and African. Japheth, apparently the best of the lot, was, naturally enough, considered to be the patriarch of the European people. Shem gave rise to the Asians, and Ham was the source for Africans. This was a neat enough arrangement for biblical literalists, but the recognition that the people Columbus had encountered were not Chinese or Japanese—and the certainty that they were neither European nor African—created a problem. There simply was no *fourth son* of Noah to provide a source for a *fourth race* of people. Though some, like Isaac de la Peyrère in 1655, suggested that Indians were part of a separate "pre-adamite" creation that had been unaffected by the biblical flood (Greene 1959), notions of polygenesis were never particularly popular. For most, Indians were ordinary human beings descended first from Adam and later from Noah. If any doubted that, Pope Paul III in a papal bull released in 1537 made the opinion of the Church clear when he stated that "the Indians are truly men and . . . they are not only capable of understanding the catholic faith but, according to our information, desire exceedingly to receive it" (as cited in Hanke 1937:72).

That led to the only conclusion possible: the natives of the New World must have reached its shores sometime after the Flood and could, therefore, be traced to one of Noah's three sons through a historically known group of people. For some three hundred years, European thinkers speculated about who that group might be.

American Indians: From Israelites to Atlanteans

Though the land they explored was not part of Asia, some early New World explorers noticed a clear physical similarity between the native people of the New World and Asians. Giovanni da Verrazano, an Italian navigator sailing for France in 1524, spent almost three weeks exploring the interior of Rhode Island and had an opportunity to examine local natives closely. He concluded:

> They tend to be rather broad in the face. . . . They have big black eyes. . . . From what we could tell in the last two respects they resemble the Orientals. (Quinn 1979:182)

Though Verrazano and others were quite perceptive in noticing these physical similarities, many others suggested different sources for the Native American population. In his *General and Natural History of the Indies* published in 1535, Spanish writer Oviedo (Huddleston 1967) suggested two sources for indigenous American populations: lost merchants from Carthage, a Mediterranean city-state of 2,000 years before, or the followers of King Héspero, a Spanish monarch who fled Europe in 1658 B.C. The latter hypothesis was appealing to the Spanish, who could therefore assert that Columbus had only rediscovered and reclaimed what the Spanish had already discovered and claimed.

Speculation concerning the source of American Indians accelerated after 1550. As shown in Chapter 7, Lopez de Gomara believed they were a remnant population from the Lost Continent of Atlantis. In 1580 Diego Duran suggested that the New World natives were descendants of the so-called Lost Tribes of Israel—ten of the twelve Hebrew tribes mentioned in the Bible were historically "lost." Duran enumerated traits that he believed Indians and Jews had in common: circumcision, stories about plagues, long journeys, and the like.

José de Acosta   From our modern perspective, perhaps the most important work examining the origin of the Indians was *The Natural and Moral History of the Indies,* by Friar José de Acosta, published in 1590. The book is a remarkably perceptive, scientific examination of the question of Indian origins.

Acosta spent seventeen years as a Jesuit missionary in Peru beginning in 1570. He recognized that however people came to the New World and wherever they came from, wild animals came with them. Acosta recognized that people might have brought with them economically useful animals, but others—predators like wolves or foxes, for example—would not have been purposely imported and must have traveled to the New World by themselves.

Figure 5.2 During parts of the Pleistocene epoch, sea level dropped substantially as water evaporated from the world's oceans, fell as snow in northern latitudes and higher elevations, and did not melt but produced glaciers. This drop in sea level produced land connections like the Bering Land Bridge—a 1,500-kilometer-wide platform of land connecting northeast Asia and northwest North America. The Bering Land Bridge provided access to the New World for animals and people in the Old World.

Acosta then made a simple yet significant suggestion; if animals could migrate on their own to the New World from the Old—where they must have journeyed from after the Flood, since Noah's Ark came to rest on "the mountains of Ararat," somewhere in western Asia—then "the new world we call the Indies is not completely divided and separated from the other world" (Acosta, as cited in Huddleston 1967:50).

Thus the Old and New Worlds must be connected; animals could simply walk from the Old World to the New, and people would have come to the Americas the same way. Based on geographical knowledge of his day, Acosta even proposed where such a connection might be found—northeast Asia/northwest North America. European explorers would not verify that northeastern Asia and northwestern North America were separated by a narrow strait (in fact, only about 82 kilometers [51 miles] of open sea) until the second half of the eighteenth century (Figure 5.2).

Acosta's argument was remarkable for its objectivity and solid reasoning. Furthermore, it did not contradict a literal interpretation of the Bible—it was, after all, based on the assumption that all animals in the New World were descended from those saved on board the Ark.

Tracing the Source of Native Americans

As firmly grounded in fact and good deductive reasoning as Acosta's argument was, most European scholars rejected his conclusions and looked for sources other than Asia for the native population of the New World. Most such thinkers based their tracing of American Indian cultures on *trait list comparisons*. They hunted through descriptions of Indian cultures, seeking practices, beliefs, and even linguistic elements that were reminiscent of those in some Old World group. Where similarities were found, it was thought that a source for the American population had been identified.

Certainly, there is some logic to cultural comparison. Within the context of American society, we recognize that immigrants and their descendants often maintain traditions from their homelands. Religious practices, holiday celebrations, craftwork, clothing, and even language may persist for generations. Chinese immigrants celebrating the Chinese New Year, African Americans wearing *dashikis*, and Puerto Ricans living in the United States celebrating Three Kings' Day are all examples of such cultural persistence.

In these three examples and in the myriad others that could be presented, the connections between the practices of immigrants and those of their homelands are clear, specific, and detailed. Each occurs within an overall cultural context of many other persistent practices.

The evidence marshalled by European scholars in previous centuries regarding the source of American Indian populations is very different. Often, the similarities they saw were vague, generic, and biased. For example, sixteenth-century Spanish cleric Gregoria Garcia contended that both Jews and Indians were cowardly, that neither believed in the miracles of Christ, that both were uncharitable, that they were ungrateful, that they loved silver, and so on (as cited in Steward 1973). These aspersions, which reflect more on Garcia's attitudes than on either Native American or Jewish behavior, were taken as strong evidence of a connection between the two peoples.

Archaeologist David L. Clarke (1978:424) has suggested that trait list comparisons can be used to trace population movements only when certain requirements of the data are met. The traits must be specifically the same, not just vaguely similar. The traits being compared cannot be isolated behaviors. They must be part of entire complexes of traits, all of which are reflected in the supposed source and immigrant populations. The traits must co-occur repeatedly, both physically and chronologically. The similarities must be so complete that the likelihood that they resulted from coincidentally parallel development or functional necessity would be minimal.

For example, a simple trait like circumcision, practiced by Jews as well as the Inka, does not, by itself, necessarily prove a connection between the two peoples. The cultural/religious context and meaning of the practice in the two groups turn out to be entirely different. It is such a general trait and so many people all over the world practice it that we would quickly run out of Lost Tribes if we tried to trace them to all world cultures that circumcised their male infants.

Archaeologist John Rowe (1966) performed a wonderful exercise that shows the inadequacy of trait list comparisons. He compiled a list of sixty practices and artifacts held in common by ancient South American civilizations and the kingdoms of Europe before the Middle Ages. Some of the common traits include animal sacrifice, belief in mythically combined animals, sister marriage, cubical dice, copper tweezers, and eunuchs. Yet there was no known contact between these cultures separated by thousands of miles of land and ocean. Rowe purposely selected traits extracted from their cultural contexts, practices dating from different time periods, and behaviors present in a few widely separated European groups and similarly few widely separated Native American groups. This is precisely the nature of the comparisons between Old and New World cultures made by the great majority of European thinkers in earlier centuries.

Out of Asia

Though Acosta was ahead of his time in tracing the human population of the New World to Asia, his reasoning in *The Natural and Moral History of the Indies* was so sound that it could not be ignored. Rather than relying on scattershot cultural comparisons or unverifiable transoceanic crossings, his theory was constructed on a solid geographical foundation. Slowly, as geographical knowledge of the northern Pacific grew, it gained acceptance. By the middle of the eighteenth century, most scholars agreed that the indigenous people of the New World were, in fact, descendants of Asians—just as the Spanish cleric Acosta had argued in the sixteenth century.

By 1794 Father Ignaz Pfefferkorn could say in reference to the narrow slip of water separating Asia from America, "It is almost certain that the first inhabitants of America really came by way of the strait" (as cited in Ives 1956:421). The people whom Columbus encountered had been Asians after all—but separated by thousands of miles and thousands of years from the people of Cathay and Cipangu.

An "American Genesis"?

Though archaeologists still argue about the timing of migration of people to the New World, they virtually all agree that American Indians are Asians who arrived via the area today known as the Bering Straits. This narrow and shallow part of the Bering Sea is today a minor impediment to human movement between the Asian and North American mainlands. In the past, during the geological epoch known as the *Pleistocene* (Ice Age), travel between the two continents was even easier. During this epoch, marked by episodes of worldwide climate much colder than those that occur at present, large bodies of ice called glaciers covered much of the surface of North America and Europe. This ice came from water that had evaporated from the world's oceans. As a result, worldwide sea level dropped as much as 125 meters (410 feet), exposing large amounts of land previously and presently underwater (Josenhans et al. 1997). A 1,500-kilometer-wide (almost 1,000-mile) land platform called *Beringia* or the Bering Land Bridge was exposed, connecting Asia and North America (see Figure 5.2). Recent analysis of submarine sediments suggests a late glacial maximum sometime between 22,000 and 19,000 years ago (Yokoyama et al. 2000). Sea level was at a low point for a period of a few hundred years sometime during this time span, and Beringia would have been at its most extensive. This same evidence indicates a general warming accompanied by sea level rise in the period immediately following 19,000 years ago. So, sometime between 22,000 and 19,000 years ago, as well as during subsequent glacial readvances between 19,000 and 10,000 years ago, the Old and the New Worlds were connected, and it would have been possible for people and animals to walk from one to the other. It should also be pointed out that when Beringia was exposed, there would have been one continuous coast arcing across from Asia to America. A maritime people living on the northeast Asian coast could have expanded east following the Beringian coast into Alaska and then south into the rest of the New World. Whether by land, through the interior of Beringia, or by sea, along its coast, the movement of people into the New World via the land bridge is well supported by geological, meteorological, biological, anthropological, and archaeological evidence (Derenko et al 2001; Dillehay 2000; Dixon 1999; Meltzer 1993a, 1993b; Yokoyama et al. 2000).

Some Native Americans object strenuously to the Land Bridge scenario because, as one told me directly, "It makes us immigrants, no different from you and your ancestors." Maybe that is the case, but the most conservative scientific view places Native Americans in the New World more than 13,000 years ago—"immigrants" they may be, but certainly not latecomers!

Indian activist, author, and historian Vine Deloria, Jr. (1995), has made this issue the core of his book *Red Earth, White Lies.* His argument is that the Bering Land Bridge model cannot be proven. Besides, Indian religion maintains that native people in the New World have always been here; they were created here and did not come from anywhere else.

There is, however, a problem with this perspective. The federal government of the United States officially recognizes more than 560 Indian tribes and native Hawaiian groups. There are many more tribal groups in Canada and hundreds more in South America. These are distinct groups of people with separate histories; different languages, cultural practices, and religious perspectives; and, most important here, different stories of their own origins.

Deloria maintains that Indian religion and not science is correct in the determination of an origin for the native people of the New World. But which *one* of the hundreds upon hundreds of very different—in fact, often mutually exclusive—Native American creation stories is Deloria talking about? They can't all be right at the same time. Deloria's take on this puzzle is interesting:

> Tribal elders did not worry if their version of creation was entirely different from the scenario held by a neighboring tribe. People believed that each tribe had its own special relationship to the superior spiritual forces which governed the universe. (Deloria 1995:51–52)

This may very well be true concerning people's beliefs, but it leaves us with Deloria's apparent belief that each tribal or traditional culture's reality about origins is different, yet each is correct. Clearly this is not a scientific approach to the question; it sounds a lot more like the deconstructionist views mentioned in Chapter 2 (see Whittaker [1997] for a scathing review of *Red Earth, White Lies* and Feder [1997] for a more general discussion of the conflict between myth and science on the issue of Native American origins).

Tracing People by Their Biology

Modern anthropologists can trace the origins of a people through their biology. The human species is polymorphic; we come in different colors, shapes, and sizes. There are variations in blood type, skeletal form, tooth shape, head shape, genetic conditions, and so on. These variations are not distributed randomly across the earth, but are geographically patterned.

Sixteenth-century explorers like Verrazano recognized this geographic patterning, noted the physical similarities between Asians and Native Americans, and hypothesized an Asian source for the indigenous human population of the New World. Today, biological anthropologists can test and verify this hypothesis through application of sophisticated analytical procedures.

For example, physical anthropologist Christy Turner examined some 200,000 teeth from the New World (Turner 1987) and found that American Indian teeth are most similar to the teeth of Asian people. Among American Indians, a particular form of incisor—so-called *shovel-shaped*—is found in between 65 and 100 percent of Indian populations in different parts of North and South America (Figure 5.3). The frequency of shovel-shaping in Africans and Europeans has been measured at less than 20 percent. In eastern Asia, 65 to 90 percent of the people exhibit the trait.

Examination of other dental traits, including the number of cusps and roots on molar teeth, also shows the similarity of the teeth of Asians and Native Americans. Other features of the skeleton exhibit the same pattern; thus, archaeologists can be fairly certain that the skeletons excavated from prehistoric sites in the Americas are those of Indians and that Indians are derived from Asia on the basis of their possession of the Mongoloid or *sinodont* pattern (Turner 1987:6).

Kennewick Chronicles   We do not know his name, and yet different groups assert that they know who he was. He has no known genealogy, yet various people claim to be his descendants. He left no last will and testament, but some assert that they are his heirs. To the best of our knowledge, he provided no instructions as to how his body was to be treated upon death, but various factions today wish to speak for him on this very point. To the Umatilla, Yakama, Confederated Tribes of Colville, Nez Perce, and the Wanapum Tribe of the Columbia River valley of Washington State, where his

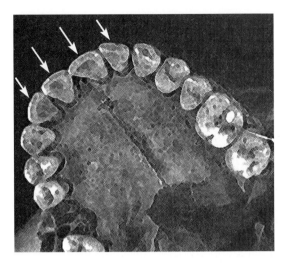

Figure 5.3   Upper jaw (maxilla) showing shoveling in the incisor teeth. This morphology is seen in a high percentage of the native peoples of East Asia and the Americas, evidencing the common biological heritage of people living on either side of the Bering Strait. (Courtesy John Seidel)

remains were discovered, he is simply the "Ancient One." To members of the Asatru Folk Assembly, a group of latter-day Vikings, his remains belong to their ancient ancestor, a brave Norse explorer of the New World, dating to long before the voyages of Christopher Columbus. To Paramount Chieftain Faumuina, he is the ancestor of modern Polynesians, his descendants having migrated from the American Northwest to South America, and from there by boat to Samoa. To scientists, both archaeologists and biological anthropologists, the bones of the individual they call "Kennewick Man" present a nearly unprecedented opportunity to peer closely at the remains of an early human inhabitant of the New World, one whose bones have been radiocarbon-dated to 9,200 years ago.

Though we can never know his name, his scientific study has allowed for a detailed postmortem (the description of the skeletal remains that follows comes from Powell and Rose 1999). He—and careful analysis of his bones provides a high degree of certainty that he was a male—lived a long and not uneventful life. He could never have conceived, however, the debate that his bones would generate 9,200 years after he breathed his last breath.

One of the surprising and controversial results of the analysis of Kennewick Man has been how different his bones look from those of modern Native Americans. In fact, he was initially identified as a white settler, largely because of the shape of his skull; his is long and narrow, while modern Native Americans tend to have short, broad skulls with tall, wide faces and broad cheekbones.

Does this mean that Kennewick Man is not related to modern Native Americans and may represent a migration of a different people to the New World? That is a fascinating possibility, but, in fact, the skeletal morphology of modern people often doesn't match that of ancient bones found in their regions, even when the bones are those of their ancestors. Skeletal morphology can change from one generation to the next as a result of changed diet

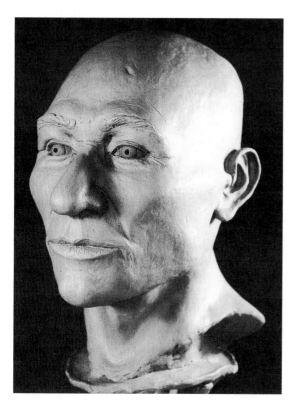

Figure 5.4 An artist's conception of the face of Kennewick Man based on a detailed analysis of his cranial anatomy. Perhaps because of its lack of hair, this version of the Ancient One bears a striking resemblance to Patrick Stewart, the actor best known for his portrayal of Jean-Luc Picard, the captain of the *Enterprise* in the television series *Star Trek: Next Generation*. (© AP/Wide World Photos)

and behavior. Certainly, over the course of 9,200 years, evolutionary processes can alter skeletal morphology as well, producing descendants whose bones are markedly different from those of their ancestors.

Though Kennewick Man did not look like a modern Native American (Figure 5.4), his skeletal remains do resemble those of Asian people, particularly the Ainu of Japan and native people of Polynesia; and there are similarities to Chukchi Eskimo of Siberia as well.

Beyond his ethnicity, we know a bit about his life. He appears to have been between forty-five and fifty years old when he died. At about 5 feet 9 inches, he was physically powerful; his bones bear unmistakable marks of extensive use, looking like those of a modern weight lifter or construction worker. Also, he was a quite healthy individual; his bones show scant evidence of illness (other than a little bit of arthritis), and there is no hint of nutritional deficiency. However, his bones also tell the story of a devastating physical trauma sometime between his fifteenth and twentieth year. In what may have been a single, terrible incident, his right forearm was broken; he cracked at least a couple of the ribs on the right side of his body; and, certainly most traumatic of all, he was stabbed by a stone-tipped spear that entered from behind, passing through his right buttock and lodging in the innominate (the flat blade of bone) of the right side of his pelvis. The spearpoint sliced into his pelvic bone before it was fully developed and actually affected its growth. By reference to standard human developmental patterns, his pelvis was clearly that of a teenager when it sustained the wound. Because other indicators of the skeleton show that he lived to be at least forty-five, we know this severe wound did not kill him. In fact, he lived for about thirty years after the injuries and, based on the location of the wounds and the degree of healing, he likely suffered no permanent disabilities. His right arm healed completely, his ribs fused as best they could, and the pierced bone of his pelvis mended itself. The spearpoint remained in his body, healing bone growing around it, from the time the wound was inflicted until his death—and even beyond. In fact, it remains there still, 9,200 years after his life ended.

The aforementioned Native American groups in Washington State hope to reconsecrate the bones of the Ancient One to the earth, where he had been placed by those who likely knew and loved him over nine millennia ago. They view him as an ancestor whose grave has been plundered and want no part of additional scientific analysis. Scientists, on the other hand, have asked to be allowed to study his remains, to learn what they can of his life and times from the story that has been coded into the bones he left behind. Scientists view him as an exceptionally important source of information whose reburial would be a tragic loss to our scientific understanding of the early settlement of America.

Unfortunately, these divergent desires have led to litigation and hard feelings on both sides. The two most recent court decisions, in February and April 2004, upheld the right of scientists to study the bones and rejected the Indians' claim of ownership of the remains. Subsequent analysis has been carried out over the objection of the Native American groups claiming descent. Unfortunately, there was no intact DNA left in the bone and, therefore, no direct biological genealogy could be drawn.

Anthropologist and Choctaw Indian Dorothy Lippert has walked in both worlds as a Native American who also is a scientist. She has seen the often-callous disregard with which some scientists have treated the physical remains of beloved ancestors, and she has been appalled and angered. But she also is troubled by the ironic loss of information that would be valuable especially to the modern descendants who might wish to return the bones of their ancestors to the earth. Lippert (1997:126) phrases it beautifully when she argues that "for many of our ancestors, skeletal analysis is one of the only ways that they are able to tell us their stories." As she maintains, these ancestors can teach us all if only we listen to their "voice made of bone." Let us all hope that, someday, we can all listen to this voice and that the Ancient One will continue to tell us about the life he lived more than 9,000 years ago. For additional information about the many issues concerning Kennewick Man, read David Hurst Thomas's (2000) *Skull Wars* and Roger Downey's (2000) *Riddle of the Bones.*

Figure 5.5 The projectile point at the far left was recovered at Meadowcroft Rockshelter in western Pennsylvania. The other artifacts here are quite similar in appearance and were also found in western Pennsylvania, at other sites. (Courtesy James Adovasio)

Archaeology of the First Americans

Most archaeologists today agree that people were in South America by at least 12,500 years ago at a place called Monte Verde, in Chile (Dillehay 1989, 1997; Dillehay and Collins 1988). The major cultural level at that site has produced spearpoints and a number of other stone tools. Organic preservation at the site is remarkable, with pieces of mastodon meat, wooden hut foundations, and plant remains recovered in the excavation. Nine of the carbon 14 dates for the main occupation date to more than 11,800 years ago; some of the dates indicate the site is as much as 13,500 years old.

Another very old New World site is the Meadowcroft Rockshelter in western Pennsylvania. At the base of the cave, the excavators recovered material that has produced arguably the oldest radiocarbon dates associated with human-made material in eastern North America (Adovasio, Donahue, and Stuckenrath 1990). Sealed beneath a rockfall from the roof of the shelter dated to 12,000 years ago were some four hundred lithic artifacts, including blades, knives with retouched edges, and a pentagonal, bifacial projectile point (Figure 5.5). Six dates in excess of 12,800 years ago were derived from material at or below this level.

The search for the first Americans has grown tremendously exciting recently with the discovery and excavation of two sites in the American

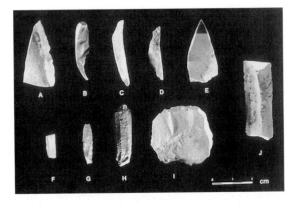

Figure 5.6   Artifacts from the Topper site in Virginia. The Topper artifacts—chipped stone flake cutting tools—were found in a stratigraphic layer below one containing Clovis artifacts and dated to 11,000 years ago and above a culturally sterile layer dated to 20,000 years ago. (SCIAA photo by Daryl P. Miller)

Southeast that might be more than 12,000 years old: Topper in South Carolina and Cactus Hill in Virginia. At Topper, sharp stone flakes (Figure 5.6) that appear to have been cutting tools were found by archaeologist Albert Goodyear (1999) and his team in a soil layer below and, therefore, older than artifacts called Clovis, which have been firmly dated to the period between 12,000 and 10,000 years ago. The layer immediately beneath the pre-Clovis artifacts has been dated to about 20,000 years ago, so the tools may be nearly that old.

In the 2004 summer field season, in another part of the site, Goodyear and his students found a deep stratum sprinkled with chipped stone flakes (Wilford 2004). Some of these pieces of stone may be tools; others may be fragments discarded in the tool-making process. Goodyear estimates the deposit with possible tools and waste flakes to be as much as 25,000 years old, but it can be extremely difficult to determine the age of a soil level accurately. The good news here is that one of Goodyear's students recovered flecks of charcoal, the possible remnants of an ancient fireplace, in the same soil level. The archaeological community eagerly awaits the results of radiocarbon dating on the charcoal for verification of Goodyear's estimate of the age of the soil layer in which the chipped stone was found.

At Cactus Hill, stone projectile points were found in an undisturbed soil layer 15 centimeters (nearly 6 inches) below a stratum in which Clovis-type artifacts were found (Figure 5.7). This implies strongly that the points in question are older than Clovis. Even more exciting, the pre-Clovis layer has been radiocarbon-dated to 18,000 years ago (Stokstad 2000), though some question whether the date was derived from older charcoal that had mixed with a younger archaeological deposit. The Cactus Hill tools are similar to some of the artifacts found at Meadowcroft, so it is possible that these sites reflect a small human population in North America that dates to sometime between 13,000 and as much as 20,000 years ago.

Not all archaeologists are convinced that there was a human occupation of the New World before the Clovis people. Objections have been raised concerning the dating of many of the sites, and it has been suggested that

Figure 5.7 Artifacts from the Cactus Hill site in South Carolina. The Cactus Hill artifacts—a stone scraping tool, stone blades, and a core—were found in an undisturbed layer 15 centimeters below one in which Clovis artifacts were found. (© Kenneth Garrett/National Geographic Society Image Collection)

some are not sites at all, but natural deposits (Fiedel 1999). This uncertainty merely reflects the way science works. We must apply a skeptical approach, demand high levels of proof, but be ready to revise our hypotheses if and when our challenges have been met, our objections responded to, our questions answered, and our skepticism soothed. Patience and skepticism are virtues in science.

If the ages of Monte Verde, Meadowcroft, Cactus Hill, and Topper hold up, the first human occupation of the New World must be pushed back further still. After all, Chile, Pennsylvania, Virginia, and South Carolina are thousands of kilometers away from the Bering Land Bridge entry point to the New World in western Alaska. Archaeologist David Meltzer (1997) has suggested that to allow people entering the New World from the Bering Land Bridge enough time to arrive at a site as far south as Monte Verde by 12,500 years ago through normal processes of migration and population expansion, they probably first entered the New World by about 20,000 years ago.

If this scenario is correct, a trail of successively older sites should exist leading from Chile, western Pennsylvania, and the American Southeast back to the land bridge. Virtually all researchers would agree that such a trail—at least an unbroken trail—has yet to be discovered.

Though it must be admitted that debate regarding the age of the earliest occupation of the New World has sometimes been acrimonious, at least those on either side, and those in between, adhere to the scientific method. There are no appeals to divine inspiration and no references to nonexistent lost continents. All the players in the game agree that the search for the first Americans is a worthwhile endeavor. And all abide by the rules of science.

Who's Next? After the Indians, Before Columbus

So we know that the ancestors of modern American Indians were the first humans to walk on the soil of the New World, perhaps more than 20,000 and certainly more than 13,000 years ago. Further, we know that Christopher Columbus arrived in the New World in 1492, though he did not know it was a "new" world. The question that remains to be addressed in this chapter is, Were there any other visitors or migrants to the New World from the Old World after the Indians arrived from Asia and before Columbus arrived from Europe? We can attempt to answer this question by examining the archaeological record.

Artifact Trails: Evidence of Visitors to the New World

Comedian George Carlin performs a hilarious routine about human beings and their possessions. An archaeologist might characterize the bit as being focused on human "material culture," but for Carlin, it's all about your "stuff" (Carlin 1997). People everywhere have stuff—the things you own, use, carry with you, and so on. In fact, Carlin maintains, a house is just a place for your stuff.

Carlin talks about what happens when you leave on vacation. Of course, you take some of your stuff—a second, smaller version—along with you. We do it today, and people in the past did it as well. And, as archaeologists can show, people invariably leave some of that stuff behind: It gets lost, stolen, used up, and discarded. This "left-behind stuff" constitutes archaeological evidence for the presence of these people in those places.

There is an important rule that resides at the core of archaeology: Everybody's stuff is different, unique, distinguishing, and diagnostic. In other words, the material remains produced by each culture are recognizable and, at the same time, recognizably different from the material remains produced by every other culture. Different cultures have different ways of doing things. They use different raw materials and use the same raw materials differently. They make different styles of tools and different kinds of pottery; they use different construction materials and use the same construction materials differently to produce very different kinds of structures. They have different rules concerning burial of the dead or even disposal of their trash. As a result, archaeological sites, because they constitute the physical remains of these unique, culture-specific practices, uniquely reflect the cultures of the particular people who produced them.

In a sense, then, archaeological sites are like fossils. The sites produced by different cultures are distinguishable much in the way that the fossils of different animal species are. When members of a foreign group enter into a new territory, they bring elements of their material culture with them. The sudden, intrusive appearance of their own unique brand of "stuff" is precisely the way archaeologists detect the presence of such intruders in the territories of other people. This holds true for all of the people we know came to the New World, including Columbus.

For example, archaeologist Charles Hoffman has recovered an enormous assemblage of European artifacts at Long Bay on Watling Island that date to Columbus's first expedition (Hoffman 1987). Also, archaeologist Kathleen Deagan has found some possible traces of the settlement of La Navidad, established by Columbus on Christmas Day in 1492 after one of his ships, the *Santa Maria*, was wrecked off the coast of what we today call Haiti. Columbus had the crew salvage whatever they could from the wreck, including wooden planks and nails for use in the construction of a small fort ashore. There was no room for the shipwrecked crew members on Columbus's two other vessels, the *Niña* and the *Pinta*, and so thirty-nine men were left at the fort when the surviving ships returned to Spain. Columbus returned to the Caribbean in late 1493 only to find that the crew members he had left behind were all dead, some having succumbed to disease but many others having died violent deaths, some possibly from fights among the crew members and some probably at the hands of the natives. The settlement itself, constructed of remnants of the *Santa Maria*, had been burned to the ground.

La Navidad was, in effect, an accidental colony, peopled by only a handful of Spaniards with a small sample of their own material culture. Deagan has recovered burned wood at what is the most likely location of the fort. That wood has been radiocarbon-dated to the second half of the fifteenth century, making it a good match with the known date of La Navidad's settlement.

The 1493 expedition was an attempt to establish a large-scale, permanent Spanish colony in the New World. The resulting settlement, located in what is now the Dominican Republic, was called La Isabela. Kathleen Deagan and José María Cruxent have excavated this site, finding a vast array of evidence of this Spanish colony, including glazed ceramics, nails, glassware, horse gear, knives, dated coins, a key, and even a crucifix (Deagan and Cruxent 2002).

The point here is simple. There is ample material evidence of the Columbus expeditions and attempts to colonize the New World; archaeologists have been successful at finding some of the stuff Columbus and his crew left behind. Any other visitors, explorers, and colonists, either before Columbus or since (for example, the Spanish exploration of the American southeast led by Hernando de Soto [Feder 1994b; Figure 5.8]), should have left physical evidence similar to what Columbus, his crew, and colonists left

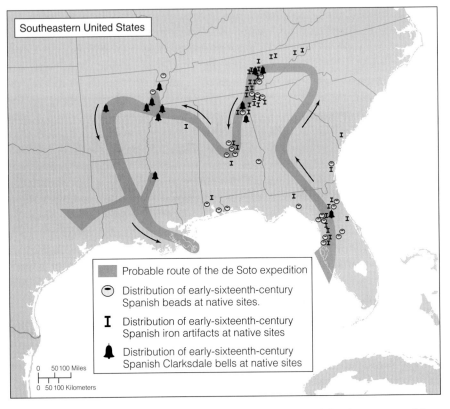

Figure 5.8 Map showing the historically documented route of the de Soto expedition (1538–42) through the American Southeast and locations where archaeological evidence of his expedition, as well as previous and subsequent Spanish expeditions, has been found.

behind at the Watling Island landfall and the settlements of La Navidad and La Isabela. The rest of this chapter assesses the evidence for other visitors to the New World in antiquity.

Europeans in America: The Norse Discovery of America

An assessment of the purported Norse discovery of the New World before Columbus begins not with artifact trails or people's stuff, but with a series of stories—the so-called Viking Sagas—passed down through oral tradition and eventually put to paper decades and even centuries later.

The *sagas* are compelling tales of adventure and discovery, life and death. The stories were handed down orally for generations and recorded hundreds of years after the events they celebrated actually transpired. Among the tales told in the sagas are a number concerning the Viking discovery, exploration, and settlement of Iceland and Greenland. Also described in the sagas is a story of the discovery of another new country. That country, it has been claimed, was North America.

Two sagas in particular tell the story of this new land: the *Greenlander's Saga* and *Eirik the Red's Saga*. The *Greenlander's Saga* relates the following tale (*Eirik the Red's Saga* differs in some particulars but describes essentially the same events); the summary is based on the English translation of the sagas by Magnusson and Paulsson (1965).

Soon after A.D. 980, Eirik Thorvaldsson, known as Eirik (Erik) the Red, was banished from his home on Iceland for having killed two men (his father before him had been banished from Norway for the same offense). The dispute had likely resulted from the growing struggle for land and power on the island nation (McGovern 1980–81). Discovered in A.D. 860 and settled initially by the Vikings in A.D. 870, Iceland's population had grown to nearly fifty thousand, and land was at a premium (Jones 1982).

Outlawed because of his crime, Eirik left his home on Iceland and sailed westward, searching for and verifying the existence of a land that had previously been sighted. Eirik, in an attempt to reestablish a land and power base, returned to Iceland, encouraging people to follow him to this newly discovered land. He called it *Greenland*. Though it was largely covered by glacial ice, Eirik gave the land its name in an early case of deceptive advertising; as the saga writers stated, "People would be more tempted to go there if it had an attractive name" (Magnusson and Paulsson 1965:50).

Established in A.D. 985–86, the Greenland colony attracted many disaffected with the political turmoil of Iceland and grew to a population of about 5,000 (McGovern 1982). The Norse succeeded in carving out a life for themselves in Greenland for 500 years; their archaeological sites are plentiful, represented by the remains of some 400 farmsteads and 17 churches clustered in two major settlements (the Western and Eastern) with a combined population of between 4,000 and 5,000 people (Ingstad 1982:24). The archaeological remains of the Greenland Norse provide a model for what such a colony in the New World might look like.

The mystery of the Greenland colony is not why it failed but, as archaeologist Tom McGovern points out, how it survived for five hundred years (Pringle 1997). In Greenland, at least initially, it seems that the Norse attempted to adhere to their traditional dairy farming economy in a place only marginally suited to that way of life. When the climate of Greenland grew dramatically cooler in the fourteenth century, that way of life became not just uncertain, but also untenable. The skeletal remains of the Norse show a major shift in their diet from the agricultural produce they previously relied on but could no longer grow to food from the sea. Chemical analysis of their bones shows that in the 1300s, fish and marine mammals made up an increasingly large portion of their diet (Richardson 2000).

Concerning climate, everything is relative to one's cultural perspective. Exactly the same change to colder conditions that ended the Norse occupation of Greenland was a boon to a Native American group known as the Thule—a group of the people commonly called Eskimo—whose culture made them supremely well adapted to a cold climate. The increasingly frigid conditions of the fourteenth century, in fact, encouraged Thule expansion south along the Greenland coast. The Thule and Norse likely came into contact at this time; it is unknown if this had any effect on the Norse abandonment of their Greenland settlements. A Norwegian priest sailing to the Western Settlement in 1361 found the entire community abandoned. All of the Norse were gone from Greenland by A.D. 1500.

A Newfound Land

The same year the Greenland colony was established, a Viking ship captained by Bjarni Herjolfsson got lost in a storm on the journey from Iceland to Greenland. After about four days of sailing he sighted land. Bjarni could not identify the country and continued to sail, sighting at least two other lands before finally reaching Greenland by sailing *east*. Bjarni and his men did not set foot on these new unidentified lands. Later, he was to be criticized for not exploring these possibly valuable territories. Bjarni was more a farmer than an explorer, yet this relatively unknown Viking is likely the first European to have sighted America.

Despite the fact that the Greenland settlement was prospering and growing at the end of the tenth century, or maybe because of its success and growth, the possibility that new lands might be found to the west intrigued many. Eirik's son, Leif, spoke to Bjarni about his accidental discovery and even purchased his boat. He set sail with thirty-five men around A.D. 1000 to search for these new lands. According to the *Greenlander's Saga*, following Bjarni's directions backward, Leif made landfalls on the three new lands. He called them Helluland (flat-stone or slab land), Markland (forest land), and Vinland (wine land) (McGovern 1980–81). On Vinland, Leif built some sod houses (called *booths*) and used these as a base from which Vinland could be explored (Figure 5.9).

After this initial exploration, Leif returned to Greenland and told of the richness of Vinland; there were salmon in the rivers, wild grains (probably wild rice) in the meadows, abundant grapes, and so on. Soon thereafter, Leif's brother, Thorvald, traveled to these newfound lands and investigated them for about a year. He encountered natives of the new land, called them *Skraelings*, and was killed in a battle with them. He was buried on Vinland, and the rest of his men returned to Greenland.

In A.D. 1022, Thorfinn Karlsefni led at least 65 and perhaps as many as 160 colonists from Greenland to attempt a permanent settlement of Vinland. Families came, and farm animals were brought along. They built homes and

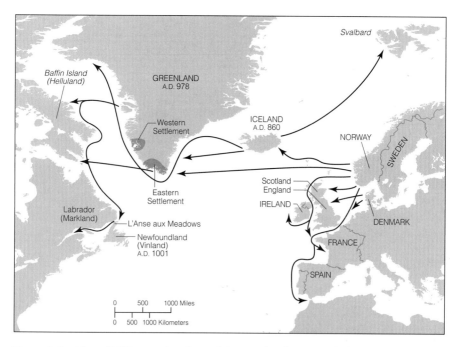

Figure 5.9   Map of Viking explorations of the North Atlantic, including their probable route to the New World in the late tenth and early eleventh centuries A.D.

began farming the land. After about a year, however, following a bitter battle with the Skraelings, the colony was abandoned. This first attempt to establish a permanent European settlement in the New World failed, according to *Eirik the Red's Saga,* because "although the land was excellent they could never live there in safety or freedom from fear, because of the native inhabitants" (Magnusson and Paulsson 1965:100). History might have been substantially different had this not been the case. One final attempt was made to settle Vinland, but this too ended in failure.

Where Was Vinland and Who Were the Skraelings?

McGhee (1984) points out that the sailing directions in the sagas, as well as the geographical and environmental descriptions of the islands Leif explored, suggest quite strongly that Helluland is Baffin Island, Markland is Labrador, and Vinland is Newfoundland, all in Canada. The Skraelings, then, were American natives, most likely Indians rather than Eskimos (Fitzhugh 1972:191–95; Jones 1986:130–34).

There is one unexplained mystery though. Vinland is named for the wine that could be made from the wild grapes that grew there, and there are a number of references to such grapes in both the *Greenlander's Saga* and *Eirik the Red's Saga.* Newfoundland was too far north, however, for wild grapes to grow even when the climate was warmer a thousand years ago. Analysis of pollen preserved at ancient sites in Newfoundland indicates that the flora during Viking occupation was not that much different from today, when grapes cannot grow (Henningsmoen 1977).

Norse Discovery of America: The Physical Evidence

Historical or legendary claims of the discovery and settlement of new lands, like those made in the sagas, can be notoriously difficult to prove. Making ancient tales fit our modern knowledge of geography, superimposing modern maps over ancient ones and trying to finesse similarities, and attempting to mine nuggets of historical truth from legendary tales are all interesting exercises, but they often fall far short of proof. We need to find physical evidence in the New World of the presence of travelers and settlers like the Norse, their unique material culture, their "stuff." And, in fact, Norse stuff, dating to as much as five centuries before Columbus, has been found throughout northeastern North America.

Some of the evidence of the Norse has been found at the archaeological sites of Native Americans. For example, a Norwegian penny minted sometime between A.D. 1065 and 1080 was found at an archaeological site in Maine. The site has been dated to between A.D. 1180 and 1235 (McKusick 1979). The coin had been perforated, perhaps to facilitate use as a pendant. It was the only Viking artifact found at the site; all of the other artifacts were clearly Indian in style and material. The fact that many of the stone tools found at the site were made of a kind of chert found only on northern Labrador may indicate that the "Norse penny," along with the chert, reached the Maine coast by trade from the north.

A growing number of native sites in Arctic Canada show evidence of widespread, occasional, but sometimes intimate contact for centuries between local people and Norse visitors (McGhee 1984, 2000; Sutherland 2000a). For example, a substantial collection of Norse material culture has been recovered from a native site on Ellesmere Island and includes pieces of European chain-mail armor, iron ship rivets, iron wedges, and a wooden carpenter's plane (Schledermann 1981, 2000). The local inhabitants of the site may have obtained these objects through trade or as plunder, or they may merely have found items left behind by a party of Norse explorers.

Archaeologist Patricia Sutherland (2000a) notes a copper pendant of native design but made from smelted (and, therefore, nonnative) copper, excavated at a site located on the east shore of Hudson's Bay, dating to the twelfth century A.D. Also in the Canadian Arctic, archaeologists have found scattered and small quantities of smelted iron, copper, and even a cast bronze pot at native sites (Sutherland 2000a). Sutherland attributes the presence of this Viking stuff to direct trade between the Norse and natives, trade of Norse objects among native groups, and even native scavenging of places where the Norse had visited and left some of their stuff behind.

Figure 5.10 Part of a bronze Norse trader's balance found by archaeologist Patricia Sutherland while working on the west coast of Ellesmere Island, in northern Canada. Artifacts like this provide conclusive evidence for the presence of the Norse in the New World hundreds of years before Columbus. (© Canadian Museum of Civilization, catalogue no. S1Hq-3:4, photo Pat Sutherland, image no. S79-7136)

Sutherland (2000b) also has discovered physical evidence at the Nunguvik site on northern Baffin Island indicating more significant contact between the Norse and native people of northeastern Canada dated to the thirteenth century A.D. She excavated artifacts there that can be traced to the Norse, including a span of about 3 meters of spun yarn made from a mixture of Arctic hare fur and goat hair. The local people did not spin yarn; there are no goats on Baffin Island; and the yarn itself is a very close match to specimens found in Norse Greenland. In addition, fragments of wooden objects were found at two sites on Baffin Island that show wood joinery techniques—for example, mortising—unknown to the native people aboriginally, but well known to the Norse. Also, red-stained holes in the wood are the remnants of corroded, square-cut iron nails, again reflecting the technology of Europe and not aboriginal America.

Sutherland (2000a) has also identified parts of a bronze balance at a site in western Ellesmere Island (Figure 5.10). This kind of artifact, used by the Norse to judge weights and measures, implies that trade was an important element behind the Norse push into the New World. Birgitta Wallace suggests that the Norse may have been looking for resources in the New World, in particular timber, walrus ivory, narwhal tusks, and even furs—especially of polar bear (as cited in McGhee 2000). The thinly scattered distribution in northeastern Canada of objects that can be traced to eleventh-, twelfth-, thirteenth-, and fourteenth-century Norse paints a picture of trade and contact between the Norse and the New World, centuries before Columbus.

It would also seem that the movement of material culture was not entirely one-sided. For example, the soapstone spindle whorl found at L'Anse aux Meadows (discussed next) was made from a fragment of a native stone bowl, and a stone lamp recovered there is also of native manufacture. In another example, two spearpoints of a style known among the Innu people (previously called the Naskapi-Montagnais Indians) on Labrador have been found by archaeologists at a Norse site on Greenland. Odess, Loring, and Fitzhugh (2000) suggest that either Norse visitors picked up the stone weapons and kept them as a curiosity or, considering the sometimes unfriendly relationship between the Norse and native people of the New World, perhaps the spearpoints had actually been shot at Norse invaders and returned to Greenland stuck in a ship's hull or even inside the body of a Viking.

This growing body of archaeological evidence—George Carlin's "stuff" mentioned earlier in the chapter—of the Norse presence in North America before Columbus stands in stark contrast to the lack of such evidence for the presence of other claimed pre-Columbian European or African visitors to the New World. The Norse explorers were small in number and spread out over a huge, forbidding territory, yet archaeologists have found the physical evidence of their presence. Surely we should expect nothing less if we are to validate claims of the presence of other nonnative people in the New World before Columbus.

L'Anse aux Meadows   Finally, one of the villages where these Norse visitors stayed has been found. In 1960 writer and explorer Helge Ingstad (1964, 1971, 1982), convinced that Newfoundland was the Vinland of the sagas, initiated a systematic search of its bays and harbors for evidence of the Viking settlement. At least the sizable colony of Karlsefni would still be archaeologically visible less than one thousand years after its abandonment. If the sagas were based on an actual attempt at colonization, the site could be found. It was only a matter of figuring out where it actually was.

On a promontory of land, at the northern tip of the northwestern peninsula of Newfoundland, Ingstad made his remarkable discovery. There he located the remains of what appeared to be eight typically Norse turf houses (Figure 5.11). Between 1961 and 1968 the site was excavated under the direction of Ingstad's wife, archaeologist Anne Stine Ingstad (1977, 1982). The archaeological evidence was more than sufficient to identify the site at L'Anse aux Meadows as Viking. This interpretation was based not on vague similarities between the excavated structures and those known from Viking colonial settlements on Greenland but on detailed identities of the artifacts and structural remains.

Figure 5.11   House remains at L'Anse aux Meadows, Newfoundland, Canada. Archaeological evidence at this site, including the house patterns, artifacts like soapstone spindle whorls and iron nails, as well as radiocarbon dates, supports the hypothesis that this was a genuine Viking settlement of the New World some five centuries before Columbus. (Photo by B. Schonback, courtesy Birgitta Wallace, Canadian Parks Service)

Along with the turf houses—the so-called booths of the sagas—they found four Norse boatsheds, iron nails and rivets, an iron smithy where local bog iron was worked into tools, a ring-headed bronze pin (Figure 5.12), and a soapstone spindle whorl used in spinning wool. As the local prehistoric Eskimos and Indians did not build boatsheds, smelt iron, produce bronze, or spin wool with spindle whorls, the evidence of an alien culture was definitive (Ingstad and Ingstad 2000).

Chunks of jasper, a flintlike stone which, when struck, produces sparks and was used by the Norse to start fires, were recovered at L'Anse aux Meadows. The jasper has been examined through trace element chemistry; its source is not Newfoundland but Greenland and Iceland, which, of course, are where the Norse inhabitants of L'Anse aux Meadows originated. We also know that the Norse who lived here traveled farther south in the New World because butternut fragments were found in the L'Anse aux Meadows hearths. Butternuts are a kind of walnut that does not grow on Newfoundland and did not grow there during the Norse occupation. Their source is Nova Scotia. The Newfoundland Norse must have visited there or traded with others to obtain them.

In the floor of one of the house structures the excavators discovered a small, stone-lined box. Called an "ember box," it was for storing embers of

Figure 5.12   A ring-headed bronze pin found at L'Anse aux Meadows. The raw material of the artifact and its form are purely Norse. Its recovery within an overall archaeological pattern that matches Viking sites in Greenland and Iceland and its clear association with a turn-of-the-eleventh-century date further support the hypothesis that the site is Viking. (Photo by G. Vandervloogt courtesy Birgitta Wallace, Canadian Parks Service)

the night fire. Remains of a very similar ember box have been found at Eirik's farmstead on Greenland (A. S. Ingstad 1982:33). Twenty-one carbon dates provide a mean age of A.D. 920 ± 30 for the settlement—a bit old by saga accounts, but this may simply be a problem in the application of the dates. Some of the burned wood used for dating purposes likely was drift-wood that already was old when used by the Viking settlers (A. S. Ingstad 1977:233). Nevertheless, a number of the carbon dates fit the chronology of the sagas quite well.

More recent excavations at L'Anse aux Meadows have recovered additional material of Norse manufacture dating to about a thousand years ago. In water-logged areas of the site where preservation was good, a team led by Parks Canada archaeologist Birgitta Wallace (2000) recovered a fragment of a notched bow, a piece of what appears to be a ship patch, a pedal-shaped object, and the top of a barrel, all made of wood. All of these objects exhibited evidence that they had been carved or cut with metal tools. Also, a glass bead, a piece of gilded brass, and a needle hone—all of typical Norse design—were found.

Was L'Anse aux Meadows the settlement initiated by Leif, occupied by his brother Thorvald, and expanded in the hope of permanency by Karlsefni? The archaeological data do not conform perfectly to the sagas. No human burials were found, though the sagas indicate that a number of Vikings died in Vinland. No evidence of European domesticated animals was recovered in the excavations, though the sagas relate that such animals were brought by the settlers. Wallace (2000) concludes that L'Anse aux Meadows is not Vinland, but that Vinland was a region with L'Anse aux Meadows located at its northern margin. The site, she suggests, was used as a base of operations (called Straumfjord in the sagas) from which Norse exploration of points farther south was initiated.

It will likely never be known for certain whether L'Anse aux Meadows is the archaeological site of Eiriksson's and later Karlsefni's settlement, but perhaps this is not so important. What is important and what is indisputable is the archaeological evidence at L'Anse aux Meadows of a Viking settlement, the westernmost outpost of their far-flung world. The settlement was planted in the fertile soil of America. It withered and died for reasons largely beyond the control of those hardy folk who attempted it: a worsening climate that would render Greenland uninhabitable for Viking farmers and render the voyage from the west coast of Greenland to Vinland virtually impossible, and a native population willing to fight to protect themselves and their lands. In the final analysis, the saga of the Vinland settlement may be a tragic story of failure. But, most important in terms of the focus of this chapter and perhaps in terms of human history as well, the physical evidence indicates quite clearly that it was a drama played out on the world stage five hundred years before Columbus set sail.

Other Evidence of the Viking Presence?

The Newport Tower   Is there evidence for a pre-Columbian Norse presence south of the modern border between Canada and the United States? The Newport Tower in Newport, Rhode Island, has been proposed as an ancient Viking construction (Figure 5.13). It is singular in appearance, at least in the New World, and has been the focus of both inquiry and speculation.

There is a significant problem, however, with the hypothesis that the tower is Viking and predates the accepted period of European settlement of the region. The English settled the area around Newport in A.D. 1639, and there is no mention made by these settlers of a mysterious and already existing stone tower. They almost certainly would have noted it had there been one.

However, there was enough controversy about the possibility of a pre-Columbus Viking connection to the tower that an archaeological investigation was conducted around and *under* the tower (Godfrey 1951). Most of the artifacts were pieces of pottery, iron nails, clay tobacco pipes, buttons, and buckles. All of these items can be traced to Scotland, England, or the English colonies in America and were manufactured between the seventeenth and nineteenth centuries (Hattendorf 1997). The investigators even found the preserved impression of a colonial bootprint in the soil beneath the stone foundation of the tower. For a seventeenth-century bootprint to have been

Figure 5.13 The Newport Tower in Newport, Rhode Island, claimed by some to be an ancient Viking church. Historical and archaeological evidence indicates quite clearly that the tower was built during colonial times. (K. L. Feder)

left under the tower, the tower must have been built either sometime during or sometime after the seventeenth century.

Finally, the lime mortar bonding the stones used to build the tower has been radiocarbon-dated. The carbon date matches quite precisely the historical record and the artifacts recovered, A.D. 1665 (Hertz 1997). The mysterious tower turns out to be, in actual fact, a windmill likely built by the then governor of Rhode Island, Benedict Arnold, the grandfather and namesake of the famous traitor (it is even mentioned in his will, dated to 1677). The architecture of the tower turns out not to be unique after all; it is a close match for a windmill built in A.D. 1632 in Chesterton, England (Hertz 1997). The senior Benedict Arnold was brought up within just a few kilometers of Chesterton; perhaps he liked the unique design and decided to have a copy built on his property in Rhode Island.

The Kensington Stone A large stone slab with ostensible Viking writing, or *runes,* was found near Kensington, Minnesota, by Olof Ohman in 1898 (Kehoe 2005). The stone contained a short message concerning a journey from Vinland and bore a date of A.D. 1362. No other Norse artifacts were found in an 1899 excavation at the stone's find-spot or in subsequent excavations (in 1964 and 2001). The written message on the Kensington stone tells the story of just thirty individuals—eight Swedes and twenty-two Norwegians—who didn't stay very long. It is possible that such a small group staying for a short time would leave no other material evidence of their presence.

It is important to consider the historical context of the time period when the Kensington Stone is supposed to have been carved. As mentioned previously, as a result of climatic deterioration, the Viking world was contracting at this time. By A.D. 1362, the Vinland colony had long since been abandoned. One of the two major Norse communities on Greenland—the so-called Western Settlement—was reported to have been abandoned by A.D. 1361. Ivar Bardarson, a Norse bishop, reported that the community had been decimated by Skraelings. Two-hundred kilometers (120 miles) to the south, the older and larger Norse Greenland community—the Eastern Settlement—was declining rapidly in the fourteenth century. Archaeological evidence suggests that the Eastern Settlement was abandoned by the middle of the fifteenth century. While it seems unlikely that Vikings were sailing to Minnesota and leaving inscriptions during this period of geographic contraction, recent geological analysis suggests that the runes were carved far earlier than 1898 (Kehoe 2005). At this point, the stone's authenticity remains a point of controversy.

The Vinland Map   When the so-called Vinland map first surfaced in 1957, a few historians and cartographers thought it might be genuine, dating to about A.D. 1440, more than fifty years before the first voyage of Columbus to the New World. It was initially suggested by those who accepted the authenticity of the map that it was a copy of an even older work based on Viking knowledge of the geography of northern Canada (Skelton, Marston, and Painter 1995). Greenland is shown and named on the map. To the west of Greenland is an island called Winilanda Insula; this is thought by some to be the earliest—and a pre-Columbian—depiction of Vinland (Figure 5.14).

Many, however, were immediately skeptical of the map's authenticity. As map scholar Douglas McNaughton (2000) has summarized, the map displayed a general style and appearance that was unlike any known fifteenth-century map: Its orientation was wrong, and it lacked the border delineating Heaven and Earth seen in other maps of this time period. Beyond this, although some thought the map's authenticity was supported by the fact that it was discovered bound into a fifteenth-century book, there is no mention of the map in the book itself, supporting the hypothesis that the map may have been added long after the book was published.

Famed microscopist Walter McCrone was brought in to examine the physical characteristics of the map (McCrone 1976, 1988). When McCrone analyzed the chemical makeup of the map ink with a scanning electron microscope and electron and ion microprobes, he found the presence of titanium dioxide, the chemical name for a slightly yellow pigment called anatase or titanium white. This was a key piece of forensic evidence. Titanium white

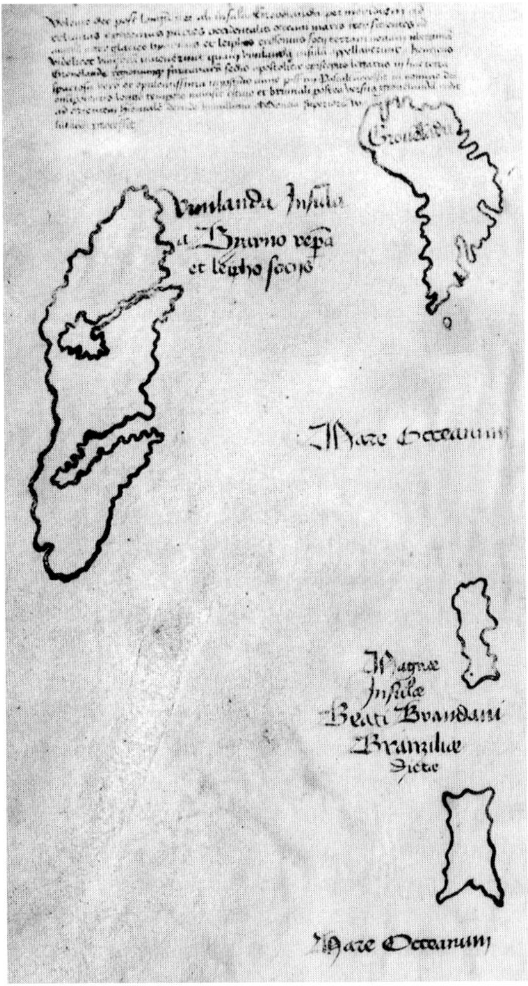

Figure 5.14   Section of the Vinland map that depicts the New World. The parchment on which the map was drawn appears to date to before Columbus, but the ink used to draw the map has been shown to be modern. (Beinecke Rare Book and Manuscript Library, Yale University)

was not manufactured until 1917 and required a technology unknown until this time. Curiously, but significantly, this pigment was not found in the ink used on the pages of the book in which the map supposedly was found.

Beyond this, McCrone found that the black ink used to outline the various continents and islands depicted on the map appeared to have diffused as a yellow band around the line itself. This is typical for old inks and normally takes hundreds of years, so its presence seemed to argue for the map's antiquity. However McCrone determined that this yellow band around the ink line was not, in reality, diffused ink, but, instead, a separately drawn, wide band of chemically distinct yellowish ink. The thin black line had been drawn over the yellow band along its center across most of the map. In other words, under the microscope it appeared that a clever forger had known that an old map would show a creeping of the ink out along the margins of the map lines. The forger could not wait, of course, for hundreds of years for this yellow band to appear, so he or she simply drew a yellow band first and then drew the black ink line over it, simulating an appearance of antiquity. The Vinland map had to have been drawn, according to McCrone, not in the fifteenth century, but in the twentieth; it was a fake.

The story does not end here, however, as a subsequent analysis by Thomas Cahill (1987) failed to support McCrone's identification of the twentieth-century pigment anatase. Cahill found only trace amounts of titanium and claimed that other, authentic documents also had trace amounts of titanium. McCrone vigorously disputes Cahill's analysis.

In a fascinating turn of events, in 2002 researchers radiocarbon-dated a small piece of the parchment on which the map was drawn. The result: The parchment dates to approximately A.D. 1434 (Donahue, Olin, and Harbottle 2002). If the map showing Newfoundland truly dates to fifty-eight years or so before Columbus set sail, it would seem to support its authenticity, but skeptics have a response; suppose the forger cleverly used an old piece of parchment which, they claim, would have been readily available? In support of this skeptical perspective, chemists Robin Clark and Katherine Brown have confirmed McCrone's earlier analysis and support his conclusion that a modern ink was used to make the map lines look antique (2004).

In other words, things are pretty much still up in the air about the Vinland map. Is the map itself an authentic depiction by Europeans of a chunk of the New World based on information collected decades—or even centuries—before Columbus? Is the parchment on which the map was drawn authentically old, but the drawn map itself a twentieth-century fake?

Though the authenticity of the map is of great concern to cartographers and to Yale University (the current owner of the map), its significance relative to the question of a Viking presence in the New World actually has diminished over the years. After all, as shown in this chapter, we know from the archaeological record that the Norse explored and attempted to settle the northeast coast of the New World 500 years before Columbus. Whether or not they drew a map of their exploits is, at least in this regard, largely beside the point.

Other Voyagers, Other Visitors

Though there was a great deal of skepticism among historians and archaeologists concerning the accuracy of the Norse sagas, today the Norse encounter with and attempted settlement of North America centuries before Columbus is an accepted part of history, as a direct result of the discovery of archaeological evidence of their presence in the New World. The artifacts found by

Patricia Sutherland and others and, of course, the excavation of the Norse community at L'Anse aux Meadows represent a series of smoking guns, definitive, physical proof that the Norse were here before Columbus.

Other proposed contacts between inhabitants of Asia, Africa, and Europe before the voyages of Christopher Columbus are fascinating possibilities but simply do not present the kinds of physical, archaeological evidence seen for the Norse.

A Chinese Discovery of the New World?

For example, there is a long-standing debate concerning the possibility of Chinese sailors, accidentally or intentionally, making it to the shores of the New World before Columbus. Like the Norse sagas, this scenario also begins with a historical legend, a Chinese "saga" of the land of Fusang, a distant place, the story tells, visited by a Buddhist monk about 1,500 years ago. Depending on how you interpret the story, Fusang was real, mythical, or some combination of the two.

As Frost (1982) points out, Fusang was placed on the Asian coast by ancient Chinese mapmakers. Nevertheless, some have tried to identify Fusang as America, carefully selecting elements of the legend that seem to reflect the biogeography of the California coast. But is there any physical evidence for the presence of Chinese explorers or lost fishermen in the New World that dates to 1,500 years ago? For a time, it was thought that there was. In 1973 a vessel dredging off the coast of California brought up a sizable rock, carved into the shape of a doughnut. In 1975, twenty or so similar stones were found by divers off the Palos Verdes peninsula in southern California. These discoveries generated a great deal of publicity at the time. Some suggested that the stones were identical to anchor stones used on Chinese sailing vessels as far back as A.D. 500.

The Palos Verdes stones were examined by the geology department at the University of California, Santa Barbara, in 1980. If the anchor stones could be shown to have been made from rock present only in China, the case for a Chinese presence in the New World before Columbus would be much stronger. Unfortunately for the supporters of this hypothesis, it was determined that the alleged Chinese anchors were made of California rock (Frost 1982:26), most likely Monterey shale, a common local rock type.

The stones looked like Chinese anchors, however, because that is precisely what they were. Chinese American fishermen commonly trawled the waters off California in the nineteenth century. They sailed in their traditional craft, the junk. Indeed, the Palos Verdes stones are almost certainly the anchors, moorings, and net weights of these fishermen. They provide no help to those who wish to prove that Fusang is, in reality, ancient California because the anchors clearly were made locally by historically recognized Chinese sailors.

The hypothesis proposed by Gavin Menzies (2002) in his book *1421: The Year China Discovered America* (the original, hardcover version was more accurately titled *1421: The Year China Discovered the World*) is breathtaking, but not so much for its timing. After all, 1421 is a mere seventy-one years before Columbus's first voyage to America and just ninety-eight years before Ferdinand Magellan became the first European to circle the earth. It is the scope of the hypothesis that is staggering: Menzies proposes that between A.D. 1421 and 1423, an armada of more than one hundred Chinese ships with a contingent of 10,000 men circumnavigated the globe, encountering and, in some instances, colonizing Africa, North America, South America, assorted Pacific Islands, as well as Australia.

Menzies begins with the fascinating historical account—largely ignored in the West (did you ever hear about this in social studies?)—of the voyages of Chinese Admiral Zheng He, who commanded a huge fleet of ships in his seven epic voyages dating from 1405 to 1433. During these voyages, Zheng He ventured westward from China along the south Asian coast, traveling as far as the east coast of Africa and then north into the Persian Gulf, a truly remarkable feat of navigation decades before Columbus or Magellan. So far, so good; but from there, Menzies, to put it mildly, extrapolates. He suggests that when Zheng He returned home after exploring the east coast of Africa in 1421, a part of the fleet, commanded by four of Zheng He's rear admirals, didn't return, as most historians contend, but continued the journey, following the African coast to the south, turning to the north after circling the southern tip of Africa, exploring the west coast of that continent, and then making a beeline to the east coast of the New World. After making landfall in South America, Menzies believes, Zheng He's fleet traveled south, circled Cape Horn (the southern tip of South America), and sailed up the western coast of South America, catching the ocean currents westward to Australia. Menzies maintains that, in a roundabout journey, part of the fleet next followed the ocean currents back eastward to North America, which they explored, trading with the natives, and from there returned home to China in 1423 (Figure 5.15).

To be sure, Menzies tells a ripping good sea tale, but the evidence for Zheng He's fleet circumnavigating the globe is quite thin. Much of his evidence consists of a number of fifteenth- and sixteenth-century maps known to have been in the possession of European explorers. Menzies interprets these maps as exhibiting a preexisting knowledge of the New World. That knowledge, he proposes, came to Europe from the Chinese. In other words, according to Menzies, Columbus, Magellan, and the rest knew where they were going on their voyages of exploration and discovery because the Chinese had already been there and mapped their routes and described the places they discovered.

Menzies's interpretation of these maps involves quite a bit of squinting at squiggly lines on ancient parchment and finding what he expects to

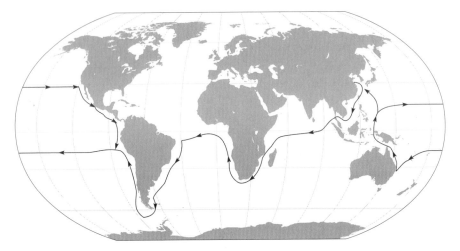

Figure 5.15   One of several routes that writer Gavin Menzies proposes was followed by a Chinese fleet to circumnavigate the globe in the early fifteenth century. In his view—as reflected in the title of his popular book published in 2002—the Chinese discovered America in A.D. 1421, seventy-one years before Columbus (based on Menzies 2002).

find. For example, we know that in 1513 the Ottoman admiral Piri Reis pro-duced a map of the world by combining the information in a number of older maps, including one produced by Columbus and a number drawn by early-sixteenth-century Portuguese explorers of the New World, especially those in the period 1500–1503. Where Menzies sees a startling accuracy in the Piri Reis map in its depiction of the New World, especially parts of South America not yet explored by any Europeans (Figure 5.16), others see great inaccuracy and mostly guesswork, about what you'd expect from mapmak-ers who had never actually seen the southern coast of South America or the shores of North America (Dutch 2003). In his definitive work on the map, Gregory McIntosh (2000) shows beyond any doubt that, though a wonder-ful historical resource, the Piri Reis map fits nicely within the context of fif-teenth- and sixteenth-century European mapmaking: It displays often accurate renderings of coastal regions actually visited and mapped by ex-plorers, guesswork in those areas that had been seen or visited only briefly, and sheer conjecture in those areas not yet visited. European mapmakers of this period apparently didn't like leaving blank areas on maps, so they used their imagination to draw what they thought might exist in those regions where geographic information was lacking. Piri Reis incorporated those con-jectures into his map. His map does not accurately render the southern coast of South America or the coast of North America. There is no geographic in-formation on the map that could only have appeared in Europe via Chinese travelers who had already visited these regions. McIntosh (2000:38–41) points to a number of European maps predating 1513 and still in existence

Figure 5.16   The famous Piri Reis map is a virtual Rorschach for amateur cartographers. Some claim that his map, produced in A.D. 1513 and based on far older maps, shows an intimate and unexpected knowledge by ancient mapmakers of the coasts of South America and Antarctica.

that were the probable sources for Piri Reis. There are no early-fifteenth-century Chinese maps of the New World in existence to support Menzies and no need to invoke them.

Beyond this, historians tell us that Zheng He's endeavor was terminated after he reached Africa, and his army does not disappear on a lengthy voyage around the world but is accounted for, having been reassigned to construction work back in China (Barrett 2002). Above all else, though Menzies recognizes the potential and necessity of the archaeological record for testing his hypothesis, he presents precious little in the way of Chinese material culture—the ever present stuff that Chinese globe-trotters would certainly have brought along on such a voyage of exploration and colonization—to back up his hypothesis. As reviewers have pointed out (Barrett 2002), there are no early-fifteenth-century Chinese artifacts found in firm archaeological context that would afford physical evidence for the early presence of Chinese explorers or colonists anywhere in the New World—nothing, for example, like the stuff Columbus and his men left behind in their exploration and settlement of the Caribbean. Make no mistake, the fifteenth-century Chinese were certainly up to the task of circumnavigating the globe and "discovering" those places we in the West give credit to European explorers for "discovering." Until definitive physical evidence like the material left behind by Columbus is found, however, the claim that China discovered the world in 1421 remains unproven.

Africans in Ancient America?

Others have suggested that Africans journeyed to the Americas long before Columbus, made contact with the native people, and may have had an enormous impact on the development of New World civilization. Although not the first to suggest it, a professor of anthropology, Ivan Van Sertima (1976), has been the most eloquent proponent of these claims.

In his book, *They Came Before Columbus,* Van Sertima presents the following evidence in support of his claim of an African presence in the pre-Columbian New World:

1. References in Columbus's writings to the presence of "black Indians" in the New World
2. The presence of a metal (*gua-nin*) purported to be African in origin, reported by Columbus
3. Pre-Columbian skeletons with "Negroid" characteristics
4. Artistic representations of black Africans at sites in the New World that predate the voyages of Columbus

While some of the kinds of evidence cited by Van Sertima are in line with the discussion earlier in this chapter concerning what is necessary to trace the prehistoric movement of people, the actual data presented fall far short of that needed for a convincing case.

For instance, Columbus does not claim to have seen black-skinned Indians; he merely passes along a story told to him by a group of Indians he did contact. Columbus also passed on the report of Indians with tails, so such evidence is highly suspect.

The report of the metal called *gua-nin* is similarly unconvincing. We do not have the metal to examine, none has ever been found in archaeological excavations in the New World, and we certainly cannot rely on five-hundred-year-old assays of the metal that Van Sertima maintains indicate its African identity.

As stated earlier, one way to trace the movement of prehistoric people focuses on skeletal analysis. Van Sertima cites analysis of a small number of skeletons found in the New World, particularly in Mesoamerica, that ostensibly have indicated the African origin of some individuals. Here again the evidence is quite weak, with either the African character of the skeletons being questionable or the dating of the bones uncertain. Europeans brought black slaves to the New World as early as the sixteenth century, and some of the skeletons found in the New World cited by Van Sertima, if actually of African origin, would most likely be those of early, but post-Columbian, slaves.

Figure 5.17   An example of a giant carved stone head of the Olmec culture of Mesoamerica. These carvings in hard volcanic rock—weighing up to 20 tons—are evidence of an advanced society in Mesoamerica three thousand years ago. For some, the facial features of the Olmec heads are evidence of an African origin for that advanced culture. However, there is no evidence for an African presence in ancient Mesoamerica. (© Richard H. Stewart/National Geographic Society Image Collection)

Van Sertima's assertion that there is ample evidence of the presence of black Africans in the New World in the form of artistic representations of individuals who look African is, perhaps, the weakest link in an already weak chain of reasoning. The weakness lies in the subjective nature of the assertion. For example, Van Sertima points to the physiognomies of the so-called Olmec heads of lowland Mesoamerica—huge pieces of basalt carved into human heads between 3,200 and 2,900 years ago by the bearers of what is almost certainly the first complex culture in Mesoamerica (Stuart 1993) (Figure 5.17). Altogether, fewer than twenty of these carved heads have been found; they range from about 5 to 11 feet in height.

Van Sertima asserts that they are clearly African in appearance, and indeed they do possess full lips and broad noses. Van Sertima, however, ignores the fact that many of the Olmec heads also have flat faces like American Indians, not prognathic profiles (jutting-out lower faces) like Africans. He also chooses not to see what appear to be epicanthic folds on the eyelids of the statues—these are typical of Old World Asians and American Indians. It is also the case that American Indians exhibit a broad range of features and some, in fact, have full lips and broad noses—at the same time, they possess other, more typically Indian physical features (Sabloff 1989). Most archaeologists interpret the Olmec heads as stylized sculptures, perhaps representing the faces of their rulers or chiefs.

Many other specific responses could be provided to refute particular claims made by Van Sertima. It is more important, however, to point out the deductive implications of his hypothesis and the lack of confirming evidence. If Africans truly were present in the New World in large numbers before Columbus and if they had a substantial impact on indigenous cultures, there should be ample evidence in the archaeological record of artifacts, raw materials, and skeletons—the kinds of cultural and biological evidence that archaeologists regularly find and analyze—to support this claim. We would find more than enigmatic statues and vague historical references. Archaeologists should find clear evidence of material remains reflecting an African rather than an Indian pattern in housing, tool making, burial of the dead, ceremonies, and so on. Without such evidence, the claim of an African discovery and settlement of the New World remains unproven.

Furthermore, to assess the origin of things like the huge Olmec sculptures, we must focus not on subjective assertions about what or whom they may look like but on the cultural context of these artifacts within Olmec society. Artifacts like the basalt heads that Van Sertima cites as evidence of an African influence cannot be viewed in a vacuum. Surely such things demanded a level of technical competence, but they also required a complex social/political/economic infrastructure. Labor had to be conscripted to quarry the stone, to transport it across many miles, and to carve it. Workers needed to be fed and housed, and their labor had to be organized and overseen. It is highly unlikely that a small group of interlopers, even if they had been present, could possibly have so altered a society over a short period of time to produce all of the manifold cultural systems needed to create the stone heads—and the pyramids, jade carvings, earthen platforms, and so on that characterize the Olmec culture. Of necessity, the sculpted heads could have been produced only as one part of a complex pattern of behaviors and abilities that must have evolved together over a lengthy period of time.

This is precisely what the archaeological record shows. In fact, there is no physical evidence to validate the claimed presence of African visitors to Mesoamerica before Columbus. The notion that this unproven presence was a crucial factor in the development of complex societies in the New World flies in the face of a wealth of archaeological evidence that clearly shows the complex and independent evolution of those societies over a lengthy period of time. For a detailed and comprehensive critique of Van Sertima's assertion that the Olmec were inspired by West African voyagers to the New World, see the articles by Mesoamericanist Bernard Ortiz de Montellano in the journals *The Skeptical Inquirer* (Ortiz de Montellano 1991, 1992), *Current Anthropology* (Ortiz de Montellano et al. 1997a), and *Ethnohistory* (Ortiz de Montellano et al. 1997b).

Afrocentrism   Unfortunately, Van Sertima's claim of an African presence in Mesoamerica long before Columbus has become entrenched dogma among some espousing an "Afrocentrist" perspective of history. Afrocentrism has a laudable goal: to disclose the enormous but often ignored contributions made by African people to the sciences, medicine, philosophy, literature, and art. Unfortunately, in this effort some Afrocentrists ignore established historical and scientific fact and make claims of an African source for things that clearly can be shown to be non-African. Some Afrocentrists assert that much of European science and philosophy was literally "stolen" from African sources (James 1954). For example, it has been asserted that the Greek philosopher Aristotle secretly visited the Egyptian city of Alexandria and pillaged the great library there, taking the best ideas of African thinkers and presenting them to the world as his own. But this is an impossibility. Aristotle died in 322 B.C., and the library at Alexandria was not established until 297 B.C.—twenty-five years after his death (Lefkowitz 1996). In fact, we know that the library was assembled by one of Aristotle's students and that most of the works there were written in Greek, not Egyptian.

In its extreme version, Afrocentrism proposes that African cultures were the source of virtually every significant development in the ancient world. For example, Afrocentrist Kwame Nantambu (1996–97) claims that the archaeological and historical records prove that Africa, specifically the culture of ancient Egypt, was the world's source for such things as pottery, the domestication of plants and animals, and writing. In each of these cases, Nantambu is factually incorrect: The world's first pottery has been found in Japan, dating to 11,000 years ago, predating African ceramics by more than a millennium; the domestication of plants and animals has been traced back to close to 11,000 years ago in Southwest Asia, while the earliest evidence for domestication in Africa dates to no more than 8,000 years ago; the first Egyptian writing has been dated to 5,100 years ago, and the earliest writing in the world has been found in Mesopotamia in Southwest Asia dating to 6,000 years ago (Feder 1998–99). The ancient and modern peoples of Africa represent some of the great cultural achievements of humankind and there is no need to exaggerate their intellectual contributions to the world.

Other Europeans in the New World Before Columbus?

Evidence for the presence of other European visitors to the New World before Columbus is not nearly as strong as for the Norse. For example, according to legend, the Irish priest St. Brendan was supposed to have embarked on a seven-year trip westward into the Atlantic Ocean sometime in the late fifth and early sixth centuries A.D. Three centuries later, his adventures were recorded in a work called the *Navigatio* (Ashe 1971).

Based on documentary and archaeological evidence, it is clear that wandering Irish monks called *anchorites* had indeed accomplished some

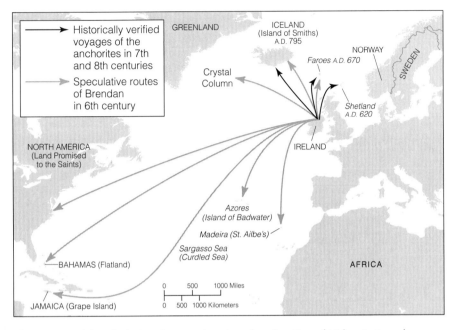

Figure 5.18   Map depicting the actual routes of exploration of Irish priests and proposed routes of Brendan in the sixth century A.D.

rather remarkable feats of navigation in the sixth through eighth centuries A.D. (Figure 5.18). Searching for places of quiet solitude where they could worship God, they settled the Orkney Islands in A.D. 579, the Shetlands in 620, and the Faroes in 670 (Ashe 1971:24). They even beat the Vikings to Iceland, settling it in A.D. 795.

Some assert that a place mentioned in the *Navigatio*—the so-called Land Promised to the Saints—is actually North America. Could Brendan have visited the New World? Adventurer Tim Severin (1977) attempted to replicate such a hypothesized voyage by sailing across the Atlantic in a replica of a *curragh*, the name given to the hide boats of the Irish. But replicative experiments of historical events merely show what may have been possible; they cannot prove that such events actually did take place. The only way to prove that Brendan made it to the shores of North America would be to find physical, archaeological evidence of a sixth-century Irish presence here—to find some of their stuff, like crosses, iron rings, or buttons—and no such confirmation has ever been found. Without such evidence, the story of Brendan remains simply an interesting legend.

Another purported European visitor to the New World is Prince Madoc. Madoc himself appears to have been an actual historical personality who lived in the twelfth century A.D. He was a renowned or, more accurately, legendary sailor. In one of the stories about his exploits, he allegedly sailed westward from Wales in about A.D. 1170 and discovered a new land. Depending on which version of the story suits you, either he never returned, or he did come back, making several trips to this new land and bringing hundreds of Welsh settlers to the territory he had discovered.

Unfortunately, many of the stories the Madoc supporters provide are secondhand and contradict each other. We can read breathless accounts published in the eighteenth century of the Navajo, Cherokee, Aztec, or Mandan Indians being indistinguishable in culture, language, and skin tone from Welshmen. In many of these stories we see an underlying racist theme similar to what we will see in reference to the *Moundbuilder* myth in Chapter 6; where Indian villages are clean, where their houses are well made and streets neatly laid out, even where agriculture is the primary mode of subsistence, it is presumed that the Indians must really be Europeans. With a ready-made legend like that of the Welsh voyage(s), it was natural to associate those groups with Madoc and his band of travelers.

There is, however, one variety of physical, archaeological evidence presented by the Madoc supporters. These supposed confirming data consist of the ridgetop stone forts of Kentucky and Tennessee. In fact, Deacon (1966:202) attempts to trace Madoc's route in America from Mobile Bay, up the Alabama River into Kentucky and Tennessee, by the distribution of these sites.

Clearly the discovery of a single iron sword, a datable Welsh inscription, artifacts made from a raw material present in Wales, or the skeleton of a western European would have gone further in support of the Welsh hypothesis than would all the stories of Welsh-speaking, light-skinned Indians. But archaeologist Charles Faulkner (1971) found no physical evidence supporting the Welsh hypothesis when he excavated one of the better-known forts in central Tennessee. Instead, the fort, which is really little more than a hilltop enclosed with a stone wall, contained artifacts made by American Indians, not Europeans. Included among the very few artifacts actually recovered were stone spearpoints and cutting and scraping tools. Carbon dates derived from charcoal found at the site and associated with its construction and use indicate that the stone fort was built and used sometime between A.D. 30 and 430.

In the mid-1960s the Daughters of the American Revolution erected a historical marker on the shore of Mobile Bay in Alabama. It reads, in part: "In memory of Prince Madoc, a world explorer who landed on the shores of Mobile Bay in 1170 and left behind, with the Indians, the Welsh language." If Madoc, indeed, did sail across the Atlantic into the Gulf of Mexico, into Mobile Bay, up the Alabama River, and eventually into Tennessee, he might have seen the stone forts credited to him and today presented as material evidence for his visits in the twelfth century. The Indians had already beaten him to it, having built them as much as one thousand years before. Here again, there is no physical evidence—no support in the archaeological record—for a Welsh presence in America before Columbus.

America B.C.?

Harvard marine biologist the late Barry Fell (*America B.C.*, *Saga America*, and *Bronze Age America*) provides ostensible evidence, not just for the discovery but also for the exploration and colonization of the Americas by Iberians (people from Spain and Portugal) 3,000 years ago, Celts 2,800 years ago, Greeks 2,500 years ago, ancient Hebrews about 2,000 years ago, and Egyptians 1,500 years ago.

Fell and adherents like Trento (1978) and Feldman (1977) do not claim that these various Old World groups simply discovered America or that they merely explored it. It is Fell's contention that these peoples settled the Western Hemisphere, apparently in large numbers, many years before Columbus. It is his further claim that there was a regular flow of commerce between the Old and New Worlds over many years and that the presence of these interlopers had a significant impact on indigenous peoples.

Most archaeologists and historians in the New and Old Worlds who have had something to say concerning Fell's claims have been skeptical, and some have been downright hostile (Cole 1979; Daniel 1977; Dincauze 1982; Hole 1981; McKusick 1976; Ross and Reynolds 1978).

The three categories of evidence Fell provides in his books are

1. Alleged linguistic connections between American Indian languages and many different European tongues

2. Inscriptions found in the New World in many ancient European alphabets

3. Architectural similarities between stone structures mainly in New England and those in western Europe

Linguistics

Two scientists at the Smithsonian Institution examined Fell's claims of linguistic similarities between American Indian and European languages such as Egyptian, Celtic, Norse, and Arabic (Goddard and Fitzhugh 1979). Fell's basic approach is to select words in particular Indian and European languages that sound alike (or can be made to sound alike) and can be interpreted as having similar meanings. He then concludes that the Indian language must be derived from that of the Old World group. Fell's approach has long ago been discredited by linguists; it is little different from that of those speculative thinkers in Europe in the sixteenth through nineteenth centuries who attempted to trace American Indians to various Old World peoples.

Goddard and Fitzhugh point out that such an approach is pointless; the correct pronunciation of many of the Indian words is very rarely known.

Furthermore, merely comparing words ignores facts of grammar that are much more important in language comparisons. With relatively few common sounds making up the countless words of most human languages, coincidental similarities are bound to show up if you look hard enough. For example, as Mesoamericanist Pedro Armillas (personal communication) points out, the Latin word for "little eyes" is *ocelli*. "Little eyes" look like little spots and in Nahuatl, the language of the Aztecs, a spotted cat is an *ocelot*. Such word-by-word comparisons can show word similarities in many different languages with absolutely no historic connection. The Indian words that Fell claims are derived from European sources can be traced; they have a linguistic history within their own languages. There is no evidence that they suddenly entered a language, which would be expected if they had been borrowed from elsewhere.

Inscriptions

Fell, though trained in biology, also claims expertise in epigraphy (deciphering ancient inscriptions). He asserts that there are literally hundreds of examples of ancient inscriptions in various Old World alphabets scattered throughout the New World. Yet here Fell ignores definitive evidence concerning some of his important artifacts. For example, he cites inscribed tablets from Davenport, Iowa, well known to be nineteenth-century fakes, as positive evidence of the exploration of midwestern North America by a fleet of Egyptian ships, under the command of a Libyan skipper, in the ninth century B.C. (1976:261–68). See Chapter 6 (Figure 6.5) for a description of the unmasking of the fakes (and see McKusick 1991 for a detailed accounting of the entire story).

Moreover, as Goddard and Fitzhugh maintain, among even those inscriptions where fraud cannot be proven, "all of the alleged ancient New World inscriptions examined by specialists to date have been found to contain linguistic or epigraphic errors or anomalies consistent with modern manufacture but inconsistent with a genuine ancient origin" (1979:167).

Beyond the fakes, Goddard and Fitzhugh point out that many of Fell's inscriptions are simply random marks on rock. Archaeologist Anne Ross and historian Peter Reynolds (1978) examined a sample of the marked stones translated by Fell. They point out that obvious marks on the stones that do not match Fell's alphabetic interpretations are simply ignored by him. They view many of the so-called inscriptions as simply the result of natural erosion or plow marks. A plow blade can repeatedly scratch a rock in the soil, leaving a series of lines. It is also possible that, in some instances, the lines are intentional, but as tally marks, not a written language. They should be read as a number (six strokes equals six days or six deer). Fell interprets these lines as conveying meaningful messages in an alphabet called *Ogam*—a well-known alphabet based on Latin that dates to the fourth century A.D. in western Europe. It was used exclusively to write in early Old Irish.

Fell claims that the Ogamic inscriptions he has interpreted in New World locations are sometimes much older than this. He further claims the New World versions were written without vowels (one simply adds the "necessary" vowels), recording words in a number of different languages. Anne Ross, a British expert on Ogam who has examined many of the alleged Ogam inscriptions in New England, finds this to be a "semantic phantasy of the wildest nature" (Ross and Reynolds 1978:106).

As Goddard and Fitzhugh state, Ogam is, indeed, a record-keeping system that consists largely of simple strokes, so any process that produces lines in rock can superficially resemble Ogam. Then, as they state, in Fell's approach "it is a matter of little further difficulty to select words from this range of languages to match against the string of consonants which have been read" (1979:167).

More recently, Celtic scholar Brendan O Hehir performed a methodical analysis of one of Fell's translations, a so-called Christmas message inscribed on a rock in West Virginia. His is an incredibly detailed, line-by-line, word-by-word, and even letter-by-letter analysis of the inscription and Fell's translation (O Hehir 1990). There is little doubt in his mind; O Hehir characterizes the "Christmas message" as "a stupid and ignorant fraud" (p. 1).

Architecture

A site that seems to be a cornerstone in Fell's argument is located in North Salem, New Hampshire (Goodwin 1946). Fell claims the site is the remnant of a 3,000-year-old settlement of migrants from western Europe. Fell and his supporters assert that the architecture of the stone structures at the site is the same as that of Europe during this period. At that time in western Europe, the so-called Megalith builders were busy working in stone, constructing monuments like Stonehenge in England (see Chapter 12), Carnac in France, and thousands of smaller sites. Their habitations, like Skara Brae on the Orkney Islands, were also built of large pieces of stone (Figure 5.19).

The New Hampshire site consists of numerous stone structures and features (Figure 5.20). William Goodwin, a retired insurance executive from Hartford, Connecticut, purchased the site in 1935 and spent the rest of his life rebuilding parts of it and trying to prove that it was the settlement of ancient Europeans—specifically Irish Culdee monks in the tenth century A.D. For years it was called Mystery Hill, though now the owners refer to it as America's Stonehenge.

The architecture at sites like Mystery Hill must be examined in an overall cultural context. The stone structures superficially resemble those found

Figure 5.19   The village of Skara Brae on the main Orkney Island in northern Scotland was built more than four thousand years ago. The walls, hearths, and even the storage areas of the seven structures found there were constructed of stone. The style of architecture seen at Skara Brae only superficially resembles much later construction in the New World. (K. L. Feder)

in ancient Celtic sites in England, Wales, Scotland, and Ireland, but is that enough to prove that ancient Celts settled in the New World?

Archaeologist Robert R. Gradie (1981) provides a good argument for a negative answer to this question. He points out that there may indeed be a relationship between the stone structures in Great Britain and New England—but not as a result of pre-Columbian, seafaring Celts.

Gradie shows that in Europe, stone chamber building very much like that of the Megalith culture continued as so-called vernacular architecture into the twentieth century. Ross and Reynolds point out that such stone structures have been built recently enough for living people to remember their construction (1978:103). In the past few centuries farmers in western Europe built root cellars and storage buildings using the same methods people had used centuries and even millennia before when they built ceremonial structures. Some of these farmers migrated to New England in the seventeenth and eighteenth centuries, naming counties and towns after their Celtic homelands and maintaining aspects of their material culture—including the style of their outbuildings. Gradie suggests that the stone structures

Figure 5.20 The admittedly strange stone structures of Mystery Hill, North Salem, New Hampshire, are part of an idiosyncratic site most likely built by colonists in the eighteenth or nineteenth century. Some insist that the site is far older, built by European settlers of the New World more than three thousand years ago. (K. L. Feder)

at sites like Mystery Hill were, indeed, built by Celts, but of a much more recent vintage than Fell asserts.

The Archaeological Verdict

If Fell's Celts were here in the numbers he claims and for the length of time he suggests, the evidence would be at least as clear, as obvious, and as recognizable as that seen for the Norse foray into North America discussed earlier in this chapter. What, then, does the archaeological record indicate for Fell's hypothesis?

Unfortunately for Goodwin and Fell, there are no archaeological artifacts to bear witness to the presence of pre-Columbian interlopers at Mystery Hill or other, similar sites. If the people Goodwin or Fell claims were here actually were here in the numbers implied, they had to have been the neatest people ever to grace the planet. They picked up everything, leaving nothing for the archaeologist to recover and analyze. This represents, by itself, a fatal blow to the arguments of Fell and his supporters.

For example, while on a visit to Mystery Hill, I asked the guide why their small museum had one large glass case of stone artifacts found at the site and clearly of local Indian manufacture and one glass case filled with the pottery, brick, and iron nails of nineteenth-century inhabitants, but no case filled with the European bronze tools of the supposed "Bronze Age" European settlers of the site. The guide responded, "You don't think those ancient people would have left all those valuable bronze tools just lying around, do you?" I responded that they most certainly had left "all those valuable bronze tools" lying around in Europe; that's how we know it was the Bronze Age—archaeologists find such objects. In other words, I was simply asking that the archaeological context be considered. I was told, in essence, that there was no archaeological context.

It has even been reported that this clear lack of any conventional archaeological evidence has been used to indicate the ritual significance of the site. An excavator of Mystery Hill, after fruitlessly searching for any confirming evidence of a Celtic presence at the site, commented in this way: "It's spooky; I've never seen a site as clean as this one" (as reported by Tarzia 1992:6). Thus, a lack of any evidence whatsoever is interpreted as enormously significant, indicating the obvious ritual significance of the place.

An archaeological excavation was conducted at Mystery Hill. In the 1950s the organization that controlled the site, The Early Sites Foundation, hired Gary Vescelius, a Yale University graduate student in archaeology, to excavate. Their hope was that artifacts would be found that would support the hypothesis that the site had been built and occupied by ancient European immigrants to the New World. In hiring an archaeologist to excavate at the site, they were recognizing that an archaeological context was necessary. They were admitting, in a sense, that architectural similarity was not enough, that it merely suggested the possibility of a connection between the Old and New Worlds. Archaeological evidence of the kind of people who lived at the site was necessary to support the hypothesis—the kind of evidence discussed earlier in the chapter, including entire complexes of artifacts found only in ancient Europe, the skeletal remains of identifiable Europeans, and artifacts made of raw materials from European sources, all in a context that could be dated to before Columbus.

Vescelius (1956) found nothing of the kind. He recovered some seven thousand artifacts in his excavation. They all were clearly of either prehistoric Indian manufacture (dating to an occupation of the site before the stone structures were built) or nineteenth-century European manufacture—ceramics, nails, chunks of plaster, and brick fragments. The archaeological evidence clearly pointed to a nineteenth-century construction date for the site. Precisely the same results were derived from excavations at *Gungywamp*, in Groton, Connecticut, a similar site that Fell claims is of ancient Celtic vintage (Jackson, Jackson, and Linke 1981). All the artifacts found at Gungywamp were of a much more recent date.

Finally, regional surveys have been performed on sites in Massachusetts (Cole 1982) and Vermont (Neudorfer 1980), where stone structures suggested by some to be of ancient Celtic origin are found. Both projects show quite clearly and definitively that the stone structures were part of historic, colonial patterns of land use and construction.

Cole found absolutely no archaeological evidence in the thirteen sites he investigated that the stone structures were built by pre-Columbian settlers; all the structures were part of a known pattern and most were, in fact, parts of complexes of buildings and features (farms, mills, a hotel) known to date to the nineteenth century.

Neudorfer (1980) conducted a three-year project, examining forty-four stone chambers in Vermont, taking measurements and searching for historic contexts for the structures. She found that with one exception, all the structures, *including seven specifically identified by Fell as being Celtic temples,* were associated with eighteenth- or nineteenth-century farm complexes (p. 56). In one case she was even able to come up with the name of the actual nineteenth-century builder of one of the chambers Fell maintains is ancient Celtic in origin.

Neudorfer found that the stone chambers, far from being enigmatic, were a common part of farm culture in historic New England. She found in some cases that the style of masonry of the chambers was identical to that of the foundations of nearby historic farmhouses. Further, she found eighteenth- and nineteenth-century publications describing the best methods for building such structures for cold storage of fruits and vegetables. Whereas Fell claims that the southerly or easterly orientation of the chamber entrances reflects ancient Celtic ceremonies, the farm publications Neudorfer located advised eighteenth- and nineteenth-century farmers to orient the openings of their root cellars to take advantage of the position of the winter sun in the southern sky, thereby preventing freezing in the cellars.

Perhaps the most significant contribution of Neudorfer's work rests in her showing the historic context of the stone chambers. Could ancient Celts have traveled to New England and built stone temples? Certainly it is possible, but it is also *possible—and far more probable—*that these structures were eighteenth- and nineteenth-century farm buildings. As archaeologist Dena Dincauze (1982) points out, Occam's razor should be applied here. The chambers fit in with everything we know about historic farmers in New England, and this explanation requires no other assumptions. As Dincauze states, Neudorfer's argument and evidence "shifts an apparently immovable burden of proof onto the shoulders of those who would claim otherwise" (1982:9–10).

Finally, Neudorfer points out that the mystery associated with the stone chambers of New England is a product of a sort of cultural amnesia. Common, everyday aspects of life like the stone chambers have been forgotten and now appear to be enigmatic. They are a reflection of a time not so distant by absolute chronological measurement, but hugely distant from the modern world of computers, space shuttles, and cell phones. As a result, for example, common nineteenth-century tools for converting lye to soft soap

(Swauger 1980) have become sacrificial altar stones for some (as stated in the pamphlet distributed at Mystery Hill), even though artifacts similar to the so-called sacrificial stone can be found in museums devoted to New England farm life (Figure 5.21). In the same manner, animal-powered bark mills have been transformed into mysterious temples, even though photographs exist of bark mills in operation—and they look remarkably similar to the feature in question at the Gungywamp site (Figure 5.22; Warner 1981). We are so removed from these once common architectural features that today we need primers to remind us of what once was part of everyday life (Sanford, Huffer, and Huffer 1995). Unfamiliar they may now be, but mysterious, alien, or ancient they are not.

Archaeological Context: Digging Pits and Recovering Evidence

During the course of their research careers, field archaeologists, of necessity, dig a lot of holes in the ground and sift much of that dirt through hardware cloth with various grid sizes (often one-quarter- or even one-eighth-inch screening). When one multiplies all of the pits dug or overseen by individual archaeologists in their careers by the number of archaeologists, over time the number of "test pits" excavated by archaeologists grows to truly staggering numbers.

Let's consider the example of southern New England. David Poirier is the staff archaeologist at the Connecticut Historical Commission (CHC). The CHC administers regional archaeological surveys within the state where sites of all types, ages, and cultural affiliation are searched for, located, and investigated. Poirier's office also oversees federally and state-mandated surveys—so-called compliance archaeology—where archaeological sites are searched for before federally or state-funded construction projects can commence. In other words, most, though by no means all, of the site survey reports produced in Connecticut are submitted to Dave's office, and every one of the forms detailing the material found in each test excavation passes across David's desk. His estimate is that during the 1990s, in each year, about 10,000 test pits were excavated by archaeologists in Connecticut.

Paul Robinson at the Rhode Island SHPO holds a position equivalent to Poirier's. Paul informed me that from the late 1980s up until about 1997, the mean number of test pits excavated by archaeologists in Rhode Island each year was in the neighborhood of 4,000 to 6,000. In the last couple of years during that span, that number declined to between 1,000 and 2,000. Using the lower numbers provided by Paul, we come up with about 34,000 test excavations for those ten years.

Brona Simon, the state archaeologist of Massachusetts, was next on my list. Brona's office publishes a listing of archaeological survey projects required by her office; in fact, she issues the permits for the surveys. According

Figure 5.21   The so-called sacrificial altar stone at Mystery Hill (top) is presented by some as a unique and romantic artifact, evidence of a population of pre-Columbian interlopers practicing ceremonial sacrifices. However, the grooved stone platform at Mystery Hill is anything but unique; it is a common artifact found in historical New England farming communities, used in the rather unromantic production of soap. The similar "lye stone" in the bottom image is located at the Farmers' Museum in western Massachusetts. (K. L. Feder)

Figure 5.22   Some claim that the seemingly mysterious circle of stones at Gungywamp, Connecticut (top), has mystical significance within an early European religious context—proof, therefore, that pre-Columbian Europeans had settled Connecticut. However, other, similar historically documented—and photographed— features are known to have been used by more recent settlers of New England as bark mills for the extraction of chemicals for hide tanning (bottom). (K. L. Feder)

to her records, over the last ten years of the twentieth century, on average, about 7,500 test pits were excavated on a yearly basis in the projects that fall under the jurisdiction of her office. So 75,000 test pits in Massachusetts is probably a fair estimate for the last ten years.

For the three relatively small states just surveyed, in the 1990s, archaeologists have excavated no fewer than 200,000 test pits in federally or state-mandated archaeological site searches. In larger states, these numbers would be proportionately larger. For example, Dr. David Snyder of the Ohio Historic Preservation Office estimates that in the 1990s archaeologists excavated an average of 50,000 test pits on a yearly basis (personal communication).

Thousands of archaeological sites, in fact, have been found in these test pit surveys, including very rare, very ancient sites (some more than 10,000 years old) of extremely low archaeological visibility; 9,000-year-old sites representing the villages of native people who were adjusting to the post–Ice Age environment of southern New England; far more abundant so-called Late Archaic sites representing a florescence of human population in the region between 6,000 and 4,000 years ago; larger, more permanent and, therefore, more archaeologically visible sites of the so-called Woodland period, late in whose sequence we find native people planting the traditional Native American triad of corn, beans, and squash; native sites of the seventeenth century showing clear evidence of contact with European settlers; and the villages, camps, burial grounds, quarries, mines, and the like of these new European inhabitants of southern New England.

Remember our discussion earlier in this chapter of our human proclivity to bring along some of what George Carlin calls our "stuff" wherever we travel and our habit of losing and discarding some of that stuff along the way? There is no reason to believe ancient visitors to the New World would have been any different. With that in mind, it must be reported that in none of those 200,000 or so test pits excavated in New England did any archaeologist report the discovery of even a single artifact attributable to the ancient Welsh, Chinese, Celts, Africans, or other non–Native American group and dating to the dim mists of antiquity. We have found none of the stuff that they would have brought along on their voyage. This alone is strong evidence that these groups were not here before Columbus.

Current Perspectives:
The Peopling of the Americas

It has been called "molecular archaeology," and it involves the metaphorical excavation for information hidden deep within the genes of living people. To connect a modern group of human beings to its initial population source, these archaeologists of our chromosomes sift through the genetic instructions of living people to determine which groups share unique codes, often representing minor genetic mistakes or small idiosyncrasies that don't mean much and that don't have an impact on a person's appearance or health status. There are so many different possible clusters and variants, it is a virtual certainty that those living groups who share the same cluster of minor differences must share a biological ancestor from whom they inherited it. It's the equivalent of what happens in the movies when long-lost siblings verify their biological connection by comparing the tiny mole each one carries like a tiny badge that identifies them as members of the same family; only here that badge is a set of genetic instructions.

For example, when researchers investigate the mitochondrial DNA (mtDNA; a variety of DNA that appears not in the nucleus of cells, but in their mitochondria, the energy factories that provide them with power) of living people across the globe, they find a number of variants called haplogroups. Native Americans exhibit a total of five such distinct haplogroups. Those five variants have so far turned up in only one other human group in only one geographic location: specifically, the Atlatians, a group of Asian natives who live along the shores of Lake Baikal in central Siberia (Derenko et al. 2001). The appearance of the five distinct haplogroups among New World natives and Asian natives provides strong evidence of close familial ties.

Mitochondrial DNA is passed down only in the female line, so the mtDNA evidence relates only to females. Analysis of specific variants in the Y-chromosome, obviously present only in males, has shown results similar to those of mtDNA. Maria-Catira Bortolini and her colleagues (2003) have identified two specific mutations on the Y-chromosome that allow us, again, to connect native Asians and Native Americans. These are minor genetic differences that do not have any impact on the appearance or health of those men who exhibit these otherwise insignificant genetic variants. She found these two Y-chromosome haplogroups to be present in native populations in the New World and Asia, specifically the fourteen populations the researchers sampled in central Siberia. This, like the mtDNA data, provides strong evidence for an ancient biological connection between the aboriginal people of the New World and those living in central Siberia.

It is truly remarkable that researchers can investigate our genes much in the way archaeologists can excavate ancient sites. Our genes, it seems, much like ancient artifacts made by past peoples, preserve the stories of our ancestors and define who we are and where we have come from. Those stories are being read by the molecular archaeologists and are telling us the story of the migration of people into the New World.

It is further interesting to point out that archaeological sites dating close to 20,000 years ago have been excavated in central Siberia, specifically near Lake Baikal where the five mtDNA haplogroups present in America have been identified, producing artifacts that bear a similarity to some of the earliest tools found in the New World. Artifacts, as well as genes, point to the people of central Siberia as the most likely source for the native people of the New World.

FREQUENTLY ASKED QUESTIONS

1. *Were there multiple migrations to the New World across the Bering Land Bridge?*

It was long thought, based on genetic and linguistic evidence, that there were three separate migrations of Asians across the land bridge: an early migration of the ancestors of most American Indians, a later migration of Eskimo-Aleuts, and an additional migration of the ancestors of Indians who now live on the northwest coast of North America. Many still believe this, but recent genetic data have led some to suggest that modern Native Americans are genetically so similar that they all may have descended from a single group of transplanted Asians (Gibbons 1996).

2. *How could the Vikings navigate to the New World without devices like a compass or a sextant?*

The Vikings navigated by ocean currents, winds, and positions of stars in the sky. It was a knowledge informed by centuries of exploration. An attempt to replicate the Norse voyage to Vinland was carried out in 2000, close enough in time to call it the millennial celebration of the original voyage. The replica ship, the *Islendingur* (Icelander), sailed from Reykjavík, Iceland, on June 17, 2000, that island nation's Independence Day. It arrived safely at L'Anse aux Meadows on July 28 to an enthusiastic welcome. The ship's design was based on that of a well-preserved Norse boat built in the ninth century A.D. and discovered by archaeologists in 1882.

BEST OF THE WEB

http://www.geraceresearchcenter.com/archaeology.htm
Home page of the Gerace Research Center, College of the Bahamas. The site has links to a listing of archaeological research and publications related to Bahamian archaeology, including the work of Charles Hoffman at the Long Bay site, where late Spanish artifacts have been found dating to the early voyages of Christopher Columbus.

http://www1.minn.net/~keithp/cclandfl.htm

An interesting site produced by Keith A. Pickering, presenting a discussion of the many possible locations of Columbus's Caribbean landfalls.

http://www.beringia.com/02/02maina9.html

The very informative Web presence of the Yukon Beringia Interpretive Center, focusing on the story of Beringia.

http://instaar.colorado.edu/QGISL/bering_land_bridge/

A very cool animation of the change in the configuration of Beringia from 21,000 years ago when sea level was at its low point and the land bridge was at its maximum to the establishment of the modern coastline about 8,000 years ago.

http://archaeology.about.com/blclovis.htm

In her *About Archaeology* Web site, K. Kris Hirst provides a useful bibliography on the debate concerning the timing of the first human settlement of the Americas.

http://www.pc.gc.ca/lhn-nhs/nl/meadows/natcul/hist_e.asp

The Canadian government's official L'Anse aux Meadows Web site, with links to brief discussions of the village's founding by the Norse in the late tenth century, the Viking sagas, and the archaeological research conducted at the site that confirms definitively the site's identification as a Norse outpost in the New World five centuries before Columbus.

http://www.pitt.edu/~dash/vinland.html

A nice site with links to photographs of some of the diagnostic, tenth-century Norse artifacts found at the site.

http://www.mnh.si.edu/vikings/voyage/

This is the companion Web site for the museum exhibit Vikings, The North Atlantic Saga, produced by the Smithsonian Institution. Extremely informative and well-produced, the site provides an enormous amount of information about the archaeology, history, genetics, and environment of the Norse.

CRITICAL THINKING EXERCISES

1. Using the deductive approach outlined in Chapter 2, how would you test these hypotheses? In each case, what archaeological and biological data must you find to conclude that the hypothetical statement is an

accurate assertion, that it describes what actually happened in the ancient human past?

- The first discoverers of America were Asians who crossed over from the Old World via a land connection.
- The first Americans were big-game hunters who entered the New World by following migratory herds of animals.
- The original settlers of America were a diverse group not limited to northeast Asians, but also including Africans, Australians, and Europeans.

2. Research the expeditions of Martin Frobisher or Francisco Vasquez de Coronado. How can their visits to the New World provide us with insights about the archaeological trail left by a small group of visitors to the New World?

6

The Myth of
the Moundbuilders

Today, the intriguing culture archaeologists know as the *Moundbuilders* is one of the best-kept secrets in the study and teaching of American history. That a complex American Indian society with great population centers, powerful rulers, pyramids, and fine works of art evolved in the midwestern and southeastern United States comes as a surprising revelation, even to those in whose backyards the ruins lie.

Yet the remnants of these ancient inhabitants of North America are nearly ubiquitous. The most obvious manifestation of their culture is their earthworks (Figures 6.1 and 6.2): conical mounds of earth, up to nearly 100 feet in height, containing the burials of perhaps great rulers or priests with fine grave goods in stone, clay, copper, and shell; great flat-topped pyramids up to 100 feet in height, covering many acres, and containing millions of cubic feet of earth and on which ancient temples once stood; and *effigy* earthworks in the shapes of great snakes, birds, and bears.

Few of us seem to be aware of the remarkable cultural legacy of this indigenous American culture. This became sadly clear to me when attending an archaeology conference in St. Louis more than twenty years ago. Much of my excitement about the conference resulted from its location. The largest and most impressive Moundbuilder site, *Cahokia,* an ancient settlement with thousands of inhabitants, sits on the Illinois side of the Mississippi River, just east of St. Louis. Wishing to take advantage of my proximity to the site, I asked the gentleman at the hotel front desk how I might get to Cahokia. The response: a blank stare. He had never heard of it. "You know," I explained, "the big Indian site." "No, no," he responded, "There haven't been any Indians around here for many years."

No one in the hotel had heard of Cahokia, and even at the bus station people thought I was just another confused out-of-towner. Luckily, I ran into a colleague who knew the way, and I finally got to the site.

Figure 6.1   Examples of mounds: Serpent Mound, an effigy earthwork in southern Ohio in the form of a coiled 1,500-foot-long snake (top). A huge, conical burial mound close to 100 feet high in Miamisburg, Ohio (bottom). (*Top:* photo by Major Dache M. Reeves. Courtesy National Museum of the American Indian, Smithsonian Institution; *bottom:* K. L. Feder)

It was worth the trouble. About 70 of the 120 or so original mounds re-main (Fowler 1989). Several of these demarcate a large plaza where cere-monies were likely held during Cahokia's peak between A.D. 1050 and 1250.

Figure 6.2   Aerial photograph of Monks Mound, an enormous, tiered pyramid of earth at Cahokia in Illinois. Monks Mound served as a platform on which a temple once stood. (Courtesy Cahokia Mounds State Historic Site)

Monks Mound (see Figure 6.2), containing more than 20 million cubic feet of earth, is one of the largest pyramids in the world (including those of Egypt and Mesoamerica). It dominates the plaza. The highest of its four platforms is raised to a height of 100 feet, where it once held a great temple. Surrounding the central part of this ancient settlement was a massive log wall, or palisade, with evenly spaced bastions and watchtowers. The palisade enclosed an area of about 200 acres in which eighteen of the largest and most impressive of Cahokia's earthworks were built. The log wall itself may have been the most monumental of the many large-scale construction projects undertaken by Cahokia's inhabitants; it consisted of some 20,000 logs, each one about 1 foot in diameter and 20 feet tall, and was rebuilt virtually in its entirety at least three times during the site's occupation.

Cahokia must have been a splendid place. At its population peak in about A.D. 1150, Cahokia represented the single largest concentration of people in North America north of Mexico. While recognizing that no firm boundaries can be drawn, archaeologist George Milner (2004:135) estimates that the mounds that define the extent of the Cahokia community with its house clusters, burial grounds, and gardens are distributed over an area of approximately 10 square kilometers (3.9 square miles). Although, again, it is difficult to estimate, Milner (2004:145) suggests that, at its peak sometime in the eleventh or twelfth century A.D., the population of Cahokia certainly numbered in the thousands and, conceivably, may have reached as high as 6,000 people. Cahokia was a trading center, a religious center, and the predominant political force of its time (Iseminger 1996; Pauketat 1994). It was,

Figure 6.3   An artist's rendition of Cahokia at its cultural peak. With a population estimated in the thousands, Cahokia was a virtual prehistoric American Indian city on the Mississippi River more than seven hundred years ago. (Painting by William Iseminger, Courtesy Cahokia Mounds State Historic Site)

by the reckoning of many, an emerging civilization created by American Indians whose lives were far different from the stereotype of primitive, nomadic hunters too many of us envision (Figure 6.3).

From atop Monks Mound one can peer into two worlds and two different times. To the west rises the modern city of St. Louis, framed by its Gateway Arch of steel. Below rests the ancient city of Cahokia with its monuments of earth, shadows of a long-ignored Indian culture.

How could people not know of this wonderful place? Suffice it to say that if people today living twenty minutes from Cahokia haven't heard of it, most New Englanders, Californians, Southerners—in fact, most Americans—are completely unaware of it and the archaeological legacy of the indigenous American society that produced it and hundreds of other sites.

Cahokia and Moundbuilder culture, however, were not always an invisible part of the history of this continent. In fact, the remains of their culture once commanded the attention of the American public and scientists alike. It was not only that the mounds themselves, the fine ceramics, sumptuous burials, carved statues, and copper ornaments were so impressive, though this was part of the fascination. Unfortunately, much of the intense interest generated by the remains of this culture resulted from a supposed enigma perceived by most; the Moundbuilders clearly lived before Columbus, the Indians were the only known inhabitants of North America before the coming of the Europeans, and it was commonly assumed that the Indians were simply incapable of having produced the splendid works of art and monumental construction projects that characterized Moundbuilder culture. With the rejection of the possibility that American Indians had produced the culture, the myth evolved of an ancient, vanished American race (see especially Silverberg 1989 for a very useful and succinct account of the evolution of the Moundbuilder myth).

The myths of a petrified giant (Chapter 3) and of a human ancestor with a modern brain and simian jaw (Chapter 4) were based on hoaxes, clever or otherwise. People suspended their critical faculties and were fooled by these frauds. The Moundbuilder myth, in contrast, was not predicated on a hoax (though, as you will see, hoaxes did play a role) but rather on a nearly complete and sometimes willful misunderstanding of genuine data.

The Myth of a Vanished Race

The myth of a vanished race of Moundbuilders was accepted by many Americans in the eighteenth and nineteenth centuries. Five basic arguments were presented to support the notion that American Indians could not have been the bearers of Moundbuilder culture. Let's deal with each in turn.

1. *Indians were too primitive to have built the mounds and produced the works in stone, metal, and clay attributed to the Moundbuilder culture.*

    The attitude of J. W. Foster, president of the Chicago Academy of Sciences, was prevalent. Describing the Indian, he states:

    > He was never known voluntarily to engage in an enterprise requiring methodical labor; he dwells in temporary and movable habitations, he follows the game in their migrations. To suppose that such a race threw up the symmetrical mounds which crown so many of our river terraces is as preposterous, almost, as to suppose that they built the pyramids of Egypt. (1873, as cited in Silverberg 1989:117)

    In his 1872 work, *Ancient America*, J. D. Baldwin is even more direct: "It is absurd to suppose a relationship or connection between the original barbarism of these Indians and the civilization of the mound-builders" (as cited in Thomas 1894:615).

    These arguments can be fairly characterized as racist and unfortunately held sway among many people.

2. *The mounds and associated artifacts were very much more ancient than even the earliest remnants of Indian culture.*

    Though the analysis of soil layering known as stratigraphy was not to become an established part of archaeology until later in the nineteenth century (for example, Dall 1877), in 1820 Caleb Atwater used a simple form of stratigraphic analysis to support the notion that the Moundbuilders were from a period far before the Indians arrived in the New World. He maintained in his book *Antiquities Discovered in the Western States:*

> Indian Antiquities are always either on, or a very small distance below the surface, unless buried in some grave; whilst articles, evidently belonging to that people who raised our mounds, are frequently found many feet below the surface, especially in river bottoms. (1820:125)

The evidence of the annual growth rings of trees also was used in the argument that the mounds were quite ancient. In 1786, the Reverend Manasseh Cutler counted the rings on a tree he had cut down on a mound in Marietta, Ohio. He found 463 rings and calculated that the mound must have been built before A.D. 1300 (Fagan 1977). Others went further, suggesting that large trees presently growing on mounds must have been preceded by several generations of trees, indicating that the mounds were more than 2,000 years old.

3. *Stone tablets were found in the mounds that bore inscriptions in European, Asian, or African alphabets.*

The best known of such artifacts were the Grave Creek Mound Stone from West Virginia (Schoolcraft 1854), the Newark Holy Stones from Ohio, the Bat Creek Stone from Tennessee (Manifort and Kwas 2004), and the Cook Farm Mound Tablets in Davenport, Iowa (Putnam 1886). Because American Indians north of Mexico were not known to have possessed a writing system before European colonization, the presence of writing in the mounds seemed to provide validation of the hypothesis that a non-Indian culture had been responsible for their construction. Where characters from specific alphabets could be discerned, sources for Moundbuilder culture could be, and were, hypothesized.

4. *American Indians were not building mounds when first contacted by European explorers and settlers. When queries were made of the local Indians concerning mound construction or use, they invariably professed complete ignorance.*

Very simply, the argument was presented that if Indians were responsible for the mounds, they should have been building such earthworks when Europeans first came into contact with them. If no longer building mounds, living Indians should remember a time when their ancestors had built them. The supposed fact that Indians were not building mounds when first contacted by Europeans combined with the fact that most Indians did not claim that their ancestors had built the mounds was seen by many as definitive, empirical evidence against any claim of Indian responsibility for Moundbuilder culture.

5. *Metal artifacts made of iron, silver, ore-derived copper, and various alloys had been found in the mounds.*

Historic Indian cultures north of Mexico were not known to use metal other than copper, which could be found in pure veins and nuggets in parts of Michigan; silver, also found in pure, natural deposits that required no further metallurgical refinement; and iron from meteorites. Smelting ore to produce copper, silver, or iron and techniques of alloying metal (mixing copper and tin, for example, to produce bronze) were unknown. Therefore, the discovery of artifacts of these materials in the mounds was a further indication that a people other than and more technologically sophisticated than American Indians had been the Moundbuilders.

With these five presumably well-supported "truths" in hand, it was clear to the satisfaction of many that Indians had nothing to do with mound building or Moundbuilder culture. This left open the question of who, in fact, the Moundbuilders were.

Who Were the Moundbuilders? Identifying the Vanished Race

From our vantage point in the early years of the twenty-first century, it is extremely difficult to imagine how intensely interested many were in the origins of the mounds and Moundbuilder culture. The fledgling Smithsonian Institution devoted several of its early publications to the ostensible Moundbuilder enigma. Another government agency, the Bureau of American Ethnology, whose job it was to preserve information concerning rapidly changing Native American cultures, devoted a considerable part of its resources to the Moundbuilder issue. Influential private organizations like the American Philosophical Society also supported research into the question and published works reporting on such research.

The mystery of the mounds was a subject that virtually all thinking people were drawn to. Books, pamphlets, magazine pieces, and newspaper articles abounded, written by those who had something to say, sensible or not, on the question that seemed so important to answer: Who had built the mounds? Though few could agree on who was responsible for construction of the mounds, there was no lack of opinions.

In one of the earliest published conjectures, Benjamin Smith Barton wrote in 1787 that the Moundbuilders were Vikings who had long ago journeyed to the New World, settled, and then died out. Josiah Priest in his 1833 work variously posited that the mounds had been built by wandering Egyptians, Israelites, Greeks, Chinese, Polynesians, or Norwegians (Silverberg 1989:66). Others suggested that the mounds had been fashioned by Welshmen, Belgians, Phoenicians, Tartars, Saxons, or Africans. A Cincinnati journalist, Lafcadio Hearn, made a number of interesting suggestions concerning the source of the mysterious midwestern moundbuilders. In an article published in 1876, he proposed that, though their source was uncertain,

> It is at least generally recognized that they were not Indians. Their monumental record little resembles that of the Aztec people; and indeed no other American Nation has left traces satisfactorily analogous to those left by the Mound-builders. But it is worthy of note that very similar remains have been left by the European Mound-builders.

So, maybe they were Europeans. Then again, in the very same article, Hearn proposed another, even more speculative origin for the Moundbuilders; he suggested that the Moundbuilders came from the Lost Continent of Atlantis (see Chapter 7)!

An Atlantean source might sound impressive, but one thinker went further still, attributing one of the mounds to a divine architect. The Reverend Landon West maintained that Serpent Mound (Figure 6.1, top) represented the snake that tempted Eve in the Genesis story in the Old Testament of the Bible (Lepper 1998b). Not content merely to make this literary connection, Reverend West went on to claim that God himself had constructed Serpent Mound to memorialize the event and placed the monument in Eden itself. Yes, that is correct; Reverend West suggested that Eden was located in Bush Creek valley, Ohio.

The Walam Olum

One of the favored themes underlying the Moundbuilder myth was that, whatever their ultimate geographical source, they had created a splendid and peaceful civilization in the dim mists of antiquity. They had been overrun and eliminated in a much more recent invasion by a wild, violent, and barbaric people. In this version of the myth, the barbarians were the ancestors of the American Indians.

One nineteenth-century hoaxer went so far as to concoct an entire epic story that followed this scenario. In 1836 Constantine Samuel Rafinesque claimed that ten years earlier he had located and deciphered an ancient historic text engraved on wooden tablets by the ancestors of the Lenape (Delaware) Indians of eastern North America (Oestreicher 1996). Rafinesque called the story he had "discovered" the *Walam Olum*. The tablets themselves had disappeared (of course), but Rafinesque claimed to have translated the saga they told of the migration of American Indians from northeast Asia 3,600 years ago across a frozen wasteland that had once connected the Old and New Worlds. There is a certain irony in this; this part of Rafinesque's fake tale bolstered part of a scenario we now know to be true—that is, humans first entering the New World from Asia across a land bridge in the far north—although his timing is far too recent (Chapter 5).

In Rafinesque's fantasy, the Moundbuilders had migrated to the New World long before the arrival of the Indians. Rafinesque went on to have his fictitious migrants overwhelm and then defeat the Moundbuilder people in battle. Where did the Moundbuilders come from in this story? According to the *Walam Olum*, the Moundbuilders originated on the Lost Continent of Atlantis (see Chapter 7). Many Lenape people rejected the authenticity of the *Walam Olum*, and researcher David Oestreicher (1996) has shown that the hieroglyphs in which the document was written were cobbled together using a jumble of Egyptian, Chinese, and Mayan characters. The *Walam Olum* was an elaborate hoax, one of a series surrounding the mystery of the Moundbuilders.

The Archaeology of the Myth

Caleb Atwater, an Ohio lawyer, performed a detailed analysis of the earthworks in his state in an attempt to establish the identity of the vanished race. Though Atwater's conclusions were typical for the time, his methods were far more scientific than the speculations of some of his contemporaries. In his work *Antiquities Discovered in the Western States* (yes, Ohio was then considered a "western" state), Atwater divided the archaeological remains found there into three categories: Indian, European Colonial, and Moundbuilder. The last of these he ascribed to "a people far more civilized than our Indians, but far less so than Europeans" (1820:120).

To his credit, Atwater was not an armchair speculator concerning the Moundbuilders. He personally inspected many sites in Ohio and produced detailed drawings and descriptions of artifacts and earthworks. But his myopia about American Indian cultural achievement clearly fashioned his view:

> Have our present race of Indians ever buried their dead in mounds?
> Have they constructed such works as described in the preceding pages?
> Were they acquainted with the use of silver, iron, or copper? Did the
> North American Indians erect anything like the "walled town" on
> Paint Creek? (Atwater 1820:208)

For Atwater the answer to these questions was a clear "no." American Indians simply were too primitive. He concluded his discourse on the question by suggesting that the Moundbuilders had actually been "Hindoos" from India.

To be sure, there were a few prescient thinkers on the question of the origin of Moundbuilder culture. Perhaps the first to approach the question objectively was Thomas Jefferson, framer of the Declaration of Independence and third president of the United States. Jefferson was curious about the ancient earthworks on and adjacent to his property in Virginia. Not content to merely speculate about them, in 1784 Jefferson conducted what is almost certainly the first archaeological excavation in North America, carefully digging a trench through a mound that contained many human skeletons (Willey and Sabloff 1993). Jefferson drew no conclusion concerning who the Moundbuilders were, calling for more work on the mystery. As the president of the American Philosophical Society, he later would encourage others to explore this question.

Interest in the mounds and debate over the source of the culture that had produced the tens of thousands of these earthworks continued to increase during the nineteenth century as white settlement expanded into the American Midwest, the heartland of Moundbuilder culture. American archaeology developed as a discipline largely in response to questions about the mounds (as well as to questions concerning the origins of the Indians; see Chapter 5).

In their chronicle of the history of American archaeology, Willey and Sabloff (1993) select 1840 as the benchmark for a shift in American archaeology from a period of speculation to one characterized by research—with a

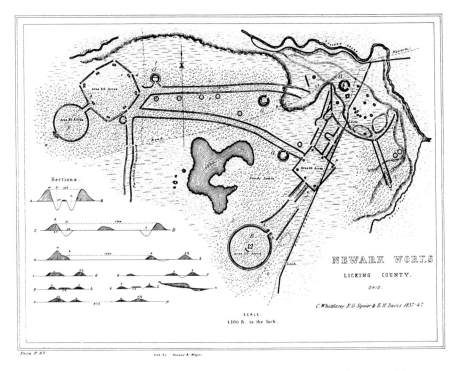

Figure 6.4 Ephraim Squier and Edwin Davis conducted a detailed survey of the mounds of the Ohio Valley and "western" United States in the 1840s, producing beautiful drawings of earthworks like these enclosures in Newark, Ohio. (From *Ancient Monuments of the Mississippi Valley*, AMS Press and Peabody Museum of Archaeology and Ethnology, Harvard University)

goal of description and classification. The work of Ephraim G. Squier and Edwin H. Davis on the Moundbuilder mystery is a good example of this shift in emphasis. Squier was a civil engineer and writer from Connecticut. Davis was an Ohio doctor. Both were interested in the Moundbuilder culture and between 1845 and 1847 carried out intensive investigation of some two hundred sites. They conducted excavations and produced detailed maps of the sites and drawings of the artifacts. Their research culminated in a book, *Ancient Monuments of the Mississippi Valley,* which was selected as the first publication of the recently established Smithsonian Institution.

Squier and Davis approached their task without many of the preconceptions and pet theories of their predecessors on the Moundbuilder question: "With no hypothesis to combat or sustain, and with a desire only to arrive at truth, whatever its bearings upon received theories and current prejudices, everything like mere speculation has been avoided" (1848:*xxxviii*).

Ancient Monuments of the Mississippi Valley is a descriptive work, with more than two hundred drawings in its three hundred or so pages. Squier and Davis were quite systematic in their investigations. Generally, they classified the various kinds of earthworks according to the empirical data of form and content as deduced from their detailed surveys and excavations. However, they also made unwarranted assumptions concerning the function of the different earthwork types.

In any event, they arranged and described the earthworks as follows:

1. *Defensive enclosures*—earth embankments surrounding high, flat plateaus

2. *Sacred enclosures*—earth embankments surrounding areas of from a few up to more than 50 acres (Figure 6.4); also, effigy mounds (mounds in the shapes of animals; see Figure 6.1 top)

3. *Altar mounds*—tumuli within sacred enclosures, with burned layers showing possible use as sacrificial altars

4. *Sepulture or burial mounds*—conical mounds, 6 to 80 feet in height, overlying human burials that contained grave goods (see Figure 6.1 bottom)

5. *Temple mounds*—truncated pyramids, some enormous, with pathways leading to the top where flat platforms, sometimes of a few acres, were found and where temples may have stood (see Figure 6.2)

6. *Anomalous mounds*—oddly shaped or unique mounds

Squier and Davis describe in great detail and depict in beautifully rendered drawings the artifacts that are found in association with the mounds: ceramics, metal implements and ornaments, stone and bone objects, sculptures, and inscribed stones. In a number of places in their book, they compare these objects with those found in other parts of the world, but never attempt to make a direct connection. Nevertheless, Squier and Davis are explicit in maintaining that the quality of artwork found in the mounds is "immeasurably beyond anything which the North American Indians are known to produce, even to this day" (1848:272).

Squier and Davis conclude their report by suggesting a "connection, more or less intimate" (p. 301) between the Moundbuilders and the civilizations of Mexico, Central America, and Peru. So they do subscribe to the idea that the Moundbuilders were a group separate from and culturally superior to the North American Indians, but at least they ascribe an indigenous, New World source for the Moundbuilders.

The Moundbuilder Mystery Solved

The late nineteenth century saw a continuation of interest in the Moundbuilders. Then, in 1882, an entomologist from Illinois, Cyrus Thomas, was hired to direct a Division of Mound Exploration within the Bureau of American Ethnology. An amendment to a federal appropriations bill in the U.S. House of Representatives directed that $5,000 of the $25,000 B.A.E. budget be devoted solely to the solution of the Moundbuilder mystery. With this funding, Thomas initiated the most extensive and intensive study yet conducted on the Moundbuilder question. The result was more than seven hundred pages submitted as an annual report of the Bureau in 1894 (Thomas 1894).

Above all else, Thomas's approach was empirical; he thought it necessary to collect as much information as possible before suggesting hypotheses about mound function, age, origins, and cultural affiliation. Whereas Squier and Davis focused on about 200 mounds mostly in Ohio, Thomas and his assistants investigated 2,000 mound sites in twenty-one states. He gathered over 40,000 artifacts, which became part of the Smithsonian Institution's collection. After amassing so much information, Thomas was not afraid to come to a conclusion on the Moundbuilder mystery. Whereas Squier and Davis devote 6 pages to their conclusions regarding the mounds, Thomas provides a 136-page discussion on the identity of the Moundbuilder culture. Thomas's work was a watershed, both in terms of answering the specific question of who had built the mounds and in terms of the development of American archaeology.

For Thomas the important question was simple and succinct: "Were the mounds built by the Indians?" (1894:21). He went about answering this question by responding to the arguments—presented earlier in this chapter—against identifying Indians as the Moundbuilders.

1. *Indian culture was too primitive.*

   To the claim that Indians were too primitive to have attained the level of civilization reached by the Moundbuilders, Thomas responded that it was difficult to conceive

why writers should so speak of them who had access to older
records giving accounts of the habits and customs of the Indian
tribes when first observed by European navigators and explorers . . . when the records, almost without exception notice the fact
that . . . they were generally found from the Mississippi to the Atlantic dwelling in settled villages and cultivating the soil. (p. 615)

For example, Hernando de Soto's chronicler, known to us only as
the "Gentleman of Elvas," mentions great walled towns of as many as
five or six thousand people encountered by these explorers (1611:122).
It is clear from his descriptions of Indian settlements that there was a
large, sedentary, "civilized" population in the American Southeast
in the sixteenth century.

In another example, William Bartram, a botanist from Philadelphia,
began his travels through the Southeast in 1773. In his book enumer-
ating his experiences, he also describes scores of heavily populated
Indian towns; in one case he mentions traveling through nearly two
continuous miles of cultivated fields of corn and beans (1791:285).
He estimates the population of a large town called *Uche* to be as many
as fifteen hundred people (p. 313), and he was very much impressed
with how substantially built their structures were.

So, in Thomas's view and in fact, evidence indicated that at least
some Indian cultures were agricultural and sedentary, with people
living in large population centers. They clearly would have been
culturally capable of constructing monumental earthworks.

2. *Mound culture was older than Indian culture.*

In reference to the presumed great age of the earthworks, Thomas
denigrates the accuracy of dating the mounds on the basis of tree-
ring counts. On this point, he was wrong; the age of at least some of
the mounds may have been more accurately estimated by some of
the ancient race enthusiasts. Thomas incorrectly thought many had
been built after European arrival in the New World. Ultimately, however, the age of the mounds was only a problem if one accepted the
then-current notion that the Indians were relatively recent arrivals.
We now know that Native Americans first arrived in the New World
more than 13,000 years ago (see Chapter 5), and the mounds are all
substantially younger.

3. *There were alphabetically inscribed tablets in the mounds.*

Thomas had quite a bit to say concerning the supposed inscribed
stone tablets. Though the myth of a vanished race of Moundbuilders
was based largely on misinterpretation of actual archaeological and
ethnographic data, hoaxes involving inscribed tablets also were
woven into its fabric.

For example, in 1838, during an excavation of a large mound in Grave Creek, West Virginia, two burial chambers were found containing three human skeletons, thousands of shell beads, copper ornaments, and other artifacts. Among these other artifacts was a sandstone disk with more than twenty alphabetic characters variously identified as Celtic, Greek, Anglo-Saxon, Phoenician, Runic, and Etruscan (Schoolcraft 1854). Translations varied tremendously and had in common only the fact that they were meaningless. The disk was certainly a fraud.

Given the popularity of the notion that the Indians may have descended from one of the Lost Tribes of Israel (Chapter 5), it is not surprising that suggestions were made that at least some of the Moundbuilders themselves represented a group of ancient Jewish migrants from the Holy Land. The so-called Newark Holy Stones (Figure 6.5) seemed to support this notion (Applebaum 1996).

In the summer of 1860, David Wyrick, a professional land surveyor and ardent amateur archaeologist, continued his ongoing explorations of the impressive group of ancient mounds and enclosures located in Newark, Ohio (Lepper and Gill 2000). Immediately to the east of the large octagonal enclosure (seen on the left of Figure 6.4), Wyrick discovered a roughly triangular, polished stone object, 6 inches long by 2½ inches at its widest. It looked somewhat like a plumb bob and was labeled the "Keystone." What made the object so intensely interesting was the fact that there was a series of clearly recognizable Hebrew letters etched onto its surface (Figure 6.5, top). Wyrick must have been ecstatic at this discovery because it seemed to supply proof for his own deeply held belief that the New World Moundbuilders were members of the Lost Tribes of Israel. Hebrew writing on an object found in association with an ancient earthwork in Ohio would lend dramatic support to this hypothesis.

Unschooled in the Hebrew language, Wyrick brought the object to a local reverend, John W. McCarty, who could translate it. Reverend McCarty determined that on each of its four faces, the messages read in Hebrew, respectively: "the laws of Jehovah"; "the Word of the Lord"; "the Holy of Holies"; and "the King of the Earth."

Some were immediately skeptical of the object's antiquity, pointing out that the Hebrew writing on this supposedly antique object was quite modern. As if made to order, several months after the discovery of the Keystone and amid growing skepticism concerning its age, none other than David Wyrick discovered yet another stone bearing a Hebrew inscription in a mound located just a few miles south of Newark. This was a far more elaborately carved object: a limestone tablet, covered on all of its faces with Hebrew letters of an entirely different, apparently older vintage than the characters on the Keystone.

Figure 6.5 The so-called Keystone, the first of the Newark Holy Stones found in Ohio, was presumed by some to have been produced by ancient Israelites who visited the American Midwest some 2,000 years ago (top). The Decalogue, the second of the Newark Holy Stones, was written in a more ancient version of Hebrew than the Keystone, bearing an enumeration of the Ten Commandments (bottom). The "Calendar Stone," one of the Davenport Tablets (middle), was found in Davenport, Iowa. The Hebrew inscription on the Holy Stones and the Calendar Stone's assortment of Old World scripts seemed to point to a non-Indian origin for the mounds. It is now accepted by most that all three were hoaxes. (*Top and bottom:* Courtesy Johnson-Humrickhouse Museum, Coshocton, Ohio; *middle:* Proceedings of the Davenport Academy of Natural Sciences, No. 1)

This stone became known as the "Decalogue" when its translation revealed it to be a version of the Ten Commandments; the person around whom the commandments were carved was identified as Moses (Figure 6.5, bottom).

Some hailed these artifacts as proof of an ancient Jewish presence in Ohio. Others were still skeptical. If both stones were legitimate, how is it that ancient Jews in North America were, at the same time, writing in two different versions of Hebrew traceable to different time periods in their homeland? Perhaps only the first stone with its modern writing was a fake and the Decalogue was the real thing? How likely was it that a genuine stone with ancient Hebrew writing would coincidentally be found by the same searcher just a few miles from the spot where hoaxers had recently planted a fake stone with modern Hebrew on it? The Decalogue stone seemed to reflect a Hebrew script dating to the presumed antiquity of the mounds, but, nevertheless, it contained apparent anachronisms that suggested that it had been carved in the nineteenth century. These questions do not even begin to approach broader, cultural issues: There is no ancient (or modern) Jewish practice of constructing conical burial mounds or earth enclosures, yet it was being proposed that the ancient Jews who had left behind the Holy Stones had also built the earthworks found in Ohio.

In a wonderful piece of detective work, Brad Lepper and Jeff Gill (2000) have traced the cast of characters in this story. They point out that in 1839, Reverend McCarty's bishop, Charles Petit McIlvaine, had already predicted that artifacts linking the Moundbuilders to the Bible would one day be found. In Lepper and Gill's solution to the mystery, McCarty simply supplied the "proof" that realized his bishop's prediction. The ambitious Reverend McCarty was demonstrably deeply involved *after* the discovery of the Holy Stones, both translating them and championing their authenticity. Lepper and Gill suggest that he was also deeply involved *before* they were "found." In other words, McCarty faked the stones, planted them, and made sure Wyrick found them. McCarty's motive may have been to lend support to his and McIlvaine's belief in the unity of the native inhabitants of the Old and New Worlds as descendants of the people of the Bible. As Lepper and Gill suggest, in a general sense, the purpose of planting artifacts bearing Hebrew writing may have been "to encompass the prehistory of the New World with the biblical history of the Old" and to show that all people could be traced to the first people whom God had created and placed in the Garden of Eden (Lepper and Gill 2000:25).

Rochelle Altman (2004), a specialist in ancient writing systems, disputes the claim that the Newark Holy Stones are fraudulent, but neither does she believe they reflect the presence in Ohio of mound-building Israelites in antiquity. She maintains that the objects in question are genuine ritual equipment, manufactured in Europe and datable to the medieval period, the heirlooms of a Jew living in Ohio in the nineteenth century. The Decalogue stone, in her estimation, is a ritual object called a phylactery, worn on the arm by observant Jews during prayer. She believes the Keystone is a "flow detector," an object for ritually determining the purity of water. In the scenario she presents, the owner of the objects was killed while praying. Altman proposes that his body, along with the Decalogue/phylactery, was disposed of, only coincidentally near the Newark earthworks. In the sort of made-for-TV-movie scenario presented by Altman, the Keystone/ flow detector was then stolen by the culprit, carried away, and disposed of elsewhere. It is another coincidence, in this scenario, that the same searcher, David Wyrick, found both of these objects.

It should be pointed out that the black limestone from which the Decalogue was made looks quite similar to rock outcrops in the area around Kenyon College in Ohio, the very institution attended by Reverend McCarty. Archaeologists employ a number of analytical procedures for tracing the sources of raw materials used by ancient people for making their artifacts. Those same procedures might be applied here to definitively determine the source of the rock used to make the Decalogue and either support or refute Altman's claim that it was made in Europe and brought to America. Whatever the case, however, neither the Lepper/Gill scenario nor Altman's proposal lends any support to the claim that the earthworks of Ohio were built by a community of ancient Jews.

The fact that the second Newark Holy Stone (the Decalogue) seemed specifically and precisely to challenge the reaction of skeptics to the first discovery is not terribly surprising. It's actually pretty common to find this kind of "on-the-job training" among archaeological hoaxers. Consider the example of the Michigan Relics, a series of some 800 faked artifacts of clay, copper, and slate discovered throughout Michigan between 1890 and 1920 (Michigan Historical Museum 2004). In their initial attempt to produce objects that seemed to show that the mounds were tied to ancient Egyptians, Israelites, Christians, and others, the fakers made some fundamental errors. For example, some of the first objects discovered were unfired clay cups. Anyone who has worked with clay can testify that if they remain unfired, clay objects will begin disintegrating soon after they are made. They will dry out, crack, and fracture in the sun and under moist conditions—for example, when embedded in soil—will simply become wet and mushy, lose their shape, and, eventually, fall apart. Unfired clay artifacts certainly would not have remained intact for hundreds or even thousands of years in the Michigan soil, so, skeptics argued, the unfired clay artifacts among the Michigan Relics were recently made and demonstrably fake. To make matters even a bit worse, in at least one instance, one of the fabricators of an unfired clay bowl apparently had set the object down on what was clearly a machine-sawed wooden board. The board left the telltale imprint of mechanized sawing on the bottom of the bowl. Since ancient "whoevers" did not have machine-sawed boards, but nineteenth-century Michiganers did, the recent origin of the bowl was clinched.

Almost as soon as this inconsistency was pointed out by skeptics, however, people began finding, certainly not coincidentally, fired clay artifacts to add to the Michigan Relics assemblage. In fact, it may be a general rule of archaeological fakery: When skeptics point out the obvious errors in the first artifacts made by hoaxers, the hoaxers learn from their mistakes and produce specimens that are more convincing.

In another hoax, the Reverend Jacob Gass discovered two inscribed slate tablets, in 1877, in a mound on a farm in Davenport, Iowa (McKusick 1991). One of the tablets had a series of inscribed concentric circles with enigmatic signs believed by some to be zodiacal. The other tablet had various animal figures, a tree, and a few other marks on one face. The reverse face had a series of apparently alphabetic characters from half a dozen different languages across the top, and the depiction of a presumed cremation scene on the bottom (see Figure 6.5, middle). Gass discovered or came into possession of a number of other enigmatic artifacts ostensibly associated with the Moundbuilder culture, including another inscribed tablet and two pipes whose bowls were carved into the shape of elephants.

Thomas launched an in-depth investigation of the tablets. He believed that he had identified the source of the bizarre, multiple-alphabetic inscription. Webster's unabridged dictionary of 1872 presented a sample of characters from ancient alphabets. All of the letters on the tablet were in the dictionary, and most were close copies. Thomas suggested that the dictionary was the source for the tablet inscription (1894:641–42).

Beyond this, McKusick (1991) has discerned the presence of lower-case Greek letters on the Davenport tablet. Lowercase Greek letters were not invented until medieval times. McKusick has also identified Arabic numbers, Roman letters, musical clefs, and ampersands (&) on the Davenport tablet. Their presence is clear proof of the fraudulent nature of the stone. In fact, no genuine artifacts containing writing in any Old World alphabet have ever been found in any of the mounds .

4. *Indians were never witnessed building mounds and had no knowledge of who had built them.*

We next come to the claim that Indians were not moundbuilders at the time of European contact, nor did they know who had built the

Figure 6.6   The notion that Indians could not have built the mounds was supported by the contention that no historical Indian group had ever been observed building or using earthworks. Yet such a claim was clearly inaccurate. A number of written reports and even artistic depictions, like this one produced by Jacques Le Moyne in northeastern Florida in the 1560s, bore witness to mound use—here in a burial ceremony—by indigenous tribes. (From *Report on the Mound Explorations of the Bureau of American Ethnology*, by Cyrus Thomas)

mounds in their own territories. Thomas shows that this is, quite simply, false. De Soto's chronicler, the Gentleman of Elvas, mentions the construction and use of mounds almost immediately in his sixteenth-century narrative. Describing the Indian town of *Ucita*, he writes, "The lordes house stoode neere the shore upon a very hie mount, made by hand for strength" (1611:25).

Garcilaso de la Vega compiled the notes of some of the 311 survivors of the de Soto expedition. He describes how the Indians constructed the mounds on which temples and the houses of chiefs were placed: "They built up such sites with the strength of their arms, piling up large quantities of earth and stamping on it with great force until they have formed a mound from twenty-eight to forty-two feet in height" (cited in Silverberg 1989:19). Beyond this, sixteenth-century artists depicted Indian burial practices that included building mounds for the interment of chiefs (Figure 6.6).

Nearly two hundred years later, at the turn of the eighteenth century, French travelers lived among the Natchez Indians at the mouth of the Mississippi River. They described the principal town of these agricultural Indians as possessing a mound 100 feet around at its base, with the houses of leaders located on smaller mounds (Du Pratz 1774). William Bartram, at the end of the eighteenth century, mentions the fact that the houses of chiefs are placed on eminences. Even as late as the beginning of the nineteenth century, William Clark, co-leader of the Lewis and Clark expedition to the American West, noted:

> I observed artificial mounds (or as I may more justly term graves) which to me is strong evidence of this country being once thickly settled. The Indians of the Missouris still keep up the custom of burying their dead on high ground. (Bakeless 1964:34)

There clearly was ample historical evidence of Indians building and using mounds. The reason for the demise of at least some of the mound-building cultures of the Southeast was that de Soto accidentally introduced smallpox into these populations (Ramenofsky 1987). Exposed to this deadly disease for the first time, the indigenous people had no immunity to it and died in great numbers. Large mound sites were abandoned as a result of the tragic consequences of this deadly epidemic.

5. *Metal objects found in the mounds were beyond the metallurgical skills of the Indians.*

Thomas carefully assessed the claim that some mound artifacts exhibited a sophistication in metallurgy attained only by Old World cultures. Not relying on rumors, Thomas actually examined many of the artifacts in question. His conclusion: All such artifacts were made of so-called *native copper* (Figure 6.7). Certainly this implied extensive trade networks. Michigan was the source for much of the raw material used in copper artifacts found as far away as Florida. There was no evidence, however, for metallurgical skills the Indians were not known to have possessed.

Thomas clearly had marshalled more evidence on the Moundbuilder question than had anyone before him. In a rather restrained fashion, he comes to this conclusion: "It is proper to state at this point, however, that the author believes the theory which attributes these works to the Indians . . . to be the correct one . . . " (1894:610).

With the publication of Thomas's *Report on the Mound Explorations of the Bureau of American Ethnology,* Moundbuilder archaeology had come of age. Its content was so detailed, its conclusions so reasonable that, though not accepted by all, the myth of a vanished race had been dealt a fatal blow.

Figure 6.7 Moundbuilder metallurgy was restricted to the use of naturally occurring pure copper without smelting, casting, or alloying. This photograph shows a hammered copper sheet depicting what may be a shaman or a priest in a bird costume. This artifact was found at a well-known mound site, Etowah, in Georgia. (© Smithsonian Institution, #91117)

Rationale for the Myth of a Vanished Race

The myth of a non-Indian, vanished race of Moundbuilders was predicated not on a hoax or series of hoaxes but on ignorance and selective acceptance of the data. Silverberg's thesis that the vanished race myth was politically motivated is well founded; it was, as he says, "comforting to the conquerors" (1989:48).

If the Indians were not the builders of the mounds and the bearers of a culture that impressed even the rather ethnocentric European colonizers of America, it made eliminating the presumably savage and primitive natives less troublesome. And, if Europeans could further convince themselves that the Indians were very recent interlopers—in fact, the very invaders who had savagely destroyed the gentle and civilized Moundbuilders—so much the better. And finally, if it could be shown that the Moundbuilders were, in actuality, ancient European travelers to the Western Hemisphere, the circle was complete. In displacing the Indian people, Europeans in the eighteenth and nineteenth centuries could rationalize that they were merely reclaiming territory once held by ancient Europe. The Moundbuilder myth was not just the result of a harmless prank or a confusing hoax. It was part of an attempt to justify the destruction of American Indian societies. We owe it to them to set the record straight.

Current Perspectives: The Moundbuilders

An enormous amount of research has been conducted on the Moundbuilder culture in the last hundred years. See George R. Milner's (2004) book *The Moundbuilders: Ancient Peoples of Eastern North America* for a terrific summary of what we now know about Moundbuilder society, and see Brad Lepper's (2005) *Ohio Archaeology: An Illustrated Chronicle of Ohio's Ancient American Indian* for a detailed and beautifully illustrated discussion of the Ohio contingent of Moundbuilders. We now realize that there was not one Moundbuilder culture but several (Figure 6.8). The oldest evidence for mound building in North America has been found at the Watson Brake site in Louisiana and dates to 5,400 to 5,000 years ago (Saunders et al. 1997). There, a people reliant on hunting and gathering for their subsistence constructed a complex of eleven earthworks, including mounds and enclosures. The largest among the mounds is 6.5 meters (25 feet) in height. The great antiquity of Watson Brake is a clear indication that mound building has a very long history in North America. It also is geographically widespread, with ancient earthworks found throughout the American Southeast, Midwest, and northern plains.

Also in Louisiana, dating to a little before 3,250 years ago, are the Poverty Point earthworks (Gibson 2000). Monumental in scale, they consist of a series of six segmented, concentric earth ridges enclosing a rough half-circle with a radius of 0.65 kilometer (2,100 feet) (Figure 6.9). Each of the ridges is about 24 meters (80 feet) wide at its base, 3.5 meters (10 feet) tall, and separated from adjacent ridges by about 45 meters (150 feet). Altogether there are 9.65 kilometers (6 miles) of these ridges at Poverty Point enclosing a central plaza of about 37 acres. If the soil to produce Poverty Point had been mounded up in 50-pound basket loads, it would have taken 30 million such loads to complete the monument (Kopper 1986).

The tops of the earth ridges were living surfaces where archaeologists have found the remains of hearths and trash pits. Though there is evidence of domesticated squash at Poverty Point, wild foods, especially fish and other aquatic resources, seem to have been the mainstays of the diet. The construction of the Poverty Point earthworks necessitated the existence of a large labor force coordinated through a complex social and political structure more than 3,000 years ago.

The conical burial mounds that developed in the Ohio River valley have been divided into two cultures: the *Adena* and the *Hopewell* (Lepper

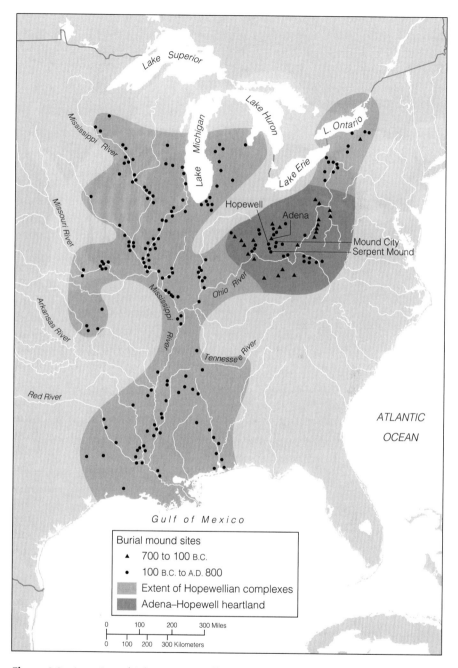

Burial mound sites

▲ 700 to 100 B.C.

• 100 B.C. to A.D. 800

▨ Extent of Hopewellian complexes

▨ Adena–Hopewell heartland

0   100   200   300 Miles

0   100   200   300 Kilometers

Figure 6.8   Location of Adena, Hopewell, and Mississippian heartlands in the United States. Clearly, the geographical focus of Moundbuilder culture was the river valleys of the American Midwest and Southeast.

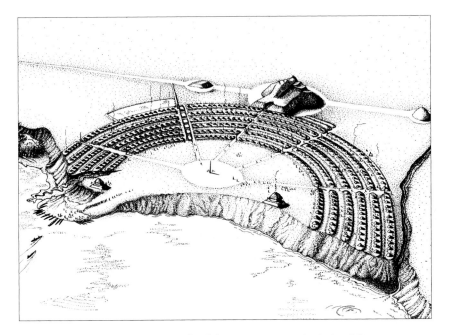

Figure 6.9 The concentric mounds of the Poverty Point site in Louisiana are more than 3,200 years old and reflect the work of a large, organized labor force among the native people whom we today call the Moundbuilders. (Drawing courtesy Jon Gibson, State of Louisiana Division of Archaeology)

1995a). These both involved burial cults, long-distance trade, and the production of fine crafts and artwork and are differentiated on the basis of certain artifact types. Adena is earlier, dating to as much as 2,800 years ago. Hopewell emerged from Adena about 2,200 years ago and likely represents what is essentially a flowering of Adena culture, though there is extensive chronological overlap between the two patterns. (In other words, not all of those we call Adena developed into Hopewell at the same time.)

Adena and Hopewell people lived in small towns located across much of southern and central Ohio and surrounding states to the south and west. Though we usually think of Native American subsistence as based on corn, very little evidence for that crop has been found at either Adena or Hopewell sites. The Hopewell people especially are known to have relied on the cultivation of local seed plants like sunflower, knotweed, maygrass, goosefoot, and marsh elder, as well as squash, crops that were part of an indigenous agricultural revolution that took place before the movement of corn into the region from Mexico (Smith 1995). Hunting and gathering wild plant foods continued to contribute to the subsistence quest.

The burial mounds themselves mark the remains of either individuals or groups of people, almost certainly the "important" religious, social, and political leaders of Adena or Hopewell society. These "important people"

Figure 6.10   Mound City in Chillicothe, Ohio, is a virtual city of the dead. The site consists of twenty-three burial mounds—a few of which can be seen here—within a 13-acre enclosure demarcated by an earth embankment. (K. L. Feder)

include both men and women and people of a broad range of ages from young children to aged adults. Some of these mounds are quite impressive, covering several acres and reaching 70 or 80 feet in height. Mound 25 at the Hopewell Mound Group in Ohio is particularly striking; it is 150 meters (500 feet) long, 55 meters (180 feet) wide, and 9 meters (30 feet) high (Lepper 1995a). Mound City in Chillicothe, Ohio, is another significant site, a virtual necropolis, or "city of the dead," consisting of twenty-three burial mounds surrounded by an earth embankment (Figure 6.10).

A widespread trade network brought natural resources to the Adena/ Hopewell from all over the United States: Copper and silver from the Great Lakes region were made into finely crafted goods and placed in the graves of those buried in the mounds; turtle shells, pearls, and conch shells from the Gulf of Mexico traveled up the major river systems of eastern North America and were also included in the burials of the Adena and Hopewell; obsidian from the Rocky Mountains, quartz crystals and mica from the Appalachian Mountains, alligator teeth from the lower Mississippi Valley, and chalcedony from North Dakota all made long journeys into the hands of the elite of Adena/Hopewell society.

Some of these sites of extensive earthworks include earthen-wall-enclosed spaces of unknown purpose. For example, in Newark, Ohio, a series of long, narrow, earthen walls about 5 feet high encloses an octagonal plot of more than 40 acres, which is in turn connected by two parallel earthen walls to an enormous circular area of more than 20 acres, also enclosed with an earth wall several feet high (Lepper 2002; see Figure 6.4). This large earth-work is located at the endpoint of what appears to have been a 60-mile-long ceremonial road demarcated by two earthen walls approximately 200 feet apart and perhaps as much as 8 to 10 feet in height (Lepper 1995b, 1995c). Altogether, archaeologist Brad Lepper (2002) estimates, the builders of the Newark earthworks piled up more than seven million cubic feet of dirt to produce the mounds, enclosures, and walls that characterize the site. Con-necting sacred or ceremonial mound sites and enclosures, these "roads" may have been used by pilgrims visiting the sites for religious observances—per-haps burial ceremonies or worship services. The earthworks located along these ceremonial roads appear to have been aligned in reference to impor-tant locations along the horizon, places where the sun and moon rise and set at certain dates during the year. Lepper (1998a, 2002) suggests that these astronomical alignments are not coincidental but indicate a detailed knowl-edge of the movements of the sun and moon, perhaps incorporated into cal-endar ceremonies practiced by the Moundbuilder people. These sites and the ceremonial roadways are examples of the ability of the Adena/Hopewell to organize a large labor force and produce works of monumental proportions.

Later developments in the Mississippi River valley and the American Southeast represent a different pattern. During this period, called the Mis-sissippian, the major temple mound sites were not just places of burial but were also the central places or capital towns of increasingly complex soci-eties, called "chiefdoms." The labor of a sizable population was conscripted by the leaders of temple mound societies to construct large, truncated (cut off at the top) pyramids of earth. Cahokia was the largest and most impres-sive of these—and the only one with a resident population of a size and den-sity that approach an urban character. There were, however, many others like Etowah in Georgia and Moundville in Alabama that, though smaller in size and complexity, with fewer and smaller monumental earthworks, nevertheless represent development of complex, indigenous societies in the period after A.D. 1000.

The temple Moundbuilders grew maize and squash and later added domesticated beans to their diet. The chemical analysis of their bones shows a dramatic shift to a diet reliant on maize at around A.D. 1000 (Smith 1995). They fished in the rivers and hunted in the forests and continued to gather wild plant foods, including acorn and hickory. The enormous food surplus made possible by agriculture likely allowed for the support of a class of priests and the attendant nobility and artisans.

Old World civilizations such as those of ancient Egypt and Sumer and New World civilizations including the Aztec and Maya are marked by strat-ified social systems. Kings, emperors, or pharaohs ruled with the help of noble and priestly classes. The nature of social stratification is exhibited

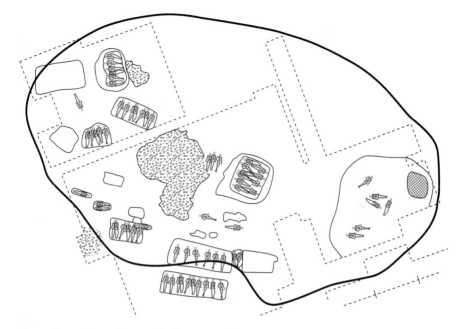

Figure 6.11 Map showing the location of the burials at Mound 72 at Cahokia. The primary burial is that of a young man, laid out on a bed of more than twenty thousand mother-of-pearl shell beads. The great wealth reflected in the materials with which he was buried and the likelihood that some of the secondary burials represent human sacrifices suggest that the primary burial in Mound 72 was that of an important person, perhaps a ruler of ancient Cahokia. (Courtesy William Fowler)

quite clearly in the archaeology of their deaths; the tombs of pharaohs and kings are large and sumptuous with concentrations of finely crafted artwork, rare or exotic (and presumably expensive) materials, and even the presence of sacrificed human beings—people killed and buried with the ruler to accompany him or her to the afterlife.

Cahokia, too, has evidence of just such a burial (Fowler 1974:20–22, 1975:7–8). Mound 72 represents the interment of members of a royal family of Cahokia (Figure 6.11). A young man was laid out on a platform of twenty thousand perforated mother-of-pearl shell beads that had, perhaps, been woven into a burial cloak. A cache of more than one thousand stone arrowpoints had been placed in his tomb (Figure 6.12). Nearby, three women and three men were buried, accompanied by stone weapons made from materials imported from Oklahoma and Arkansas as well as by sheets of mica from North Carolina. A 2- by 3-foot sheet of copper from Michigan had also been included in their burial.

Another part of the mound contained the burials of four men, decapitated and with their hands cut off. Close by were the remains of fifty women,

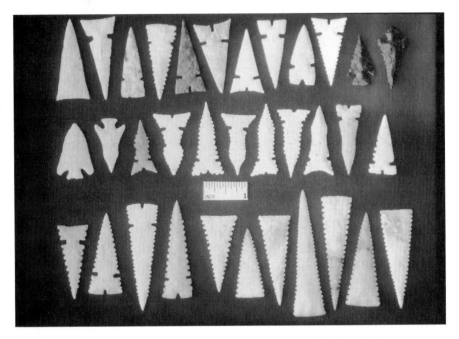

Figure 6.12   A small sample of the more than one thousand finely crafted stone projectile points buried with one of Cahokia's leaders in Mound 72. (Courtesy Cahokia Mounds State Historic Site)

all in their late teens and early twenties. These may have been individuals whose lives were sacrificed for the presumed needs of the rulers in their lives after death, but this remains speculation.

The evidence at Cahokia and other temple mound sites, as well as at sites of the Adena and Hopewell cultures, is clear. American Indians produced cultures of great sophistication and complexity. The only mystery that remains is why more Americans are not aware of the legacy of these indigenous civilizations.

◈ ◈ ◈   FREQUENTLY ASKED QUESTIONS   ◈ ◈ ◈

1. *Some of the mounds are huge. Where did all the dirt come from to build the mounds?*

The dirt came from the immediate vicinity of the mounds. Huge quantities were excavated using wooden shovels and stone- and shell-bladed hoes. The dirt was carried by basket. In the vicinity of some of the larger mounds, enormous borrow pits (extensive, but not terribly deep) represent the source areas for the dirt used to build the mounds.

2. How long did it take to build a mound?

The time it takes to build a mound depends on how many people are working and the size of the mound being constructed. In the early 1980s an experiment was conducted in mound building at the Kampsville campus of the University of Illinois. About twenty-five people constructed a small mound, transporting and piling up more than six hundred basket loads of dirt. They did not have to dig the dirt up; it had already been loosely piled for them. This certainly saved them quite a bit of time and effort. It took this group the better part of an afternoon to construct a mound about 5 feet high with a diameter of about 20 feet at its base for a volume of a little more than 500 cubic feet. Compare this to Monks Mound at Cahokia, with its volume of 20 million cubic feet. Certainly large mounds were an enormous undertaking, demanding the labor of large numbers of people for extended periods of time.

BEST OF THE WEB

http://www.cahokiamounds.com/cahokia.html

The official page of the Cahokia Mounds State Historic Site. View photographs, read about the archaeology of the site, and see a listing of events open to the public at the site and museum.

http://www.ua.edu/academic/museums/moundville/

Visit the Moundville site in Alabama, by some measurements second only to Cahokia among temple mound sites in terms of the size of the community—and size of the earthen pyramids.

http://www.ngeorgia.com/parks/etowah.html

Web page of the impressive Moundbuilder archaeological site, Etowah, in Georgia.

http://cas.memphis.edu/chucalissa/

Take a virtual tour of the Chucalissa mound site in Tennessee.

http://www.mississippian-artifacts.com/

A wonderful resource, loaded with photographs—accompanied by thoughtful discussions—of some of the fine art and craft of Mississippian Moundbuilder stone, ceramic, shell, and beadwork.

http://www.cr.nps.gov/aad/feature/feature.htm

Lengthy discussion of Moundbuilder culture.

http://www.sos.state.mi.us/history/michrelics/index.html
Read the incredible story of the so-called "Michigan Relics," on this virtual museum exhibit (the actual exhibit was hosted by the Michigan Historical Museum). The relics were clumsy fakes produced in the early 1890s to make money by taking advantage of people's curiosity concerning the ancient inhabitants of the New World.

CRITICAL THINKING EXERCISE

Using the deductive approach outlined in Chapter 2, how would you test these hypotheses? In each case, what archaeological and biological data must you find to conclude that the hypothetical statement is an accurate assertion, that it describes what actually happened in the ancient human past?

- The mounds found throughout the American Midwest and Southeast were the product of an indigenous people.

- The mounds found throughout the American Midwest and Southeast were the product of invaders from Europe who later were displaced by the ancestors of American Indians.

◈◈◈◈◈◈◈ 7 ◈◈◈◈◈◈◈

Lost: One Continent—Reward

It was a beautiful land. Its people, gentle and fair, artistic and intelligent, created the most wonderful society the world has ever known. Their cities were splendid places, interwoven with blue canals and framed by crystal towers gently arching skyward. From its seaports, ships were sent out to the corners of the globe, gathering in abundant raw materials needed by its artisans and giving in return something far more valuable—civilization. The wondrous achievements of the archaic world can be traced to the genius of this singular ancient land. The cultures of the ancient Egyptians and the Maya, the civilizations of China and India, the Inka, the Moundbuilders, and the Sumerians were all derived from this source of civilization (Figure 7.1).

But tragedy was to strike down this great nation. In a cataclysmic upheaval of incomprehensible proportions, this beautiful land and its people were destroyed in a day and a night. Earthquakes, volcanic eruptions, and tidal waves, with forces never before or since unleashed by nature, shattered the crystal towers, sank the great navy, and created a holocaust of incalculable sorrow.

All that remains are the traces of those derivative cultures that benefited from contact with this most spectacular source of all culture. But ancient Egypt, the Aztecs, the Maya, the Chinese Shang, the Moundbuilders, and the rest, as impressive as they were, could have been only the palest of shadows, the most tepid of imitations of the source of all human civilization.

This is the great irony of prehistoric archaeology; the most important of ancient cultures is beyond the grasp of even those archaeologists who investigate the corpses of great civilizations. For the original civilization of which I speak, the source of all human achievement, is *Atlantis,* the island continent whose people were obliterated beneath the seething waters of the Atlantic more than 11,000 years ago. Atlantis the fair; Atlantis the beautiful; Atlantis the source.

Figure 7.1   Artists have long imagined what Atlantis may have looked like. In this rendering, the artist has remained true to the Greek philosopher Plato's description, depicting a series of concentric rings of habitation, separated by canals but linked by gracefully arching bridges. (© AKG Images/Peter Connolly)

Atlantis: Where Are You?

I live in a charming, bucolic, and rather woodsy part of Connecticut, tucked into the green and lush Farmington River valley. Along with terrific schools, wonderful people, and a farm store that sells the best ice cream anywhere, my little town has another thing going for it. West Simsbury, Connecticut, Zip code 06092, appears to be almost the only place left on the planet that someone has *not* claimed is the actual location of the Lost Continent of Atlantis. Or so it seems.

I am exaggerating here a bit, but check it out (Figure 7.2). The lost civilization of Atlantis was located on a continent-size landmass positioned outside of the Straits of Gibraltar, in the Atlantic Ocean, and was destroyed in a natural cataclysm more than 11,000 years ago (Plato in Hutchins 1952). No, that can't be right. Atlantis must have been located on the island of Crete in the Mediterranean, and it was destroyed by a volcanic eruption 3,600 years ago (Galanopoulos and Bacon 1969). No, that's not right either; instead, it was located on the much smaller island of Santorini, also in the Mediterranean, and destroyed by the aforementioned volcanic eruption (Pellegrino 1991). If that doesn't work for you, how about moving it a bit north and to the east, and make it not an island continent, but a city in western Turkey (James 1998)? No? Maybe it was actually situated in the Antarctic, of course during a time when the climate of the South Pole was far more hospitable and a lot less "arctic" than it is now (Flem-Ath and Flem-Ath 1995). No,

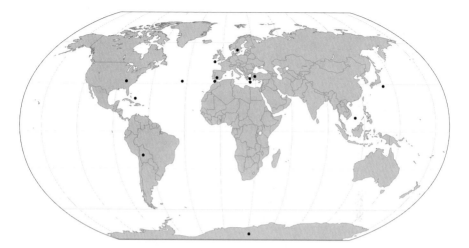

Figure 7.2 Where has Atlantis been found? Better to ask, Where hasn't Atlantis been found? This map shows just some of the better-known locations where assorted researchers have claimed Atlantis has definitively been located. All of these places share one important characteristic; there is no archaeological evidence indicating that any one of them represents the actual location of Plato's Atlantis, which was, after all, an invention of his imaginative mind.

that's not right either; I have it: Atlantis was located on Spartel Island, a tiny, not-so-continent-size landmass, located immediately west of the Straits of Gibraltar, between Morocco and Spain (Collina-Girard 2001). No, forget the island; Atlantis was in Spain proper, right there on the mainland of Europe (Kühne 2004). That can't be right. Let's place it farther to the north, in Scandinavia (Spanuth 1979). I suppose that would make the Atlanteans Vikings. You don't like that? Okay, let's push it to the west and locate Atlantis in the North Atlantic, about 160 kilometers (100 miles) from the coast of Great Britain, on an island just off Cornwall (a claim made by unspecified Russian scientists and reported by the BBC in 1997). No, wrong ocean; the continent of Atlantis was actually situated in the South China Sea (dos Santos 1997). No, it's not there either. I've got it: Atlantis was in North America (Lopez de Gomara back in 1555 as cited in Huddleston 1967). No, not there? How about this: Atlantis was located in South America, specifically, Bolivia (Allen 1999). No, not Bolivia or anywhere in South America, but perhaps farther north, just off the coast of Cuba (Collins 2002). Or was it (or something very much like Atlantis) located off the coast of Japan (Hancock 2003)? Wait. I just found it. Of course, Atlantis is on an island in the Bahamas, just offshore of the island of Bimini (Cayce 1968). No, wait; we can trace it, not to Bimini, but to another island in the Bahamas. I have documentary evidence right here in this brochure. Whoops; that "Atlantis" is just a modern and rather pricey resort that calls itself Atlantis, but it isn't the original Atlantis. Hold it! Stop the presses! The latest news flash shows that Atlantis is back in the Mediterranean. The spectacular architectural remains of walls, a canal, and even an acropolis have been found beneath the sea, just 97 miles off the coast of Cyprus (as announced in late 2004 by the explorer Robert Sarmast; Hamilton 2004). No; it's not there either. Maybe Atlantis is in Connecticut after all.

Or maybe Atlantis isn't in any of these proposed locations because it wasn't anywhere. It was a mythical place, a construct intended not to join the inventory of historical civilizations, but merely to be used as a literary tool to convey a lesson about the political, social, and economic organization of a well-run society. When looking for Atlantis, it turns out that satellite photographs, sonar, ground-penetrating radar, deep-sea submersibles, and other modern tools of the archaeologist may be of no help. Atlantis can't be traced underwater or under mud or rock or volcanic ash. In fact, Atlantis is traceable to no geographical place at all, but to the mind and imagination of one of the world's best-known and most highly respected thinkers (Jordan 2001). That mind belonged to the Greek philosopher Plato.

Atlantis: The Source of the Legend

Plato was born in 429 or 428 B.C. He became a disciple of another great philosopher, Socrates, in about 410 B.C. and established his own academy in 387 B.C. He was well known in his own time and is, of course, still studied and considered a great thinker more than 2,000 years after his death.

Plato apparently believed that the best way to teach was to engage his students in dialogues. Plato wrote many of his philosophical treatises in a dialogue format as well. Readers who insist that the entire Atlantean dialogues are genuine history may be unaware, however, that even the context of Plato's dialogues is fictitious. The dialogues were largely imaginary conversations between Socrates and his students. The actual discussions Plato reported on never really took place; the published dialogues were not simply stenographic records. They usually included real people, but some of them lived at different times. In fact, the Critias who tells the Atlantis story has been identified as Plato's maternal great-grandfather (Lee 1965).

The late entertainer and writer Steve Allen once produced a fascinating television show using a similar device. In his *Meeting of Minds,* actors and actresses portraying famous historical figures discussed and debated important philosophical issues. In one episode nineteenth-century evolutionist Charles Darwin, nineteenth-century poet Emily Dickinson, renowned sixteenth- and seventeenth-century scientist Galileo, and fifth-century general and king Attila the Hun sat down together for a chat. And wouldn't you have liked to have been a fly on the wall when Plato himself showed up to thrash out a few ideas with eighteenth-century French author and philosopher Voltaire, sixteenth-century church reformer Martin Luther, and late-nineteenth-/early-twentieth-century medical pioneer Florence Nightingale? Each of these historical figures was portrayed by an actor or actress well versed in the perspective of the individual he or she was playing. Of course, the real people being depicted never actually had these discussions. The point was to imagine how such conversations might have gone. Plato used a similar technique to challenge, teach, and entertain his readers.

It has been suggested that Plato used this format to present sometimes quite controversial ideas of his own without getting in trouble with the authorities—he could always claim that the opinions were not his but those of the people engaging in the dialogues (Shorey 1933). The format also allowed Plato to argue both sides of an issue without taking a stand himself.

The story of Atlantis was presented in two of Plato's dialogues: *Timaeus* and *Critias*, named, respectively, after the major participant in each conversation. We know that Timaeus and Critias were real people; Timaeus was an astronomer from Italy, and Critias was an Athenian poet and teacher. The dialogues that bear their names were written sometime after 355 B.C. and before Plato's death in 347 B.C. and describe conversations that supposedly occurred in 421 B.C. (Jordan 2001:11). If you have already done the math, you realize that Plato would have been only seven or eight years old at the time; the dialogues certainly could not have been stenographic transcriptions written by an eight-year-old who listened in on a real conversation.

The Timaeus Dialogue

The Timaeus dialogue begins, oddly enough, with Socrates taking attendance. Socrates then refers to the previous day's discussion of the "perfect" society. It is clear in this context that the discourse Plato is referring to is his most famous dialogue, the *Republic,* actually written several years before *Timaeus.* Here, we are being asked by Plato to go along with the fiction that the *Republic* dialogue, where the nature of a perfect society had been discussed in great detail, was the product of yesterday's conversation.

Socrates next summarizes the characteristics of the conjectural perfect culture presented in the *Republic.* Artisans and husbandmen would be separated from the military; and those in the military would be merciful, would be trained in "gymnastic" and music, would live communally, and would own no gold or silver or any private property.

Socrates, however, then despairs of hypothetical discussions, like the one presented in the *Republic,* of such a perfect society:

> I might compare myself to a person who, on beholding beautiful animals either created by the painter's art or, better still, alive but at rest, is seized with a desire of seeing them in motion or engaged in some struggle or conflict to which their forms appear suited. (Hutchins 1952:443; all quotations from Plato's dialogues are from this translation)

Socrates next gives what amounts to an assignment:

> I should like to hear some one tell of our own city [his hypothetical perfect society] carrying on a struggle against her neighbors, and how she

went out to war in a becoming manner, and when at war showed by the greatness of her actions and the magnanimity of her words, in dealing with other cities a result worthy of her training and education. (p. 443)

Socrates even explicitly instructs his students to engage "our city in a suitable war" to show how the perfect society would perform. One of those present, Hermocrates, tells Socrates that a fellow student, Critias, knows the perfect story. Critias then begins to give the account: "Then listen, Socrates, to a tale which though strange, is certainly true . . ." (p. 444).

Critias says that he heard this "true" story from his grandfather, who related the tale at a public gathering on a holiday called Apatouria that Plato scholar Paul Friedlander refers to as a kind of April Fool's Day (1969:383) when prizes are awarded for the best narrative. Critias's grandfather (also named Critias) said that he heard it from his father, Dropides, who heard it from the Greek sage Solon, who heard it from some unnamed priests in Egypt when he was there about 590 B.C. So at best, when we read Plato, we are reading a very indirect account of a story that had originated about 240 years earlier.

According to the tale told by Critias, the Egyptian priests tell Solon that the Greeks are little more than "children" and know nothing of the many cataclysms that befell humanity in ancient times. They then go on to tell him of ancient Athens, which "was first in war and in every way the best governed of all cities" (p. 445). In fact, it is this ancient Athens which in Critias's story will serve as the model of the perfect state.

The priests tell Solon of the most heroic deed of the ancient city of Athens; it defeated in battle "a mighty power which unprovoked made an expedition against the whole of Europe and Asia" (pp. 445–46). They continue by describing and identifying the evil power that so threatened the rest of the world: "This power came forth out of the Atlantic Ocean . . . an island situated in front of the straits, which are by you called the Pillars of Heracles" (p. 446). (Today they are called the Straits of Gibraltar.) The Egyptian priests told Solon the name of this great power in the Atlantic Ocean: the island nation of Atlantis.

Ancient Athens was able to subdue mighty Atlantis, which had held sway across northern Africa all the way to Egypt. After her defeat in battle, all of Atlantis was destroyed in a tremendous cataclysm of earthquakes and floods. Unfortunately, ancient Athens also was destroyed in the same catastrophe.

After outlining the Atlantis story, Critias remarks to Socrates:

When you were speaking yesterday about your city and citizens, the tale which I have just been repeating to you came into my mind, and I remarked with astonishment how, *by some mysterious coincidence,* you agreed in almost every particular with the narrative of Solon. (p. 446, emphasis mine)

Of course, it was no coincidence; it was how Plato worked Atlantis and ancient Athens into the dialogue.

Following this brief introduction to the story, Critias cedes the floor to Timaeus, who provides a very detailed discussion of his theory of the origins of the universe. In the next dialogue, *Critias*, details of the Atlantis story are provided.

The Critias Dialogue

Critias appears to have listened well to his teacher's description of the perfect society; for in his tale ancient Athens, even in detail, matches precisely the hypothetical society of Socrates. According to the story Critias told, in ancient Athens, artisans and husbandmen were set apart from the military, military men owned no private property and possessed no gold or silver, and so on.

Only after first describing ancient Athens does Critias describe Atlantis. He relates that Atlantis was originally settled by the Greek god Poseidon and a mortal woman, Kleito, who bore him five sets of male twins. All Atlanteans were descended from these ten males. The Atlanteans became quite powerful and built a 15-mile-wide city of concentric rings of alternating land and water, with palaces, huge canals, towers, and bridges. They produced artworks in silver and gold and traded far and wide. They possessed a great navy of twelve hundred ships and an army with ten thousand chariots. Their empire and their influence expanded exponentially.

After a time, however, the "divine portion" of their ancestry became diluted and the human portion became dominant. As a result, their civilization became decadent, the people depraved and greedy. The dialogue relates that after Athens defeated the Atlanteans in war, Zeus, the chief god in the Greek pantheon, decided to teach the inhabitants of Atlantis a lesson for their avarice and prideful desire to rule the world. Zeus gathered the other gods together to relate his plan. The dialogue ends unfinished at just this point, and Plato never returned to it, dying just a few years later.

The Source and Meaning of Timaeus and Critias

Though briefly summarized here, this is the entire story of Atlantis as related in Plato's dialogues. All else written about Atlantis is derivative, contrived, or invented.

It is ironic, however, that this source of the popular myth of Atlantis, while having spawned some two thousand books and articles (de Camp 1970) along with a number of periodicals (*Atlantis, The Atlantis Quarterly,* and *Atlantis Rising*), isn't really about Atlantis at all. The lost continent is little more than a plot device. The story is about an ostensible ancient *Athens.* Athens is the protagonist, the hero, and the focus of Plato's tale. Atlantis is the antagonist, the empire gone bad in whose military defeat by Athens the functioning of a perfect society as defined by Socrates can be exemplified.

Now consider the story that Plato tells: A technologically sophisticated but morally bankrupt, evil empire—Atlantis—attempts world domination by force. The only thing standing in its way is a relatively small group of spiritually pure, morally principled, and incorruptible people—the ancient Athenians. Overcoming overwhelming numerical and technological odds, the Athenians are able to defeat their far more powerful adversary simply through the force of their spirit.

Sound familiar? Plato's Atlantean dialogues are essentially an ancient Greek version of *Star Wars*! Think about it: Plato placed Atlantis nine thousand years before his time, off in the little-known (to the ancient Greeks) Atlantic Ocean. *Star Wars* takes place "a long time ago, in a galaxy far, far away." Atlantis, with its sophisticated military and enormous navy, parallels the Empire with its Stormtroopers and Death Star. The Athenians are the counterparts of the ragtag group of rebels led (eventually) by Luke Skywalker. The rebels and the Athenians both are victorious, certainly not because they are militarily superior, but—why?—because "the Force" is with them both. One more connection can be made; if 9,000 years from now people ask whether the *Star Wars* saga is actual history, not fiction, it would not be too different from our suggesting today that Plato's story of Atlantis really happened. Both stories are myths, used to entertain and to convey moral lessons. They are both equally fantastical.

Who Invented Atlantis?

In the Timaeus dialogue, Plato has Critias state that Atlantis was destroyed more than 9,000 years before *Solon's* time (590 B.C.). He contradicts this somewhat in the Critias dialogue, where Critias states that Atlantis was destroyed 9,000 years before *his* present time (350 B.C.). This adds up to a discrepancy of about 240 years. Whichever date Plato intended, it is important to point out that there are no records of the Atlantis story in Egypt, where Solon is supposed to have been told the tale. It is equally instructive to point out that chroniclers of the history of Athens, including those who discussed that city's military triumphs in great detail, do not mention a war with a nation called or even vaguely sounding like the Atlantis of the dialogues. The best-known Greek historian, Herodotus, who lived 100 years before Plato, never mentions Atlantis. Also in the fifth century B.C., Thucydides provides a detailed discourse on the military and political struggles of ancient Athens in his book *Archaeology*, yet he is absolutely silent about Atlantis. He doesn't mention it, even to dispute its existence. It certainly seems that, before Plato, there was no tale about Atlantis circulating among Greek thinkers.

There was a book called *Atlantis* written by the Greek author Hellanicus that predated the Timaeus and Critias dialogues by about one hundred years (Gantz 1993). Only fragments of this work survive and, beyond possibly providing inspiration for the name Plato gave the lost continent (Castleden 1998), there is no indication Plato derived any of the details of his story from Hellanicus.

Imagine that the War of Independence in the United States had become a dimly remembered event, discussed only occasionally by people, many of whom were skeptical that it had actually occurred. Now, imagine that, many years after that war took place, a respected scholar found an ancient manuscript that focused entirely on that war, providing a wealth of information about the roots of our nation, the heroism of its founders, as well as the nature of the empire that held us in subjugation. In revealing a crucial part of our history and detailing events that formed us as a nation, that manuscript certainly would generate intense discussion after its discovery. Even those who were aware of the "legend" of such a war, but still skeptical it had actually taken place, would be expected to talk or write about the newly discovered document, presenting their arguments for why they were still skeptical about the historicity of the war.

Now consider Plato's story of a conflict between Athens and Atlantis, which surely would have been viewed as being as singularly formative for Athens as the War of Independence was for the United States. It is inconceivable that there would be no mention of a great military victory by ancient Athens over Atlantis—or any place even vaguely like it— in the works of Greek historians who followed Plato (Fears 1978). Yet this is precisely the case. For example, there is no mention of Atlantis in the historical work *Panathenaicus* by Isocrates, written between 342 and 339 B.C., even to deny its reality (Fears 1978:108). The same is true in later versions of Athenian history. This must mean that Greek historians didn't view the story as anything more than the fiction Plato intended it to be. They felt no more need to discuss it in their histories—even to refute it—than a modern historian feels compelled to mention the Evil Empire of the Star Wars saga, even to remind readers that it didn't actually exist. Everyone already knows that; and, it appears, Greek writers of history and their readers already knew that about Atlantis too.

But wait; Plato has Critias assert that the story of Atlantis was true. Isn't this evidence that Plato believed he was relating genuine history? Absolutely not. As historian William Stiebing, Jr., states, "Virtually every myth Plato relates in his dialogues is introduced by statements claiming it is true" (1984:51). It is not only the Atlantis account but also tales about heaven and hell (Isles of the Blessed and Tartarus) in *Georgias,* immortality and reincarnation in *Meno,* antiquity in *Laws,* and the afterlife in the *Republic* that are prefaced with statements attesting to their truth (Stiebing 1984:52).

Remember also that the story Critias relates here is the direct result of Socrates having asked his students the previous day to come up with a tale in which his hypothetical perfect state is put to the test by warfare. In other words, it's a homework assignment! Critias relates the story of a civilization conveniently enormously distant from his Athens in both time and space, whose remnants are below the Atlantic, certainly beyond recovery or testing by the Greeks of Plato's time. He also has ancient Athens, which would not have been beyond the purview of contemporary Athenians to study, conveniently destroyed. Finally, though maintaining it is a true tale, he admits that "by some mysterious coincidence," it matches Socrates' hypothetical society almost exactly. As A. E. Taylor has said, "We could not be told much more plainly that the whole narrative of Solon's conversation with the priests and his intention of writing the poem about Atlantis are an invention of Plato's fancy" (1962:50).

Where Did Plato Get the Details of the Story? A Minoan Source

The final question to be asked is, If the Atlantis story was Plato's invention, did he at least base it on a real event or a series of events? In other words, did Plato construct elements of his story—of a great civilization destroyed by a cataclysm—from historical events, perhaps only dimly remembered by the Greeks at the time he was writing? The answer is almost certainly yes; in a sense, all fiction must be based on fact. All writers begin with knowledge of the real world and construct their literary fantasies with the raw material of that knowledge. Plato was no different, and there were plenty of historical events of which Plato was well aware that he could have used in constructing his Atlantis tale.

For example, as early as 1909, a scholar at Queen's University in Belfast suggested a connection between historical Minoan Crete and the Atlantis legend (cited in Luce 1969:47). Using more recent archaeological evidence, researchers Spyridon Marinatos (1972), J. V. Luce (1969), and Angelos Galanopoulos and Edward Bacon (1969) have expanded on Frost's suggestion, arguing that Plato based at least elements of his Atlantis story on historically accurate aspects of Minoan civilization.

The spectacular temple at the Minoan capital of Knossos was built beginning about 3,800 years ago (Figure 7.3). At its peak the temple covered an area of some 20,000 square meters (more than 210,000 square feet or about 5 acres), contained about one thousand separate rooms, and had a central courtyard with a pillar-lined hallway, a ceremonial bath, and grand staircases. Some parts of the temple were three and even four stories tall. The walls of some of the living quarters and large halls were covered with artfully produced fresco paintings of dolphins and bulls. Where the Minoans depicted themselves in these paintings, we see a graceful and athletic people. The Greeks of Plato's time were aware of this even more ancient and impressive culture.

There are, however, many problems in attempting to assign a Minoan source to Atlantis. Crete is far too small and in the wrong place to conform

Figure 7.3   Those who support the hypothesis that the eruption on Thera is the source of the story of the destruction of Atlantis have suggested that the Minoan civilization on Crete was the historical model for Atlantis culture. Pictured here is the ancient temple at Knossos on Crete, dating to Minoan times. (M. H. Feder)

with Plato's description of Atlantis. Further, it is not nearly as old as Atlantis is purported to be. In addition, there are no elephants on Crete, though Plato maintains that the Atlanteans had a large stock of elephants.

A key element in the possible connection between Plato's fictional Atlantis and the historical Minoan civilization rests in a catastrophe that affected the island of Crete in 1628 or 1627 B.C. At that time, a volcano erupted on the island today called Santorini (the ancient Greeks called it Thera), 120 kilometers (72 miles) north of Crete (Figure 7.4). The explosive force of the eruption of Thera was four times as powerful as that of Krakatoa in the Dutch East Indies in 1883 (Marinatos 1972:718), which killed some 36,000 people.

It should come as no surprise that the obliteration of Thera did have a significant impact on the Minoan civilization (Marinatos 1972). The eruption itself, accompanied by severe earthquakes, badly damaged many settlements on Crete. Devastating waves, or tsunamis, produced by the eruption of Thera wiped out Minoan port settlements on the north coast of Crete.

The Minoan civilization developed, at least in part, as a result of trade. The loss of ports through which trade items passed and the probable destruction of the Minoan fleet of trading vessels must have had a tremendous impact on the Minoan economy. Also of great significance for the Minoans

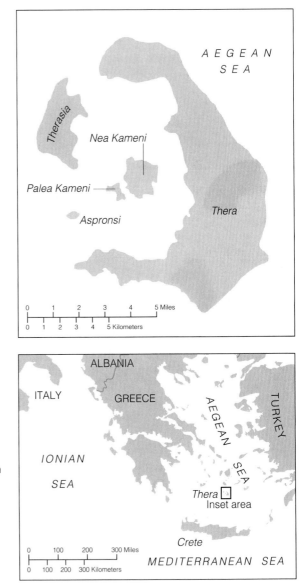

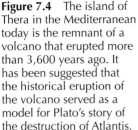

Figure 7.4   The island of Thera in the Mediterranean today is the remnant of a volcano that erupted more than 3,600 years ago. It has been suggested that the historical eruption of the volcano served as a model for Plato's story of the destruction of Atlantis.

over the long term was the thick deposit of white volcanic ash that blanketed the rich farmland of Crete, interrupting for a time the agricultural economy of the Minoan people.

Though the eruption on Thera and the devastation it wrought on Minoan Crete might, at first glance, seem to conform to Plato's story of the destruction of Atlantis, in fact it is a very poor match. Archaeological evidence clearly shows that, despite being adversely affected by the eruption on Thera, Minoan Crete was not destroyed by it. As historian William Stiebing

(1984) points out, there is plenty of evidence of destruction on Crete coinciding with the eruption of Thera, but equally plentiful evidence of repair work afterward. There is evidence of construction of Minoan structures on top of the volcanic deposit soon after the eruption (Bower 1990).

In fact, the Minoan civilization continued to thrive for 100 years after the eruption on Thera—actually, for a time, rising to new heights. It did not collapse until 1320 B.C., more than 300 years after the eruption on Thera. As the instantaneous obliteration of Atlantis is a key component of Plato's story, this alone would seem to rule out Crete as the model for Atlantis in anything but the most general sense.

There is another major problem with identifying Minoan Crete as the single source for Plato's Atlantis. Significantly, the major theme of Plato's story, the defeat by Athens of a great military power, remains unexplained here. Minoan Crete did not suffer a major military defeat at the hands of Athens. If Minoan Crete was Plato's inspiration for the Atlantis story, this key aspect of the tale was entirely fictional.

As long ago as 1872, the French writer Louis Figuier made the correlation between Atlantis and the very impressive Minoan settlement on Santorini/Thera (Castleden 1998). Others have followed (Pellegrino 1991). Though this site better conforms to Plato's description of Atlantis's fate, having been utterly destroyed by the volcanic eruption there in 1628 B.C., it is plagued by all of the other objections to any direct correlation between the Minoan civilization and Atlantis. Clearly, Thera is far too small, it is far too recent, and it is still in the wrong location to be Plato's Atlantis.

More recently, Rodney Castleden (1998), the highly respected author of a number of books on Mediterranean prehistory, has attempted to show that not Minoan Crete and not Thera, but both together were Plato's inspiration and that Atlantis was not a single, enormous island, but several. Plato, however, certainly does not state or imply this; he is quite clear that Atlantis was a single, island continent.

Most of the attempts to directly correlate a historical place with Atlantis are afflicted by the same problem; part of Plato's story must be revised or ignored to make a reasonable fit. One is forced to ask the question: How many alterations can be made to a historical location and have it still be reasonable to argue that it is the place Plato described?

While arguing that Plato's Atlantis was a combination of Thera and Crete, Castleden (1998) clearly recognizes elements of many other historical places and events enfolded in Plato's description of Atlantis in the Critias dialogue. For example, he suggests that elements of the political structure of Sparta, a competitor and sometime enemy of Athens, were grafted by Plato onto his Atlantis (Castleden 1998:160–63). Athens and Sparta fought against each other in the Peloponnesian War, which started when Plato was twelve years old; yet, again, there is no perfect match here as Athens was not victorious but suffered a humiliating defeat by Sparta in that war. Castleden

(1998:154–60) also suggests that many architectural features of the fifth-century B.C. Italian city of Syracuse closely match Plato's description of Atlantis.

Searching *Critias* for characteristics of Atlantis that closely parallel specific ancient societies almost certainly misses Plato's primary point. The specifics that Plato has Critias speak are not intended as history but as part of the parable. To make his point, Plato makes Atlantis sound like a nearly insurmountable adversary. Plato's detailed description of Atlantis was intended to impress the reader with its material wealth, technological sophistication, and military power. That the smaller, materially poorer, technologically less well endowed, and militarily weaker Athenians could defeat the Atlanteans imparts the fundamental message of *Critias:* It is not just wealth or power that is important in history; even more important is the way a people govern themselves. For Plato, the intellectual achievement of a perfect government and society is far more important—and triumphs over—material wealth or power. As Plato scholar Paul Shorey concludes, "Atlantis itself is wholly his [Plato's] invention, and we can only divine how much of the detail of his description is due to images suggested by his reading, his travels, and traveler's tales" (1933:351).

After Plato

After Plato died, leaving the Critias dialogue and the Atlantis story incomplete, we find no mention of the lost continent for more than 300 years (de Camp 1970:16). As noted previously, Greek historians who followed Plato made no mention of it even to dispute its reality. Atlantis was entirely ignored. We have to rely on later writers like the Greek geographer Strabo, who was born in about 63 B.C., for some insight into what those who followed Plato thought about his account of a lost continent. Strabo claimed, for example, that, in reference to Atlantis, Plato's best-known student Aristotle said, "He who invented it also destroyed it" (as cited in de Camp 1970:17). It seems that many, though not all, who followed Plato viewed Atlantis as an invention, part of a story whose moral is, as A. E. Taylor has said,

> transparently simple. It is that a small and materially poor community [ancient Athens] animated by true patriotism and high moral ideals can be more than a match for a populous and wealthy empire [Atlantis] with immense material resources but wanting in virtue. (1962:50)

It was not until the Age of Exploration and the discovery of the New World that consideration of the veracity of the Atlantis story became popular. For example, as we saw in Chapter 5, Huddleston (1967) points out that in 1552 the Spaniard Lopez de Gomara suggested that American Indians were a remnant population of emigrés from the Lost Continent of Atlantis. Gomara based his interpretation on a linguistic argument concerning a

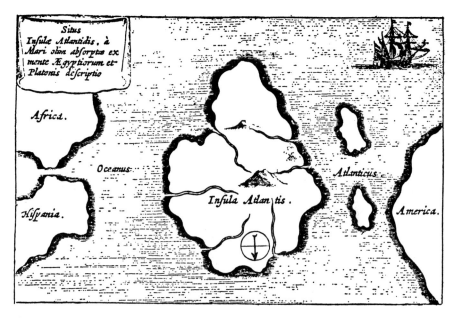

Figure 7.5   This 1644 map shows the location of Atlantis in the Atlantic Ocean. Note that south is to the top of the map. (From *Mundus Subterraneous* by Athanasius Kircher)

single word; in the Aztec language of Nahuatl, the word *atl* means water (Huddleston 1967:25).

Later, in 1572, Pedro Sarmiento de Gamboa maintained that the great civilizations of the New World were partially derived from Atlantis. In the seventeenth century, maps were drawn placing Atlantis in the Atlantic Ocean (Figure 7.5). Some, like Englishman John Josselyn (1674), even identified the New World *as* Atlantis.

A French scholar, Abbé Charles-Étienne Brasseur (called de Bourbourg) "translated" a Maya Indian book, the Troano Codex, in 1864. It was a complete fantasy and contained elements of the Atlantis story, particularly destruction by flood. Using the same delusional alphabet, Augustus Le Plongeon also translated the Codex, coming up with an entirely different story, connecting the Maya to the ancient Egyptians. It was all complete fabrication, but it kept alive the notion that perhaps the civilizations of the Old and New Worlds could somehow be connected and explained by reference to Atlantis.

Ignatius Donnelly: The Minnesota Congressman

Speculation concerning the possible reality of Plato's Atlantis story might have ended in the eighteenth or nineteenth century, as other myths were abandoned when scientific knowledge expanded (see Chapter 5). We have one man to thank, or blame, for this not happening: Ignatius Donnelly.

Donnelly was born in 1831. He studied law, and at only twenty-eight years of age became the lieutenant governor of Minnesota. He later went on to serve several terms in the federal House of Representatives and twice ran for vice president of the United States.

By all accounts, Donnelly was an exceptional individual, a voracious reader who collected an enormous body of information concerning world history, mythology, and geography. Clearly, however, he was less than selective in his studies and seemingly was incapable in his research of discriminating between the meaningful and the meaningless. Donnelly is the father of modern Atlantis studies; and, as writer Daniel Cohen (1969) has aptly put it, Donnelly's book *Atlantis: The Antediluvian World*, published first in 1882, is the "bible" of belief in the legend. (It is interesting to note that in his book *The Great Cryptogram*, Donnelly is also an early source for the claim that Sir Francis Bacon wrote all of Shakespeare's plays.)

Donnelly's *Atlantis: The Antediluvian World* is an amazing piece of inductive scholarship. While obsessive in his collecting of "facts," Donnelly had very little scientific, skeptical sense. His approach was indiscriminate. Essentially, he seems never to have met a claim about Atlantis that he didn't like and accept.

He begins by asserting he will prove that the Atlantis story as told by Plato is not legend but "veritable history" (1882:1); that Atlantis "was the region where man first rose from a state of barbarism to civilization" (p. 1); and that it was the source of civilization in Egypt, South America, Mexico, Europe, and North America, where he specifies the Moundbuilder culture (Figure 7.6).

Donnelly's argument is a confusing morass of disconnected claims and ostensible proofs. He does little more than enumerate supposed evidence; this is diagnostic of the purely inductive method of reasoning he employed. Nowhere does he attempt to test the implications of his hypotheses—what must be true if some of his specific claims also are true. To be sure, we cannot fault Donnelly for failing to apply to the argument data unknown during his lifetime. We can, however, fault his general approach and do what he failed to—test the implications of his claims.

For example, he cites numerous flood legends in various world cultures, all of which he presumes are part of some universal memory of the destruction of Atlantis. His reasoning is that lots of legends referring to a similar event must indicate that the event actually happened. If this were true, we should be able to show that the legends were all independently derived stories that match, at least in terms of their important generalities. This turns out not to be true. Several of his supposed corroborating myths sound quite similar, not because they relate to an actual historical event but because they can be traced to the same source.

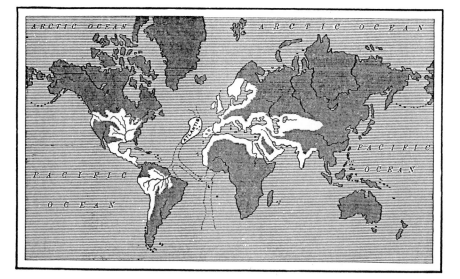

Figure 7.6   Ignatius Donnelly saw all of the world's ancient civilizations as having been derived from that of Atlantis. Here, Donnelly maps (in white) the extent of Atlantis's influence, including the cultures of ancient Egypt, Mesopotamia, Meso-america, and the Moundbuilders of the United States.

For example, the biblical flood story (Donnelly says it is really about the cataclysm that destroyed Atlantis) and the Babylonian flood story are quite similar in their particulars because the ancient Hebrews spent time in Babylonia and picked up the older flood legend from local people. When American Indian tribes related flood stories, they often did so to missionaries who had already instructed them in Genesis. Some tribes already possessing flood stories could easily have incorporated the details of Genesis into their mythology. Applying Occam's razor here, which is the simpler explanation? One requires a lost continent for which there is no evidence; the other simply presumes that Indians would have incorporated new stories told them by missionaries into their own myths.

Although Donnelly spends quite a bit of time arguing that catastrophes like those that presumably befell Atlantis could and did happen, this is not the crux of his argument. Reasoning based on *cultural* comparisons is central to his methodology. He maintains: "If then we prove that, on both sides of the Atlantic, civilizations were found substantially identical, we have demonstrated that they must have descended one from the other, or have radiated from some common source" (1882:135).

This argument for the significant role of *diffusion* in cultural development was common in anthropology in the late nineteenth and early twentieth centuries (Harris 1968). The presumption seems to have been that cultures are basically uninventive and that new ideas are developed in very few or even single places. They then move out or "diffuse" from these source areas. It was fairly common to suggest that Egypt was the source of all civilization, that agriculture, writing, monumental architecture, and the like were all invented only there. These characteristics, it was maintained, diffused from Egypt and were adopted by other groups. As mentioned in Chapter 5, today, in the more extreme varieties of Afrocentrism, Africa is seen as the source for all cultural development throughout the world. Pottery, writing, and even agriculture are all traced to Africa by the most extreme of the Afrocentrists.

Donnelly was a diffusionist. For him the common source of all civilization was Atlantis, rather than Egypt, Sumer, or some other known culture. In his attempt to prove this, he presents a series of artifacts or practices that he finds to be identical among the civilizations of the Old and New Worlds. In these comparisons, Donnelly presents what he believes is the clearest evidence for the existence of Atlantis. His evidence essentially consists of trait list comparisons of the sort discussed in Chapter 5. Let us look at a few of these and do what Donnelly did not—test the implications of his claims.

1. *Egyptian obelisks and Mesoamerican stelae are derived from the same source* (Donnelly 1882:136).

   Donnelly finds that the inscribed obelisks of Egypt are virtually identical to the inscribed stelae of the Maya civilization. He does little more than make this assertion before he is off on his next topic. But it is necessary to examine the claim more closely and to consider the implications. If it were, in fact, the case that Egyptian obelisks and Maya stelae were derived from a common source, we would expect that they possessed similarities both specific and general. Yet, their method of construction is different; they are different in shape, size, and raw materials; and the languages inscribed on them are entirely different (Figure 7.7). They are similar only in that they are upright slabs of inscribed rock. It is not reasonable to claim that they must have been derived from a common source. They are simply too different.

2. *The pyramids of Egypt and the pyramids of Mesoamerica can be traced to the same source* (Donnelly 1882:317–41).

   Here again, if this hypothesis were true, we would expect that these pyramids would share many specific features. The pyramids of the Old and New Worlds, however, do not look the same (Figure 7.8). New World pyramids are all truncated with flat tops, whereas the Egyptian monuments are true geometric pyramids with a pointed apex. New World pyramids have stairs ascending their faces; Egyptian pyramids do not. New World pyramids served as platforms for temples, and many also were burial chambers for great leaders. Egyptian pyramids had no temples on their summits, and all were

Figure 7.7 Donnelly asserted that Egyptian obelisks and Maya stelae were so similar in form and function, they must have originated in the same place: Atlantis. Yet here it can be seen that obelisks, like this one currently residing in the Piazza del Popolo in Rome and dedicated to the pharaoh Ramses II (top left), were quite tall, inscribed, four-sided columns, whereas Maya stelae (bottom) were far different, being flat blocks of inscribed limestone. Beyond this, though both bear written inscriptions, Egyptian hieroglyphs (see top right for a closer image of the inscription on Ramses II's obelisk) and Maya hieroglyphs are entirely different. (*Top:* K. L. Feder; *bottom:* © Gianni Dagli Orti/CORBIS

burial chambers for dead pharaohs or their wives. Construction methods were different; most Egyptian pyramids represent a single construction episode, whereas Mesoamerican pyramids usually represent

Figure 7.8   Egyptian pyramids, like this one from Giza (top), and Mesoamerican pyramids, like this one from Tikal (bottom), are quite different in construction, form, function, and chronology. Donnelly was thoroughly unjustified in claiming a connection—via Atlantis—between pyramid building in the Old and New Worlds. (*Top:* M. H. Feder; *bottom:* Courtesy Chris Wibby)

several building episodes, one on top of another. Finally, if Mesoamerican and Egyptian pyramids are hypothesized to have been derived from the same source (Atlantis or elsewhere), they should date from the same period. But Egyptian pyramids were built between about 5,000 and 4,000 years ago. Those in Mesoamerica are all less than 3,000 years old—most are considerably younger, dating to less than 1,500 years ago. All pyramids date to well after the supposed destruction of Atlantis some 11,000 years ago.

3. *Ancient cultures in the Old and New Worlds possessed the arch* (Donnelly 1882:140).

This statement reflects an imprecise use of language. Cultures in the Old World possessed the true arch with a keystone—the supporting wedge of stone at the top of the arch that holds the rest of the stones in place. New World cultures did not have knowledge of the load-bearing keystone, constructing, instead, the entirely different corbelled arch where stones are set in layers (Figure 7.9).

4. *Cultures in the Old and New Worlds both produced bronze* (Donnelly 1882:140).

This is true, but Donnelly does not assess the implications of the claim that Old and New World metallurgies are derived from a common source. For this to be the case, we would expect the technologies to share many features in common. Bronze is an alloy of copper and some other element. Old World bronze is usually an alloy of copper and tin. In the New World, bronze was generally produced by alloying copper and arsenic (though there is some tin bronze). With such a basic difference in the alloys, it is unlikely that there is a common source for Old and New World metallurgy.

5. *Civilizations in both the Old and New Worlds were dependent on agricultural economies for their subsistence. This indicates that these cultures were derived from a common source* (Donnelly 1882:141).

It is almost certainly the case that cultures we would label "civilized" are reliant on agriculture to produce the food surplus necessary to free the number of people required to build pyramids, produce fine artworks, be full-time soldiers, and so on. But again, for this to support the hypothesis of a single, Atlantean source for Old and New World agriculture, we would expect there to be many commonalities, not the least of which would be the same or similar crops. That this was not the case certainly was known to Donnelly. Even during his time, it was established that cultures in the Old World domesticated one set of plants and animals, whereas people in the New World domesticated an entirely different set.

Figure 7.9   Though Donnelly claims that the arch was present in ancient buildings in both the Old and New Worlds and that this architectural feature had a single source on Atlantis and spread out from there, even the first assertion is not true. Although the true arch with a "keystone" was present in the ancient Old World, as shown in this ancient Israeli building (top), the true arch was unknown in the pre-Columbian New World. A corbelled arch like this one found at the Maya site, Chichén Itzá, in Mexico, was used by Native American architects (bottom). (*Top:* M. H. Feder; *bottom:* K. L. Feder)

We now know that even within the Old World, different ancient societies relied on different mixtures of agricultural crops for their subsistence. In the Middle East, wheat, barley, chick peas, lentils, and vetch were most significant (Henry 1989; Hole, Flannery, and Neely 1969). In the Far East, foxtail millet and rice were major crops (Crawford 1992; Solheim 1972). In Africa, sorghum, pearl and finger millet, and a host of tropical cultigens like the cereals fonio and tef, as well as the banana-like enset, provided subsistence to agricultural people (Harlan 1992; Phillipson 1993). In the Old World, animals like sheep, goats, cattle, and pigs added meat to these various diets.

The list of crops used aboriginally in the New World is just as varied and is entirely different from the lists of Old World domesticates. In Mesoamerica, maize (corn), beans, and squash were predominant with crops like tomato, avocado, chili pepper, amaranth (a grain), and even chocolate rounding out the diet (de Tapia 1992; MacNeish 1967). In South America, maize and beans were important, as were a number of other crops including (most significantly to our modern diets) potato, but so were less well known crops like oca, jícama, and ulluco (Bruhns 1994; Pearsall 1992). In North America, native people produced their own agricultural revolution, domesticating such crops as sunflower, sumpweed, pigweed, goosefoot, and a local variety of squash (Smith 1995). Turkeys were bred by the ancient inhabitants of the American Southwest. In Mesoamerica, turkeys, Muscovy ducks, and dogs were raised for food, and in South America, llamas, alpacas, and guinea pigs were domesticated and provided meat. The llama was also a serviceable pack animal and the alpaca was a source of wool.

It is readily apparent that the agricultural bases of Old and New World cultures were entirely different. This is far more suggestive of separate evolution of their economies than of their having been derived from a common source.

Archaeological investigations have further supported this fact by showing that, in both the Old and New Worlds, agriculture evolved in place over thousands of years. In several world areas after 12,000 years ago—notably in southwestern Asia, southern Europe, eastern Asia, Africa south of the Sahara, Mesoamerica, the North American Midwest and mid-South, and South America—lengthy evolutionary sequences reflect the slow development of agricultural societies. The archaeology in these areas has revealed long periods during which people hunted wild animals and gathered wild plants that later became domesticated staples of the diet.

The physical evidence in these areas in the form of animal bones and carbonized seeds similarly reflects the slow development of domesticated species. Over centuries and millennia, human beings "artificially selected" those members of wild plant communities that produced the biggest, or densest, or quickest-maturing seeds, allowing only those that possessed these advantageous (from a human perspective) characteristics to survive and propagate. Similarly, the ancient people in these regions selected those individuals in an animal species that were the most docile or that produced the thickest wool or the most meat or milk, again allowing only those that possessed these features to survive, breed, and pass these traits down. The continuum through time visible in the archaeological record of increasing seed size, decreasing size of dangerous animal teeth or horns, and so on is clear evidence of the evolutionary process that resulted in fully agricultural people. Agriculture does not simply appear in the archaeological record of the Old and New Worlds. It has deep roots and a lengthy and distinct history in each. Clearly agriculture was not introduced wholesale from Atlantis; rather, it was developed separately in many world regions (Smith 1995).

By failing to consider the implications of his claims of connections between the cultural practices of Old and New World civilizations, Donnelly was easily led astray by their superficial similarities. Ever hopeful and convinced of the legitimacy of his argument, Donnelly ended *Atlantis: The Antediluvian World* by stating:

> We are on the threshold. Scientific investigation is advancing in great strides. Who shall say that one hundred years from now the great museums of the world may not be adorned with gems, statues, arms, and implements from Atlantis, while the libraries of the world shall contain translations of its inscriptions, throwing new light upon all the past history of the human race, and all the great problems which now perplex the thinkers of our day? (p. 480)

It has been more than 100 years since Donnelly wrote these words, and Atlantis the fair and the beautiful is as distant as it was when Plato constructed it out of the stuff of his imagination more than 2,000 years ago.

Atlantis After Donnelly

Donnelly was the most important of the Atlantis scholars, but he was not the last. Although today we may criticize his reasoning, it is far superior to that of many who followed him. Scottish mythologist Lewis Spence (1926), for example, eschewing the "tape-measure school" (p. 2) of archaeology, opts for "inspirational methods" (p. 2). Where Plato placed one imaginary continent in the Atlantic, Spence put two; he added an Antilla to accompany Plato's invention. Spence suggests that not one but a series of cataclysms befell Atlantis. One of the first of these occurred about 25,000 years ago. It resulted in the earliest settlement of Europe by modern humans. Spence identifies so-called Cro-Magnon Man, the oldest fossils of completely modern-looking humans in Europe, as refugees from Atlantis (1926:85). Spence identifies the famous cave paintings and sculptures of ancient Europe (see Figures 12.1 and 12.2 of this book) that date to as many as 32,000 years ago as reflecting the artwork of the displaced Atlanteans.

Among the most extreme Atlantis speculators were the *Theosophists,* members of a strange sect founded by Helena P. Blavatsky (1831–91) in the late nineteenth century. Their philosophy included peculiar beliefs about stages of human evolution—they called them "root races." In one stage we humans were, apparently, astral jellyfish, and in another stage four-armed, egg-laying hermaphrodites. The fourth stage, or race, lived on Atlantis, flew around in airplanes, bombed enemies with explosives, and grew a form of wheat imported from extraterrestrial space aliens. Theosophists also believed that there was a Pacific counterpart to Atlantis called *Mu.* Blavatsky and her followers—not surprisingly, I think—made little effort to support the veracity of such claims.

The web of Atlantis speculation and fantasy continued to be spun in the twentieth century. For example, between 1933 and 1944, the so-called sleeping prophet, Edgar Cayce, gave an enormous number of psychic readings to people, many of whom, according to him, had actually lived on Atlantis in previous lives (Cayce 1968; Noorbergen 1982). In these readings, Cayce's descriptions of Atlantean technological sophistication are stunning. Cayce's Atlanteans had developed things that sound suspiciously like nuclear weapons, lasers, and television. It should go without saying that there is nothing like any of this in Plato. As author Paul Jordan points out (2001:97), Cayce's Atlanteans seem to have possessed, thousands of years ago, many of the technological trappings of the mid-twentieth century, about the period Cayce was giving his readings. They did not, Jordan points out, have personal computers or anything like the Internet. This would seem to fit with the interpretation that Cayce's descriptions were a product of his mid-twentieth-century imagination.

Cayce maintained that at least some Atlanteans who survived the destruction of their homeland migrated to Egypt before 10,000 B.C. and there constructed an underground pyramid in which they housed the historical records of their nation. Cayce said that this "Hall of Records" was located near the Great Sphinx. To date, archaeological research has located no such feature. Cayce also made a number of firm predictions about coming geological catastrophes on the scale of the destruction of Atlantis: Japan will disappear beneath the waters of the Pacific, New York City will similarly disappear as will parts of Georgia and Carolina, and new land will rise up off the east coast of America. When will this all occur? Cayce says this will all begin in 1968 or 1969 (Cayce 1968:157–59). It should go without saying that these predictions were not accurate.

Certainly the most odious appropriation of the Atlantis story was attempted in the 1940s by Heinrich Himmler, head of the Nazi SS. Himmler believed that members of the so-called Aryan race—that is, Germanic people—were actual descendants of an Atlantean master race. Himmler went so far as to order German scientists to look all over the globe for the descendants of the Atlanteans, measuring and gauging people, searching for similarities with Germans that might indicate a common descent from the Atlanteans. Not surprisingly, the master race turned out to be not so masterful, and the Germans fared no better in World War II against the Allies than did Plato's Atlanteans against the Athenians.

Indeed, the legend of Atlantis did not die with Plato, nor did it die with Donnelly. It seems constantly to shift, filling the particular needs of each era for a Golden Age when great warriors, ingenious scientists, astral jellyfish, or egg-laying hermaphrodites walked the earth. Ultimately, in trying to convey a rather simple message, one of the great rational minds of the ancient world produced fodder for the fantasies of some of the less-than-great, nonrational minds of the modern world. If only we could trance-channel Plato, I wonder what he would say. I doubt that he would be pleased.

Current Perspectives: Atlantis

According to Plato's story, Atlantis was defeated in battle by a humble but quite advanced Athenian state some 11,000 years ago. What does modern archaeology tell us about ancient Greece from this period? Is there any physical evidence in the Atlantic Ocean for the civilization of Atlantis? What does modern geology tell us about the possibility of a lost continent in the Atlantic?

Ancient Greece

Simply stated, there was no Athenian state 11,000 years ago. Such a statement is based not on legends and stories but on the material remains of cultures that inhabited Greece. South of Athens, for example, a site has been investigated that dates to around the same time as the claimed Athenian defeat of Atlantis. The site, Franchthi Cave, has been excavated by archaeologist Thomas Jacobsen (1976).

More than 10,000 years ago the inhabitants of the cave were not members of an "advanced" culture. They were simple hunters and gatherers, subsisting on red deer, wild cattle, and pigs. They also collected mollusks, snails, small sea fish, and wild plant foods, including barley and oats. They were a Stone Age people and obtained obsidian—a volcanic glass that can produce extremely sharp tools—from the nearby island of Melos. It is not until 6000 B.C. that there is evidence of the use of domesticated plants and animals by the inhabitants of the cave. Evidence at other sites in Greece conforms to the pattern seen at Franchthi. Cultures that we would label as "civilized" do not appear in Greece for thousands of years. The Greek world of 11,000 years ago is nothing like Plato imagined.

Archaeological Evidence in the Atlantic: The Bimini Wall

Claims have been made that there is archaeological evidence of submerged walls and roads off the coast of Bimini in the Bahamas. Just as Edgar Cayce maintained that the island of Bimini was a remnant of Atlantis, modern Atlantis popularizers have claimed that the features constitute direct empirical evidence for the existence of the lost continent (Berlitz 1984).

Apparently in the 1960s some divers indeed found tabular limestone blocks that they interpreted as being parts of a road and wall as well as supposed columns from a submerged building. They based this interpretation on the unwarranted assumption that patterned features of the landscape cannot be natural. In fact, natural geological forces and processes are capable of producing extraordinarily symmetrical geometric shapes laid out in precise patterns. The surface of the top of the Devils Postpile National Monument in California exhibits a perfect example (Figure 7.10, top). What might appear to be a floor of hexagonal pavers neatly laid out by a flooring contractor turns out to be, instead, the tops of a series of long and entirely natural columns of volcanic rock. Though the geological process is different, the so-called Bimini Wall also is the product of natural erosional processes (Harrison 1971; McKusick and Shinn 1981). What had been interpreted by the divers as the interstices of masonry blocks were nothing more than the natural joints of limestone beachrock that forms rapidly underwater. Such rock erodes as a result of tidal forces, and breaks or joints tend to occur at regular intervals and at right angles to each other. Similarly jointed natural beachrock has been observed off the coast of Australia (Figure 7.10, bottom; Randi 1981).

Analysis of the so-called columns shows that they are simply hardened concrete of a variety manufactured after A.D. 1800 (Harrison 1971:289). The columns likely resulted when barrels of the dry ingredients of the concrete were thrown or washed overboard. The concrete hardened after mixing with water and the wood barrels decayed, leaving what may appear to some to be fragments of building columns.

The Bimini wall, road, and columns simply are not archaeological artifacts derived from Atlantis. They are, instead, readily understood natural and recent cultural features.

The Geology of the Atlantic

There is no evidence in the Atlantic Ocean for a great submerged continent. In fact, our modern understanding of the geological processes of *plate tectonics* rules out this possibility.

Figure 7.10 Devils Postpile National Monument in California (top). The patterned jointing seen at the top of the individual columns of the volcanic rock that formed this feature is entirely natural. Not an artificial construction, these rectangular blocks of stone from the southeastern coast of Tasmania (south of Australia) are the result of natural processes of erosion (bottom). A similar geological feature located off the Bimini coast in the Caribbean has been misidentified by nongeologists as a wall built by inhabitants of Atlantis. (*Top:* K. L. Feder; *bottom:* Courtesy Sonja Gray)

The earth's crust is not a solid shell but consists of a number of geologically separate "plates." The plates move, causing the continents to drift. In fact, we know that the present configuration of the continents was different in the past. More than 200 million years ago, the continents were all part of a single landmass we call *Pangaea*. By 180 million years ago, the continents of the Northern Hemisphere (*Laurasia*) parted company with the southern continents (*Gondwanaland*). The separation of the continents of the Eastern and Western Hemispheres and the formation of the basin of the Atlantic Ocean occurred sometime before 65 million years ago. The Atlantic has been growing ever since, as the European and North American plates have continued to move apart, the result of expansion of the seabed along the intersection of the plates. Movement along the Pacific and North American plates resulted in the destructive earthquake that hit the San Francisco/Oakland area in October 1989.

A ridge of mountains has been building for millions of years at the intersection of the two crustal plates that meet in the Atlantic. Material is coming up out of the plate intersection; landmasses are not being sucked down below the ocean. The geology is clear; there could have been no large land surface that then sank in the area where Plato places Atlantis. Together, modern archaeology and geology provide an unambiguous verdict: There was no Atlantic continent; there was no great civilization called Atlantis.

◈ ◈ ◈ FREQUENTLY ASKED QUESTIONS ◈ ◈ ◈

1. *Could the legend of Atlantis somehow be connected to the mystery of the Bermuda Triangle?*

The belief that there are mysterious and inexplicable disappearances of boats and planes—and all the people aboard—in a triangular area with Bermuda at its apex and Puerto Rico and the southern tip of Florida as the other two vertices is a myth, just like Atlantis. Writer Lawrence Kusche (1995) has investigated most of the major disappearances in the Triangle and found that all of these supposedly mysterious incidents had rational explanations. Bad weather, equipment failure, dangerous cargo, and pilot error account for virtually all of the occurrences. There is no evidence that the area enclosed by the Bermuda Triangle has experienced worse nautical or aviation luck than any other similar-size part of the globe. Atlantis was supposed to be nowhere near the Bermuda Triangle anyway. The only connection between Atlantis and the Bermuda Triangle mystery is the fact that both are myths.

2. *Is there a "lost continent" in the Pacific?*

There is a *legend* of a lost continent in the Pacific Ocean: Mu, or Lemuria. Mu is entirely mythological; the geology of the Pacific basin shows that there was no—and could not have been any—large landmass that sank below the waters in a cataclysmic upheaval.

BEST OF THE WEB

http://www.classicallibrary.org/plato/dialogues/17_timaeus.htm
Complete Timaeus dialogue online.

http://www.classicallibrary.org/plato/dialogues/18_critias.htm
Complete Critias dialogue online.

http://www.activemind.com/Mysterious/Topics/Atlantis/
Though not the most skeptical Web site, there is some valuable summary information here about the lost continent. Vital statistics for the lost continent, an Atlantis history timeline, and some background on Plato are found here.

CRITICAL THINKING EXERCISE

Using the deductive approach outlined in Chapter 2, how would you test this hypothesis? In other words, what archaeological and biological data must you find to conclude that this hypothetical statement is an accurate assertion, that it describes what actually happened in the ancient human past?

- The civilizations of ancient Egypt and Mexico share many general cultural similarities. This is most likely the result of both of these societies having been influenced by the civilization of the Lost Continent of Atlantis.

❖❖❖❖❖❖❖ **8** ❖❖❖❖❖❖❖

Prehistoric E.T.:
The Fantasy of
Ancient Astronauts

It was a remarkable, even audacious, suggestion when first made in an article published in 1963. It began with the proposition that even under the most conservative of scenarios, the universe likely is teeming with life. The argument continued that some of that life has, in all probability, evolved into highly intelligent life forms that have, in turn, produced technologically sophisticated civilizations. A subset of those civilizations, the author of the article maintained, is old enough to have developed technologies that enabled its inhabitants to explore our galaxy. Though the author admitted there is no evidence that these extraterrestrial civilizations are currently visiting Earth, he went on to maintain that there was a strong likelihood that, at some time during the evolution of the human species, they had explored our planet and that "It is not out of the question that artifacts of these visits still exist . . ." (p. 496). The author was making the incredible suggestion that, perhaps, ensconced in the archaeological record there might be archaeological artifacts that were direct evidence of these extraterrestrial visitations: pieces of Mr. Spock's communicator, Luke Skywalker's light sabre, or even E.T.'s bones.

It was amazing, indeed—an extraterrestrial archaeology on Earth. Who would make such a bold suggestion? Was it a UFO afficionado? A believer in flying saucers, extraterrestrial abductions, and alien invasions? In fact, no. This scenario was drawn up by none other than Carl Sagan (1963)—brilliant scientist, prolific writer, noted rationalist, and supreme skeptic (Poundstone 1999; Sagan, 1996).

Gods in Fiery Chariots

Sagan's article, published in a technical journal, *Planetary and Space Science*, read only by astronomers and astrophysicists, made no impression on the nonscientist public and is long forgotten. But five years after its publication, the notion that extraterrestrials had visited Earth at some time in the distant past, leaving evidence of their prehistoric visits in the form of archaeological artifacts, became wildly popular.

The ancient astronaut bubble began inflating in 1968, first in Europe with the publication in German of a book titled *Erinnerungen an die Zukunft* *(Recollections of the Future)* and then in the United States with the publication in English of the same book, now with the question-mark-bearing title *Chariots of the Gods?* The Swiss author of the book, Erich von Däniken, proposed that there was indisputable and copious archaeological support for his claim that extraterrestrial aliens had visited the earth in prehistory and had played a significant role in the development of humanity.

In *Chariots of the Gods?* it seemed that Sagan's remarkable suggestion had been blown up into a full-scale anthropological fairy tale (though von Däniken does not cite Sagan's article in his book).

There seemed to be three implicit hypotheses behind von Däniken's ideas (1970, 1971, 1973, 1975, 1982, 1996, 1997a, 1997b, 1998, 2000, 2002):

1. All over the world there are prehistoric pictorial and three-dimensional representations—drawings on cave walls, pottery, and sculptures—as well as early written accounts that most reasonably can be interpreted as the drawings, sculptures, or literary descriptions by primitive people of actual extraterrestrial visitors to Earth.

2. The biological evolution of the human species cannot be understood unless we assume the involvement of a scientifically advanced extraterrestrial civilization.

3. Some ancient artifacts and inventions are far too advanced and complex to have resulted from simple, prehistoric human intelligence and ingenuity. These advanced artifacts and great inventions must instead be the direct result of purposeful introduction by extraterrestrial aliens.

Let's assess these claims one at a time.

The Inkblot Hypothesis

The first implicit claim concerns the existence of prehistoric drawings or sculptures of aliens from outer space and early writings about their visits. It is an intriguing thought. Hundreds, thousands, even tens of thousands of years ago, spaceships landed on our planet in a burst of fire and smoke. Out came space-suited aliens, perhaps to take soil samples or study plant life (just like E.T. in the Spielberg movie). On completion of their mission, they got back into their spaceships and took off for home.

Secreted in the bushes, behind the rocks, an ancient human sat transfixed, having watched the entire scene unbeknownst to our alien friends. This prehistoric witness to extraterrestrial visitation rushed home to tell others of the marvelous sight of the fiery "chariots" of the "gods" (thus, the English title for von Däniken's book) that had come down from heaven. He or she would tell of how the gods had silver skins (space suits) and bubbleheads (space helmets) and wielded marvelous devices (communicators, lasers, and so forth). Artistic renderings would be made on cave walls and pots. Descriptions would be passed down from generation to generation, especially if the space gods came back again and again, reinforcing the entire idea of gods from the heavens. Descriptions would be written of the wondrous spectacle of the gods coming to Earth. Our ancestors would wait for their return, as perhaps we wait to this very day.

Fascinating? Undoubtedly! Wonderful, if true? Absolutely! Would this forever alter our understanding of our place in the universe? Definitely. Backed up by evidence and proof? Absolutely not.

This first von Däniken scenario can be called the *Inkblot Hypothesis*. I am sure you are familiar with "inkblots" used in psychological testing (called Rorschach tests after their originator). A person looks at a series of inkblots (images made by dripping ink on paper, which is then folded and pressed while the ink is still wet) and then describes what he or she sees. The rationale for such an exercise is quite simple. Since there really are no specific, identifiable images in the random inkblot pictures, the image you recognize comes entirely from your imagination. Therefore, your description of what you see in the inkblots should give a psychologist an idea of what is going on in your mind. It might tell him or her something about your personality, feelings, and so on.

The point is that the picture seen in an inkblot is entirely dependent on the mind of the viewer. The images themselves are not necessarily anything in particular. They are whatever you make them out to be, whatever you want them to be.

Von Däniken's approach is analogous to an inkblot test. Although he is describing actual images, these images belong to a different culture. Without an understanding of the religious, artistic, or historical context of the drawings or images within the culture that produced them, von Däniken's descriptions of the images tell us more about what is going on in his mind than about what was in the minds of the ancient artists.

For example, an image identified by von Däniken as an astronaut with a radio antenna might be more easily explained as a shaman or priest with an antler headdress or simply a mythical creature (Figure 8.1). Von Däniken sees spacemen because he wants to, not because they really are there.

Here is another example. On the desert southern coast of Peru, prehistoric people called the *Nazca* constructed a spectacular complex of shapes (Kosok and Reiche 1949; McIntyre 1975; Reiche 1978). Most are long lines,

Figure 8.1 Applying von Däniken's perspective to artifacts like this antler mask from the Moundbuilder site of Spiro (see Chapter 6) in Oklahoma (right) and this petroglyph (rock carving) in Colorado (below), one might conclude that they both depict space-helmeted aliens, complete with antennae. The application of Occam's razor demands that we first consider more mundane explanations. The mask likely was used in ceremonies where a priest or *shaman* portrayed a deer spirit, and the petroglyph is most likely the depiction of a mythical creature. (*Top:* Photo by David Heald. Courtesy National Museum of the American Indian, Smithsonian Institution; *bottom:* K. L. Feder)

etched into the desert surface, criss-crossing each other at all angles. The most interesting, however, are about three hundred actual drawings, rendered on an enormous scale (some are hundreds of feet across), of animals such as fish, monkeys, birds, and snakes (Figure 8.2).

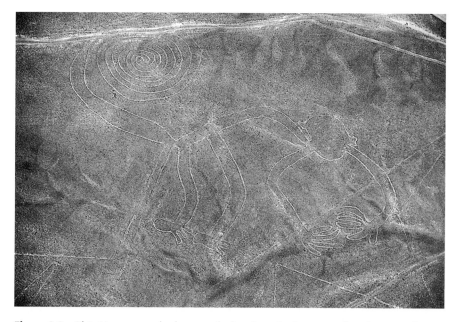

Figure 8.2   This Nazca *geoglyph*, or earth-drawing, depicts a monkey. Large-scale drawings like those at Nazca are known from a number of places in the world. They likely were intended to please the gods and were constructed with the use of scale models. They certainly did not require the intervention of extraterrestrials—and why would aliens from outer space instruct ancient humans to draw giant monkeys, spiders, snakes, and the like in the first place? (© Bates Littlehales/National Geographic Society Image Collection)

The figures and lines were made by clearing away the darker surface rocks, exposing the lighter desert soil beneath. They are remarkable achievements because of their great size, but certainly not beyond the capabilities of prehistoric people. Remember, these drawings were not carved into solid rock with extraterrestrial lasers; they were not paved over with some mysterious substance from another world. They were, in essence, "swept" into existence. Science writer Joe Nickell, an investigator of extreme claims whom we will encounter again when we examine the Shroud of Turin in Chapter 11, has duplicated the technique of making Nazca-like designs. With a crew of six people and several bags of lime (the white powder farmers and backyard landscapers use to cut soil acidity; it's also used to lay out lines on athletic fields), Nickell was able to outline a nearly perfect replica of a 120-meter-long (400-foot) Nazca bird in a single day. The other raw materials were some rope and a few pieces of wood (Nickell 1983).

What does von Däniken have to say about the Nazca markings? Almost yielding to rationality, he admits that "they could have been laid out on their gigantic scale by working from a model and using a system of coordinates" (1970:17), which is precisely how Nickell accomplished it. Not to disappoint us, however, von Däniken prefers the notion that "they could also have been built according to instructions from an aircraft" (p. 17). Relying on the "inkblot approach," he says, "Seen from the air, the clear-cut impression that the 37-mile-long plain of Nazca made on me was that of an airfield" (p. 17).

Please remember Occam's razor here. On the one hand, for the hypothesis that the ancient people of South America built the lines themselves, we need only assume that they were clever. The archaeological record of the area lends support to this. On the other hand, for von Däniken's preferred hypothesis, we have to assume the existence of extraterrestrial, intelligent life (unproven); assume that they visited Earth in the distant past (unproven and not very likely); assume that they needed to build rather strange airfields (pretty hard to swallow) and then, for added amusement, instructed local Indians to construct enormous representations of birds, spiders, monkeys, fish, and snakes. Those assumptions are bizarre, and the choice under Occam's razor is abundantly clear.

We can go on and deduce some implications for our preferred hypothesis: We should find evidence of small-scale models, we should find the art style of the desert drawings repeated in other artifacts found in the area, and we might expect the Nazca markings to be part of a general tradition in western South America of large-scale ground-drawings called "geoglyphs." When we test these predictions, we do find such supporting evidence: For example, Wilson (1988) has reported on a more recently discovered set of large-scale earth drawings in Peru. Archaeological and historical information indicates that the lines were ceremonial roads leading to sacred origin places for families or entire communities. Far from being entirely enigmatic or without any cultural or historical context, they were made and used by some local native groups until fairly recently as a regular part of their religious festivities (Bruhns 1994).

Consider another example of the inkblot approach from a more recent von Däniken book, *The Eyes of the Sphinx* (1996). Deep in one of the subterranean chambers of the Egyptian temple dedicated to Hathor, goddess of music, love, and dance, located in Dendera, is a relief sculpture depicting two strange objects (Figure 8.3). In each, a slightly sinuous snake emanates from a flower and is enclosed in an elongate object attached to the flower. Altogether, the relief looks like two giant eggplants with enclosed snakes facing off against each other. A strange image, to be sure, but what does it mean?

To answer this riddle, von Däniken considers the challenge of providing enough light for Egyptian artisans to have produced the wall reliefs deep in the temple and postulates an extraordinary light source. Egyptologists assume, rather unimaginatively, that these workers used oil lamps and torches to light their way. From Egyptian sources we know that pieces of linen were soaked in oil or animal fat and then twisted into wicks, which, when lit, provided a bright light. Salt was applied to these wicks to reduce

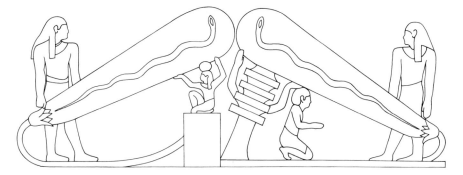

Figure 8.3   Image from a wall deep in the temple of Hathor at Dendera, Egypt. These objects can be interpreted as representations of ancient lightbulbs only by applying von Däniken's inkblot approach. Absolutely no physical evidence supports the claim that ancient Egyptians produced electrically powered lightbulbs.

smoke and soot. Lamps that burned oil or animal fat also were used; again, salt was added to the mix to cut down on smoke. Beyond this, the ancient Egyptians made candles to light their way in the darkness of subterranean rooms and pyramid tombs. These candles were manufactured to burn a predetermined amount of time. Pyramid and tomb workers knew their shift was complete when the candle began to burn down to its base. Finally, there also is clear physical evidence that the Egyptians constructed clever arrays of polished metal mirrors to bring reflected light down inside deep corridors.

Not one to accept such simple explanations, von Däniken complains that absolutely no lamp soot was found on the walls or ceilings and that the light reflected by mirrors would have been too weak. Occam's razor forces a scientist to suggest the rather mundane possibility that salt was effective in reducing the amount of soot produced and that workers cleaned the soot that was produced from the chamber's surfaces when they were done. Also, experimental testing of mirror replicas shows that they work quite well, and these produced no soot at all.

Von Däniken, however, is not bound by Occam's razor, experimental testing, or any other rule of logic or method of science. His suggestion? The snake encased in an eggplant motif is a depiction of an electric lightbulb! The flower is its socket, the snake the filament, and the eggplant its glass enclosure.

Electrical lights more than 4,000 years ago in ancient Egypt? That is an extraordinary hypothesis. However, like any hypothesis, extraordinary or otherwise, it can be—in fact, must be—tested through the scientific method. Electrically powered lightbulbs in ancient Egypt or anywhere else must have been invented, manufactured, and used within a broader context. What are the deductive implications of the hypothesized existence of such lighting devices in ancient Egypt? What should we find in archaeological excavations to support this interpretation? Even modern lightbulbs burn out or break, so we would expect to find in archaeological excavations in Egypt dead but, perhaps, intact bulbs, fragments of broken glass bulbs, metal sockets, pieces of the necessarily durable filaments, and stretches of the electric cable needed to bring electricity to the bulbs from its source. This last requirement leads us to the most important and most problematic deduction—we also must find evidence for the production of electric power by ancient Egyptians for these lightbulbs.

Little of this seems to occur to von Däniken, although using a thoroughly discredited interpretation of a 2,000-year-old artifact from Iraq he does claim that electricity was produced in the ancient world (Eggert 1996).

Is there any hard, archaeological evidence of the kind just listed that ancient Egyptians produced electricity and manufactured lightbulbs? The answer is no. In his analysis of the images on the wall in Hathor's Temple in Dendera, von Däniken does not even ask whether such evidence exists. He certainly doesn't prove that Egyptians had electric lighting but merely that his inkblot speculations have become even more wildly imaginative in recent years.

Because prehistoric pictorial depictions and even early written descriptions are sometimes indistinct or vague and—perhaps more important—because they are part of a different culture and have a context not immediately apparent to those who do not explore further, you can see or read anything you want into them, just as you can with inkblots.

Try this experiment. Using any of von Däniken's books, look at the photographs, but do not read the captions where von Däniken tells you what the item pictured must be (spaceship, extraterrestrial alien, or whatever). Now figure out what *you* think it looks like. You probably will not agree with what von Däniken says. For example, Figure 8.4 is a photograph of a sarcophagus lid from the Maya site of Palenque. Does it evoke in your mind any extraterrestrial images? Probably not. Yet, for von Däniken, the coffin lid is a clear representation of a space-suited alien piloting a spacecraft (1970:100–101).

The inkblot principle is at work again. When you are unfamiliar with the culture, you can make just about anything you want out of these images, but you are most decidedly not practicing science. Von Däniken does not understand the cultural context of the Palenque artifact. He does not recognize the Maya symbols in the carving of the Ceiba Tree and the Earth Monster. What are mysterious devices for von Däniken are simply common artistic representations of Maya jewelry, including ear and nose plugs. Again, not understanding the context of the artifact, von Däniken apparently does not think it important or even relevant that the person depicted on the sarcophagus lid was a dead Maya king represented in a position between life, the Ceiba Tree above him, and death, the Earth Monster below (Robertson 1974; Sabloff 1989).

As for the individual depicted on the lid and buried in the tomb, he is anything but some mysterious, out-of-place enigma whose origins can be

Figure 8.4   Using what we here call the inkblot approach, von Däniken interprets the image on the sarcophagus lid from the Temple of Inscriptions at the Maya site of Palenque as depicting an astronaut with antennae and oxygen mask, peering through a telescope and manipulating the controls of a rocket. Maya archaeologists prefer to interpret this scene within the context of Maya cosmogony—a king poised between life and death in his journey to the afterlife. (© 1976 Merle Greene Robertson/Pre-Columbian Art Research Institute)

Figure 8.5   The magnificent Temple of the Inscriptions, the final resting place of Pacal, ruler of Palenque. Pacal's tomb with its famous sarcophagus lid was found at the bottom of a staircase leading from the top to a point beneath the pyramid. (© Barry Kass/Anthro-Photo)

traced to outer space. In fact, we know a great deal about him; the information was provided by the Maya themselves (Schele and Freidel 1990). He was Pacal, ruler of the ancient city of Palenque from A.D. 615 until his death and placement in the tomb at the base of an impressive pyramid in A.D. 683 (Figure 8.5).

Fortunately for students of Maya history, Pacal had a detailed king list inscribed in the temple atop his pyramid tomb, and an additional listing placed on his sarcophagus. We know the names of his ancestors and the names of his descendants. We know what he accomplished during his reign as ruler of Palenque. And we have his physical remains in the coffin. Although he was once the all-powerful ruler of a splendid society, nothing is left of Pacal save his very human bones.

Pacal's story needs no tired speculation about extraterrestrial visitors to Earth. Pacal was a dynamic and vibrant historical personage, a real human being who lived, ruled a great city, and died more than 1,300 years ago, and whose story has been revealed by archaeology and history.

One needs to be familiar with Maya cosmogony, writing, and history to recognize the context of the Palenque stone within Maya culture. Von Däniken, however, seems wholly ignorant of Maya beliefs and therefore can come up with such an unsupported speculation concerning the image on the coffin lid.

Once you become familiar with von Däniken's own particular brand of illogical thinking, you can probably guess what he says renderings in ancient art actually represent. Doing so might be fun, but it is in fact just a game of trying to guess the meandering of his mind. That is not archaeology; that is psychotherapy. The Inkblot Hypothesis merely shows how suggestible people are ("Hey, doesn't that cave painting look like a spaceman?" "Gee, now that you mention it, I guess it does."). Inkblots, however, or strange drawings on cave walls, weird creatures on pots, odd sculptures, or mystical visions written down in ancient books can never prove the visitations of ancient astronauts, as much as von Däniken might like them to.

The Amorous Astronaut Hypothesis

Von Däniken's second hypothesis suggests that extraterrestrial aliens played an active and important role in the actual biological development of our species. There has been some controversy on this particular point. An episode of the public television series *Nova* ("The Case of the Ancient Astronauts" 1978) focused on von Däniken's ideas. During an interview that was part of the episode, he maintained that he never really made such a claim. Let's see.

In *Chariots of the Gods?* von Däniken proposed the following scenario. A group of extremely advanced, interstellar space travelers lands on Earth, for the first time perhaps millions of years ago. They find a primitive race of creatures, very apelike, with small brains, but with a lot of potential. Then, von Däniken claims, "A few specially selected women would be fertilized by the astronauts. Thus a new race would arise that skipped a stage in natural evolution" (1970:11).

If the previous claim can be called the *Inkblot Hypothesis*, I can call this one the *Amorous Astronaut Hypothesis*.

According to this hypothesis, extraterrestrial aliens have streaked at near light speed to get to Earth. The speed of light is fast (186,000 miles per second), but the universe is large, and our space*men* (for von Däniken, the extraterrestrial visitors always seem to be males) have been cooped up in their spaceship, perhaps in suspended animation, for at least four years. The star nearest to our sun is about four light-years away, and so—even traveling at the speed of light—four years is the absolute minimum. Our extraterrestrial friends land, are wakened from their deep sleep, and exit their spaceship to explore the new frontiers of an unexplored planet in an alien solar system. And what do you think they do? They look for females to "fertilize." The human species is not the product of evolution, but of interstellar miscegenation.

Even von Däniken's most ardent supporters must admit that he has some very strange ideas concerning the ability of different species to mate and produce offspring. For example, the mummy of ancient Egyptian priestess Makare, daughter of Pharaoh Pingdjem (c. 1075 B.C.), was placed in her tomb with a small mummified bundle. It had been assumed that the bundle was her child until it was x-rayed in 1972. The small mummy turned out to be that of a baboon. This was not so surprising. Egyptians commonly mummified animals, and most Egyptologists assumed that the baboon baby was Makare's pet or, perhaps, a symbolic child entombed with Makare as a surrogate for a human baby. Von Däniken (1996:63) suggests, instead, that Makare may have actually given birth to what he implies was a human/baboon hybrid. Von Däniken recognizes that humans and baboons cannot mate and produce offspring, so he proposes that extraterrestrial aliens conducted genetic experiments, hybridizing a wide variety of earth species. Makare's baby baboon is just one example. The many mythological creatures seen all over the ancient world—Pegasus, the Sphinx, griffins—are not mythological at all for von Däniken but are accurate depictions of these hybrids! Why did ancient astronauts conduct these seemingly bizarre genetic experiments? According to von Däniken (1996), it was solely for entertainment: "The extraterrestrials had found a way to keep themselves busy. They merrily invented one monster after another . . . and they observed with much amusement the reactions of the flabbergasted humans" (p. 58). The extraterrestrials appear to have had a rather twisted sense of humor, if you ask me.

As Carl Sagan so astutely pointed out in "The Case of the Ancient Astronauts," the chances of any two different species from even our own planet being able to mate and produce offspring are quite remote. Horses and donkeys are one of the very rare exceptions to this. Even here, when these two very closely related species mate, the offspring are sterile. The possibility of two species that evolved on different planets in two different solar systems even having the appropriately matching physical equipment for mating, much less having matching DNA necessary to produce offspring, is so incredibly unlikely that it is beyond calculation. Yet these are precisely the implications that must be deduced from von Däniken's hypothesis. As Sagan pointed out, a human ancestor would likely have been more successful mating with a petunia than with a creature from outer space; at least the human ancestor and the petunia both evolved here on Earth. Extraterrestrial astronauts, amorous or not, simply could not have mated with our ancestors to produce us.

The "Our Ancestors, the Dummies" Hypothesis

This leads us to the final von Däniken hypothesis, the notion that the archaeological record is replete with evidence of highly advanced artifacts beyond the capability of ancient humans. This can be called the *Our Ancestors, the Dummies Hypothesis* (after Omohundro 1976). Von Däniken is claiming that our human ancestors were too dumb to have, all by themselves, using their own creative abilities, intelligence, and labor, produced the admittedly spectacular works of engineering, architecture, mathematics, astronomy, botany, and zoology evidenced in the archaeological record. Mind you, von Däniken is not saying that archaeologists are hiding the physical evidence of ancient flying saucer parts or laser torpedoes found at prehistoric Indian villages or ancient Chinese temples. That would be an easy claim to check scientifically; such artifacts either exist or they do not. No, instead, von Däniken simply points to artifacts such as pyramids or temples, statues, or carvings. He makes reference to prehistoric accomplishments such as the domestication of plants and animals, the development of metallurgy, and especially astronomical abilities—all things for which archaeological evidence is abundant. Von Däniken simply cannot understand how, and therefore doesn't believe that, prehistoric people could have managed all this without some sort of outside help. This help, for von Däniken, comes in the form of aliens from outer space.

Extraterrestrial Calendars?

For example, in his third book, *Gold of the Gods* (1973), von Däniken makes reference to the hypothesis of science writer Alexander Marshack (1972). Marshack maintains that some inscribed bone, antler, and ivory tools from Paleolithic Europe, dating from 30,000 to 10,000 years ago, represent the oldest calendars in the world. He hypothesizes that these first calendars were based on the cycle of changes in the phases of the moon. Amazed as always, von Däniken asks:

> Why did Stone Age men bother about astronomical representations? It is usually claimed that they had their hands full just to procure sufficient nourishment on endless hunts. Who instructed them in this work? Did someone advise them how to make these observations which were far above their "level"? Were they making notes for an expected visit from the cosmos? (1973:203–4)

Von Däniken has lots of questions, but precious few answers. Let's look at one of these artifacts and see if it indeed looks like something only an extraterrestrial alien might have devised. Probably the most famous of the artifacts in question is the Abri Blanchard antler plaque found in southern France and dated to about 30,000 years ago (Figure 8.6). This ancient piece of ivory has close to seventy impressions carved into it along a sinuous arc. If you begin in the center of the antler and work your way along the arc, a rough pattern emerges. Each design element appears to be a fraction of a circle. As you follow the arc of impressions, the marks seem to grow in terms of the proportion of a circle represented and then, once a whole circle is produced, to diminish. The similarity between the sequence of impressions and the phases of the moon is apparent. It is Marshack's well-reasoned, though still-debated, hypothesis that this is precisely what these ancient people were trying to convey.

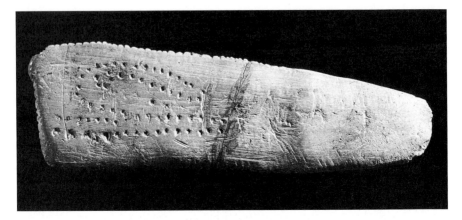

Figure 8.6   Von Däniken sees evidence for knowledge far beyond the capabilities of ancient people in 30,000-year-old bone implements of the Upper Paleolithic. But perhaps the best known of these, the antler plaque at Abri Blanchard in France, though a compelling argument for the great intelligence of our prehistoric ancestors, is really just the simple depiction of lunar phases. The pattern of lunar waxing and waning was likely well known to these people. (© Alexander Marshack)

No one can deny that it is fascinating to think that 30,000 years ago prehistoric people may have looked at the mysterious light in the night sky and wondered about it. Based on this and similar artifacts from the period 30,000 to 10,000 years ago, it appears quite possible that these ancient people recognized the cyclical nature of the lunar phases. But as interesting as it might be, does the antler plaque look like the calendar of an extraterrestrial alien?

Certainly it took intelligence to watch the nightly change in the moon's phases and conclude that it was not random, that it was patterned and predictable. But remember, these were people who, of necessity, were attuned to the natural world around them. Their very survival depended on their observations of nature, and nature is filled with predictable cycles. Day followed by night followed by day is an unending, constant pattern that is easily recognized. The fact that summer follows spring, is replaced by fall and then winter, which leads inevitably back to spring, was a cycle that had to be known, followed, and relied on by our prehistoric ancestors. Long before 30,000 years ago their brains had become as big as ours, and they were just as intelligent as we are. The fact that they may have recognized the phases of the moon as another cycle in nature and that they recorded these changes to be used, perhaps, as a kind of calendar is a wonderful achievement, but not really so unexpected.

Extraterrestrial Aliens in the Pacific?

Easter Island is one of the most remote places on Earth, 3,200 kilometers (2,000 miles) west of the coast of South America and 2,000 kilometers (1,250

Figure 8.7   The remarkable Moai of Easter Island number in the hundreds and reflect the great intelligence, technical skill, and organizational abilities of so-called primitive people. The photograph on the right shows a Moai that was not finished, still lying in place in its quarry. No laser burns have been found in the quarries, only the stone tools the Easter Islanders used to carve out the statues from the surrounding rock. (Courtesy Sonja Gray)

miles) southeast of the nearest inhabited island. The island was first settled sometime after A.D. 300 by Polynesian explorers from the west.

On the island, 883 large stone statues called Moai have been located, and there may be as many as fifty others not yet recorded (Van Tilburg 1987, 1994, 1995). Carved from a relatively soft volcanic rock called *tuff,* they are impressive indeed. The largest is over 20 meters (60 feet) high and weighs about 55,000 kilograms (60 tons). The "average" statue is over 14½ feet high and weighs 14 tons. Even the smaller statues would have taken consider-able labor to quarry, sculpt, transport, and erect (Figure 8.7).

Not surprisingly, von Däniken does not believe that the Easter Is-landers could have accomplished these tasks by themselves. In *Gods from Outer Space* (1971), he suggests that the statues (or at least some of them) were erected by extraterrestrial aliens marooned on Easter Island. What was their motive for erecting the statues? According to von Däniken, it was sim-ple boredom (p. 118).

Intensive archaeological investigations have been carried out on Easter Island since 1955 (see Van Tilburg 1994 for a detailed discussion of this work). Quarries with partially completed statues have been discovered—along with the simple stone picks, hammers, and chisels used to quarry the rock and carve the images. Roads have been identified on which the statues were transported. Statues accidentally broken during transport have been located along the roads. Experiments have been carried out in techniques of quarrying, carving, transport, and erection (Heyerdahl 1958). Six men roughed out a 5-meter-long statue from the stone quarry in just a few days. A group of several islanders erected an ancient Moai in a short time period, using levers and ropes. Statues have been moved along the old roads using wooden sledges and rope.

More recently, researcher Jo Anne Van Tilburg (1995) has applied computer technology to approach the question of how the statues were moved. In her analysis, the Moai could have been moved either face down or up on a sledge consisting of a large V of two wooden beams about 18 feet long and 10 inches in diameter, connected by a series of wooden cross-braces. According to the computer model, it would have been possible to transport the stone several miles in this way. Then, using ramps, levers, and wedges, the statue could have been slowly tilted upright onto its ceremonial platform, called an *ahu*.

The Moai are certainly impressive and show what human ingenuity and labor can accomplish. But there should be no mystery about that. The mystery is why von Däniken did not realize that simple fact.

And how were Samoa, Hawaii, Fiji, Easter, and all of the other inhabited islands of the Pacific originally populated? In attempting to answer this question, science has focused on archaeological evidence on the islands themselves, analysis of the watercraft used in the Pacific, and study of the superb traditional navigational skills of the native people (Shutler and Shutler 1975; Terrell 1986). Computer models have been developed that show the likelihood of the success of ancient explorers of the Pacific given certain parameters of wind, current, and direction taken (Irwin 1993). From these sources of data, we think we have a pretty good handle on the original human exploration of and migration into the Pacific.

But our answers do not satisfy von Däniken. He finds hypotheses of human intelligence, endurance, and curiosity too outlandish. What is his explanation for how these islands were settled, how the first human inhabitants got there? He says, "I am convinced with a probability bordering on certainty that the earliest Polynesians could fly" (1973:133). There is very little that can be said in the face of such absurdity.

A Real Mystery

But the absurdity doesn't end there. Not content merely to write preposterous books, von Däniken has recently devised another way to spread the gospel of the ancient astronauts. *It's a theme park!* Disney proclaims Mickey's Magic Kingdom, "The Happiest Place on Earth," and I see no reason to dispute that. I would like to here proclaim von Däniken's Mystery Park the *silliest* place on earth, and I dare anyone to dispute that (Powell 2004)! On the associated Web site (http://www.mysterypark.ch/), von Däniken is quoted as saying "People should learn the meaning of astonishment," and I will admit that he has accomplished his primary mission with this archaeologist. I am deeply astonished and, I must say, impressed. Von Däniken was able to convince a number of major corporations, including Coca-Cola, Sony, Fujitsu, and Swatch, among others, to bankroll (to the tune of $62 million) his Mystery Park, a sort of world's fair of silliness, dedicated to the ancient astronaut hypothesis. For those of you planning your summer vacations, Mystery Park is located in Interlaken, Switzerland, a major European resort town.

The park itself consists of seven major attractions, each one constructed to represent what is, to von Däniken, a great mystery of the ancient world. For example, one pavilion is built in the shape of an Egyptian pyramid (see Chapter 9), another mimics the Maya Pyramid of the Feathered Serpent in Chichén Itzá (see Chapter 12). Each pavilion's name represents its theme in von Däniken's universe of absurdity: Maya, Orient (focusing on Egypt), MegaStones (Stonehenge and the like), Contact, Challenge, Nazca (South America), and Vimana (ancient India). Each pavilion's exhibit consists of a movie, dioramas, and artifacts. The seven main pavilions form a ring around a central Earth base for the ancient astronauts; von Däniken himself maintains an office and library there. Oh, and don't forget the Mystery Park mascot, "Mysty" (get it?), a bluish, sort-of-extraterrestrial critter who shows up on the Web site and some of the Mystery Park merchandise (though, to be frank, they are missing a great marketing opportunity by not offering any Mysty plush toys for their kiddie visitors).

The park is filled with bizarre juxtapositions and incredible anachronisms. For example, among the exhibits of ancient Mesoamerican cities and Maya stelae within the Maya pavilion, there also is a diorama of a mariachi band (Powell 2004). What, exactly, is von Däniken trying to tell us (or sell us) here? Mariachis of the Gods?

As deliciously bizarre as this all is, writer Eric Powell, who attended the grand opening of the park for *Archaeology* magazine, points to a far more serious, depressingly familiar von Däniken theme that permeates Mystery Park. It's "our ancestors, the dummies" all over again. Powell notes that the foundation of amazement that underlies Mystery Park doesn't honor the great capabilities of our ancient human ancestors, but, instead, reflects an assumption of their intellectual incompetence. The great engineering and intellectual achievements of the ancient world were made possible not by human ingenuity and brain power, but by extraterrestrial tutoring. Powell's (2004:66) description of the Mayaland movie reveals the core of the von Däniken mind-set: Ancient astronauts land on Earth, abduct a band of children from the primitive native people, take them to their home planet, instruct them in the ways of pyramid building and calendar making, and then return them to the Mesoamerican jungle where they share their new-found knowledge, pulling their people from a life of savagery up to the pinnacle of intellectual, civilized life. It would be funny, if it were not fundamentally an egregious libel against the human species.

The Archaeology of Mars

If at this point you are wondering "what on earth" motivates von Däniken and his supporters, you might want to rephrase that question less restrictively. It is not just "on Earth" that they see archaeological evidence for the presence of extraterrestrial visitors. They also see such evidence on Mars.

In the summer of 1976 the National Aeronautic and Space Administration (NASA) had two unmanned Viking spacecraft in orbit around the red planet Mars. There has been unremitting speculation about the possibility of life on Mars at least since 1877 when astronomer Giovanni Schiaparelli observed rectilinear markings on the Martian surface, calling them *canali* (Italian for channels). American astronomer Percival Lowell became the chief proponent of the claim that Schiaparelli's *canali* were broad bands of vegetation bordering irrigation canals dug by an ancient Martian civilization.

None of the NASA engineers expected anything quite so dramatic as canals, but they were hopeful that some evidence of life on Mars—of a microscopic, not monumental variety—would be found. Viking *Orbiter 1* dispatched a lander to the surface of the planet on July 20. The lander possessed a robotic arm that was able to collect Martian soil samples. Chemical analyses were conducted on board, searching specifically for the presence of organic molecules as well as chemical traces of life, the diagnostic waste products left behind by bacteria and other single-celled organisms. If there were life on Mars, and if it were at all chemically similar to life on Earth, these soil tests would have produced unambiguous results.

The letdown was obvious when the NASA scientists announced that the soil tests showed no definitive evidence of life had been found. No organisms or organic molecules were detected. Although some intriguing chemical processes were noted, these were almost certainly the product of ordinary, nonbiological chemical reactions. Our planetary neighbor bore no evidence of life. Our Earth remained the only planet known to us in the universe that had produced living things.

But not everyone was convinced. As the result of a single photographic exposure taken by the orbiter camera from an altitude of about 1,000 miles above the Martian landscape in an area called Cydonia, a few individuals became convinced that, although there might not be any microscopic or chemical evidence for life on Mars now, there is mind-boggling archaeological evidence of monumental proportions for life there in the past (DiPietro

Figure 8.8   The so-called Mars Face (upper right) is almost certainly a natural product of Martian geology—a natural feature of the landscape that happens to look like a human face under the right lighting conditions—and not a monument built by an ancient Martian civilization. (Courtesy NASA)

and Molenaar 1982). On exposure 35A72, in a grainy pastiche of shadow and light, is the image at the heart of this extraterrestrial archaeological controversy (Figure 8.8). It is called, simply, "the Mars Face," and it is enormous, roughly a mile long from the top of its head to its chin.

Undeniably, it does look like a human face, or at least a part of one. But it also seems to be explainable as an interesting and coincidental play of light and shadows, the kind of image trickery that causes us to see faces, animals, or even household appliances in rock exposures, cave formations, and clouds. These images do not really exist except for our mind's tendency to coax familiar pictures out of natural features. I have been in countless underground caverns where the tour guides have pointed out features like "the Capitol Dome," "Two Eggs, Sunnyside Up," and the "New York City Skyline." A rock face in Wisconsin presents a lifelike, entirely natural profile of the Indian leader Black Hawk. None of these often astonishingly real-looking images were conjured up by some ancient geological intelligence. They are a product of our own imaginations, another version of the inkblot effect.

Most geologists who viewed the original Mars Face photograph ascribed it to something like the inkblot effect. Sure, it sort of looked like a face, but so what (Figure 8.9, left)? The resolution of the image—each tiny pixel on the photograph corresponds to a whopping 43 meters (141 feet) on the ground—is far too low to accurately determine what the feature actually looks like (Malin 1995).

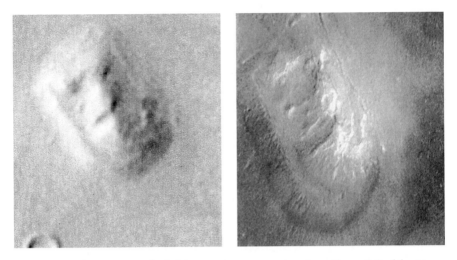

Figure 8.9   The image on the left is an enlargement taken from Figure 8.8 of the Mars face seen in the original 1976 Cydonia photograph taken by the Viking spacecraft. The image on the right was taken of the same feature in April 1998 with the camera on board the Mars Global Surveyor. It is amazing what a better angle and a higher-resolution camera can accomplish. Even a casual glance at the new image of the so-called Mars Face shows nothing that is particularly facelike. Clearly, the "face" is nothing more than a natural feature of the Martian landscape. (Courtesy NASA)

At least partially as a result of public interest about what the photograph depicted, additional images of the Cydonia region were taken on April 1998 by another interplanetary voyager, the Mars Global Surveyor (MGS) satellite. The 1998 photographs taken by the much more sophisticated camera on board were of a resolution ten times higher than that of the original Viking images; each pixel represents only 4.3 meters (14.1 feet) of the Martian surface. This much sharper photograph showed that the feature looked nothing at all like a face, but more like an eroded mesa, entirely natural in appearance (Figure 8.9, right). Then, on April 8, 2001, the MGS photographed the region yet again. The resulting photograph has an even higher resolution than the April 1998 image, with each pixel now representing only about 1.56 meters on the ground (about 5 feet, the maximum resolution possible with this camera; Figure 8.10). According to NASA (2001), an object the size of a small building would be discernible in the photograph; genuine cultural features, like a giant, mile-long sculpted face, would be easily recognized. But no such feature is present in the new photograph; the Mars Face has disappeared completely. All that is left is an eroded mesa with an irregular depression where the "eye" was located and a valley where people saw a mouth. NASA scientist James Garvin (2001) has even determined the easiest trail to the top of the mesa, should astronauts ever make it to Mars

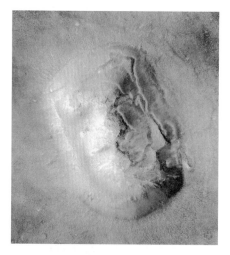

Figure 8.10   The Mars Global Surveyor photographed the Mars Face again in April 2001, producing the highest possible resolution with the camera on board. An object the size of a small building would be discernible in the photograph; genuine cultural features, like a giant, mile-long sculpted face, would be easily recognized. But no such feature is present in the new photograph; the Mars Face has disappeared completely. (Courtesy NASA)

and have a desire to stroll around the geological feature once called the Mars Face.

There are other interesting features on the Martian landscape. One looks like the "happy face" symbol (Gardner 1985), but it is simply a meteorite impact crater about 215 kilometers (134 miles) across with fortuitously positioned smaller features located inside it: a smaller crater and a cluster of eminences for eyes and a curved cliff for the smiling mouth (Figure 8.11, top left).

In June 1999, the Mars orbiter camera photographed a geological feature on Mars that specialists identified as a natural pit formed by collapse within a straight-walled trough. Though it was a bit late for the holiday, the 2.3-kilometer- (1.4-mile-) wide feature looked remarkably like a Valentine's Day heart (Figure 8.11, top right).

Finally—my personal favorite—another photo of the Martian surface shows a lava flow that bears a remarkable resemblance to Kermit the Frog (Figure 8.11, bottom)! No one has claimed, at least not yet, that this is evidence of an extraterrestrial origin for the Muppets.

To scientists, the Face, the "happy face," the Valentine heart, and Kermit the Frog are rare, but by no means unique, images of landscape features on a planetary body; the images look artificial, but they are entirely natural.

This has not prevented some from going far beyond just the supposed human face. Writer Richard Hoagland (1987) has scanned a series of the Viking photographs and views the Face as just the tip of an extraordinary extraterrestrial iceberg. Hoagland sees the Face as just one feature in the ruin of a vast and ancient Martian city filled with huge pyramids, fortresses, roads, and other artificial features.

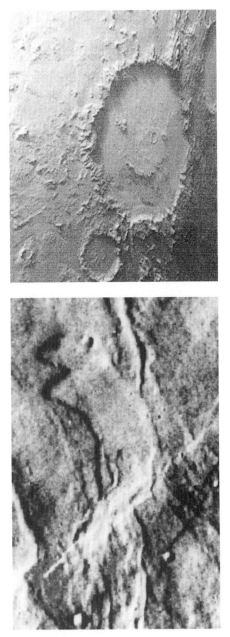

Figure 8.11   Natural features that appear to be patterned or even those that look as if they were made by some intelligent force are actually quite common on Earth as well as on Mars. Three images from Mars show this rather humorously: a meteorite impact crater 8 kilometers (5 miles) wide NASA refers to as "the largest known Happy Face in the solar system" (top left; the smile and eyes were formed by natural fractures); an erosional feature that is a perfect match for a Valentine's Day heart (top right); and a remarkable Martian lava flow that bears an uncanny resemblance to the Muppet character Kermit the Frog (bottom; Kermit's eye is a meteorite impact crater). (Courtesy of Jet Propulsion Laboratory, NASA)

Hoagland's claims, if borne out, would represent the most spectacular archaeological *and* astronomical discovery of all time: an advanced and sophisticated extraterrestrial civilization dating to, Hoagland estimates, more than 500,000 years ago!

Since the 1976 Viking touchdown on Mars, the United States has landed three more spacecraft on the surface of that planet: the tiny Sojourner robot vehicle in 1997 and the two far more sophisticated rovers Spirit and Opportunity, which have been exploring the Martian surface since their separate bouncy landings in January 2004.

It is truly remarkable when you consider that human beings have designed spacecraft and launched them from Earth and that those craft have endured the harsh environment of space, rendezvoused with another planet in our solar system, landed safely, unpacked themselves, and scooted around the surface taking incredible photos, drilling holes in rocks, and performing chemical analyses on the resulting rock dust. I admit, it would have been spectacular had a living creature walked up to one of the Mars Rover cameras and waved or flashed the peace sign, but, alas, that did not happen. Furthermore, none of the down-to-Mars missions have encountered anything whatsoever that could be interpreted—or even naively misinterpreted—as a cultural feature, the product of an intelligence past or present. Go to the home page of the Mars Rovers (http://marsrovers.jpl.nasa.gov/home/index.html) and look at the photographs (press images, raw images, panoramic images, and 3-D images). They are amazing, remarkable, and astonishing, reflecting in exquisite resolution the geology of our sister planet, the fourth rock from the sun; but there is no visual evidence, at least on the surface, of past life or ancient intelligence, no foundations, roads, trash heaps—and yes, no canals. Mars appears to be a dead planet and not a terribly fruitful place to conduct archaeology.

Current Perspectives: The von Däniken Phenomenon

Von Däniken repeatedly underestimates the intelligence and abilities of our ancestors and then proposes an extraordinary hypothesis to explain the past. That is clear. However, what is not so clear is the second reason I have suggested for von Däniken's inability to accept prehistoric peoples' ability to produce the great achievements seen in the archaeological record (the first was simple ignorance). I have already mentioned it briefly—European ethnocentrism.

What I mean by this becomes clear when you read *Chariots of the Gods?* It is curious that von Däniken is ever ready to provide examples as proof of his third hypothesis (Our Ancestors, the Dummies) from archaeological sites in Africa, Asia, North America, and South America; but he is curiously and atypically silent when it comes to Europe. My feeling about this was so strong on reading *Chariots of the Gods?* that I actually went through the book and tallied the specific references to amazing accomplishments of prehistoric people that von Däniken believes were too advanced, too sophisticated, or too remarkable for mere humans to have produced. I paid careful attention to where in the world (which continent) these specific examples were from. The following chart resulted (Feder 1980a):

Continent of the Example	Number of Examples	Percentage
Africa	16	31
Asia	12	23
Europe	2	4
North America	11	22
South America	10	20
Total	51	100

The great majority of von Däniken's examples here are from places other than Europe. It appears that he is utterly astounded by the archaeological records of ancient Africa, Asia, and North and South America. He is so astounded, in fact, that he thinks that only through the assistance of men from outer space could those black, brown, yellow, and red peoples have produced the prehistoric works that archaeologists find on these continents.

It is curious that von Däniken never wonders who helped the ancient Minoans build the great temple at Knossos or the Greeks the Parthenon, or which spacemen instructed the Romans in constructing the Colosseum. Why not? These monuments are every bit as impressive as those that von Däniken does mention. The temple at Knossos is more than 3,500 years old, the Parthenon is almost 2,500 years old, and the Colosseum is close to 2,000. Even in the case of Stonehenge in England, von Däniken is strangely quiet and only briefly mentions it in *Chariots of the Gods?*—though he finally does get around to Stonehenge in a more recent book, *Pathways to the Gods*.

This may be a key point in von Däniken's success. *Chariots of the Gods?* is listed in the *Publishers Weekly* inventory of all-time best-sellers, having sold over seven million copies—that is more than *The Diary of a Young Girl* (Anne Frank), *Catch-22*, or *All Quiet on the Western Front*, for example (So Big 1989). It is such an incredibly silly book that we must ask why it has done so well.

Many people are aware of phenomena like the pyramids of Egypt, the ruins of Mexico, and the ancient Chinese civilization. Some, however, may wonder how the prehistoric ancestors of contemporary people whom they consider to be backward and even intellectually inferior accomplished such spectacular things in the past. After all, today Egypt is a developing nation, the Indians of Mexico are poor and illiterate, and the Chinese are just beginning to catch up with the technology of the modern world. How could the ancestors of such people have been advanced enough to have developed pyramids, writing, agriculture, mathematics, and astronomy all by themselves?

Along comes von Däniken with an easy answer. Those people did not produce those achievements on their own. Some sort of outside help, an extraterrestrial "peace corps," was responsible. If I am correct in this suggestion, it really is a pity; human prehistory is a spectacular story in its own right. All peoples have ancient pasts to be proud of, and there is no place for, nor any need to fall back on, the fantasy of ancient astronauts.

◈ ◈ ◈ FREQUENTLY ASKED QUESTIONS ◈ ◈ ◈

1. Carl Sagan predates von Däniken in publishing the suggestion that there might be archaeological artifacts that bear witness to the visitation and exploration of our planet by extraterrestrial astronauts sometime in the distant past. Does that make Sagan a pseudoscientist?

Of course not. Merely suggesting a potentially fruitful line of investigation—even if other scientists are skeptical—doesn't make somebody a pseudoscientist. Sagan recognized, of course, the kind of evidence needed to uphold his hypothesis and clearly concluded, in the years following his suggestion, that the requisite evidence was not found. Read any of Sagan's more recent works, especially *The Demon-Haunted World* (1996). One of Sagan's great wishes was that, during his lifetime, there would be proof that we are not alone, that our Earth is not the only repository of intelligent life forms in the universe. Disappointed he may have been that this did not happen, but deluded he was not. There is no archaeological evidence for ancient extraterrestrial visits to Earth; Sagan knew and accepted this fact.

Remarkably, a form of Sagan's idea has been resurrected more than forty years after he first proposed it. Astronomers Christopher Rose and Gregory Wright (2004) have calculated that, in certain scenarios, it would be more efficient for an extraterrestrial civilization hoping to communicate with other societies in the galaxy to send a message in the form of a physical object (they call it "inscribed matter") than as a radio communication. They suggest that such a civilization may have long ago sent such objects hurtling off toward developing solar systems where they have been designed to land—on an asteroid or planet—to await their discovery, recognition, and decoding. In a discussion of this fascinating possibility, science writer Woodruff T. Sullivan III (2004) even refers to those who might someday search for these messages as "astroarchaeologists."

In a sense, our own civilization has done this already. The message plates affixed onto our two Pioneer spacecraft (launched in 1972 and 1973) and the more detailed recorded disks attached to the two Voyager craft (launched in 1977) are exactly this: artifacts representing a message announcing "We are here." It should come as no surprise that the messages attached to these spacecraft were designed by Carl Sagan.

2. Is there any evidence for the use of electricity by ancient people?

No, but the claim has been made that a primitive 2,000-year-old electrical battery was found in Iraq. No one knows precisely what this object was used for, but it certainly was not producing any electrical power when it was found in 1936. The so-called Baghdad Battery is a ceramic vase with a closed bottom, a cylindrical tube of copper inserted through the neck, and a rod of iron inside the copper tube. The metals were held in place with a plug of asphalt. A number of modern experiments, often with inaccurate models of this object, have produced mild and short-lived electrical currents when an appropriate electrolyte (liquid that conducts electricity) is poured into the vessel. However, this will happen whenever two different metals are immersed in an electrolyte, and there is no evidence that any such liquid was ever placed into the original jar. Just because it can be used to produce a weak electrical current using modern knowledge does not prove that it ever was used in that way in the past. It is a rather odd artifact, but it in no way proves the use of electricity by ancient people (Eggert 1996).

BEST OF THE WEB

EASTER ISLAND

http://www.netaxs.com/~trance/rapanui.html

Especially useful for an extensive series of links to Easter Island Web sites as well as breaking news about archaeological work on the island and potential threats to the Moai as a result of recent plans to develop parts of the island.

http://www.pbs.org/wgbh/nova/easter/

PBS companion Web page to the *Nova* "Secrets of Easter Island" documentary.

MARS FACE

http://barsoom.MSSS.com/education/facepage/face.html

Web page dating to 1995 presenting a discussion of the Mars Face based on the 1976 Viking *Orbiter 1* photograph.

http://mars.jpl.nasa.gov/mgs/msss/camera/images/4_6_face_release/

1998 NASA Web page revisiting the Mars Face phenomenon on the basis of new, high-resolution photographs taken by the Mars Orbiter camera.

http://www.msss.com/mars_images/moc/extended_may2001/face/index.html

Web page presenting the May 2001 NASA press release announcing the most recent (April 2001) image of the Mars Face. The download can take a long time with a telephone modem, but the full-sized image of the mesa (no, there's no face there at all) is more than worth the wait.

http://science.nasa.gov/headlines/y2001/ast24may_1.htm?list540155

NASA Web page presenting a brief history of the Mars Face phenomenon, including the April 2001 photographs taken by the Mars Global Surveyor, the highest-resolution photos yet taken of the feature. Scroll down to the end of the site for James Garvin's trail map to the top of the mesa.

CRITICAL THINKING EXERCISE

Using the deductive approach outlined in Chapter 2, how would you test this hypothesis? In other words, what archaeological and biological data must you find to conclude that this hypothetical statement is an accurate assertion, that it describes what actually happened in the ancient human past?

• The prehistoric record contains evidence of enormous and unexpected leaps forward in science and technology—agriculture, pyramid building, writing, and so on. These leaps are evidence of the introduction of such innovations by extraterrestrial aliens.

Mysterious Egypt

Hours before I wrote these words, I stood in the literal shadow of one of the iconic monuments of the ancient world: the Colosseum in Rome. The Colosseum is a building of spectacular beauty, breathtaking majesty, and remarkable functionality, all of which are all the more mind-boggling when one considers that it was built nearly 2,000 years ago (Figure 9.1).

The emperor Vespasian oversaw much of the Colosseum's construction, carried out between A.D. 72 and A.D. 80. The walls of the ancient amphitheatre rise a dizzying 48.5 meters (almost 160 feet), the equivalent of a modern nearly fifteen-story building. The amphitheatre's three tiers of seating could accommodate an audience of upward of 50,000 people, about the capacity of many modern major league baseball stadiums. Like many of its modern counterparts, the Colosseum had a protective partial roof (of cloth) shielding at least some of those in attendance from the sun, something anyone who has endured August in Rome will appreciate. The Colosseum served as the primary Roman venue for gladiatorial matches, staged animal hunts, and even mock naval battles for which the several-acre playing surface and basement were flooded.

When Did People Get That Smart?

It is perfectly reasonable for modern people to marvel at the end products of ancient technologies, structures like the Colosseum, monuments like Stonehenge (see Chapter 12), and memorials like the Egyptian pyramids (this chapter). When did ancient people get that smart? How could they possibly have developed the engineering, architectural, mathematical, and even the practical skills necessary to build things that continue to astound us thousands of years after they were built? Who were the geniuses who first solved

Figure 9.1 Completed in A.D. 80, the three tiers of seating in the justifiably famous tourist destination, the Colosseum in Rome, could hold nearly 50,000 spectators. Monumental structures like the Colosseum beg the question: "How did ancient people get so smart?" (K. L. Feder)

the many complex challenges involved in building these remarkable structures, and how did they do it? Scientists and nonscientists alike have long pondered these apparent mysteries.

Grafton Elliot Smith, whom we met in Chapter 4, was one of those thinkers. Smith's intellectual legacy will, perhaps, forever be tainted by his association with the Piltdown Man hoax. You will remember that, though almost certainly not materially involved in perpetrating the fraud, he became one of the false fossil's strongest proponents.

At least as important as his association with Piltdown, however, was Smith's role as one of the chief architects of the diffusionist perspective that characterized the British school of anthropology in the early years of the twentieth century. An underlying theme of this school of thought, put most simply, was that human beings were, in general, dull, unimaginative, and uninventive. From this, Smith deduced that most ancient human groups were, in large measure, culturally static and, if left on their own, would have changed very little through time.

Of course, Smith understood that humanity had, nevertheless, undergone vast cultural changes since human beings first burst onto the scene. He explained these changes as the result of exceptions—or perhaps a single exception—to this characterization of human groups as culturally inert. Smith and the other diffusionists maintained that there had been only one or, perhaps, a very few "genius" cultures in antiquity. The cultural precocity of such a group or groups was ascribed by some diffusionists to their superior genetic endowment and by others to their location in a privileged, exceptionally generous natural habitat.

For Smith, the single genius culture, the source of all human cultural development, was ancient Egypt. In his view, before 6,000 years ago, people all over the world were living in a natural, primitive, and more or less fixed state. At about this time, a group of humans settled along the Nile and, as the result of an incredibly rich subsistence base made possible by the fertile valley soil, were liberated from the time-consuming requirements of subsistence production that so dominated the human condition nearly everywhere else. Using that free time to their advantage, Smith believed, the ancient Egyptians single-handedly produced most, if not all, of the key inventions that made civilized life possible: agriculture, animal domestication, ceramic technology, writing, metallurgy, monumental construction, and urban settlements.

In the diffusionist view, these cultural inventions spread like ripples on a still pond, emanating from Egypt and moving across the face of the earth. For Smith, the Egyptians alone had independently evolved a complex civilization. In his view, a number of other societies—including some located across the Atlantic Ocean in the New World—only later developed complex civilizations, inspired by contact with Egypt and by adoption of advanced technologies that had "diffused" from that ancient source. The proverb may be correct when it states that "all roads lead *to* Rome," but in Smith's view, all intellectual roads in the ancient world led *from* the Nile valley.

Though Egypt was viewed as a cultural font by many diffusionists, not all embraced that land as the ultimate source of civilization. Some diffusionists supported the notion that, instead of Egypt, a civilization now lost in the clichéd "dim mists of antiquity" had been the source of all human progress. We have already encountered this view in Chapter 7 in the form of Ignatius Donnelly's vision of the Lost Continent of Atlantis as articulated in his book *Atlantis: The Antediluvian World* (1882). You will recall that Donnelly believed Egypt was not the source but, instead, was only one of the many recipients of the wisdom and technological prowess of a singularly advanced society, that of the Atlanteans.

We have seen in the previous chapter how, instead of pointing a finger toward Egypt or out to a spot in the middle of the Atlantic, Erich von Däniken points his finger up to the heavens, electing to find the ultimate source for human civilization and technological achievement in the cosmos. Ultimately, von Däniken's writings amount to a space-age application of the diffusionist view. If intrinsically dull, uninventive, and unimaginative human beings had, in deep time, exhibited remarkable technologies, marvelous architectural skills, and mathematical sophistication, these abilities must have come from somewhere else. No human source underpins von Däniken's diffusionist argument—not remarkably advanced Egyptians and not denizens of a lost continent. For von Däniken, instead, human societies had progressed technologically through the good works of what amounts to an extraterrestrial Peace Corps.

This brings us to the writings of Graham Hancock (1995). Here again, we encounter a writer who is understandably and justifiably amazed at the remarkable technological accomplishments of the ancient world: celestially aligned monumental structures, meticulous stone masonry, precise calendrical systems. And clearly, Hancock recognizes in his writings that ancient people *could* have developed sophisticated calendars, built magnificent monuments, and so on, independent of outside help. Unfortunately, he largely rejects such an explanation, preferring one that requires the existence of a super-civilization far older than any of those recognized by archaeologists and historians—one that was, in his view, the ultimate source of human achievement.

Consider the following. In his book *Fingerprints of the Gods,* Hancock refers to the great sophistication of the calendar used by the ancient Maya of Mesoamerica (see Chapter 12) and maintains that we should be greatly skeptical of their ability to have developed it by themselves. He proposes that, in fact, they didn't develop it, but "inherited it" from a much older, super-sophisticated, lost civilization. This ancient civilization is the functional equivalent of Donnelly's Atlantis: a technologically sophisticated society that existed thousands of years before those recognized by archaeologists and historians and from whose shores diffused the advanced technologies found in the much more recent societies of ancient Egypt, Mesopotamia, and the Maya.

To support his thesis that a lost civilization must have been responsible, Hancock must show that the Mesoamerican calendar is inexplicably, even shockingly, out of character with the rest of Mesoamerican culture; otherwise, no hypothesis of an outside source for the calendar is warranted. Here, Hancock has painted himself into a methodological corner and has no choice but to characterize the noncalendrical achievements of the Maya, recognizably an impressive and awe-inspiring ancient civilization, as "generally unremarkable" (Hancock 1995:158) and to portray their way of life as being only "semi-civilized" (Hancock 1995:161). He must maintain this nonsense because an objective analysis of the remarkable achievements of the Maya in architecture, agriculture, artwork, and mathematics indicates that their calendar is not out of character at all, but was just one marvelous achievement in a long list. The sophistication of the Maya calendar is not so surprising at all when one fairly assesses the sophistication of the rest of their culture. Any hypothesis of an external source for the calendar for no given reason other than the fact that it is sophisticated presupposes that which it is attempting to test.

Ancient Egypt

Are the achievements of the ancient world the product of independent invention, or diffusion from a source unrecognized by traditional science? A good historical test case can be found in the story of Egyptian civilization.

Most people are at least passingly familiar with the Egypt of the great pharaohs: the awe-inspiring pyramids, the mysterious Sphinx (Figure 9.2), the fabulous treasures of Tutankhamun, and so on. How did such a remarkable civilization develop, culminating in the construction of the Great Pyramid at Giza more than 4,500 years ago?

The mystery is amplified and exploited by von Däniken when he claims, "If we meekly accept the neat package of knowledge that Egyptologists serve up to us, ancient Egypt appears suddenly, and without transition with a fantastic, ready-made civilization" (1970:74). Echoing this sentiment, Hancock (1995:135) asserts that "The archaeological evidence suggested that rather than developing slowly and painfully, as is normal with human societies, the civilization of Ancient Egypt [like that of the Olmecs] emerged *all at once and fully formed.* . . . Technological skills that should have taken hundreds or even thousands of years to evolve were brought into use almost overnight—and with no apparent antecedents whatever" (emphasis in the original).

In a sense, von Däniken and Hancock are correct; if we hypothesize that Egypt or any other civilization was transplanted full-blown from somewhere else—whether that somewhere else is simply a neighboring society, Atlantis in whatever guise, or even aliens from outer space—we should expect that it appeared quickly, fully formed, and without evolutionary an-

Figure 9.2 The Sphinx, at Giza, emblematic of ancient Egypt, is the product of human ingenuity and hard work. It was not built or inspired by ancient astronauts. (M. H. Feder)

tecedents. An important point needs to be brought up, however. Any claim of the sudden appearance, fully formed, of Egyptian civilization is, at best, entirely misleading and, at worst, absolutely incorrect.

Egyptologists have been digging up the past of Egypt for nearly 200 years now and can construct a fairly detailed scenario for the evolution of this civilization. This scenario represents precisely the long and painful process that von Däniken and Hancock deny (Brewer and Teeter 1999; Clayton 1994; Kemp 1991; Shaw 2000). In fact, the roots of this "sudden" civilization can be traced back more than 12,000 years, to when nomadic hunters and gatherers began to settle down along the Nile (Butzer 1976). Excavations at sites like Wadi Kubbaniya show that at this time people were living in small villages along the Nile and harvesting the wild wheat, barley, lentils, chick peas, and dates that abounded there (Wendorf , Schild, and Close 1982). Their villages are littered with the grinding stones, mortars, and pestles they used to make flour. They supplemented their diet with wild game and fish, so they weren't entirely settled or "civilized," but they were on the path toward civilization. By beginning to rely on the crops of wild wheat and barley, they were laying down the roots of an agricultural revolution that was to form the subsistence base of Egypt of the pharaohs.

We have archaeological evidence for small villages along the Nile where the people were living no longer on wild but on domesticated plants and animals fully 8,000 years ago. Cultivating crops and raising animals provided a more secure, more dependable, and much more productive food base for these people. The archaeological evidence indicates clearly that in response to this, both the number of villages and the population of individual villages grew (Lamberg-Karlovsky and Sabloff 1995). After 7,000 years ago, the shift to agriculture at sites like Merimde, Tasa, and Badari was complete. The inhabitants grew wheat and barley and raised cattle, goats, pigs, and sheep. Eventually these villages began competing with each other for good farmland along the Nile.

Seen from satellite photographs, the Nile is a thin ribbon of green and blue flowing through a huge yellow desert. Clearly, the Nile is the "giver of life" to the plants, animals, and people of Egypt. As the circumscribed, precious, fertile land along the Nile became filled up between 8,000 and 6,000 years ago, competition for this rich land intensified.

Some Nile villages were quite successful and grew at the expense of others. One example is *Hierakonpolis,* a town that grew from an area of a few acres in size to over one hundred, and from a probable population of a few hundred to several thousand (Hoffman 1979, 1983). A local pottery industry also developed here.

Pottery manufactured in the kilns that archaeologists have discovered at Hierakonpolis can be found at sites all along the Nile. As the demand for the pottery of this successful town grew, so did the wealth of the people who owned the pottery kilns. It is here at Hierakonpolis that we first see large tombs where perhaps these wealthy pottery barons were laid to rest. Their tombs were sometimes carved out of bedrock and covered with mounds or small, crude pyramids of earth. Finely crafted goods were placed in the tombs of these men, perhaps to accompany them to the afterlife.

However, just as the small towns had previously competed for land, Hierakonpolis and other, larger villages began to compete for space and wealth. Again, based on the archaeological evidence for this period, we can conclude that power struggles leading to warfare were common after 5,200 years ago. One hundred years later, a ruler of Hierakonpolis, whose name has been passed down to us through later Egyptian writings as *Narmer*, was able through military conquest to subdue and then unify the competing villages along the Nile. Now with the wealth of not just one town but of every town along the Nile to call on, Narmer and his successors lived and were buried in increasingly sumptuous style.

Eventually, the old practice of burying a leader in a bedrock tomb with a small earthen pyramid on top was deemed insufficient for pharaohs. However, the pyramid did not appear "suddenly," as von Däniken would have us believe. The first generations of Egyptian pharaohs were buried in the royal cemetery complex located in the desert at a place call Abydos. Their tombs, called *mastabas,* are single-story square-block structures made of mud brick (O'Connor 2003). As the mastabas over the tombs got larger through time, pharaohs began to build stepped mastabas, with one block on top of another, culminating in a stepped pyramid for the pharaoh Djoser at Saqqara (Figure 9.3). Djoser ruled Egypt from 2668 to 2649 B.C. in what is referred to as the Third Dynasty of ancient Egypt.

Based on records kept by the ancient Egyptians themselves in their hieroglyphic language, we even know the name of the designer of Djoser's stepped pyramid: Imhotep. Imhotep was no mysterious intruder from Atlantis or outer space; he is a well-known historical figure in Egypt. Along with being a master architect, Imhotep became well known as a physician, priest, poet, and advisor to the pharaoh. Egyptologists even have a pretty good idea who his parents were and have a short list of Egyptian towns in which he most likely was born. It should also be pointed out that in the statues found depicting Imhotep, most show him as an ordinary Egyptian man dressed in plain attire; none portray him as a mysterious foreigner and, most assuredly, none show him as an alien from outer space (Figure 9.4).

The stepped pyramid Imhotep designed for Djoser was built of clay and stone, rising through six steps to a height of roughly 60 meters (197 feet— and, yes, that's taller than the Colosseum). Its base covers a rectangular footprint of more than 13,200 square meters (more than 142,000 square feet, or about 3.25 acres), and it is part of a mortuary complex of multiple structures built for the pharaoh.

A number of pharaohs ruled for short periods after Djoser's death. Then, in 2613 B.C., the pharaoh Sneferu ascended to the throne. He initiated

Figure 9.3   Von Däniken's claims about the "sudden" appearance of the Egyptian pyramid are simply incorrect. The Egyptian pyramid was not introduced by aliens, extraterrestrial or otherwise, but evolved through several phases in Egypt itself. One of these phases is represented by the stepped pyramid of Saqqara, which had itself evolved from the single-tiered *mastabas*. (M. H. Feder)

Figure 9.4   This ancient Egyptian depiction of the brilliant architect, physician, priest, and poet Imhotep shows the designer of the pharaoh Djoser's pyramid, not as an Atlantean intruder or an extraterrestrial from another star system, but as a typical Egyptian of his time. (© Erich Lessing/Art Resource, NY)

construction of his funerary monument to the south of Saqqara at a place called Meidum (Perez-Accino 2003b). Sneferu's monument was begun as another stepped pyramid, this time with seven distinct platforms. During construction, however, Sneferu decided to alter the form of the pyramid, first adding an eighth platform and then deciding to change the exterior to the shape we are more familiar with today, with flat, triangular faces leading to a common apex at the top, which was intended to rise to a height of 92 meters (302 feet). The work was only partially completed when the project was abandoned as a result of the king's decision to move his funerary monument to Dashur, north of Meidum and closer to Saqqara. The Meidum pyramid ultimately was stripped of much of its polished exterior casing stone for recycling in other construction projects. Today it looks like an abandoned and then cannibalized construction site—which is what it is (Figure 9.5, top). As Egyptologist Mark Lehner (1997) characterizes it, though never completed, Meidum marks the transition between stepped and true pyramids in Egypt.

At Dashur, Sneferu commanded the construction of a true pyramid. The faces of individual platforms of Egyptian stepped pyramids were sloped at between 72 and 78 degrees. This angle would have been far too steep for an entire true pyramid. Construction of Sneferu's pyramid at Dashur was commenced with its surfaces sloped at about 54.5 degrees. Even at this gentler angle, however, severe instability of the walls of the pyramid was recognized partway through construction. At that point, the pyramid architects and engineers changed the angle of each of the four pyramid faces to an even more gentle 43.5 degrees. This gentler angle allowed for the completion of Sneferu's pyramid, but the change is readily apparent in the appearance of the monument; it is today called the Bent Pyramid as a result (Figure 9.5, bottom).

Finally, by about 2589 B.C., Sneferu's builders got it right, constructing an entire, true pyramid (Figure 9.6). They began construction of this monument at a 43-degree angle, and maintained that slope throughout. The Red, or North, Pyramid that resulted fits our conception of what an Egyptian pyramid should look like, with four flat, triangular faces joined at an apex, here rising to a stunning 105 meters (345 feet).

These pyramids are all remarkable achievements, wonderful examples of the architectural, mathematical, engineering, and organizational skills of ancient Egyptians. But, understand, the pyramids were not an abrupt or overnight accomplishment. The timeline of Egyptian pyramid building shows that it was only through years of trial and error, attempt and mistake, challenge and solution, that the architects and engineers of ancient Egypt were able to perfect their craft.

Consider the evolution of the pyramids as a function of their height, beginning with the oldest of the monuments. Djoser's stepped pyramid, finished in 2649 B.C., is about 60 meters (197 feet) high. The next pyramid in

Figure 9.5   Errors and false starts in construction like those exhibited in the Collapsed Pyramid at Meidum (top) and shoddy construction and work-arounds like those seen in the Bent Pyramid at Dashur (bottom) reflect the very human process that characterizes the evolution of Egyptian pyramid-building technology. Problems like these contradict any assertion that pyramid building arrived fully formed in Egypt from an outside superhuman source like ancient astronauts. (M. H. Feder)

Figure 9.6   The Red Pyramid was constructed after the Collapsed and Bent Pyramids. Mistakes made in those projects and the lessons learned led to the more standard appearance—and greater durability—of the Red Pyramid. (M. H. Feder)

the chronology, Sneferu's first attempt—the Collapsed Pyramid—was designed to stand 92 meters (302 feet) tall, a 53 percent jump in height compared to Djoser's pyramid. As we have seen, it was a failure, too big a jump, perhaps, over the step pyramid, and never completed. Sneferu's next try, the Bent Pyramid, was another less-than-sterling success. It had a planned height of 128.5 meters (421.6 feet). This would have been a 40 percent rise in height over the Collapsed Pyramid. Its actual finished height was considerably less because, as noted, its architects were forced to decrease the angle of its rise midway through construction. The Bent Pyramid, nevertheless, is a still impressive 105 meters (344.5 feet) high, a jump of about 14 percent over the Collapsed Pyramid. Sneferu's final construction, the Red Pyramid, is about the same height as the Bent Pyramid, exhibiting no growth at all in pyramid size.

Perfection of the craft of pyramid building occurred subsequently in the burial monument of the pharaoh Khufu, whose pyramid can be found north of Dashur, at Giza (Figure 9.7). Finished in 2566 B.C., Khufu's pyramid is one of the Giza triad of monuments (the other two are the pyramids of Khufu's son Khafre and grandson Menkaure). Khufu's is the largest, a stupendous 146.6 meters (481 feet) high, a 40 percent jump in height compared to the previous successful monument, his father Sneferu's Red Pyramid. Khufu's was the tallest pyramid ever built in ancient Egypt and, rather

Figure 9.7 The three spectacular pyramids at Giza represent the pinnacle of Egyptian pyramid-building technology. They clearly reflect the endpoint along a continuum of technological refinement with the process of trial and error evident in the structures that preceded them. (M. H. Feder)

remarkably, was the tallest human-made structure in the world until the construction of the Washington Monument and the Eiffel Tower in the 1880s (even so, it cannot be seen from the moon with the naked eye, as one urban legend would have you believe).

The pattern reflected in the timeline of pyramid construction in ancient Egypt is clearly evolutionary, showing the step-by-step development of the architectural form by Egyptians over the course of more than eight decades, from Djoser's stepped pyramid in 2649 B.C. to Khufu's masterpiece completed in 2566 B.C. The progression shown in the archaeological and historical records is unlike anything that would be expected if pyramid building had been developed somewhere else and then introduced into Egypt in its perfected form (Figure 9.8). The evidence is unequivocal; pyramid construction was developed over time in Egypt by Egyptians. It was not introduced by anyone from Atlantis, outer space, or anywhere else.

Unfortunately, everybody in ancient Egypt knew that the pyramids contained great wealth, and most were broken into soon after the pharaoh was laid to rest. Eventually the Egyptians gave up pyramid building completely and buried pharaohs underground, where their tombs might be better hidden and protected.

Remember, in science we propose a hypothesis to explain something, we deduce those things that must also be true if our hypothesis is true, and

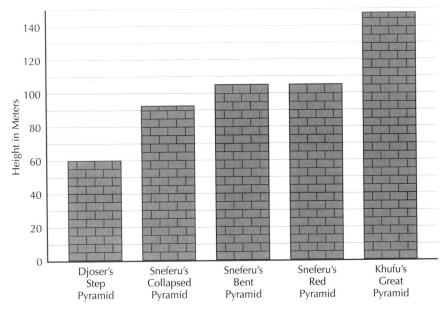

Figure 9.8   This histogram shows growth in the height of pyramids built by the ancient Egyptians from the construction of Djoser's Step Pyramid through Khufu's Great Pyramid more than eighty years later. The pattern shown here of slowly increasing height is a clear indication of the evolutionary development of pyramid-building technology within Egypt and contradicts any notion that pyramid building was introduced by a more advanced intelligence, whether terrestrial or extraterrestrial in origin.

then we do further research to determine if our deduced implications can be verified. Only then can we say that our hypothesis is upheld. Here, our hypothesis is that the ancient Egyptians built the pyramids using their own skill, intelligence, ingenuity, and labor. We can deduce that if this were true, then we should find archaeological evidence for the slow development of these skills and abilities through time.

This is precisely what we have found. Egyptian civilization evolved not "suddenly" but after some 12,000 years of development marked by

- The adoption of agriculture
- Increasing village size
- Intervillage competition
- Village differentiation
- Concentration of wealth
- Increase in tomb size
- Consolidation under a single leader or pharaoh
- Obvious trials and errors in the development of the pyramids as monuments to their dead kings

The Egyptians kept accurate historical records of their kings. The so-called Royal Canon of Turin contains the names of about three hundred pharaohs (Kemp 1991:23). It is a detailed and virtually complete listing of Egyptian rulers for the first part of their history, providing the duration of their reigns, sometimes to the exact numbers of years, months, and even days. This list traces Egyptian kingship for 958 years, all the way back to Narmer. Not surprisingly, there's not a single Atlantean or extraterrestrial in the bunch; it is, instead, a clearly connected family lineage of descent from father to son, pharaoh to pharaoh.

How Did They Build the Pyramids?

Any building project, ancient or modern, no matter how large, difficult, impressive, or even seemingly impossible, ultimately involves the coordinated execution of a large number of smaller jobs that are individually achievable. The pyramids, including the largest, are, after all, just very impressive construction projects which, when broken down into their component tasks, certainly were within the capabilities of a large workforce laboring for long stretches of time.

Broken down most simply, pyramid construction involved several steps, including quarrying the rock, mostly limestone, that made up most of the structure; preparing the work site by producing a flat surface on which to construct the pyramid; moving the quarried stone to the work site; shaping the building materials—in the case of Khufu's pyramid, more than 2.3 million blocks of limestone—into their desired final form; moving the building materials into place—both horizontally and vertically—to produce the final form of the pyramid; and, finally, carving rooms, chambers, passageways, and tunnels from the artificial mountain of pyramid blocks.

Though we cannot travel back through time and actually watch as a pyramid project progresses, the Egyptians themselves left a substantial body of evidence indicating how the component steps in the undertaking were carried out. For example, the limestone quarry from which much of the material used in the construction of the Great Pyramid was extracted has been located and studied by Egyptologists. Just like abandoned quarries of a more recent vintage—for example, the nineteenth-century sandstone quarries of Connecticut that produced building materials for all of those "brownstone" buildings in New York City—the imprint of the quarriers in ancient Egyptian quarries is obvious in the form of channels, grooves, trenches, and other tool marks left in the face of the exposed rock (Figure 9.9).

Today, the Khufu quarry is a huge gash about 30 meters (almost 100 feet) deep from which, it has been estimated, the Egyptians extracted more than 2.75 million cubic meters (more than 97 million cubic feet) of limestone (Jackson and Stamp 2003:50). By no small coincidence, the volume of the Great Pyramid is about 2.6 million cubic meters (91 million cubic feet). The location of the pyramid project was selected, almost certainly, with the location

Figure 9.9   Photograph taken from inside the Giza limestone quarry from which most of the blocks making up the Great Pyramid were extracted. In the background can be seen the straight, flat wall of the quarry face. Seen in the foreground, the pattern of squares separated by a gridwork of channels reflects the manner of stone block extraction employed by the Egyptians. Using simple copper tools, channels were cut at right angles to isolate cubes of limestone that constituted much of the raw material of pyramid construction. (Courtesy Frank Roy)

of the source of building materials in mind; the Great Pyramid is positioned just 300 meters (1,000 feet) away from the quarry. Copper chisels used in quarrying and shaping stone as well as wooden mallets used to hammer on the chisels have been found, providing additional evidence of how the stone was extracted. Also, archaeologists have recovered a set of perfectly preserved measuring tools in the tomb of an architect at Deir el Medina; an examination of these tools indicates that Egyptians would have been perfectly capable of accurately measuring the quarried stones for their fit into the scheme of the pyramid.

The methods used by ancient Egyptians to move the pyramid stones are evidenced in a number of ways (Arnold 1991). The stones themselves sometimes exhibit "handling bosses"—extra ridges or knobs left on surfaces that wouldn't be visible on the finished structure—used to facilitate the attachment of a rope. Beyond this, some stones exhibit carved grooves and sockets to accommodate the positioning of a lever. Wooden pulley wheels

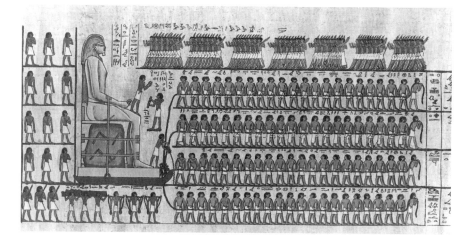

Figure 9.10   Von Däniken cannot conceive how the ancient Egyptians were able to build pyramids and move the enormous stone blocks and statues that are a part of the archaeological record of their civilization. But the ancient Egyptians themselves left records, like this image copied from a wall panel, of how they did it. Here, a crew of 168 men pull ropes attached to a sled on which sits a statue more than 20 feet tall. A worker on the sled pours a lubricant—perhaps an oil—onto the ground in front of the sled. (K. L. Feder)

and even some of the rope have been found, further indicating how Egyptians solved the problems presented by moving large, heavy stones.

Archaeologists have also found wooden sleds that were used to facilitate the transport of heavy blocks of stone and even finished sculptures. The sleds were moved along on flat surfaces, ramps, and maybe even trackways of "sleepers," flat slabs of wood laid in the ground perpendicular to the direction of sled movement. To reduce friction and ease movement, surfaces of the sleepers were lubricated with vegetable oil or even just water. We are fairly certain that this was at least one common way in which large, heavy blocks were moved because the Egyptians themselves recorded these activities in artistic form. For example, a nearly 3,900-year-old wall painting in the tomb of Djehutihotep depicts the movement of an enormous statue of this regional leader which, based on its size relative to the size of the men hauling it, is more than 20 feet tall (Figure 9.10). The statue, which we know weighed more than 52,000 kilograms (57 tons), is tied down to a sled; and 176 men set out in four rows of forty-four men each are pulling it (it is difficult to see in the artist's re-creation of the painting in Figure 9.10, but each man in the image has another man right behind him) (Arnold 1991:61). Along with other workers shown around the statue, one additional worker is shown standing on the sled, emptying the contents of a jar, clearly lubricating the ground in front of the statue.

So we have clear evidence of where and how the Egyptians quarried stone and how they moved the stone to the building site. The greatest challenge awaited them at the site itself, in having to raise the stones, to place course upon course, reaching up to a height of 50, or 100, or even nearly 150 meters in the case of the apex of Khufu's pyramid. How did the ancient Egyptians accomplish this remarkable feat? The honest answer is, we just don't know for sure because the facilities built to raise up the stones were large and obtrusive, and had to be dismantled when the job was complete. Based on existing evidence from places where this dismantling didn't occur—for example, at an early pyramid that was never finished at a place called Sinki—and in the Egyptians' own artistic depictions of the construction process, we know with certainty that they built ramps made of rubble, and in some cases tracked those ramps with sleepers, mentioned previously, to ease the movement upward of large stones attached to sleds. In some cases the ramps may have climbed the pyramid directly as it was built; at Meidum, a large, broad depression is visible on the surface of a portion of what's left of the collapsed pyramid, most likely where a ramp had been attached before it was dismantled (Arnold 1991:83). In other cases, a ramp may have been built along one face of the pyramid in the form of a series of switchbacks or even as a continuous corkscrew along all four faces of the pyramid, spiraling its way to the top (Figure 9.11).

An episode of the *Nova* science series on PBS (titled "This Old Pyramid") put many elements of ancient Egyptian pyramid construction to the test. Using traditional techniques to quarry, transport, and raise the stones, an archaeologist, a Massachusetts stonemason, a sculptor, and a crew of Egyptian laborers were able to reproduce a small-scale pyramid over the course of about three weeks. Though not perfect—and not without disagreements erupting among the participants about the best way to proceed—the

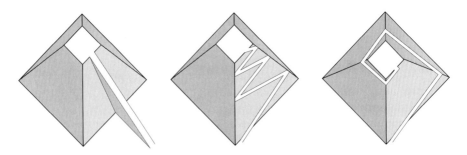

Figure 9.11   Three different conceptions of how ramps may have been built by ancient Egyptians to facilitate raising courses of pyramid blocks: a steeply inclined direct ramp; a series of switchbacks; a ramp that corkscrews around the four faces of the pyramid. There is direct evidence of such construction ramps having been built by ancient Egyptians.

mini-pyramid the team constructed was a successful test of many of the individual elements of pyramid construction.

Stuart Kirkman Weir (1996) has calculated that a workforce of about 10,000 people, laboring for the entirety of Khufu's twenty-eight-year reign, could have constructed his burial tomb, the largest pyramid in Egypt. That is an enormous workforce, and, to be sure, the pyramid of Khufu was built on such a gigantic scale that it is easy to lose track of the individual human in the construction equation. We need always to remind ourselves, however, that the pyramids were built by individual people working together in a coordinated way toward a common goal.

The best example of this was revealed when explorer Howard Vyse entered Khufu's pyramid in 1837. Vyse was fascinated by the ceiling of the so-called King's Chamber located in the heart of the monument's interior. The roof of the chamber consists of nine huge granite slabs, above which—Vyse knew from the work of previous investigators—was a mysterious chamber. From the interior of that chamber, Vyse detected even more open space above its ceiling. He smashed his way through and found a stack of four more small chambers built, one on top of the other, apparently to relieve the incredible stresses produced by the enormous weight of the overlying limestone. It was in the highest of those chambers that the human factor in the construction of the Great Pyramid was most poignantly exposed. There on the ceiling was a written message more than 4,500 years old left by the workers, the real people who actually built the pyramid: "We did this with pride in the name of our great King Khnum-Khuf," the formal name of the pharaoh Khufu (Jackson and Stamp 2003:78). In that short message, the utter humanness of the gigantic project is revealed: real people responding to the enormous challenges laid out before them, constructing an eternal resting place for the spirit of a real person who ruled over a real nation. The genuine discoveries of archaeology, like that small moment frozen in time when an exhausted but exultant worker left a message of pride and accomplishment in a sealed chamber he could not have imagined would ever be seen again, are more wonderful than any of those the purveyors of nonsense about the human past would like you to believe.

Tutankhamun

I don't know particularly much about insurance, but I do know from experience that insurance companies set their rates at least in part on the basis of statistics. For example, my eighteen-year-old son, an enormously responsible kid and a safe driver, is charged an absurdly high premium for his automobile insurance because he is a member of a demographic category—teenage boys—statistically far more likely than other groups to take risks, drive fast, drive stupidly, and get into accidents.

It seems reasonable that insurance companies, who are, after all, not in business to lose money, base their rates on the statistical histories of the groups they insure. That being the case, one might assume that archaeologists are paying huge sums for their medical and life insurance premiums. After all, don't archaeologists, especially Egyptologists, regularly break into ancient tombs protected by deadly curses whereupon they (1) are driven insane, (2) spend the rest of their blighted lives on life support, or (3) immediately and mysteriously drop dead?

Guess what? Insurance companies charge archaeologists not a penny more than anybody else for medical or life insurance. Apparently, insurance adjusters do not believe that archaeologists are any more likely than any other cohort in the population to be afflicted by a pharaoh's—or anybody else's—curse.

You might conclude from this fact alone that there is nothing to such curses. Insurance adjusters are not stupid. If there really were effective curses that killed archaeologists, it would be clear statistically and our insurance premiums would be astronomical. Medical and life insurance adjusters don't charge archaeologists any more to insure their health and their lives, because there are no such things as effective curses on the ancient tombs we discover, excavate, and investigate.

Where then does the notion of cursed tombs come from? The best known of these mythological curses was one supposedly placed on the tomb of Egyptian pharaoh Tutankhamun. It might seem an insurmountable problem to those who spread the tale of Tut's curse that, in actual fact, there was no such curse, effective or otherwise, on his tomb. We can argue about whether or not entering Tut's tomb was bad for your health, but in fact there was no curse—no dire hieroglyphic warning of the consequences of despoiling the pharaoh's final resting place etched into the tomb's portal; no threat of a horrible fate to those who dared to enter his burial chamber; not even a pitiful, plaintive plea to leave the dead at rest; nothing (Figure 9.12). Nevertheless, the myth of the terrible consequences of Tut's nonexistent curse is astonishingly popular. Remember my most recent survey of student opinions discussed in Chapter 1 (see Figure 1.2); 22 percent of that sample accept the reality of a curse on Tut's tomb and believe that it actually killed people.

The real story of Tutankhamun is remarkable, filled with palace intrigue, power struggles, even mysterious deaths, and is far more interesting than any mythological curse. Tut himself is one of those historical characters who fits the modern sarcastic remark; he is well known because he is famous. Tut's father, the pharaoh Akhenaten, is a far more significant historical figure, having led a revolution against the powerful priests of ancient Egypt in the so-called Amarna Revolt. Akhenaten displaced the traditional Egyptian pantheon, perhaps because the priests who represented these gods

Figure 9.12   An iconic scene in Egyptology—archaeologists gazing in wonder into the freshly opened tomb of Pharaoh Tutankhamun. Howard Carter is shown crouching, his face barely visible in the center of the photograph. (© Hulton-Deutsch Collection/Corbis)

on earth were getting too rich and too powerful. Akhenaten also replaced the traditionally important gods, instituting the worship of a single, previously minor deity, Aten, the god of the disk of the sun.

One can imagine that this did not make Akhenaten particularly popular among the priests of the other gods. In fact, his death in 1334 B.C. may have been the result of an assassination plot sponsored by these priests in their attempt to wrest power back from the pharaoh. When Akhenaten's son, then called Tutankhaten, ascended to the throne, he was only nine years old. Not long after the death of his father, Tutankhaten had his name changed to Tutankhamun, thereby eliminating reference to Aten and reestablishing his loyalty to Amun, one of the gods Akhenaten had replaced and the most powerful in the Egyptian pantheon.

Only a child, Tutankhamun served as little more than a figurehead ruler for ten years and then, in 1325 B.C., he too died, again under mysterious circumstances. Some have argued that, like his father, he was killed in a power struggle over the throne (King and Cooper 2004).

Tut was not an important pharaoh; he fought no great battles, negotiated no significant treaties, and undertook no impressive construction projects. He was, in the end, only a boy who got caught up in historical, religious, and political forces that he played no role in shaping and of which he may have been only vaguely aware (Figure 9.13). He died, tragically, a

Figure 9.13 One of the most beautiful and evocative objects ever extracted from an ancient Egyptian tomb, the gold and lapis lazuli funerary mask of the "boy king": the pharaoh Tutankhamun. (© Robert Holmes/Corbis)

teenager and was buried in a tomb meant for someone of lesser rank; his demise was so sudden, there wasn't even time to build him a final resting place appropriate for a pharaoh. And, in the biggest insult of all to a pharaoh, he was essentially forgotten, a barely remembered "boy king" whose sad, short life was not to be exalted by history. Of course, the irony here is that precisely because he was unimportant and largely forgotten, his tomb remained unplundered, not subject to the depredations of those who regularly raided the tombs of important rulers. When Tut's tomb was discovered in 1924 by Egyptologist Howard Carter, it was largely intact, drew the attention of the world, and inspired the public's fascination with ancient Egypt, a fascination that continues unabated to this day.

But the simple fact is that no curse had been written anywhere in or around Tut's tomb. The myth of not just a curse but an effective, working, deadly curse that actually killed people got started after the wealthy benefactor who funded the excavation, Lord Carnarvon, died four months after the tomb was opened. It was no great shock at the time; he was old and weak, and he was sick even before the tomb was discovered. As much as he wished to be there to share in the glory, a sickly Carnarvon had no business making an arduous trip to Egypt to witness the opening of the tomb that his money helped discover. Not surprisingly, he fell ill, and, after additionally suffering a serious insect bite that became infected, he died. Assertions about the lights going out in Cairo at the moment of his death mean little, as electrical service was entirely unpredictable there and failed regularly. Similarly, tales about Carnarvon's dog's death back in England simultaneous with the death of his master are irrelevant and unverifiable.

But, the curse purveyors maintain, a large number of people did die after the tomb was opened, and their deaths cannot be so easily dismissed. In actual fact, however, the allegation that the tomb was a death trap can be disproved with the kinds of statistics insurance adjusters regularly rely on. For example, the twenty-three people most intimately involved with the opening of the tomb, including Howard Carter (director of excavations), as well as other archaeologists, photographers, guards, and the like, lived an average of twenty-four years (yes, *years*) after the opening of the tomb, and their average age of death was seventy-three (all data from Hoggart and Hutchinson 1995). Carnarvon's daughter, who was with her father when the tomb was first entered, lived for another fifty-seven years, and Howard Carter, the man who discovered the tomb and who would have been the most obvious target of a curse, lived for sixteen more years after entering the tomb—during which time he analyzed and wrote about the splendid objects found there.

Epidemiologist Mark R. Nelson (2002) recently conducted another statistical test of the efficacy of the nonexistent curse on Tut's tomb. Howard Carter listed forty-four Europeans and Americans in Egypt at the time of the tomb's opening, of whom twenty-four likely entered the tomb at some time or came into contact with objects from the tomb and, therefore, would have been exposed to a curse, had there been one. The other twenty people on Carter's list had no contact with the tomb or its contents. Of those for whom Nelson could determine age of death, there was no significant difference between how long the two groups lived; those who entered the tomb or had been in contact with the objects from the tomb lived just about as long as those who had no opportunity to enter the tomb or handle the recovered artifacts.

Recognizing that the longevity of the tomb's discoverer and chief excavator seems the clearest evidence against the existence of a curse, one especially silly television "documentary" went so far as to assert that, though he lived a long life, Howard Carter actually was the individual most sorely afflicted, having been "cursed" to spend the rest of his life examining the objects found in Tut's tomb. Imagine that: an archaeologist "cursed" to spend his life analyzing, discussing, and writing about the most spectacular archaeological discovery of the twentieth century. Poor Howard! Where do I sign up for a curse like that?

Current Perspectives: Secrets of the Pyramids

It cannot be concluded from this chapter that there are no surviving mysteries of ancient Egypt that demand solution, no secrets left still hidden deep within the stone-lined corridors of the Great Pyramid. There are, of course, many fascinating stories of ancient Egypt yet to be told and scholars of various stripes eager to tell them.

One such mystery concerns the four so-called airshafts that slice through the Great Pyramid (Figure 9.14). The shafts are small rectangular tunnels running through the monument, far too narrow and shallow for a person to traverse—at one point, one of the shafts is a mere 11 centimeters (4.3 inches) high. Two of them, a northern shaft and a southern shaft, begin in the lower room called the Queen's Chamber, and two others originate in the higher King's Chamber. The two shafts emanating from the Queen's Chamber dead-end within the pyramid itself while those beginning in the King's Chamber extend to the surface, though it is not certain that they re-

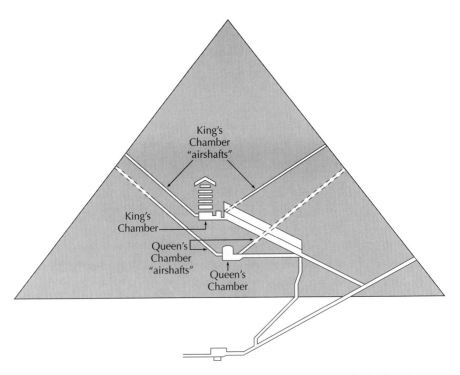

Figure 9.14   Location of the so-called airshafts of the Great Pyramid. The function or meaning of these shafts is unknown. Some have proposed that they were simply functional features, providing ventilation for workers laboring inside the pyramid. Others suggest that they were ceremonial, pointing the entombed pharaoh's spirit to particular stars in the night sky.

mained as openings when the polished limestone casing that blanketed the interior pyramid blocks was intact.

The shafts have fascinated and frustrated Egyptologists for decades. What were they for? Why did the pyramid builders go to such trouble to build them into the monument? Did at least the King's Chamber shafts serve the simple and practical purpose of ventilation, bringing in fresh air from the outside to those working deep within the pyramid during its construction? Were the shafts of astronomical significance, pointing to important celestial bodies during crucial days in the yearly cycle of ancient Egypt's calendar, providing a line of sight to some distant star for the spirit of the pharaoh?

Intrigued by the shafts, in the early 1990s engineer Rudolf Gantenbrink designed mobile mini-robots to explore them. A camera was attached to the front of each robot, allowing it to send images back to Gantenbrink at his command center on the surface or in the King's or Queen's Chamber. The resulting view provided by the camera is extraordinarily eerie and not terribly appealing for anyone with even a hint of claustrophobia; you can find several remarkable still images at http://www.cheops.org/.

Though the project is currently in a quiet phase, its contribution has been significant. We now know, for example, that the shafts do not make a straight run through the pyramid, but take angled deflections that render moot any hypothesis concerning a direct line of sight between the Queen's or King's Chamber and a particular star or constellation. What, then, could their purpose be? We still cannot answer that fundamental question.

Perhaps the most remarkable camera image from inside the shafts was taken in March 1993 when one of the mobile robots was unable to complete its mission in the southern shaft originating in the Queen's Chamber. After traveling approximately 59 meters (194 feet) up the shaft, the robot, called Upuaut-2, was stopped dead in its tracks when it encountered a plug of stone blocking any further progress. This stone plug's existence was intriguing and made little sense; why did the builders go to the trouble of building a shaft only to block it? The neatly shaped stone filled the shaft from side to side and from the top to nearly, but not quite, the bottom surface, leaving a tantalizing sliver of open space below the plug. The stone plug's surface facing the camera was smoothed and polished and, intriguingly, had been pierced from its opposite side by two copper spikes whose ends were bent at right angles at the stone plug's surface (Figure 9.15).

Gantenbrink and others involved in the project began referring to the stone slab as the "Door," but is it a door at all, and, if so, a door to where? Of course, the question that occurred to virtually everyone who saw the stone plug was, "Is there something secreted on the other side?"

An answer—a not-terribly-satisfying answer—to that question was obtained in September 2003 when Zahi Hawass (the director of research at Giza) and National Geographic sent another robotic device into the shaft. This robot carried with it not only a camera but also a drill. After slowly

Figure 9.15 Originally discovered in 1993 by researcher Rudolf Gantenbrink through the use of a small remotely operated vehicle, a mysterious stone plug blocks the passage about 59 meters (194 feet) up the southern shaft originating in the Queen's Chamber of the Great Pyramid. (© NGT& F/NGS Image Collection)

grinding away at the stone plug, the drill passed through it, providing a small opening large enough for insertion of the camera lens and a light. The tension was palpable as the researchers, in a live television broadcast, focused intently at the monitor hooked up to the camera. The moment was eerily similar to the opening of King Tut's tomb in 1924, when Howard Carter alone peered in and the world waited for the report of what he had seen. In the case of Tut's tomb, when his benefactor, Lord Carnarvon, anxiously inquired, "Can you see anything?" Carter responded with one of the most famous statements ever made by an archaeologist: "Yes, wonderful things!" (Buckley 1976:13). Unfortunately, the answer to the same question, "What do you see?" in the case of what lay beyond the stone plug was, simply, "another damn stone plug!" It was, to be frank, an incredibly disappointing and frustrating letdown. But it also was fascinating and to be expected that the Great Pyramid does not so readily reveal its secrets. It is not obvious what lies beyond this second block of stone. Perhaps a third. I hope not. What is clear is this: There are mysteries yet to be solved in the Great Pyramid that, it is hoped, archaeology—working with modern technology—can someday reveal.

FREQUENTLY ASKED QUESTIONS

1. Were the pyramids built by slaves?

If you have read the book of Exodus in the Old Testament of the Bible or seen the Hollywood epic *The Ten Commandments* (with no less a figure than Charlton Heston playing Moses), you probably have the impression that the pyramids were built by a large population of mistreated, oppressed, and expendable slaves. It turns out that this common conception is incorrect. There are no written records in Egypt that support this notion: no mention of the use of slaves in pyramid building and no hieroglyphic "spreadsheets" keeping track of an enslaved workforce listing, for example, the number of slaves, where they came from, their skill levels, ages, or names (such listings were, in fact, standard operating procedure in the American South before the Civil War). Beyond this, recent archaeology indicates that the living conditions of the pyramid workers themselves were quite good by the standards of ancient Egypt; pyramid workers ate well, had reasonably nice places to live, and, when they died, were buried in tombs reflecting a rather high status in Egyptian society (Pérez-Accino 2003c; Shaw 2003). Apparently, it was considered by many a privilege to help build and maintain the eternal home of the dead pharaoh's spirit, and workers drafted into service could expect a better diet and an elevated social status for their work for the king's spirit.

2. Are the mummies of ancient pharaohs so well preserved that one day science may be able to bring them back to life?

Erich von Däniken (Chapter 8) actually claims this (1970:81), but it's not likely. In the mummification process, the Egyptian priests disemboweled the body, sticking the heart, lungs, liver, and other organs in containers called canopic jars. These same priests removed the deceased's brain by picking it out, a little at a time, through the nose.

This can be seen directly in the computerized tomography (CT) scans of the mummy of the Egyptian priest Nesperennub that are part of an exhibit on mummification at the British Museum (http://www. thebritishmuseum.ac.uk/mummy/). CT scanning technology provides a peek through this priest's coffin and then past his mummy wrappings, allowing a clear view of his mortal remains. A careful examination reveals that his vital organs are gone, having been removed during the mummification process, as is his brain. The evidence of how the brain was removed is apparent; the fine bones of the nasal cavity have been broken through to get at the gray matter (Hopkin 2004). There could be little hope for bringing Nesperennub or anybody else in that state back to life.

BEST OF THE WEB

http://guardians.net/egypt

About as all-inclusive as you can get in a Web site devoted to as broad a topic as ancient Egyptian culture. Great graphics, terrific discussion, links to everything from the official Egyptian Supreme Council of Antiquities to tour groups, online catalogs of Egyptian goods, and chat groups. If you visit one Web site on Egypt, this is the one.

http://www.seas.upenn.edu/~ahm/history.htm

The University of Pennsylvania Egypt Web site. There are lots of links to Web sites on the culture of ancient Egypt, online tutorials on hieroglyphic writing, an encyclopedia of Egyptian deities, and much more.

http://www.pbs.org/wgbh/nova/pyramid/textindex.html

Web site on ancient Egypt produced by PBS. Features an online interview with famed Egyptologist Mark Lehner and virtual tours of the pyramids at Giza.

http://www.catchpenny.org/

Larry Orcutt's entertaining site exploring some of the supposed mysteries of ancient Egypt. "Mysteries of the Sphinx," "Pyramid Enigmas," and pharaoh's curses are explored here, all within the context of the application of the scientific method to the investigation of the Egypt of the pharaohs. Lots of fun and enormously informative.

CRITICAL THINKING EXERCISE

Test the following hypothesis: Pyramid building was introduced into Egypt by bearers of an alien, non-Egyptian culture. What should the archaeological record in Egypt look like if this hypothesis is an accurate description of Egyptian history? What does the archaeological record actually show regarding the history of pyramid construction in Egypt?

❖❖❖❖❖❖❖❖ **10** ❖❖❖❖❖❖❖❖

Good Vibrations:
Psychics and Dowsers

The McLean Game Refuge consists of approximately 4,000 acres of thickly forested hills marked by deeply incised, meandering streams. Since 1993, our team of archaeologists has been surveying this nature preserve in north-central Connecticut, and we have located about twenty prehistoric occupations of the refuge.

Finding ancient, buried archaeological remains may seem like magic, but there is no magic to it. How do archaeologists come into an area like McLean, identify the areas most likely to have ancient buried villages and camps, dig in those very places, and find the material evidence of those pre-historic habitations? We are guided, in part, by experience. Archaeologists are practiced at identifying the kinds of environmental features that at-tracted ancient settlement: proximity to fresh water, relatively flat and dry land, and places where the surrounding territory would have supplied basic resources, including food, wood to fuel fires and build dwellings, stone for tools, and clay for pots.

Areas so identified represent hypotheses that need to be tested. The test is in the search for artifacts in those places, the physical objects people made and used, and then lost or discarded. Over the course of ten years of research, we have investigated large swaths of the subsurface of the game refuge, but, of course, we have not stripped back all of the soil in our 4,000-acre research domain. To minimize disruption of the ecology of the game refuge and to use our time efficiently, we have employed a sampling strat-egy (Orton 2000; Shafer 1997). Since 1993, we have excavated a large num-ber of individual, shovel-dug test pits, each 50 centimeters (close to 20 inches) on a side, 10 meters (about 33 feet) apart, along a series of widely dispersed transects, or lines. We have positioned these transects to pass through all of the various habitats and landforms in the refuge. We don't want to sample only areas along streams or places near rock outcrops. Doing so would guarantee that we find sites only near streams or outcrops, but we do not know that these are the only kinds of places where the ancient inhabitants lived or worked. Our goal is representative coverage of all of the many different game refuge habitats. No area is oversampled and no place is underrepresented in our test pit sample. In this way, we have attempted to increase the likelihood that the kinds of sites we have discovered are a representative subset of the kinds of sites present in the game refuge. All of the soil we dug in these test excavations was passed through ⅛-inch-mesh hardware cloth (screen). Soil passes through the screen, but artifacts like stone flakes, sherds of pottery, burned bone, and charred nut fragments are caught and represent clear evidence of ancient habitation.

It's not magical, and it certainly is not easy. Much of the survey work is in pretty rough territory, far from the gentle, established trails. Our backpacks are laden with heavy equipment, and we carry shovels and screens that are awkward to negotiate through the dense growth. Mosquitoes (some carrying West Nile virus), ticks (some carrying Lyme disease), snakes (some poisonous), poison ivy, stifling heat, and thick humidity add to the mix. Certainly, for those dedicated few who devote themselves to this task, the rewards are great when an ancient site whose people lived thousands of years ago is revealed. When we are the first to encounter the remnants of the daily lives of people who lived and died so long ago, it is worth every mile, every mosquito bite, every sprained ankle.

Once sites are discovered, the laborious process of excavation begins. Even the small (less than ¼ acre in extent), 4,000-year-old streamside encampment we excavated in the field season of 2003 commanded our attention for months of excavation and laboratory analysis (Figure 10.1). Scraping back the soil incrementally in 2-meter-square excavation units, passing all soil through hardware-cloth screening, and keeping accurate and meticulous records of the site all take time but are crucial parts of the process. The excavation of a site necessarily involves its destruction, so great care and thorough documentation are absolutely vital if we are to preserve the information about past lives that the site can provide (see Fagan 2000; Feder 2004; Sharer and Ashmore 2003; Thomas 1999, for discussions of survey and excavation methodology).

Finally, we hope to be able to reconstruct as completely as possible an ancient way of life. To do so, archaeologists have had to devise methods to coax information out of the often meager remains we recover; the artifacts are mute, the bones silent. Detailed examination of stone tools under the microscope can tell us how they were made and used. Chemical analysis of human bone can provide insight into ancient diets. Physicists can help us to determine the age of sites. Nuclear reactors are used to trace raw materials to their prehistoric sources. Pollen, starch grains from plants, and even blood

Figure 10.1   Archaeological excavations are time-consuming enterprises. Here, at the Firetown Meadow site in Granby, Connecticut, a crew of archaeology students is shown revealing the remnants of a 4,000-year-old occupation of the Farmington River valley. (K. L. Feder)

residue can survive for thousands of years on the interior surfaces of ancient pots, on the smoothed façades of grinding tools, and even on the cutting edges of sharp-edged stone knives; these organic remnants can be recovered and analyzed, providing a wealth of information about the tasks people performed with these artifacts. Powerful computers are needed to map the distributions of artifacts within sites and of sites within regions to help us illuminate the nature of human behavior. Archaeologists are like detectives of the human past. We try to reconstruct not a crime but a way of life from the fragmentary remains people accidentally and incidentally left behind.

But is there a better, easier way of going about our various tasks? Can we locate sites by simply looking at a map of an area and intuiting their existence? Can we know where to dig at a site simply by walking over the ancient habitation and "feeling" where artifacts are? Can we reconstruct, in exquisite detail, the lives not just of general "cultures," but also of specific, identifiable human beings simply by handling the objects they touched in their daily lives? Is there a methodology that could obviate the tedious and hard work of archaeology and get right at that which interests us most—ancient people and their cultures? Though virtually all archaeologists would wish the answer to this question were yes, most would realistically answer no.

Some new methodologies have been suggested, however—mostly by nonarchaeologists—that are alleged to do precisely this.

Psychic Archaeology

For example, some claim that "psychic power" is a tool that can be applied to the archaeological record (Goodman 1977; Jones 1979; Schwartz 1978, 1983). There are many fine books in which the reality of subjects such as telepathy and clairvoyance are assessed with a scientific and skeptical eye (see Table 1.1). A detailed examination of so-called paranormal phenomena is beyond the scope of this book; nevertheless, we can assess the application of such alleged powers in archaeological research.

Remember, whatever one's preconceptions might be regarding the existence of psychic power, hypotheses regarding the reality of such phenomena and their utility in archaeological site survey, excavation, and analysis can be tested just as all hypotheses are tested—within a scientific, deductive framework. When a psychic predicts the location of a site, we must test the claim archaeologically. When a certain artifact or feature is predicted at a particular spot in a site, such a claim also must be tested by digging. Finally, when a psychic attempts to reconstruct the activities at a site or the behavior of the people at a site, those involved in testing the legitimacy of such an ability must devise a way to test such reconstructions with independent archaeological data.

In such testing, sources of information other than psychic must be controlled for. Here the application of Occam's razor should be clear. If the information reported by the psychic is correct but could have been obtained in some more pedestrian way (through such simple avenues as reading the available literature on a site or time period or the application of common sense), then Occam's razor would demand that we accept the simpler explanation before we accept the validity of a paranormal phenomenon. Unfortunately, as you shall see, such tests of psychic archaeology either are not conducted or are conducted so poorly as to render the results meaningless (Feder 1980b, 1995a).

The Roots of Psychic Archaeology

When the Church of England purchased the site and ruins of the ancient Benedictine Abbey of St. Mary at Glastonbury near Bath in 1909, Frederick Bligh Bond, a local architect, was hired to stabilize the standing walls of the abbey, to produce a map of the ruins, and to prepare a guidebook for tourists. Bond studied ancient historical records and conducted archaeology at the site, gathering as much data as he could to better understand the appearance, construction history, and functioning of the church.

Though Bond withheld the information from the Church at the time, he later maintained in a book devoted to his study of the abbey that his archaeological investigation had been directed by a host of dead monks present in its ruins (Bond 1918). Other deceased historical figures who commiserated with him about his work were a Danish warrior; the abbey's sixteenth-century builder, Abbot Beere; and even Julius Caesar. Bond claimed to have had regular discussions with these ancient spirits, who directed the investigators to the best places to excavate.

Bond's claim of a ghostly source for his discoveries exhibits a fundamental problem in testing the validity of psychic archaeology—or any psychic claim—in an uncontrolled setting. Simply stated, it is virtually impossible to eliminate the possibility that prior knowledge on the part of the participants in the study may have directed them to the right parts of the site to dig.

For example, Bond claimed that the spirits of dead monks directed him to the locations of the ruins of two chapels in the abbey—Edgar and Loretto chapels—and also to the foundations of enormous church towers. But Bond was an expert on medieval churches, and we know that he had access to and had examined many of the documents, maps, plans, and drawings of the abbey before initiating field research. Although much of the abbey was a ruin, some walls and foundations were visible at the surface. Previous subsurface investigation had been conducted at the abbey, so areas where little had been found could be, and were, eliminated in Bond's study.

As Marshall McKusick (1982:104) points out, the tall church towers actually were recorded and located in a historical document Bond almost surely had already seen. An early drawing of the abbey, as well as structural remains visible on the surface, provided clues about the location of these towers. The Edgar and Loretto chapels were known to church historians before Bond began his work and had been generally located in historical documents. Previous searches for the chapels had been unsuccessful, so Bond did not have to look in those same areas. Instead, he searched for and found the chapels in the only reasonable places left for them to be (McKusick 1982:104).

As archaeologist Stephen Williams (1991:288) points out, "Culture is patterned behavior, and medieval cathedrals are some of the most patterned pieces of construction in our culture." Bond's knowledge of the spatial patterning of medieval church construction allowed him to use that pattern as a guide in discovering additional architectural elements in the ruins of the abbey that were not readily apparent on the surface. Modern archaeologists give Bond high praise for his work in the abbey (McKusick 1982; Williams 1991), but they credit his success to his great knowledge and skills, not to any messages from the great beyond.

Stefan Ossowiecki was another spiritualist who became involved in psychic archaeology. Ossowiecki was the subject of a number of experiments conducted between 1937 and 1941 by the ethnologist Stanislaw Poniatowski. The methodology employed was simple. Poniatowski provided Ossowiecki with Paleolithic artifacts about which the psychic had no prior knowledge. Ossowiecki then provided details concerning the sites, time periods, people, and cultures associated with the artifacts.

One might think that the controlled setting of these experiments should render the results less ambiguous than Bond's claims. Unfortunately, this is not the case, and the Ossowiecki experiments are extraordinarily difficult to assess, not the least because the original records kept by the ethnologist disappeared during World War II. Psychic researcher Stephan Schwartz (1978) maintains that a mystery man provided Ossowiecki's wife with those records in 1952, but it is difficult to determine whether these were the original materials documenting the experiments.

Psychic Site Location

In reference to the claimed ability to locate archaeological sites through the application of psychic skills, it is most important to consider the fact that archaeologists regularly discover sites by employing some rather commonsense techniques. Human beings—prehistoric, ancient historic, and modern—do not locate their habitations randomly. Among the more important factors considered by a human group when deciding where to settle are distance to potable water, distance to a navigable waterway, topographic relief, defensibility, protection from the elements, soil type, food resources, and the availability of other resources such as stone, clay, or metal for tools.

Using such a list, even an untrained person can examine a map of an area and point out the most likely places where ancient people might have settled. In my own introductory course in archaeology, after lecturing on settlement location choice, I distribute United States Geological Survey maps (1:24,000 scale) of areas in Connecticut where we have conducted archaeological surveys (Figure 10.2). I ask students to peruse the maps and to suggest areas where sites might be located. It is quite common for students to come up with precise locations where, indeed, sites have already been discovered. Therefore, even if a psychic could come up with an accurate prediction for the location of an unknown site, we would have to consider the simple explanation that, consciously or not, the psychic was merely relying on commonsense cues rather than ESP to make the prediction. The lack of control of these variables renders such tests impossible to assess.

For example, Stephan Schwartz (1983) led a psychic archaeology project in Egypt. A team of ten self-proclaimed psychics was used to find sites now located underwater in the city of Alexandria's harbor. Indeed, sites were found, but, according to Egyptian archaeologists, this was not surprising. The harbor was used in ancient times, and divers had often found ancient remains in the mud at the bottom. The use of psychic archaeology need not be invoked simply because sites were found in the general area the psychic predicted.

I guess I could claim to have psychic abilities as well when it comes to predicting the location of archaeological sites. Certainly, my field crew

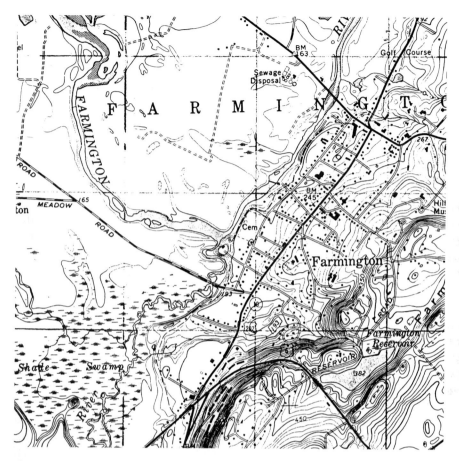

Figure 10.2   An understanding of the factors that influenced ancient people in settlement location choice helps us find archaeological sites. United States Geological Survey maps (1:24,000 scale) like this section of the New Britain Quadrangle, Connecticut, provide a valuable picture of topography and drainage—significant considerations for people in the past, as well as the present. (Courtesy U.S.G.S.)

was mightily impressed by my seemingly paranormal abilities when I placed an X on the map we were using in our search for sites in Peoples State Forest in northwestern Connecticut, predicting that they would find a site in that very location (Feder 2004). Sure enough, when I next saw my crew chief later that same day, she expressed her amazement at my prescience. I assure you, as I assured her, no psychic skills were employed. I based my guess on the nearby presence of a permanent stream, a relatively flat surrounding area in an otherwise topographically rough and irregular part of the forest, and an abruptly rising slope to the west, offering a bit of protection from winds that usually come in from that direction. I wasn't psychic; I was merely aware of previous archaeological research that had already revealed the general pattern of settlement location among the prehistoric inhabitants of the region. And I was lucky. A little knowledge and a little luck may be all that is needed in many instances to accurately predict the location of a site.

Psychic Excavation

Jeffrey Goodman (1977, 1981) claims to have used psychic revelations to locate an outpost of immigrants from the Lost Continent of Atlantis in Arizona (see Chapter 7). Goodman's psychic predicted that excavators would find the following at the "site": "carvings, paintings, wooden ankhs, cured leather, and parchment scrolls with hieroglyphiclike writing" (1981:128). Also predicted among the finds were an underground tunnel system, domesticated horses and dogs, and corn and rye (p. 134). Goodman admits, "My beliefs may appear to outstrip the physical discoveries at Flagstaff so far" (p. 134), showing that he is nothing if not a master at understatement. *None* of the predicted items was, in fact, discovered at the site. The utility of psychic archaeology as a method for supplementing excavation has not been supported experimentally.

Psychic Cultural Reconstruction

Archaeologist Marshall McKusick (1982, 1984), who played a key role in clearing up the myth of the Davenport Tablets discussed in Chapter 6, has produced useful summaries of the claims of the psychic archaeologists. Regarding the psychic reconstruction of prehistoric cultures, he has come up with the phrase "the captive-of-his-own-time principle" (1982:100). He uses this phrase to underscore the fact that when psychics have attempted to reconstruct past lifeways, invariably they have done so within the framework of popular notions of those lifeways with all their biases, inconsistencies, and errors. In other words, the "vibrations" psychics allegedly receive by walking over a site, studying a map, or "psychometrizing" an artifact (holding the object to link up in some way with the person who made and used it thousands of years ago) do not come from some other plane of reality but rather from more mundane sources like popular books, newspaper articles, and the like.

For example, McKusick points out that when, in the 1930s, Stefan Ossowiecki had visions of the Old Stone Age, they were in line with perspectives of ancient people that were then current but are now known to be erroneous. Ossowiecki described *Magdalenian* people of the Late Paleolithic as being short with large hands and low foreheads (McKusick 1982:100). McKusick points out that Ossowiecki was likely simply providing a commonly held stereotype of Neandertals. But the Neandertals became extinct more than 10,000 years before the Magdalenian culture came into existence. Ossowiecki should have described a tall people with high foreheads, not short, squat Neandertals. Clearly his description reflects not on his psychic connections but on his own ignorance of Paleolithic archaeology.

As McKusick (1982) shows, when another self-proclaimed psychic and witch, Sybil Leek, tried applying her psychic gifts to ostensible Viking sites in the New World (Holzer 1969), she described the wrong kind of sailing vessel, but one that matched then-current presumptions. When Leek encountered the ghost of one of the Viking settlers, she identified him by reading a part of his name: ". . . KSON" (Holzer 1969:118). Later, in Leek's dream, the ghost wrote his initial: "E" (p. 126). Presumably we are to believe that the spirit of Leif Eiriksson appeared to Ms. Leek (by the way, at a supposed Viking site in Massachusetts rather than the more likely setting of Newfoundland as discussed in Chapter 5). Also, presumably, we are to believe that this Norse explorer learned Roman letters on "the other side," since in their time Vikings wrote in their own Runic alphabet.

Also in this regard, self-proclaimed seer Edgar Cayce, whom we encountered in Chapter 7, saw his paranormal abilities fail him terribly. In the 1920s, after the discovery of Piltdown but years before its unmasking as a fraud (see Chapter 4), Cayce obtained information from another plane of reality informing him that *Eoanthropus* was one of a group of ancient Atlantean settlers of England (McKusick 1984:49). Apparently, Cayce's other-worldly sources were not aware that the whole thing had been a fake.

As mentioned in Chapter 7, in the 1940s Cayce predicted that sometime during the 1960s parts of Atlantis would rise from the depths of the ocean, and much of the Atlantic seaboard would be inundated. New York City was to have disappeared, the Great Lakes were to drain into the Gulf of Mexico, and most of Japan would be drowned (Cayce 1968:158–59). During Cayce's career as the "sleeping prophet," he produced some fourteen thousand predictions. With all that predicting, the odds are good that at least some would turn out to be accurate. Obviously, the predictions mentioned here were not among those.

Psychic cultural reconstruction is, at its heart, nonscientific if only because the vast majority of such reconstructions cannot be tested. There simply are no data with which these often detailed descriptions can be judged. Take Stefan Ossowiecki's detailed description of a sexual encounter between two premodern human ancestors:

> He makes advances to her. Takes her breasts and pulls to himself . . . he moves around her to and fro. There are no kisses. She strokes his neck, back, he lies down. She sits on him equestrian style. He embraces her with his whole strength, she is active not he. There are no normal movements, they are like monkeys. (In Schwartz 1978:89–90)

This, of course, is nothing more than fantasy. The archaeological record can provide no data that would enable us to assess such a scene. It may be titillating, but it most decidedly is not science.

Psychic Archaeology: The Verdict

As an archaeologist, I wish psychic archaeology worked. As an archaeologist committed to a scientific and skeptical approach, I can only say that wishing doesn't make it so. The verdict on psychic archaeology based on experiments under controlled conditions is decidedly negative.

Dowsing Instead of Digging

Dowsing for subterranean water is a venerable tradition. Using a Y-shaped stick, a pendulum, or two metal wires with a 90-degree bend in each, some claim the ability to walk over the ground and, depending on the motion of the device, identify the location, the depth, and even the flow rate of underground water (Chambers 1969; see Vogt and Hyman 1980 for a skeptical analysis by an anthropologist and a psychologist).

Although "water witching" goes back hundreds of years—the first recorded reference is in 1568 (Chambers 1969:35)—its application to the discovery of archaeological artifacts or buried structures is more recent. Schwartz (1978:108–35) details the alleged abilities of Major General James Scott Elliot in Britain; respected archaeologist Ivor Noël Hume (1974:37–39) describes its use at colonial Williamsburg in Virginia; Bailey (1983) and Bailey, Cambridge, and Briggs (1988) detail the use of dowsing in medieval church archaeology in England; Goodman (1977) discusses "map dowsing," where sites are supposedly discovered by using a dowsing technique on maps.

For some (Schwartz and Goodman, for example) dowsing is simply a method for enhancing or facilitating the psychic abilities of the user. Others maintain that the dowsing device allows them to locate, through some unknown but normal process, magnetic anomalies caused by the buried objects. Major General Elliot, as cited in Schwartz (1978), eschews the psychic label; Noël Hume (1974) uses dowsing to find only metal objects, ostensibly as a result of their magnetism.

Small but discernible magnetic effects, indeed, are known to result from human activity and have been used in locating archaeological artifacts or features through a process called *proton magnetometry* (Aitken 1970; Weymouth 1986). In a related approach, the *electrical resistivity* of soil has been measured and used to locate buried foundations and walls (Clark 1970). In the former case a device called a proton magnetometer can be used to locate anything displaying magnetism that differs from the background magnetism of the earth: iron objects, fired clay, or ancient pits (pit fill is more loosely packed than surrounding soil, resulting in differences in what is called *magnetic susceptibility*). For example, archaeologist David Hurst Thomas (1987) was very successful in using a magnetometer in the search for Santa Catalina, the most important sixteenth- and seventeenth-century Spanish mission in Georgia. In the case of *electrical resistivity surveying*, soil resistance to an introduced electrical current varies depending on the compactness of the soil or medium (rock, brick) through which the current is passing. Buried walls and pits will possess different resistivity to the current than will surrounding soil. Differences can be mapped, and buried objects or features causing the differences in resistivity can be investigated.

Measurable phenomena do exist. But can people detect these without the thousands of dollars of equipment ordinarily considered to be required?

Testing the Dowsers

A number of experimental tests of water dowsing have been performed by skeptics; in one case the president of the American Society of Dowsers was involved (Randi 1979, 1984; Martin 1983–84). Nineteen dowsers from all across Europe were tested in 1990 by the German Society for the Examination of Parasciences (König, Moll, and Sarma 1996). A test was even performed on the ABC television newsmagazine program *20/20*. In each case the self-proclaimed dowsers agreed to the scientific controls imposed and to the design of the experiment. All maintained that they could easily detect flowing water under test conditions (water flowing in randomly selected routes, through buried or covered pipes).

In all cases here cited, the dowsers failed utterly. They simply could not detect flowing water using their rods, sticks, or pendulums, even when a prize of $110,000 was at stake. The prize challenge was made under the aegis of a long-standing offer to anyone who can, under controlled conditions, prove the existence of a paranormal phenomenon—extrasensory perception, astrology, UFOs, dowsing, and so on. Now set at $1 million, the challenge is administered by the James Randi Educational Foundation; you can read the details and even find an application for the prize money at http://www.randi.org/research/index.html.

If you believe everything you read on the Internet—not a good idea—it is easy to get the impression that dowsing rods are a regular part of the archaeologist's tool kit and that dowsing is commonly used both to find sites and to select the most promising areas within sites to excavate. You might further believe that you don't read or hear much about this simply because we archaeologists don't like to admit that we employ the technique for fear of ridicule from our colleagues. Though I do know archaeologists who think that dowsing actually works in finding buried objects, in fact, not many do. I conducted a survey in 1983 of teaching archaeologists in the United States, only about 13.5 percent of whom anonymously responded positively to a question regarding the efficacy of dowsing in archaeology (Feder 1984). The vast majority of archaeologists don't use dowsing because they don't believe it works.

Perhaps the most support for dowsing comes from British archaeologists, where the procedure has been tested in a number of investigations of old churches (Bailey, Cambridge, and Briggs 1988). As researcher Martijn van Leusen (1999) has pointed out, however, just as was the case in the application and testing of alleged psychic power in church archaeology, the predictability of church architecture makes them a poor choice for an objective testing of the efficacy of dowsing. As van Leusen shows, when accurate predictions of the locations of buried architectural features are made by dowsers, it is impossible to distinguish between those actually based on dowsing and those based on a simple knowledge of how churches were built.

In another archaeological test, Martin Aitken (1959), pioneer in the use of proton magnetometry and electrical resistivity surveying in archaeology, tested dowser P. A. Raine of Great Britain. Raine could not successfully dowse the location of an archaeologically verified buried kiln that had been initially identified by magnetometry (it had produced extremely high readings). Aitken concluded from this that dowsing for archaeological remains simply did not work.

Then why, it might reasonably be asked, do some people swear by the ability of dowsers to find water or archaeological sites in the field? An answer can be found in a simple statistic. The regional government of New South Wales, Australia, keeps accurate records of the several thousand water wells drilled in its territory, including those located by local dowsers. According to these records, the dowsers were very successful, with about a 70 percent hit rate; about seven out of every ten of the wells they directed drillers to produced water (Raloff 1995:91). This sounds impressive until you compare the dowsers' success rate with that of all other (nondowsing) methods for locating wells. Here the hit rate was 83 percent (p. 91).

That dowsers seem to be almost as successful as geologists and others at finding water is not so surprising. As Robert Farvolden of the Waterloo (Ontario) Centre for Groundwater Research pointed out in an interview, "In most settled parts of the world it is not possible to dig a deep hole or drill a well without encountering groundwater" (in Raloff 1995:91). So you will be right more often than not, whether you locate a well by dowsing, geological and hydrological principles, ESP, tea leaves, or anything else.

Like their success at locating water, dowsers (as well as psychics—and even psychic dowsers) will often be right in locating archaeological sites. This might sound provocative, but it really means little. Archaeological remains are not nearly as rare as many people assume. In some favored locales, buried archaeological materials may be virtually continuous. In some places, even along lengthy transects it is almost impossible to dig a test pit without exposing archaeological remains. In such places, a dowser might direct an archaeologist to dig in a particular spot and artifacts will be found. But virtually anyone using virtually any technique could have accomplished the same feat in these archaeologically rich zones. So, without success in the lab, under controlled conditions, the efficacy of dowsing cannot be upheld and will not become part of the archaeologist's repertoire.

Current Perspectives: Archaeology Without Digging

All over the world archaeologists are leaving many of their traditional tools—shovels, trowels, brushes, and screens—back in the lab and toolshed, at least in the initial phases of some projects. Deeply buried artifacts, the outlines of ancient farmers' fields, human burials, houses long since turned to dust, and enclosed sacred spaces are being found—all without moving a cubic centimeter of dirt (Kvamme 2003).

These archaeologists are not involved in an occult movement, nor are they applying paranormal procedures to extract secrets from the earth. They are not relying on dowsing, ESP, or other unsubstantiated phenomena. Instead, these archaeologists are employing new and sophisticated technologies to perform a cutting-edge, noninvasive, and nondestructive kind of archaeology that allows us to produce an image of what is entombed in the ground beneath our feet without digging it up.

For example, in an archaeological survey conducted at Fort Benning, Georgia, at the historic Creek Indian village of Upatoi, Frederick Briuer, Janet Simms, and Lawson Smith (1997) used a proton magnetometer and *ground penetrating radar* (GPR) to scan the subsurface to determine patterns of activity in the eighteenth-century native settlement. The proton magnetometer measures local changes in the earth's magnetic field that may be caused by metal artifacts, buried walls, or alterations in the soil caused by previous disturbance resulting from excavation of old irrigation canals or even the digging of human burials. In GPR, an electromagnetic pulse is transmitted into the ground. The nature of the return signal is a factor of the medium through which the pulse travels and can be interpreted as the result of some previous activity that involved disturbing the ground. In both instances, measurements are taken at regular intervals on the surface with no disturbance of the soil (Conyers 2004; Conyers and Goodman 1997).

It may sound like dowsing, but there are major differences: Proton magnetometry and GPR are based on known, understood natural phenomena—and they work. After taking a series of readings at fixed intervals by walking across the area where a part of the Upatoi village had already been located, these researchers located six probable human burials that can now be protected without any further disturbance.

In another example, it would simply not have been practical to pepper a popular Key West, Florida, beach with test pits looking for what amounted to a handful of needles in a very large haystack. Local authorities desired to pinpoint the locations of the unmarked burials of a small group of African

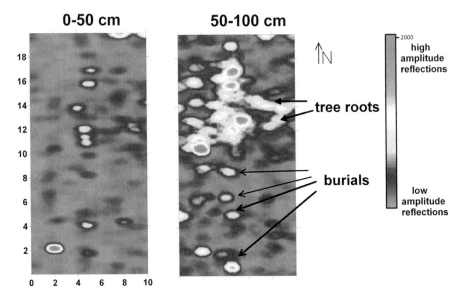

Figure 10.3   GPR (ground-penetrating radar) readout showing a clear pattern of buried remains along a beach in Key West, Florida. Being able to see through soil and sand and to recognize archaeological remains may seem like magic, but it really is based on the application of modern scientific technology. The apparent blobs on the readout are, in actuality, human burials. (Courtesy Laurence Conyers)

slaves who had shipwrecked and died there just before the Civil War, but how could they do it without a major disturbance to the beach? University of Denver archaeologist Larry Conyers and his GPR team were called in to attempt to solve the problem and locate the graves (Conyers 2003).

The images on Conyers's GPR printouts from the beach are eerie and ghostlike (Figure 10.3; see a color version at http://www.du.edu/~lconyer/grids1,3_annotated.jpg). Small, vaguely oval blobs of red and green float on an otherwise homogeneous blue background. The green and red do not appear to be randomly distributed on the sea of blue, but are neatly lined up and clustered. The red and green blobs represent the computer depictions of discontinuities in radar reflectivity beneath the surface sand and were the right size and a reasonable depth to have been the result of human burials. Excavation verified that these radar anomalies, indeed, were the graves of the African slaves.

Elsewhere, GPR has been used to locate an entire buried Viking ship in Norway that may be the ninth-century tomb of Halfdan the Black, the father of Norway's first king (Bjornstad 1998). Here, and in the other examples cited, noninvasive archaeology through geophysical prospecting may never entirely replace digging. We still need to test the "ground truth" of the clues suggested by the application of magnetometers and radar. Nevertheless, these new procedures can be incredibly useful in isolating those areas where digging will be fruitful, an accomplishment that psychics and dowsers can only promise, but not deliver.

❈ ❈ ❈ FREQUENTLY ASKED QUESTION ❈ ❈ ❈

Didn't the "prophet" Nostradamus accurately predict future events, including things that have happened in the twentieth century?

Though the allegedly accurate prognostications of sixteenth-century prophet Michel de Notredame (Nostradamus was his pen name) are beyond the scope of this book, I get this question so often in class that a brief answer is in order—no.

Specifically, Nostradamus was a physician and writer who became quite popular in France for his supposed prophetic abilities. Nostradamus made a name for himself with his book *Centuries*—a reference not to time but to the nine groupings of 100 predictions of four lines each (quatrains) contained in the book (the final edition published during his lifetime had 940 quatrains).

The vast majority of the quatrains are incredibly obscure, dense, vague, and incomprehensible. For example, you may read that Nostradamus accurately predicted the rise of Napoléon Bonaparte, actually naming the French emperor more than 200 years before he was born. You may also read that Nostradamus predicted World War II and even named the German leader Hitler nearly 400 years before the fact. Neither of these claims is true. In the former case, the Nostradamus quatrain in question states what seems like gibberish:

PAU, NAY, OLORON will be more in fire than in blood.
Swimming the Aude, the great one fleeing to the mountains.
He refuses the magpies entrance.
Pamplona, the Durance River holds them enclosed.

(Translations are taken from James Randi's book, *The Mask of Nostradamus* [1993], a terrific place to learn the truth behind the legend.) What this quatrain has to do with the ascendance of Napoléon is anybody's guess. PAU, NAY, and OLORON (uppercase in the original) are three towns located in southwestern France, near the Spanish border. The tortured attempts by Nostradamus boosters to coax Napoléon's name out of the letters of these town names is pretty lame.

The so-called Hitler quatrain is no better:

Beasts mad with hunger will swim across rivers,
Most of the army will be against the Hister.
The great one shall be dragged in an iron cage
When the child brother will observe nothing.

This is more meaningless prattle, but what about "Hister"? It is very close to "Hitler," and even though the meaning of the quatrain is completely obscure, does this hint that Nostradamus actually had prophetic abilities? No. On ancient Roman maps of Austria, the lower reaches of the Danube River were named the "Hister." Nostradamus certainly is referring to some unnamed army encamped or trapped against the Lower Danube River.

And while we are on the subject, despite what you may have heard, Nostradamus did not predict the September 11 terrorist attack on America. A quatrain circulated on the Internet soon after the attack seemed to show that he had done just that, with references to a "city of God" (New York), a "great thunder" (the sound made by the World Trade Center's towers collapsing), and "two brothers torn apart by chaos" (the two buildings falling). The delicious irony here is that this quatrain, in fact, was not written by Nostradamus, but by a college student, Neil Marshall, a few years before 9/11, in the style of the prophet. This fake quatrain was picked up by someone who, apparently, didn't realize it was a fake, and the next thing you know, everyone is speaking in hushed tones about the incredible abilities of Nostradamus.

I guess Marshall succeeded, in a way he could not possibly have imagined, in showing how Nostradamus-like quatrains could be interpreted in so many ways as to render them meaningless. Apparently, this made-up quatrain next morphed into something even spookier, with references to "two steel birds falling from the sky." This version, sounding even closer to the actual event, is akin to P. T. Barnum's fake of the Cardiff Giant; it is an intentionally faked version of the original fake Nostradamus quatrain, written, of course, after the 9/11 attack.

Even Nostradamus could not have predicted the extreme measures his twenty-first-century followers have taken to force his quatrains to match recent events. Unfortunately, it is all a sham. Nostradamus exploited the gullibility of a jaded nobility; he was the "psychic friends network" of his day. He predicted nothing.

BEST OF THE WEB

http://www.science.uwaterloo.ca/earth/waton/dowsing.html#dowsing
Brief, skeptical commentary about dowsing by the late Robert N. Farvolden of the Department of Earth Sciences at the University of Waterloo, Canada.

http://www.lysator.liu.se/~rasmus/skepticism/dowsing.html
Fantastic and very thorough discussion—and debunking—of dowsing. There is even a brief mention of the application of dowsing in archaeology.

CRITICAL THINKING EXERCISE

Design an experiment to test each of these claims.

- After a self-proclaimed psychic successfully locates a previously unknown archaeological site, the claim is made that archaeological sites can be discovered, excavated, and interpreted by the application of psychic power.

- After a dowser successfully locates a previously unknown archaeological site, the claim is made that archaeological sites can be discovered by dowsing.

❖❖❖❖❖❖❖ 11 ❖❖❖❖❖❖❖

Old Time Religion—
New Age Visions

Imagine scientists in a remote corner of the globe, scraping away the soil surrounding a remarkable discovery, peering through a microscope at a previously enigmatic artifact, or examining their computer printouts, and scarcely believing what they perceive. Incredulous, they realize that there is no other rational explanation; in the artifact they hold before their eyes, in the magnified image of their discovery, or in the results contained in their printouts, the remarkable truth is impossible to deny. The scientists have uncovered concrete proof of a miracle and, at least indirectly, proof of the existence of God. It sounds like a potential theme for a movie. But the imaginary scene I've described is not a movie scenario or a television script. It reflects actual claims made on a number of occasions by self-styled scientists.

Although the purpose of this book is certainly not to assess the veracity of anyone's religious beliefs or to judge the philosophical basis of anyone's faith, when individuals claim there is physical, archaeological evidence for a basic belief of a particular religion, the argument is removed from the field of theological discourse and placed squarely within the proper boundaries of scientific discussion.

We can assess such a claim or claims as we have assessed all other claims made in the name of the science of the past—within the context of the scientific method and deductive reasoning. This is precisely what I will attempt in this chapter for claims of the existence of Noah's Ark, the validity of biblical chronology as evidenced by the contemporaneity of dinosaur and human footprints, the reality of the Shroud of Turin, esoteric information encoded in the calendar and writing of the ancient Maya Indians, and New Age archaeology.

Scientific Creationism

You may have heard of the so-called Scopes Monkey Trial, which took place in Tennessee in 1925. That trial focused on a high school teacher, John T. Scopes, who broke Tennessee state law by teaching Darwin's theory of evolution in a public school classroom—a law that stayed on the books until 1967. The celebrated trial attracted international attention; famous defense lawyer Clarence Darrow served as counsel for Scopes, and thrice-failed presidential aspirant William Jennings Bryan served on the prosecutorial team. You can find excerpts from the trial transcript, plus a lot of interesting material related to the trial, at http://www.law.umkc.edu/faculty/projects/ftrials/scopes/scopes.htm.

Though Scopes was convicted and fined a mere $100 (he never did have to pay the fine), most presume that the notoriety—and ridicule—that accrued to Tennessee as a result of the trial resulted in a victory for science and the teaching of evolution. As scientist Stephen Jay Gould (1981, 1982) points out, however, this was not the case. Emotions ran high both during and after the trial. To avoid controversy that might hurt sales, most publishers began a practice of regularly ignoring evolution in their high school texts. Generations of American students went unexposed to evolution—the most essential principle underlying the biological sciences.

This changed rather drastically in the 1950s after the Soviets successfully launched Sputnik, the first artificial satellite to orbit the earth. American complacency regarding our superiority in all fields was shaken, and among the results was a revamping of science curricula from elementary school on up. Evolution once again took its rightful place in the biology classroom.

This development, in turn, spawned a new attempt by fundamentalist Christian groups to at least alter the teaching of evolution, a concept that they saw as directly contradictory to their religious faith. Realizing, however, that as a result of constitutional protections, religion could not be injected into public education, the fundamentalists attempted a different approach. A new and ostensibly religion-free perspective called *scientific creationism* was invented. Herein it was proposed that there was ample *scientific* evidence for the recent (usually dated to within the last 10,000 years) and spontaneous creation of the universe by an intelligent force, the recent and instantaneous creation of human beings by that same force, and the destruction of at least a part of that creation by an enormous, worldwide deluge (Gish 1973; Morris 1974, 1977; Whitcomb and Morris 1961).

Although their beliefs sound suspiciously like the story related in the Book of Genesis in the Old Testament of the Judeo-Christian Bible, scientific creationists claim that they do not base their perspective on faith. They claim simply to be scientists with an "alternate" hypothesis for the origins of the universe, the earth, life, and humanity. Scientific creationists have founded institutes (for example, the Institute for Creation Research), published books, founded schools, and debated evolutionists. Finally, they have attempted, through legislation on the state level, not to eliminate evolution from the classroom, but to impose what they call a "two-model approach" in teaching. This would involve providing equal time for creationist models of biology, geology, astronomy, and anthropology in public schools—in other words, ten minutes of Darwin, ten minutes of creationism.

It should be emphasized that although most scientific creationists are Christians, their brand of Christianity does not reflect the mainstream of that religion. As you will see, the strict literal interpretation of the Bible upon which scientific creationism is based is not adhered to by most Christian groups. Many Christian theologians believe that scientific creationism represents bad theology as well as bad science.

The creationists have failed virtually every time their equal time requests have been legislated, carried out, and then litigated. The courts have seen creationism for what it is: not an alternate scientific model but a restatement of a religious ideology. Statutes passed by state legislatures requiring the teaching of creationism in public schools have been deemed unconstitutional by the courts in several states, including Arkansas and Louisiana (Scott 1987). The Louisiana statute came before the Supreme Court of the United States in 1987, and seven out of the nine justices agreed that creationism represented little more than a restatement of a particular religious ideology—that presented in the Old Testament of the Judeo-Christian Bible. Therefore, its teaching could not be mandated in public school science classrooms. (Michael Shermer's 1997 book, *Why People Believe Weird Things*, contains a concise summary of the arguments presented in this Supreme Court case.)

The 1987 Supreme Court decision has not ended attempts by creationists to inject what the court decided was a religious doctrine into public school classrooms (Schmidt 1996). For instance, in 1995 the Alabama state legislature ordered that a pasted insert be placed in all secondary school biology textbooks stating that evolution has not been proven. The disclaimer begins by stating: "This textbook discusses evolution, a controversial theory some scientists present as a scientific explanation for the origin of living things, such as plants, animals and humans. No one was present when life first appeared on earth. Therefore, any statement about life's origins should be considered as theory, not fact." Note the misuse of the word "theory" here to imply that scientists are not certain of the validity of evolution (see Chapter 2). The claim that "no one was present when life first appeared on earth" and, therefore, we can't know what really happened is nonsense, ignoring uniformitarian principles that underpin sciences such as geology, archaeology, and paleontology.

In 1996, in a fairly close vote (20 to 13), the Tennessee Senate voted down a bill already passed by the state House of Representatives that would have provided for dismissal of any public school teacher who taught evolution as a fact. Also in 1996, the Ohio state legislature debated and then defeated a bill that would have required public school teachers to present evidence against evolution. Even though such efforts largely have been unsuccessful, an air of controversy has resulted, and some schoolteachers have revealed that they simply avoid any discussion of evolution in their biology classes (Schmidt 1996:421).

Opting for a slower, quieter, from-the-bottom-up approach, some creationists have run for positions on their local school boards, in some cases espousing a "back to basics" academic philosophy that is becoming increasingly popular, while at the same time hiding or at least soft-pedaling their agenda to inject their religious views into public school curricula. In one instance where exactly this happened, the Kansas Board of Education's standards for the high school science curriculum were altered. The standards had long required the teaching of evolution in life science courses; an understanding of evolution was one of a set of seven knowledge "benchmarks" required of all students in these courses.

After the election of several new members, in August 1999 a majority on the Kansas board voted to reduce the required knowledge benchmarks in the life sciences from seven to six, eliminating evolution as one of the required topics. This resulted in a local outcry by many parents concerned that their children would no longer be receiving a thorough grounding in science, as well as a national uproar by scientists and science educators who viewed the action of the board as an attack on science itself. It took more than two years, but members of the anti-evolution majority on the Kansas Board of Education were voted out of office, and in January 2001 the board voted to restore evolution as one of the knowledge benchmarks of the life science curriculum.

Kansas may have returned evolution to its science curriculum in 2001, but in the following year the Ohio state legislature considered passing a bill to encourage schoolteachers to disclose in their teaching the uncertainty of evolution. At the same time, the statewide Ohio Board of Education was considering, in its deliberations about a new curriculum, arguments for the removal of evolution from the science requirements. In the spirit of the Ohio legislature's deliberations, those proposing removal suggested, as a compromise, instructing science teachers to emphasize the tentative and uncertain nature of evolution as an explanation for life on the planet. The irony here is that most scientists would agree that specific evolutionary hypotheses concerning the origins of life and the significance of various mechanisms for biological change are, indeed, tentative, but that the fundamental fact of evolution is anything but uncertain. Following a bit of agonizing, in October 2002, the Ohio school board voted to adopt a science curriculum that included evolution without any disclaimers. Interestingly, the Ohio board has maintained that, though evolution is a required element of the science curriculum, teachers can elect to include a discussion of a perspective called "intelligent design" (ID) in their treatment of evolution, but students won't be tested on it (Holden 2002a, 2002b).

What is intelligent design? Though many of the details presented in the ID argument are fairly recent, dating to the last couple of decades (for example, Dembski 1999), as philosopher Niall Shanks (2004) points out, the underpinnings of ID date back to the ancient Greeks. Essentially, advocates of intelligent design, both ancient and modern, assert that the regularity, patterning, and order seen in the universe and, especially, the exquisitely complex regularity, detailed patterning, and incredible ordering seen in living things could only have been the product of an intelligence (call this intelligence God, if you wish) who designed them. As Shanks points out, a significant problem with this argument is that it ignores the fact that many known natural processes produce regularity, patterning, and order without the intervention of an intelligent force. The shape of a snowflake, the spiral of a sunflower's seeds, and a rainbow's form and color are dictated directly by chemistry, biology, and physics and not necessarily by the hand of an intelligent designer.

Even just the term "evolution" is viewed as problematic by some school boards. In January 2004, new guidelines for junior high and high school science courses in Georgia eliminated the word "evolution" altogether, substituting the less precise phrase "changes over time." The state school superintendent defended this action by asserting that "evolution is a buzz word that causes a lot of negative reaction" (Jacobs 2004). Even phrasing that casually referred to the great antiquity of the earth was altered; previous wording in the curriculum that made reference to the "long history of the earth" now merely spoke of "the history of the earth." Fortunately, the reaction of teachers, scientists, and parents to these changes resulted in the reinstatement of evolution into the Georgia science curriculum description in February 2004.

There are several fine books on the nature of creationism and the threat it poses to science education in America and elsewhere (McKown 1993; Strahler 1999). Paleontologist Chris McGowan (1984) provides a lively refutation of creationism, and writer Michael Shermer (1997) presents a point-by-point refutation of twenty-five creationist claims. For a detailed treatment of the way the intelligent design argument is being used in an attempt to include creationism in school curricula, see Barbara Carrol Forrest and Paul R. Gross's *Creationism's Trojan Horse* (2003). These are all excellent sources on the topic of creationism. We needn't go into this issue in more depth here.

However, the purported existence of physical evidence supporting biblical literalism is often used to support the *scientific* underpinnings of creationism. Such physical evidence falls into the field of focus of this book. The two pieces of ostensible evidence I will assess here are (1) the existence of the "artifact" of Noah's Ark and (2) evidence of the recent creation of the earth in the form of proof of the contemporaneity of human beings and dinosaurs.

Noah's Ark

The biblical version of the flood story was first written down between 500 and 450 B.C., and similar tales had been circulating in the Middle East since at least 1800 B.C. (Cohn 1996). In most versions, an angry and vengeful God decides to destroy his creation in an enormous flood. A single, righteous man (variously: Ziusudra, Atrahasis, Utnapishtim, or Noah) is warned of the impending deluge and is given specific instructions to build a boat with compartments, to coat it with pitch, and to fill it with plants and animals (Figure 11.1). Even the story of sending first a raven and then a dove out from the boat or ark to search for dry land after the rain ends is found in some of the older versions of the legend. This shows quite clearly that the biblical flood story was not unadulterated history but was borrowed and adapted by the ancient Hebrews from other people in the Middle East.

With this in mind, using a deductive approach as applied elsewhere in this book to nonreligious claims about the past, we can ask the following

Figure 11.1   An artist's rendition of the gathering of animals boarding Noah's Ark. Geological, biological, paleontological, and archaeological evidence indicates that Noah's Flood was not a historical event. (*Noah's Ark,* 1846, by Edward Hicks. Philadelphia Museum of Art. Bequest of Lisa Norris Elkins)

questions: (1) Could the Ark as described in the Bible have actually been built? (2) Could the people involved have saved representatives of each animal species? (3) Is there any geological evidence of a universal Flood? (4) Is there archaeological evidence of the Flood? (5) Are there actual remains of the Ark itself resting where the Ark landed after the Flood? And, finally, (6) Is there evidence of a catastrophic flood not of global but of local proportions that might have served as the inspiration for the biblical story? Let's consider these questions individually.

1. *Could the Ark have been built?*

Robert A. Moore (1983) and Mark Isaak (1998) have written point-by-point examinations of the Flood story. They conclude independently that building the Ark would have been impossible. According to the biblical account, the Ark measured 300 cubits in length and 50 cubits in width. Remember from Chapter 3, in our comparison of the biblical giant Goliath to the Cardiff Giant archaeological hoax, that a cubit equals approximately 18 inches. Using this measurement, Noah's Ark, built entirely with hand tools by a few people, would have been about 450 feet long and more than 75 feet wide! This was an enormous ship. Vessels this size did not become common in the U.S. Navy until the 1940s, and these ships were built by enormous contingents of experienced workers, not a handful of untrained people like Noah's family. The technology necessary for building a seaworthy vessel with anything approaching these dimensions did not even exist until the nineteenth century A.D. We do know what boats looked like 5,000 years ago when the Ark was supposed to have been built. Egyptologists have unearthed the oldest example of an engineered boat—something other than a hollowed out log. It has been dated to between 3100 and 2890 B.C. Its substantial size—75 feet long and 7 feet wide—still makes it just a bit more than 1.5 percent of the claimed size of the Ark. There is no archaeological or historical evidence that anything bigger than this Egyptian boat was built during this period.

2. *Could the people involved have saved representatives of each and every animal species on earth?*

Noah and his family (his wife, three sons, and their wives) could not have gathered and accommodated all the animals allegedly saved on the Ark—some from as much as 12,000 miles away, from continents not even known to Noah. Beyond this, some of the landmasses that supplied animals to the Ark were separated from Noah's location by enormous expanses of open ocean. How exactly did llamas and alpacas (from South America) or even kangaroos and koalas (from Australia) manage to get to the Ark in the first place?

We can estimate that, had the Ark housed representatives of every animal species alive in the world before the flood—as the Bible indicates was done—this would mean that 25,000 species of birds, 15,000 species of mammals, 6,000 species of reptiles, 2,500 species of amphibians, and more than 1,000,000 species of insects, all multiplied by two for each kind of the "beasts that are not clean" and by seven for each kind of the "clean beasts" (Genesis 7:2), were brought on board and taken care of for about a year (Schneour 1986:312). The small number of people on the Ark could not possibly have fed, watered, and tended this vast number of animals—and imagine cleaning out all those stalls!

Beyond this, even considering the enormous size of the Ark, there would have been less than 1 cubic meter (a stall a little more than 3 feet by 3 feet by 3 feet) for each vertebrate and its food supply—more than enough for small animals, but how about a rhinoceros, a giraffe, or an elephant (Schneour 1986:313)? And remember, as we will see in the next section, many creationists believe that dinosaurs lived during Noah's time and were among the animals saved on the Ark (Taylor 1985a). Obviously, a 30-ton, 40-foot-tall, 100-foot-long *Supersaurus* would have been more than a little cramped in its quarters.

Further, even in the twenty-first century, zoos have trouble keeping some species alive in captivity; their dietary and other living requirements are so finely adjusted in nature that they cannot be duplicated. How did Noah accomplish this?

Finally, though extinction technically occurs when the last member of a species dies, species extinction effectively occurs when numbers fall below a certain threshold. For example, the population of about one thousand pandas left in their natural habitat may be too small a number to prevent eventual disappearance of the species in the wild (Dolnick 1989). Yet, if the Flood story were true, we would have to believe that the panda and all of the other species we see today were able to successfully survive after their numbers had dwindled to either two or seven of each. Genetic variability is so small with such a limited population size that most species would have disappeared.

3. *Is there geological evidence for the Flood itself?*

Certainly such a catastrophic event occurring so recently in the historic past would have left clear evidence. In fact, worldwide geological evidence does not support the claim of a great Flood. The vast majority of the features of the earth's surface are the result of gradually acting, uniform processes of erosion repeated over vast stretches of time, not short-lived, great catastrophes (though occasional catastrophic events like asteroid impacts do occur and may have had significant effects—one large asteroid strike may have been the cause for dinosaur extinction about 65 million years ago).

For example, paleontologists have long recognized the *biostrati-graphic* layering present in the earth. Biostratigraphy refers not just to the layering of geological strata but also to the occurrence of plant and animal fossils in these strata. These biological traces are not present in a hodgepodge; they are not randomly associated in the layers but tend to be neatly ordered. That ordering—older species are found in deeper layers, more recent species are found in higher strata—is a reflection of lengthy chronology, not a recent catastrophe.

If a recent, universal Flood simultaneously destroyed virtually all plants and animals, their remains would have been deposited together in the sediments laid down in that Flood. Dinosaurs and people, trilobites and opossums, giant ground sloths and house cats, *Australopithecus* and the Neandertals—all would have been living at the same time before the Flood and should have been killed together during the Flood. We should be able to find their fossils together in the same geological layers.

Of course, we find no such thing. Plant remains are found in layers older than those containing animals. Single-celled organisms are found in layers below those containing multicelled organisms. Reptiles are found in older strata than are mammals. Layers containing dinosaurs never show evidence of human activity and are always far older than layers containing human fossils. (See "Footprints in Time" later in this chapter.)

Creationists recognize this powerful contradiction to their view. They speculate that biostratigraphy, instead of representing an ancient chronological sequence, represents differences in animal buoyancy during the Flood. In other words, reptiles are found in lower strata than are mammals because they don't float as well. Not only is this rationalization weak, it is not even original. Here creationists are only recycling an explanation put forth by John Woodward (1695) in *An Essay Toward a Natural History of the Earth*. Of course, we can forgive Woodward—he suggested this more than 300 years ago.

4. *Is there archaeological evidence for the Flood?*

If a universal Flood occurred between five and six thousand years ago, killing all humans except the eight on board the Ark, it would be abundantly clear in the archaeological record. Human history would be marked by an absolute break. We would see the devastation wrought by the catastrophe in terms of the destroyed physical remains of pre-Flood human settlements. Above all else, we would see sharp discontinuity in human cultural evolution. All advances in technology, art, architecture, and science made up until the point of the catastrophe would have been destroyed. Human cultural evolution, as reflected in the archaeological record, would have necessarily started all over again after the Flood.

Imagine the results of a nuclear war that left just a handful of people alive. Consider the devastation such a war would visit upon human culture. Think about what the remains of the pre- and postwar societies would look like from an archaeological perspective. This is comparable to what the differences would have been between pre- and post-Flood societies and their archaeology.

Unfortunately for the Flood enthusiasts, the destruction of all but eight of the world's people had no discernible impact on ancient culture and left no mark whatsoever on the archaeological record. The cultural records of the ancient Egyptians, Mesopotamians, Chinese, and Native American civilizations show no gaps in development. Either cultural trajectories in these world areas were affected not at all by the destruction of their entire populations, or there simply was no universal Flood. Applying Occam's razor, we have to conclude that, based on the archaeological record, there could have been no universal Flood like that described in the Bible.

5. *Do remains of Noah's Ark still exist?*

Are there archaeological remains of a great ship located on the slopes of a mountain in Turkey? Are these, in fact, the actual physical remains of Noah's Ark? For years various groups associated with numerous fundamentalist organizations have searched for remains of the Ark on Mount Ararat in Turkey (LeHaye and Morris 1976). One of these groups included former astronaut James Irwin. They have, as yet, all been unsuccessful.

Local Kurdish tribesmen who claim to have visited the largely intact Ark on the 17,000-foot peak have been interviewed. Stories have been collected of the Russian discovery of the Ark in 1916. That legend maintains that when the communists took control in the Soviet Union all photographs of the Ark were destroyed, and eyewitnesses to the Ark were executed. Some have circulated stories of an American discovery of the Ark in the 1960s. Here, a joint, secret expedition of the Smithsonian Institution and the National Geographic Society supposedly discovered the Ark but suppressed the information "in order to preserve the dominance of Darwinian theory" (Sallee 1983:2). An obvious question that might have been asked is, naturally enough, Then why did they go looking for the Ark in the first place?

Eyewitnesses have invariably been unable to relocate the Ark and bring people to it. Other alleged evidence for the Ark has consisted of photographs and movies. These have always either mysteriously disappeared or turned out to be of images of misidentified rock formations.

In 1959, a French explorer, Fernand Navarra, claimed to have visited the Ark and even brought back wood samples. Unfortunately for the "arkeologists," radiocarbon dating applied to the wood indicated that it dated not to 5,000 years ago as it should have according to biblical chronology, but to between the sixth and ninth centuries A.D. (Taylor and Berger 1980).

6. *Was the story in the Bible of a worldwide flood inspired by a local event?*

The newspaper headlines of early September 2000 were breathtaking in their implications. "New Evidence of Great Flood," read one. Another read, "Found: Possible Pre-Flood Artifacts." Of course, the "flood" referred to in the newspaper headlines likely wasn't interpreted by most readers to mean just any old flood: not the 1955 flood that wrought such devastation in southern New England or the catastrophic flooding of the American Midwest in 1993. Just in case you weren't sure what flood they were talking about, the Web site accompanying the research project made it transparently clear, characterizing the investigation as "The Search for Noah's Flood" (Ballard and the Black Sea 1998).

In actuality, the hyperventilated headline writers and the author of the Web site were being a little disingenuous about an intensely interesting research project being directed by underwater explorer Bob Ballard, who was also responsible for discovering the remains of the *Titanic*. Ballard is testing the hypothesis of geologists William Ryan and Walter Pitman (1998).

The scenario these geologists lay out is based on the indisputable fact that as a result of lowered worldwide sea level during the Pleistocene, the waters of the Mediterranean Sea and Black Sea, today connected indirectly by way of the Bosporus Strait, the Sea of Marmara, and the Dardanelles Strait, were entirely distinct bodies of water, separated by a rocky plateau that is now entirely underwater (Figure 11.2).

When the Pleistocene ended and glacial ice melted off, sea level rose all over the world. The same process that inundated the Beringian land connection between the Old and New Worlds (see Chapter 5) caused the Mediterranean to rise, eventually surpassing the height of the plateau, allowing its water to pour into the basin of the Black Sea. Most geologists believe this occurred gradually and relatively gently, beginning about 10,000 years ago, and that it transpired over the course of decades (Aksu et al. 2002). These same geologists also maintain that the water level in the Black Sea was only about 18 meters (60 feet) lower than modern sea level. The "in-filling" of the Black Sea as water spilled over the plateau may have produced an impressive waterfall, but it was in no way cataclysmic; its height would have been the aforementioned 60 feet (Schiermeier 2004). Compare this, for example, to the Canadian side of Niagara Falls, which is 167 feet high.

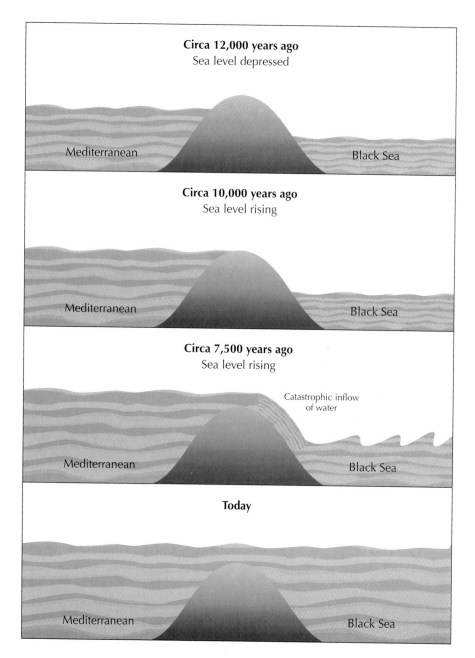

Figure 11.2 Simplified schematic drawing of a cross section across the plateau separating the Mediterranean and Black Seas. When worldwide sea level is depressed sufficiently—for example, during glacial maxima of the Pleistocene—sea level drops to below the level of the top of the plateau, and the Mediterranean and Black Seas are entirely separate. When the sea rises, eventually its level exceeds the height of the plateau, and the Mediterranean spills into the Black Sea. Researchers Ryan and Pitman (1998) assert that this in-filling of the Black Sea was catastrophic, inspiring the biblical tale of Noah's Flood.

Ryan and Pitman suggest, instead, that this water spill occurred about 7,500 years ago and was sudden and catastrophic. Those who support this scenario assert that, by the time the Mediterranean reached the height of the plateau, the water on the Black Sea side wasn't 18 meters lower but at least 50 meters (164 feet) and as much as 150 meters (nearly 500 feet) lower than the water on the Mediterranean side (Shiermeier 2004). In this scenario, the result was a stupendous waterfall in-filling the Black Sea with the force of as many as 200 Niagaras. The water poured precipitously into the shallow, post-Pleistocene Black Sea, raising its level and reestablishing a connection between it and the Mediterranean over the course of only a very few years.

Such a deluge would have been quick, unexpected, and devastating, annihilating entire communities of people who lived on the shores of the Black Sea. Ryan and Pitman propose that this historical event is the basis for the story told in the Bible of Noah's flood: not a global event, to be sure, but one stupendous enough that anyone living near the Black Sea at the time would have thought the entire world was being destroyed.

It's not quite the biblical flood, and its cause is entirely natural, but it is a fascinating historical possibility, nonetheless. A recent attempt to model the geology of a catastrophic flooding of the Black Sea by geologist Mark Siddall (Schiermeier 2004) supports a somewhat catastrophic in-filling (over the course of more than three decades), but the jury is still out (Aksu et al. 2002). Ballard's team is looking for corroborative evidence in the Black Sea itself, using an undersea ROV (remotely operated vehicle) with cameras and sonar to search for archaeological evidence of the communities that would have been destroyed by the proposed inundation. Discovery of the remains of lots of settlements, all destroyed about 7,500 years ago along the ancient Black Sea coast, would lend support, at least to the claim of a historical catastrophe; but it is difficult to see how this sort of evidence can be used to make a firm connection between the Black Sea scenario and the biblical Flood.

To date, along with shipwrecks that date to a time period far more recent than 7,500 years ago, Ballard and his crew have located the remains of a building at a depth of about 90 meters (300 feet), likely positioned on what in antiquity was dry land, an ancient shore of the Black Sea. Radiocarbon dating, however, indicates that it too is much younger than the proposed 7,500-year-old cataclysm (Mitchell 2002). Research is continuing, and you can read about the work on the National Geographic Web site (http://www.nationalgeographic.com/blacksea/).

One might suppose that with the stunning lack of any corroborative evidence, interest in the Ark would have waned after the years of fruitless searching. It hasn't, but this is because the search for the Ark has little to do with objective, scientific testing of a hypothesis and everything to do with supporting a religious ideology. As one searcher stated: "My motive is just to show to the world that the Bible is God's word, and that the stories in the Bible are truth, not fiction" (Sallee 1983:1).

The desire to find some evidence of the Ark and the Flood remains strong. An example of this was a two-hour, prime-time television special titled *The Incredible Discovery of Noah's Ark*, which aired on CBS in February 1993. It was independently produced and sold to CBS by Sun International Pictures (see Jaroff 1993 for a brief discussion of the special, and for a detailed exposé see Lippard 1994).

The show was a hodgepodge of unverifiable stories and misrepresentations of the paleontological, archaeological, and historical records. The presentation was filled with interviews of individuals identified as "Noah's Ark eyewitnesses." One particularly convincing (in the dramatic sense) "eyewitness," identified as George Jammal, claimed to have climbed through a hole in the glacial ice atop Mt. Ararat in 1984 and to have dropped down into the Ark itself. He and his companion "Vladimir" photographed the wooden animal stalls in the huge boat, and Mr. Jammal used his ice-ax to hack out an actual piece of the biblical ship.

Though tragically Vladimir was killed in an avalanche and the photographic evidence lost beneath many tons of ice, Jammal made it back to civilization with his piece of the Ark. "This wood is so precious, and a gift from God," he told the viewing audience as he displayed the remarkable artifact.

There is, however, a significant problem with Mr. Jammal's testimony—it is entirely false. It all began in 1985 when, motivated by little more than a dislike of religion, Jammal contacted the Institute for Creation Research (ICR) in California, telling them the story of his discovery of the Ark. A cursory examination of his letter should have alerted any reader with even a modicum of skepticism that it was a sham: Pronouncing the names of the individuals who Jammal told the Institute had helped him in his quest—Mr. Asholian, Vladimir Sobitchsky, and Allis Buls Hitian (Lippard 1994)—should make it clear why.

When representatives of Sun International were conducting research for their Ark show, they contacted ICR and were given Jammal's name. Inexplicably, the ICR was much impressed by Jammal's absurd tale, though Jammal had not provided even a shred of evidence to back it up. Biblical scholar Gerald Larue was a friend of Jammal's and had become close enough for Jammal to reveal his fabricated Ark story. Coincidentally, Larue had been interviewed by Sun International for a previous show. He was angry with his treatment on that show and encouraged Jammal to continue his Ark hoax when Sun contacted him.

There had been no trip to Turkey, there were no photographs, and there was no Vladimir Sobitchsky. How about the wood Jammal so reverently presented on camera as a piece of the Ark? It was never tested or seriously examined by Sun International. Had they examined it closely, it should have become apparent that it was just a slab of California pine that had been aged by microwaving it after soaking it in, among other things, teriyaki sauce! Jammal's story should have been verified by the show's producers. Even simply checking Jammal's passport would have revealed no travel to Turkey, and that should have ended it. Jammal and Larue had intentionally made it easy; in fact, all one had to do was sniff the wood. After all, why would a piece of Noah's Ark smell like an Oriental marinade? The point had been made. If the producers of *The Incredible Discovery of Noah's Ark* could be fooled by a hoax with so many obvious and intentional clues, they certainly could not be trusted on anything else.

When confronted with this, CBS responded rather lamely, "It was an entertainment special, not a documentary." Note the similarity of the excuse CBS is using for presenting the public with patent nonsense to the disclaimer discussed previously (see Chapter 2) that appears in each issue of the *Sun* tabloid paper. It is sad to believe that CBS is comfortable placing some of its "science" programming in this same category.

Footprints in Time

It is a little more than 65 million years since dinosaurs thundered across the landscape. Some fundamentalist Christians deny this dating of the extinction of the dinosaurs. In fact, it is their view that the universe, including our world and ourselves, is only about 6,000 years old. In 1650, Irish archbishop James Ussher determined that God had created the universe in 4004 B.C. Some fundamentalists still accept the validity of that date and so claim that human beings and dinosaurs walked the earth during the same period— that is, before Noah's Flood.

Such a remarkable scenario, although in agreement with some awful Hollywood movies and *The Flintstones* cartoon, stands in contradiction to the accumulated wisdom of the fields of biology, zoology, paleontology, geology, and anthropology. Basing conclusions on the seemingly indisputable evidence of stratigraphy, fossils, artifacts, and radiometric dating, these fields show quite clearly that the last of the dinosaurs died off about 60 million years before the appearance of the first upright walking hominids.

Many creationists reject all these data in favor of one bit of presumed evidence they claim shows the contemporaneity of dinosaurs and human beings—footprints from the Paluxy River bed in Glen Rose, Texas (Morris 1980).

Fossilized dinosaur footprints along the Paluxy River were first brought to the attention of scientists and the general public in 1939 when scientist Roland Bird (1939) mentioned their existence. In the same article, Bird noted that giant, *fake* human footprints were being made and sold by people who lived in the area of the genuine dinosaur prints (Figure 11.3).

Figure 11.3   These obviously carved human footprints were found by scientist
R. T. Bird (1939) in a store in Arizona. He traced them back to Glen Rose, Texas,
where he subsequently located a rich deposit of genuine, fossilized dinosaur footprints in the Paluxy River bed. (Neg. #2A17485. Photo by K. Perkins and T. Beckett.
Courtesy Department of Library Services, American Museum of Natural History)

Thereafter, claims were published in a Seventh Day Adventist church
periodical that there were *genuine* "mantracks" side by side with, in the same
stratum with, and sometimes overlapping dinosaur prints in the Paluxy
River bed (Burdick 1950). Similar claims were made in a major creationist
publication purporting to prove the validity of the biblical Flood story
(Whitcomb and Morris 1961). Throughout the 1960s, 1970s, and 1980s, creationists of various denominations and perspectives conducted "research"
in the area, looking for trackways and other evidence that dinosaurs and
humans lived during the same recent period of the past—in Texas, at least.

Certainly, the association of dinosaur and human footprints in the
same geological stratum in Glen Rose would contradict the biostratigraphic
record of the rest of the world and would seem to indicate that human beings and dinosaurs, indeed, were contemporaries.

The footprint data have been summarized from a creationist perspective by John Morris (1980) in his book *Tracking Those Incredible Dinosaurs and the People Who Knew Them*. It is clear from his descriptions that there are at least three distinct categories of features in the Paluxy River bed: (1) indisputable dinosaur footprints, (2) indisputably fraudulent, carved giant human footprints, and (3) long (some more than 50 cm; almost 20 inches), narrow, ambiguous fossilized imprints.

Little needs to be said of the first two categories. Physical anthropologist Laurie Godfrey (1985) has shown quite clearly that the fraudulent "mantracks" were known to have been carved and sold by at least one local resident during the Depression. Extant examples of these frauds (see Figure 11.3) bear no relationship to the anatomy of the human foot or the way human footprints are produced (their *ichnology*).

The third category has caused the greatest amount of confusion. Those impressions available for study are invariably amorphous imprints that, while exhibiting only in a very general sense the outline of huge human feet, bear no actual humanlike features (Cole, Godfrey, and Schafersman 1985; Edwords 1983; Godfrey 1985; Kuban 1989a). Interestingly, many of the creationists who discovered the prints admit that, as a result of erosion, the prints are now unimpressive, while maintaining they were clearly human when first discovered (Taylor 1985b).

Godfrey (1985) shows quite clearly that the elongate fossil impressions are a mixed lot of erosional features and weathered, bipedal dinosaur footprints (Figure 11.4). Most of the prints are vague—even creationists cannot agree on the length, the width, or even the left/right designation of the same prints. None of the so-called mantracks exhibit anatomical features of the human foot, nor do the tracks exhibit evidence of the biomechanics of human locomotion. As Godfrey points out, humans have a unique way of walking that gets translated into the unique characteristics of our footprints. When we walk, each foot contacts the ground in a rolling motion—the heel strikes the surface first, then the outer margin of the foot, next the ball of the foot, and finally the big toe, or *hallux*. Godfrey's analysis shows that the Paluxy "mantracks" do not exhibit these aspects of human locomotion.

In recent years, most creationists have changed their minds concerning at least the tracks discovered before 1986 (Morris 1986; Taylor 1985b). Kuban (1989b) discovered that the exposed tracks had weathered, revealing the claw impressions of the three-toed dinosaurs who had made the prints creationists claimed were made by humans. Though hopeful that earlier, now-destroyed discoveries might have been genuine human footprints or that future discoveries might be made of real "mantracks," most creationists for a time accepted what evolutionists had been saying all along; there is no evidence for the contemporaneity of human beings and dinosaurs in the Paluxy River bed.

Figure 11.4   Creationists have claimed there are fossilized footprints of giant human beings in the same layer with, and side by side with, the dinosaur prints in the Paluxy River bed. These turn out to be misinterpreted portions of genuine dinosaur footprints. Impressions left by three claws can be discerned at the front (left) of this print. (© 1985 Glen J. Kuban)

Other Guises of Creationism

Certainly, not all creationists are fundamentalist Christians. Many ultra-orthodox Jews, for example, also reject evolution and take seriously the date on the Jewish calendar, the year 5765 (corresponding roughly to A.D. 2005), as representing the age of the universe—that is, 5,765 years. Not coincidentally, this is pretty close to the age of the universe as determined by Archbishop Ussher.

In a different kind of creationism with an entirely different time scale, devout believers in the Hindu religion maintain that human beings have been around for millions or even billions of years exactly as we are now, with no evolutionary sequence leading up to the present. This anti-evolutionary perspective has been expressed in two books written by individuals affiliated with the Hare Krishnas of the Bhaktivedanta Institute (Cremo and Thompson 1993, 1994). Reflecting their belief in what amounts to a conspiracy of silence on the part of scientists, Cremo and Thompson use terms like "forbidden archaeology" and "hidden history" in the titles of their books (see Feder 1994a and Lepper 1995a for reviews of these books).

Modern followers of various creation myths ignore the fundamental difference between myth and science. By definition, creation myths are not hypotheses that have been tested, refined, reformulated, and retested until they conform closely to reality. Just as important, these myths likely were not intended as actual history. The purpose of myth is not to describe reality in an objective, scientific way but to show people how to live a moral life. This was articulated best by a prominent modern thinker when he said:

> Sacred scripture wishes simply to declare that the world was created by God, and in order to teach this truth, it expresses itself in the terms of the cosmology in use at the time of the writer. . . . *The sacred book . . . does not . . . teach how heaven was made but how one goes to heaven.* (Emphasis mine; as cited in Lieberman and Kirk 1996:3)

This is not a scientist or atheist or secular humanist speaking. These are the words of someone who has devoted his life to God, the Bible, and his church. You might be surprised to learn that this was written by Pope John Paul II. If only those arraying religion against science would realize this—and, equally, if scientists stuck to discussions of how the universe and life evolved rather than why—much of the problem would be eliminated. That this has not happened is to the detriment of both science and religion.

The Shroud of Turin

In discussing scientific epistemology in Chapter 2, I pointed out that science does not proceed through a simple process of elimination. We do not simply suggest a number of hypotheses, eliminate those we can, and then accept whichever one is left. Yet just such an approach is at the heart of much of the pseudoscience surrounding the so-called *Shroud of Turin.*

Some presume that this 14-foot by 3½-foot piece of cloth is the burial garment of Jesus Christ. It is further asserted by some that the image on the cloth of the front and back of a man, apparently killed by crucifixion (Figure 11.5), was rendered not by any ordinary human agency but by miraculous intervention at the moment of Christ's resurrection (Stevenson and Habermas 1981a, 1981b; Wilson 1979). Some of the scientists who participated in the Shroud of Turin Research Project (STURP) in 1978 reached such a conclusion (Weaver 1980).

Over five days in 1978, using seventy-two crates of high-tech equipment, STURP conducted an intensive examination of the shroud. The quality of a scientific investigation, however, cannot be assessed by the tonnage of the equipment brought to bear. The STURP research ultimately was a scientific failure. Even before they began, according to some reports, many of those involved had already made up their minds that the shroud housed in the cathedral in Turin, Italy, was the result of a supernatural occurrence (McCrone 1997; Mueller 1982).

Beyond this, their approach was not consistent with scientific methodology. In essence, they considered a limited number of prosaic explanations for the image on the shroud (oil painting, watercolors, stains from oils used to anoint the dead body). They applied their high-tech equipment in testing these hypotheses and found none of the explanations to their satisfaction. They ended up suggesting that the image was actually a scorch mark created by an inexplicable burst of radiation (Stevenson 1977). Though, officially, STURP did not conclude that the image had been miraculously wrought, Mueller (1982) points out that STURP's "burst of radiation" from a dead body would most certainly have been miraculous.

Some STURP members (in particular, Stevenson and Habermas 1981a) were forthcoming in explicitly concluding that the image must have been

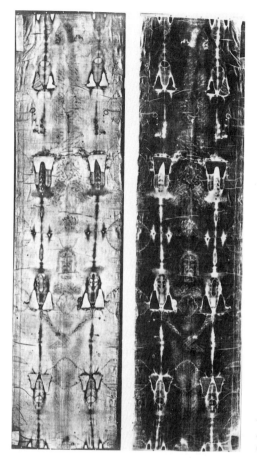

Figure 11.5   Positive (left) and negative (right) images of the Shroud of Turin. Some have claimed that the shroud was the actual burial garment of Jesus Christ and that the image on the shroud was miraculously wrought at the moment of resurrection. However, historical evidence, microscopic analysis, and a recently derived radiocarbon date show that it was the work of a fourteenth-century artist. (Photo by G. Enrie. Courtesy of the Holy Shroud Guild)

the result of a miracle. They further maintained that the image is that of a person bearing precisely the wounds of Christ as mentioned in the New Testament (scourge marks, crown of thorns, crucifixion nail holes, stab wound). They finally concluded that the image on the shroud is, in fact, a miraculously wrought picture of Jesus Christ.

Not all were convinced by STURP's official argument or the more religious claims of Stevenson and Habermas. One member of the original STURP team (he subsequently resigned) was the world-renowned microscopist Walter McCrone. McCrone and his associates examined more than eight thousand shroud fibers and collected data on thirty-two so-called sticky-tape lift samples—samples collected on a clear adhesive-coated tape that had been in direct contact with the shroud (1982). McCrone and his team used a number of techniques, including high-power (400×–2500×) optical microscopy, to examine the physical characteristics of the image and ostensible bloodstains and used x-ray diffraction, polarized light microscopy, and electron microprobe analysis in determining their chemical makeup (McCrone 1990).

McCrone found that, far from being an enigmatic or inexplicable imprint on the cloth, the shroud body image and the supposed bloodstains contained evidence of two distinct artist's pigments made and used in the Middle Ages. The image itself showed the existence of red ochre, a common historical component of paint (McCrone 2000). The bloodstains showed the presence of a synthetic mercuric sulfide, a component of the artist's red pigment vermillion. The particular characteristics of the vermillion pigment found on the shroud are consistent with a type made in Europe beginning about A.D. 800. According to McCrone, the alleged bloodstains produced only negative results when a series of standard forensic blood tests were applied. From this he concluded that there was no blood on the shroud, only an artist's red pigment.

Joe Nickell (1987) has suggested a plausible artistic method for the production of the shroud. This involved daubing powdered pigment on cloth molded over a bas-relief of a human being. His method seemed to explain the curious fact that the image on the shroud appears more realistic in negative reproductions; that simply is a product of the technique of image manufacture (as in a grave rubbing). Though his method has been used by European artists for 700 years, and his replica of the face on the shroud bears a strong resemblance to the original, not surprisingly his suggestion was rejected outright by those who believed that the shroud represented an authentic miracle (Figure 11.6).

Another attempt at replicating the shroud has been conducted recently by forensic scientists Randall Bresee and Emily Craig (1994). Using a technique familiar to medical illustrators called "carbon-dust imaging," they produced a very "shroudlike" image. Whereas Nickell's replica has been criticized on the microscopic grounds that his pigment was present at a much greater depth in the fibers than in the shroud, the Bresee/Craig replica is both macroscopically and microscopically similar to the shroud image.

Walter McCrone's (1996) approach to replicating the shroud uses the simplest technique. He asked the artist Walter Sanford to paint on linen an image of the man on the shroud with a very dilute iron-oxide tempera paint, a formula McCrone produced based on his analysis of the paint residue he found on the shroud. The "negative imaging," the lack of absorption into the fibers of the linen, and the three-dimensional features of the Turin shroud were faithfully reproduced by Sanford and McCrone (see Figure 11.6). McCrone's painted shroud and the Turin shroud look virtually identical in a naked-eye comparison (compare Figures 11.5 and 11.6, right); in addition, McCrone (2000) has demonstrated that a microscopic comparison (between 400× and 1500×) of his painted shroud and the Turin shroud shows a very close match.

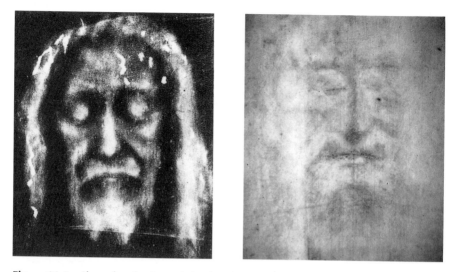

Figure 11.6 Shroud enthusiasts claim that there is no natural explanation for the image on the shroud. However, using different prosaic and entirely natural methods, Joe Nickell (left, 1987) and Walter Sanford (right, cited in McCrone 1996) have produced reasonable facsimiles of the image on the shroud. (*Left:* Courtesy of Joe Nickell; *right:* Courtesy Walter McCrone)

So, was the shroud daubed, dusted, fingerpainted, or brush-painted into existence? Ultimately, the answer to this question is not so important. Whatever process may have been used, it is clear that any assertion that the process that produced the image on the shroud is mysterious or miraculous and cannot be replicated using mundane artistic techniques is simply false.

Testing the Shroud

It must be admitted that if the image on the shroud is miraculous, it is, of course, beyond the capability of science to explain it. Nonetheless, we can apply scientific reasoning concerning the historical context of the shroud. In other words, if the shroud is the burial cloth of Jesus, and if the image appeared on the shroud through some inexplicable burst of divine energy at the moment of resurrection, then we might expect to find that

1. The shroud was a regular part of Jewish burial tradition.
2. The shroud image was described by early Christians and, as proof of Christ's divinity, used in proselytizing.
3. The Shroud of Turin can be historically traced to the burial garment of Christ mentioned in the New Testament.
4. The Shroud of Turin can be dated to the period of Jesus Christ.

We can test these implications of the hypothesis of the shroud's authenticity.

1. *Was the shroud a regular part of Jewish burial tradition?*

The story begins with the crucifixion of Jesus Christ. Whatever one's perspective concerning the divinity of Jesus, a few things are indisputable. Christ was a Jew and one among a handful of alleged messiahs about 2,000 years ago. As such, from the perspective of the Roman occupiers of Israel, Christ was one in a series of religious and political troublemakers. The Romans dealt harshly with those who directly or indirectly threatened their authority. Crucifixion—execution by nailing or tying the offender to a wooden cross in a public place—was a way of both eliminating the individual and reminding the populace of the cost of defying Roman rule.

As a Jew, Christ would have undergone a Jewish burial ceremony. In fact, the Gospel of John clearly states that Jesus was to be buried in the "manner of the Jews" (19:40). At the time, this would have involved scrupulously washing the body and anointing it with oils, shaving the face and head, and wrapping the body with a burial shroud of linen. According to *halacha* (Jewish law), burial ordinarily should occur within twenty-four hours of death or soon thereafter.

According to the New Testament, Christ was removed from the cross and placed in a cave whose entrance was sealed with a large rock. Christ is then supposed to have risen from the dead, and his body disappeared from the cave.

Taking an anthropological perspective, analysis of Jewish burial custom suggests that a burial sheet or shroud is to be expected in the case of the death and burial of Christ. But what should that shroud look like? Old Testament descriptions of shrouds seem to imply that the body was not wrapped in a single sheet (like the "winding sheets" used in burials in medieval Europe), but in linen strips, with a separate strip or veil placed over the face. In the Gospel of John, there is a description of the wrapping of Jesus' body in linen clothes and a separate face veil.

The image on the shroud has "blood" marks in various places. Shroud defenders have pointed to these supposed blood marks in an attempt to authenticate the shroud, comparing the wounds on the image to those of Christ as described in the New Testament. But there is a problem with this interpretation. If the image on the shroud is really that of Jesus produced through some supernatural agency, then the body of Christ could not have been ritually cleaned. Yet this would have been virtually unthinkable for the body of a Jew. Such ritual cleansing of a dead body is an absolute requirement for Jews, even on the Sabbath—Christ died on Friday around sundown when the Jewish

Sabbath begins—when all other work would have been halted. The marks alleged to be Christ's actual blood, therefore, contradict the claim that the body of Jesus was wrapped in the shroud; he would already have been ritually cleaned for burial before being placed in his burial clothes.

Further, if the Turin shroud is authentic, then the cloth itself should be of a style consistent with other shrouds and other cloth manufactured 2,000 years ago in the Middle East. However, textile experts have stated that the herringbone pattern of the shroud weave is unique, never having been found in either Egypt or Palestine in the era of Jesus Christ (Gove 1996:243).

In sum, there are significant inconsistencies between what the burial garments of Jesus should look like and what the Gospel of John says it looked like on one hand and the actual appearance of the Shroud of Turin on the other.

2. *Was the shroud image mentioned in the Gospels?*

The Gospel of John states specifically, "took they the body of Jesus and wound it in linen clothes" (19:40). When the disciples entered the tomb, Jesus was gone but his burial garments were still there. Again, the Gospel of John provides a short but succinct description: "And the napkin, that was about his head, not lying with the linen clothes, but wrapped together in a place by itself" (20:7). This description matches Jewish burial custom—but not the Shroud of Turin.

Certainly the Gospels were not averse to proclaiming the miracles performed by Christ. A miraculous image of Jesus would have been noticed, recorded, and, in fact, shouted from the rooftops. But though the burial linens are seen and mentioned in John, there is no mention of an image on the cloth. In fact, there is no mention of an image on Jesus' burial garments anywhere in the New Testament. This is almost certainly because there was no image.

3. *Can the current shroud be traced to the burial of Jesus?*

With the preceding argument in mind, can we nevertheless trace the burial linens of Jesus mentioned in the New Testament to the shroud housed in the cathedral in Turin? The answer very simply is no.

To be sure, other burial shrouds of Christ are mentioned in ancient stories. The earliest may be a second-century account of a shroud; there is a brief mention of it in later, secondary sources. An 8-foot-long burial shroud is mentioned in A.D. 877. But in none of these accounts is there any discussion of an image on the burial linen.

Historical references to miraculous images of the face, but not the entire body of Christ, are fairly plentiful. Probably the best known is called the "Image of Edessa," which dates to the fourth century. Christ is said to have wiped his face on a towel, whereupon a miraculous image of his face appeared. The cloth had healing properties. But this is a story of a supposedly miraculous image of Christ's face alone on a small piece of cloth. The Image of Edessa was called a "mandelion," which means "kerchief"—hardly an appropriate term for a 14-foot-long winding sheet. The Image of Edessa as described is nothing like the shroud.

The very earliest mention of the current shroud is A.D. 1353. Between the death of Jesus and A.D. 1353, there is no historical mention of the shroud and no evidence that it existed. It makes little or no sense, if indeed a shroud existed with a miraculous image of Christ on it, for it to have gone unnoticed and unmentioned for more than 1,300 years. Applying Occam's razor, a more reasonable explanation might be that the shroud with the image of Christ did not exist until the fourteenth century.

The history of the shroud after 1353 is quite a bit clearer. It has been described in an excellent book, *Inquest on the Shroud of Turin*, by science writer Joe Nickell (1987). A church named Our Lady of Lirey was established in 1353 to be a repository for the shroud, and it was first put on view there a few years later. It was advertised as "the true burial sheet of Christ," and admission was charged to the pilgrims who came to view it (Nickell 1987:11). Medallions were struck (and sold) to commemorate the first display of the shroud; existing medallions show an image of the shroud.

The Church in Rome took a skeptical approach to the shroud. As a result of the lack of reference to such a shroud in the Gospels, Bishop Henri de Poitiers initiated an investigation of the shroud, and a lengthy report was submitted to the Pope in 1359. The report pulls no punches; it concludes that the shroud was a fake produced to make money for the church at Lirey. It was even discovered that individuals had been paid to feign sickness or infirmity and to fake "miraculous" cures in the presence of the shroud. The report goes even further, mentioning the confession of the forger: "the truth being attested by the artist who had painted it, to wit, that it was a work of human skill and not miraculously wrought or bestowed" (as quoted in Nickell 1987:13).

As a result of the Church-sponsored report, Pope Clement VII declared that the shroud was a painted cloth and could be exhibited only if (1) no candles or incense were burned in its presence, (2) no honor guard accompanied it, and (3) the following disclaimer was announced during its exhibition: "It is not the True Shroud of Our Lord, but a painting or picture made in the semblance or representation of the Shroud" (as quoted in Nickell 1987:17).

Even with the disclaimer, the shroud attracted pilgrims and believers. The shroud became an article of commerce, being bartered for a palace in 1453. In 1578 it ended up in Turin, Italy, where it was exhibited in the sixteenth through twentieth centuries.

4. *What is the age of the shroud?*

Even if the Shroud of Turin turned out to be a 2,000-year-old piece of cloth, the shroud-as-miracle would not be established. It still could be a fraud rendered 2,000 years ago—or more recently on old cloth. However, a final blow would be struck to any hypotheses of authenticity if the cloth could be shown to be substantially younger than the time of Jesus. Recent analyses have shown just this.

The Church agreed to have three radiocarbon dating labs date the shroud. A postage-stamp-size sample was cut from the shroud. That is all that was needed for all three labs to date the cloth using accelerator mass spectrometry, a very precise form of carbon dating requiring very small samples (see Gove 1996 for a detailed description). A textile expert was on hand to make certain the sample was removed from the shroud itself and not patches added later to cover holes burned in a fire in A.D. 1532. Also, the entire process was videotaped to preserve a chain of evidence from the shroud to each of the labs. In this way, everyone would be certain that the labs actually received material cut from the shroud, and not material substituted for some nefarious purpose. Each lab was also provided with three control swatches: one small piece from each of three fabrics of known age that they also dated. This was done to determine the accuracy of the dates from each of the labs on known cloth, providing a measure of accuracy for a cloth of unknown age (the shroud). Furthermore, none of the labs knew which fabric sample was which; this was a blind test. In that way, no one could knowingly replace the actual shroud sample in an attempt to make it appear to be older (by replacing it with a sample known to be 2,000 years old) or younger (by replacing it with a sample known to be much more recent than 2,000 years old) than it actually is.

The shroud dates determined from all three labs indicate that the flax from which the shroud was woven was harvested sometime between A.D. 1260 and 1390 (Damon 1989; Nickell 1989; Vaughan 1988:229). These dates correspond not with the time of Jesus but with the first historical mention of the existence of the shroud.

How accurate is this date? In all certainty the date is very accurate. In dating the samples of known age, the labs were virtually perfect, and there is no reason to believe their shroud dates are any different (Table 11.1). Some have claimed that the shroud sample was

Table 11.1   *Results of Radiocarbon Dating for Historic Cloth Control Samples and Shroud of Turin*

	Known Date (historical records)	Carbon Date (three-lab average)
Thread from cloth cape	A.D. 1290 to 1310	A.D. 1273
Egyptian mummy wrapping	60 B.C.	A.D. 35
Nubian tomb linen	A.D. 1000 to 1300	A.D. 1093
Shroud of Turin	not known	A.D. 1325

Source: Gove 1996.

contaminated, but Harry Gove, the physicist who is the "father" of the radiocarbon dating technique used, has determined that for a 2,000-year-old cloth to have enough contamination to make it appear to date to the fourteenth century A.D. the sample would have to be at least one-third pure contamination and only two-thirds cloth (1996:265)—an unlikely situation and one that would have been clearly visible to the naked eye. That the Shroud of Turin was a medieval artifact was fairly certain before the dating. After the dating the issue is settled.

A recent analysis of pollen grains adhering to shroud sample fibers by botanists Avinoam Danin and Uri Baruch (1998) has been presented to support the hypothesis that the shroud originated near Jerusalem, supporting a claim of authenticity. This pollen analysis may indicate that the shroud linen originated in or passed through Israel before its "discovery" was announced in the fourteenth century, but this does not speak to the essential issue of the shroud's age. Only radiocarbon dating can supply a date in this case, and that date shows a source in the thirteenth or fourteenth century A.D., not 2,000 years ago.

Some who wish to believe in the shroud have, however, continued to maintain its miraculous nature while accepting the validity of the radiocarbon dates. Writer John Frodsham (1989:329) maintains that although the shroud cannot have been the actual burial garment of Jesus, it may be a fourteenth-century miracle, the image appearing as a sign from God, "perhaps in response to fervent prayers, during an epoch noted for its mysticism, when the Black death was raging throughout Europe." This is an interesting hypothesis, though perhaps European peasants dying in the tens of thousands might have better appreciated a more utilitarian miracle on God's part—say, elimination of the Black Plague—than an image on a piece of linen.

In one of the strangest takes on the shroud, there even is a Web site that consists of a side-by-side comparison of the image of the face on the shroud and, are you ready, the face on Mars (http://www.aadm.com/cydonia/

shroudfonMars.html). The creator of this Web site leaves it up to you to decide the cosmic significance of the similarities. I believe I will do the same.

New Age Prehistory

Sedona, Arizona, is a red rock jewel of a place. Clean air contributes to a piercingly blue sky. The exposed bedrock, shading from deep brown through magenta to lipstick red all the way to pale pink, has been eroded into endless phantasmagoric shapes. It is no wonder that the area has attracted a wonderful mix of people, some of whom perceive a magic and power in their community, the source of which cannot be explained by science.

The Sedona New Agers believe that this magic and power emanate from the red rocks of their region, and reside in the remnants left behind by the prehistoric inhabitants of northern Arizona. New Age Sedonans talk endlessly about vortexes, sacred places, and healing spots—which skeptics might suggest are merely particularly beautiful rock formations, architecturally impressive prehistoric ruins, or interesting ancient rock carvings (petroglyphs) and paintings (pictographs) (Figure 11.7).

Figure 11.7   Pictograph painted by Native Americans onto a cliff face located in Sedona, Arizona. (K. L. Feder)

Tourists can travel into Sedona's backcountry by taking any one of a number of jeep tours with companies called "Earth Wisdom Tours," "Mystic Tours," or "Crossing Worlds Journeys." Archaeological sites often are important elements in these tours. One tour pamphlet suggests that "some will sense the ancient resonance still present at these sites." Other tours promise healing ceremonies, revelation of ancestral secrets of the "Medicine Wheel," and various other cosmic insights.

The two most important archaeological sites located in Sedona are rather small cliff dwellings called Palatki and Honanki (Figure 11.8). The Palatki dwellings were occupied from about A.D. 1150 to 1300, though many of the nearby pictographs are much older. Honanki overlaps in time with the end of the Palatki occupation. I have heard these sites described as "sacred" or "mystical" places. One Web site author tells of "basking in the huge heart energy" during a visit to the Palatki ruins (http://www.visionsofheaven.com/journeys-sedonadocs/sedPalatki.html). That's fine; the archaeological

Figure 11.8 The cliff dwellings of the American Southwest reflect the architectural sophistication and the construction skills of the Native Americans who built them. But they were, after all, simply people's homes. Claims by New Agers that sites in Sedona like the Palatki ruins shown here are "power vortexes" are devoid of any scientific meaning. (K. L. Feder)

remnants of these ancient communities are fascinating and deserving of our attention and respect. If people wish to read spiritual significance into the ruins of ancient dwellings or artifacts tossed by the inhabitants onto their trash heaps, so be it. However, some Native Americans are uncomfortable with the prospect of a group of mostly white, financially well-off people romanticizing and appropriating indigenous religious beliefs and native cultural images for their own cosmic salvation. In fact, some are downright hostile.

For example, Rick Romancito, a Taos and Zuni Indian, is unhappy about the New Age fascination with all things Indian. He decries their melding of different beliefs taken from different tribes into an all-inclusive "Indian religion" that never existed among actual Indians (Romancito 1993). He characterizes this as "selectively picking and choosing spiritual concepts from several different Indian religions, as if they're products for sale in a cosmic marketplace" (p. 97).

Romancito is especially angry at the cloying New Age assumption that Indians are "repositories of 'indigenous spiritual knowledge'" (p. 97), gurus one and all just ripe for the intellectual picking. He tars such a stereotype of Indians as spiritual mystics with the same brush he does more obviously negative popular images such as "the drunken Indian" or the noble but defeated savage. Though New Agers might accuse Romancito of giving off a lot of "negative energy," his complaint should be heeded.

Current Perspectives:
Religions Old and New

Around 1885 a Paiute Indian named Wovoka had a vision in which God came to him and told of a new order that was to come. God instructed Wovoka to teach his people a new dance. If enough Indians from different tribes would only join in, this dance would lead to miracles. All sick or injured Indians would regain their health. All dead Indians from all the ages would come back to life and join in the dance. These countless Indians dancing together would float into the air, and a great flood would decimate the country, destroying in its wake all the white settlers. When the floodwaters subsided, the Indians would gently return to the ground to begin a paradisaical life of plenty, with lots of food, no sickness—and no white settlers (Kehoe 1989; Mooney 1892–93).

The *Ghost Dance*, as it came to be called, was what anthropologists label a *revitalistic movement*. Movements such as the Ghost Dance occur when a people sees its way of life threatened by a terrible, impending calamity. The old ways, including the old gods, seem to have no effect. A new, revolutionary belief system or sometimes simply a return to a previous, "purer" way is seized on as offering a solution.

In the case of the Ghost Dance, Indians faced with cultural extinction at the hands of the European colonists looked for some way out of their terrible predicament. There could be no military solution, and there appeared to be no spiritual recourse.

Wovoka's vision of salvation gave them a way out. Thousands of Indians in hundreds of groups across the United States believed in Wovoka's vision and joined in the dance.

One cannot help but be struck by the common thread running through this revitalistic movement of over a century ago and the spiritual and religious upheavals in the modern world. Fundamentalist Christians and Moslems see all of the modern world's ills as spiritually based; if we could just return to the one true belief, all would be cured. At the same time, New Age beliefs seem to provide spiritual relief for those who perceive the precariousness of modern existence but who do not see the solution in old-time religion.

A century ago Wovoka and the Indian people were faced with the destruction of their way of life and even their own extinction. The terrors of our own century are just as great and include the quick death of nuclear extinction and the slow decay wrought by pollution, terrorism, poverty, drugs, and disease. Science seems to offer little in the way of solution and, in fact, is seen by many as being at the core of the problem.

How comforting to believe that we can change all this simply by returning to a more fundamental belief in the Bible or that the solution to our problems is just a few years away in the guise of godlike extraterrestrial aliens who have been here before and who will save us, ultimately, from ourselves.

It is all the better, then, if the archaeological record can be interpreted as supporting such beliefs. In this perspective, both fundamentalism (of all sorts) and the New Age philosophy can be viewed as twenty-first-century revitalistic movements, offering hope to people desperate to believe there is a spiritual solution to our otherwise seemingly insoluble dilemmas.

It is easy to understand why so many Indians embraced the Ghost Dance: Their situation was desperate, and this new religion offered them the promise of salvation. It is no wonder, as anthropologist Alice Kehoe (1989) states, that the religion survived even massacres like that of Wounded Knee, where, on December 29, 1890, more than three hundred Indian men, women, and children were slaughtered (Brown 1970). Even though their "ghost shirts" did not protect Indian warriors from the spray of bullets spit out by Gatling guns, the desire to believe the promises of the Ghost Dance was so strong that the religion continued to have followers well into the twentieth century.

It is more difficult by far to empathize with modern, well-off people who seem to be afflicted by little more than existential angst, general depression, or a vague feeling of dissatisfaction with their lives and who then turn to New Age nonsense. Harmonic convergers, fundamentalists, and the good and kind New Agers of Sedona and elsewhere might do well to heed this message: Revitalistic movements, whether based on a literal interpretation of the Bible, remarkable interpretations of the archaeological record, or a search for enlightenment in beautiful canyons or fascinating rock carvings, can do little to address the real problems facing the world.

◈ ◈ ◈ FREQUENTLY ASKED QUESTIONS ◈ ◈ ◈

1. Are all scientists atheists?

No, though it is true that a greater proportion of scientists are nonbelievers than is the case for the general public. A Gallup poll conducted in 1991 indicated that about 87 percent of Americans believe in God, 9 percent do not, and 3 percent say they do not know (Gallup and Newport 1991). A 1996 survey among American scientists revealed that close to 40 percent believe in God, about 45 percent do not, and about 15 percent are agnostics (Larson and Witham 1997). So, although belief in God measures at less than half the level it does among the general public, and a far greater proportion of scientists than nonscientists are atheists, a sizable minority of scientists do believe in a personal God.

2. Aren't religion and evolution irreconcilable?

Again, the answer is no. Two popes, including John Paul II, six major Protestant organizations, and the Conference of American Rabbis, among others, have all published statements accepting at least the possibility that evolution was the process by which God created life (Lieberman and Kirk 1996). They accept the scientific evidence for an ancient and changing earth and accept the evidence for change in plant and animal species.

◈ ◈ ◈ BEST OF THE WEB ◈ ◈ ◈

CREATIONISM

http://www.natcenscied.org/

Web site of the National Center for Science Education, an organization devoted to defending the teaching of evolution in public schools. A good source for current events concerning the creation/evolution debate.

http://www.talkorigins.org/

Fantastic site devoted to the creation/evolution debate. A great place to find specific and detailed responses to creationist claims.

NOAH'S ARK

http://www.talkorigins.org/faqs/faq-noahs-ark.html

A Web page at the talkorigins site providing an enormously detailed enumeration of the impossibility of the biblical Flood.

CLAIMED CO-OCCURRENCE OF DINOSAUR AND HUMAN FOOTPRINTS

http://paleo.cc/paluxy/paluxy.htm

The Web site of Glen J. Kuban, probably the most knowledgeable person concerning the actual dinosaur and misidentified giant human footprints at Paluxy. The claims of those few creationists who still maintain that the Paluxy "mantracks" are genuine are thoroughly debunked here.

THE SHROUD OF TURIN

http://www.mcri.org/Shroud.html

A brief, skeptical note regarding the shroud. Click on the link to the carbon 14 graph to see how unlikely it is that recent contamination has contributed to its late-thirteenth–early-fourteenth-century radiocarbon date.

CRITICAL THINKING EXERCISE

Using the deductive approach outlined in Chapter 2, how would you test these hypotheses? In each case, what archaeological and biological data must you find to conclude that the hypothetical statement is an accurate assertion, that it describes what actually happened in the ancient human past?

- The world was all but destroyed in a cataclysmic flood about 5,000 years ago. Only a small group of people and animals were saved.
- Human beings and dinosaurs lived at the same time a relatively short time ago (within the past 6,000–10,000 years).
- The Shroud of Turin was the actual burial shroud of Jesus Christ.

◈◈◈◈◈◈◈◈ 12 ◈◈◈◈◈◈◈◈

Real Mysteries
of a Veritable Past

The past never ceases to surprise, fascinate, intrigue, and amaze people. Many are drawn to it and revel in reconstructions of what happened and what it was like to live in the times that preceded our own.

Perhaps it is this built-in interest that makes so many of us susceptible to frauds, myths, and supposed mysteries like those detailed in this book. Note that I have here repeated the book's title but inserted the word *supposed*, since the mysteries of the Moundbuilders, Atlantis, ancient astronauts, and the rest have been shown to be not mysteries at all but simply confusion resulting from misinterpretation or misrepresentation of human antiquity.

Eliminating the false "mysteries" does not, however, leave us with a dull or mundane human past. There are still plenty of mysteries and some enormously interesting, open questions about what has gone before. Three such examples of genuine mysteries of the past relate to the Paleolithic cave paintings of Europe, the development—and fall—of the Maya Indian civilization, and the European Megalithic site of Stonehenge.

The Cave Painters of Europe

Imagine this scene. In the dark, dim, and distant recesses of a cave's narrow passageway, a flickering oil lamp smears dancing shadows on a flat rock wall. A young woman, tall and lithe, her muscular arms coated with a thin layer of grime and sweat, carefully places a dark slurry in her mouth. With one hand she picks up a hollow reed and holds it to her lips. She places her other hand, palm down, on the rock face. Aiming the reed at the area around her hand, she begins puffing up her cheeks and blows, spraying a fine mist of pigment out of the end of the reed. Some of the paint thinly coats her hand, but much of it covers the cave wall immediately around the area

Figure 12.1   A 20,000-year-old "signature" left by a Paleolithic artist; a negative hand-print produced by placing a hand flat on a cave wall and then blowing paint through a hollow reed all around the hand. From the cave of Peche-Merle in France. (© Musée de l'Homme)

hidden by her palm and fingers. After a few puffs through the reed, she removes her hand from the cave wall and we see in our mind's eye her remarkable artistic creation: a negative image of her own hand, a signature some 20,000 years old calling out across time (Figure 12.1).

By her side, a young man, tall and broad, with a deeply lined face belying his years, dips a frayed twig into a thick red paste. Using skills of observation and artistry developed during his short life, he conjures up a vision held in a part of his memory as deep as where he now labors breathlessly in the cave.

The horse, wild and free, runs across his mind, her legs leaving the ground as she gallops in her desperate but doomed attempt to flee from the hunters. A deep, red gash on her belly where a stone-tipped spear pierced her hide leaks her life blood. Soon, he remembers, very soon she falls, and his comrades are upon her, thrusting their spears deep into her. Then, at last, she is quiet and still. He shudders, thinking of her spirit now returned to the sky. Then he remembers the taste of her still warm flesh in his mouth—her life lost, the life of his people maintained. It is the way of life and death in the world that he knows.

Though long dead and no longer of this life but of another world, a world of stories and magic, the mare lives again in a creation of pigment, memory, sorcery, and awe. Once a creature of blood and bone, of sinew and

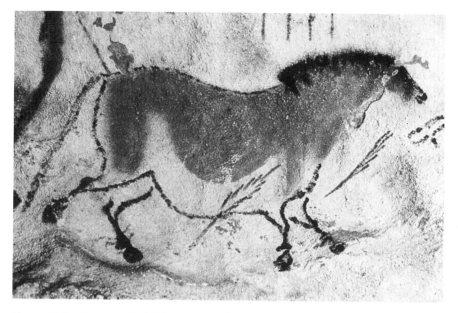

Figure 12.2   The so-called Chinese Horse from the cave of Lascaux in France. The animal was depicted in full gallop by visitors to the cave nearly 20,000 years ago. (© Art Resource, NY)

muscle, she is now a creature of color and binder. No longer running across the ice-shrouded plains of western Europe, she now runs and bellows on a flat sheet of rock, straining against her fate and bleeding eternally in the deep recesses of a dark cave. In this incarnation she has lived for 20,000 years, and in this life of pigment and memory and magic, she will live forever (Figure 12.2).

Explaining the Cave Paintings

The imagined scene just described took place more than 20,000 years ago in the period called the Upper Paleolithic of prehistoric Europe. The individuals described are emblematic of the people who painted the fabulous and now famous depictions of their ancient and extinct world in the deep recesses of more than three hundred caves in western Europe (Chauvet, Deschamps and Hillaire, 1996; Clottes and Courtin 1996; Clottes and Lewis-Williams 1998; Ruspoli 1986; Saura Ramos 1998; White 1986).

A bestiary of ancient animals stands frozen in time on the walls of the caves of Lascaux, Altamira, Chauvet, Cosquer, and Niaux. Rendered in pigments of orange, yellow, red, and brown derived from iron oxides, along with black produced from manganese, many of these paintings are astonishingly lifelike, displaying a realism unexpected among a people so ancient and supposedly so primitive.

There are horses and elk, woolly mammoths and wild cattle, rhinoceroses and bison, all captured in exquisite detail by the ancient artists' skill and talent. Often, the animals are shown not in simple, static poses but in fluid motion. A red horse flees from spears on the cave wall at Lascaux. Two woolly mammoths confront each other, locked in a dance for dominance, on a wall in the cave of Rouffignac. Two spears hang from a dying bison at Lascaux. Four stiff-maned horses graze on the wall at Chauvet; frozen in eternal stillness, they nervously probe for the scent of a predator dead now for some twenty millennia.

In some caves, there seems to be a clear relationship between the animals depicted on the cave walls and the actual remains of animals killed and eaten by the people who lived at the same time. Small, nonaggressive animals such as reindeer and red deer were important in the diet of the cave painters and were depicted on cave walls in a frequency proportional to their economic importance (Rice and Paterson 1985, 1986).

The ancient artists, however, did not depict only those animals that the archaeological record indicates were hunted for food. Bears, lions, and other carnivores also are rendered. These were often placed on walls far from the central parts of the caves, down long, sinuous, rock-strewn passageways. At Chauvet Cave in southeastern France, paintings of cave bears, cave lions, and an astonishing count of fifty rhinoceroses are among the perhaps more than three hundred images found there that also include wild horses, cattle, and elephants (Chauvet, Deschamps, and Hillaire 1996; Hughes 1995).

And there is more. Animals were not the only objects commanding the attention of Paleolithic artists. Abstract designs, geometric patterns, human handprints, and mythical beasts also adorn the cave walls. Rarely, we even find depictions of the humans themselves. Intriguingly, such "self-portraits" are often vague and indistinct—quite unlike the realistic depictions of the animals with whom our ancestors shared their ancient world.

In the cave paintings, as well as in the rest of what is called "Paleolithic art," rests a mystery. What prompted our ancient ancestors to produce these works on the cave walls? Was it simply "art" done for the sake of beauty (Halverson 1987)? Were the painted caves the equivalent of today's art galleries or museums where great artists exhibited their finest work? We can recognize the beauty in the work and today can appreciate it as art, but was that the intention of those who produced it (Conkey 1987)?

Was there some more complex reason for painting the images on the cave walls beyond simply a "delight in appearance" (Halverson 1987:68)? Were the cave paintings of food animals sympathetic magic—an attempt to capture the spirit of animals and thereby assure their capture in the hunt (Breuil 1952)? Were the paintings the equivalent of our modern trophy heads—in effect, historically recording the successes of actual hunts (Eaton 1978)? Were the paintings part of a symbolic system that revolved around male and female imagery (Leroi-Gourhan 1968)? Or were the animal paintings part of a system of marking territory by different human groups during periods of environmental stress (Conkey 1980; Jochim 1983)?

And how about the geometric designs—the dots, squares, wavy lines, and the rest? An intriguing suggestion has been made by researchers J. D. Lewis-Williams and T. A. Dowson (1988). They propose that these images are visual artifacts of the human nervous system during altered states of consciousness. These "visions" result from the structure of the optic system itself and are therefore universal. You can even see some of these visual patterns simply by rubbing your eyes. Perhaps through sleep deprivation, fasting, gazing for hours at a flickering fire, or even ingestion of hallucinogenic drugs, Upper Paleolithic shamans or priests induced these images in their own optic systems and then translated these images to cave walls as part of religious rituals.

Several prehistorians are focusing on the meaning of the cave art; see the book *The Shamans of Prehistory: Trance and Magic in the Painted Caves,* by Jean Clottes and David Lewis-Williams (1998), for a detailed and innovative analysis of the paintings. There are as yet no definitive answers; there may never be. In that sense, the art of the Paleolithic—though certainly recognizable as the work of ancient human beings and not attributable to refugees from Atlantis or extraterrestrial visitors—is a fascinating legacy of our past and can, indeed, be labeled an unsolved mystery of human antiquity.

The Civilization of the Maya

Chichén Itzá, Uxmal, Tikal, Copán, Sayil, Palenque—the names resound with mystery. These were all cities of the ancient Maya civilization that flourished more than ten centuries ago in the lowlands of Guatemala, Honduras, El Salvador, Belize, and the Yucatán Peninsula of Mexico (Figure 12.3). Archaeological research in the past few decades has brought to light some of the remarkable accomplishments of this indigenous American Indian civilization (Sabloff 1989, 1994).

The architectural achievements of the Maya match those of any of the world's ancient cultures. The imposing, elliptical Pyramid of the Magician at Uxmal is a stunning piece of architecture and engineering (Figure 12.4). The eighty-eight room "Governor's Palace" at Sayil, with its columned façade and imposing stone staircase, is similarly impressive. The Temple of Inscriptions at Palenque, El Castillo at Chichén Itzá, and the Temple of the Jaguar at Tikal all provide mute testimony to the splendid architecture of the Maya world.

Beyond their ability at construction, the Maya also developed their own hieroglyphic writing system and left a fascinating legacy of written work in the form of relief carvings, paintings, and books called *codices.* Recent advances in translating the written language of the Maya have enabled

Figure 12.3   Map of eastern Mexico (including the Yucatán Peninsula), Belize, Guatemala, Honduras, and El Salvador showing the location of some of the most important villages, ceremonial centers, and cities of the Maya civilization.

researchers to begin studying Maya history from a Maya perspective, much in the way we can study European history (Coe 1992; Montgomery 2002; Schele and Freidel 1990).

The Maya were precise mathematicians and developed the concept of zero. They also were great astronomers and even built an observatory at Chichén Itzá (Figure 12.5). With their mathematical and astronomical genius, the Maya developed a system of two calendars that together enabled them to chart time more accurately than we do with our standard calendar. In all ways the Maya were a remarkable people.

Explaining the Maya

Hypotheses of von Dänikenesque extraterrestrials are silly and superfluous for explaining the Maya. Though the story of the Maya is still being written, there is no great enigma or mystery to their origins or history. Maya roots can be traced back more than 2,800 years. Initially the Maya lived in small hamlets; by 2,300 years ago some settlements, including Nakbe, El Mirador,

Figure 12.4   The elliptical Pyramid of the Magician at the Maya site of Uxmal, located in the Yucatán Peninsula of Mexico. Unlike Egyptian pyramids, Maya pyramids have steps leading to temples placed at their apexes. (K. L. Feder)

Figure 12.5   El Caracol, or the Observatory at Chichén Itzá. Along with being an impressive piece of architecture, the tower has a number of openings through which, it is thought, Maya astronomer priests observed the night sky. (K. L. Feder)

Lamanai, Cerros, Cival, and Tikal in the south and Dzibichaltún and Komchén in the north, had become larger with evidence of public architecture in the form of large stone platforms. Settlements like Cerros, located on a bay by the mouth of a river, became trading centers where raw obsidian and jade, as well as finely crafted goods from these raw materials, were concentrated, adding to the power of the developing elite class of people (Sabloff 1994).

Some of these Maya villages evolved into true urban settlements that became the capitals of a series of independent kingdoms that shared a common religious iconography and economic system. A highly productive agricultural system focusing on maize provided food for a growing population. A developing class of Maya leaders had the power to command the construction of monuments like pyramids and temples.

Dense settlements marked by monumental architecture, as well as magnificent artwork produced by specialists, are diagnostic of early civilizations. Recent discoveries indicate that such urbanization, monument building, and specialist art began as much as 2,300 years ago among the Maya. Dating to this time, the recently excavated Cival is the largest of the earliest Maya cities (Skidmore 2004). Cival had an estimated population of 10,000 people, and the main part of the settlement was encircled by a defensive wall of earth. The 800-meter- (half-mile-) long ceremonial center of this teeming ancient metropolis was marked by three major plazas demarcated by five flat-topped pyramids. In the middle of this ceremonial heart of the city, archaeologist Francisco Estrada-Belli has found the remains of two enormous carved terra-cotta masks, each one approximately 3 meters (9.8 feet) tall and 5 meters (16.4 feet) wide. When the city was occupied, these huge masks dramatically flanked a stairway leading to the top of a pyramid 33 meters (108 feet) high (Lovgren 2004). Estrada-Belli describes the masks as having faces part human and part jaguar; one is adorned with carved corn husks over its eyes, the other has snake fangs. In the center of the main city plaza, archaeologists found a cluster of 120 finely polished green and blue jade cobbles; nearby, five polished jade axe heads were also found. Jade was a stone sacred to the Maya and associated with their main crop, maize.

Farming, focused in part on the production of maize, provided a major portion of Maya subsistence. David Webster (2002:86) estimates that maize comprised about 60 percent of the Maya diet. In many regions the Maya practiced slash-and-burn agriculture, cutting and burning forest land to produce fields that were abandoned after only a short period of use and allowed to grow over, to be used again after a period of dormancy. This is the primary agricultural technique used by the modern Maya. To this, as archaeologists have documented, the ancient Maya added a number of other, more intensive techniques, including terracing hill slopes, building raised fields in swampy areas (as indicated by radar imaging), planting kitchen gardens, and tree-cropping, the specialized use of tree crops in rainforests and within settlements (McKillop 1994; Turner and Harrison 1983). Of necessity, the

Maya relied on a number of techniques, both extensive and intensive, to feed the large and dense populations in their cities.

The inception of what is called the Classic Maya civilization dates to A.D. 250. Copán, Caracol, Lamanai, Palenque, and Tikal, with their temples, pyramids, and palaces, flowered at this time. By about 1,350 years ago Tikal, in Guatemala, had a resident population of at least 40,000 people and perhaps thousands more in the surrounding countryside. Segments of the population at Tikal were devoted to the production of certain fine works of art or craft. Many of these products were included in elite Maya burials (like Pacal's at Palenque, discussed in Chapter 8), reflecting the high status and great wealth of the upper classes.

Though some cities in the southern lowland—Lamanai, for example—continued their regional dominance, after about A.D. 800 the great cities in the southern portion of the Maya realm stopped building temples and pyramids, and their populations declined dramatically. The geographical focus of the Maya shifted to the north and east where the great cities of Chichén Itzá, Uxmal, and later Mayapán developed and thrived (Webster 2002).

The Mysterious Collapse of the Maya?

When the Spanish arrived in the sixteenth century, the Maya world was vastly different than it had been just a few centuries previously. The large urban centers of the south had been abandoned, and Maya cities in the north were, for the most part, on the decline. To be sure, Spanish chroniclers reported the existence of complex agricultural societies with densely occupied towns marked with tall temples and neatly laid out plazas, but their descriptions clearly do not match the spectacular archaeological remains of the Classic Maya. The vast difference between Classic Maya cities and those encountered by the Spanish in the early 1500s has long been a great historical mystery. Indeed, what happened to the Maya to cause such a great "collapse" of their civilization?

Mayanist David Webster (2002) maintains that this notion of an absolute, abrupt disintegration of Maya society is mistaken. In fact, he points out that the great collapse of the Maya was anything but sudden and, in light of Maya history, anything but unexpected. The first hints of the collapse of the Classic Maya are traced to the middle of the eighth century A.D., and the breakdown wasn't complete until about A.D. 950. Furthermore, the breakdown was essentially a geographically limited phenomenon, centered in the western lowlands of Maya territory. Finally, as Webster shows, the great collapse was merely the most dramatic in a series of smaller breakdowns and resurgences that marked the fundamental cycle of Maya history.

In Webster's view, Maya civilization always represented a delicate balance between nature, a growing population, and the land-hungry system of slash-and-burn agriculture. That balance, in fact, was upset several times during Maya history, leading to a series of collapses. Slash-and-burn agriculture was an effective subsistence strategy in this tropical lowland habitat; but as population grew in Maya communities, the need for more intensive use of the land to produce crops grew as well. However, slash-and-burn agriculture requires an enormous amount of land (perhaps as much as 20 acres for each family) and quickly depletes the soil of nutrients, requiring a long rest or fallow period to allow the soil to regain its productivity. When the Maya agricultural fields, previously allowed to rest and regain nutrients, were pressed back into service more quickly in order to produce more food, ultimately and ironically productivity declined even more rapidly.

Adding other, more intensive agricultural techniques—terraced hill slopes, raised fields in swamps, kitchen gardens, and tree-cropping—certainly helped feed more mouths. For example, by artificially mounding up fields in wetlands, the Maya were able to exploit rich floodplains previously too wet to farm and were able to farm the same plots every year. At the Pulltrouser Swamp site in Belize, for instance, the Maya essentially reclaimed part of the swamp by building fields into the wetlands, producing extremely rich agricultural plots that could have yielded multiple crops each year (Turner and Harrison 1983).

Ultimately, however, the more intensive use of farmland like that evidenced at Pulltrouser Swamp was not enough to solve the Maya's food production problems. Another strategy employed by individual Maya cities was to expand their land base by aggressively appropriating the agricultural fields of their neighbors. Warfare for land capture may have been a short-term solution by growing a community's farmland base; but, as population continued to grow and productivity to decline, the need accelerated for ever more land, and warfare became endemic, an everyday, unpleasant fact of life for the Maya peasants who may have made up 80–90 percent of the population (Webster 2002:140). As foot soldiers, these peasants bore the major burden of these wars. Webster suggests that as agricultural productivity declined further and as the need to fight wars to capture land increased, the peasants, whose labor and lives were required for the system to work, lost faith in the ability of their kings to solve the problems plaguing them, to ease their increasing burden either materially or spiritually. As Webster points out, a civilization is no longer viable when farmers/foot soldiers/workers simply walk away; Webster calls it "voting with their feet." In his view, many peasants, disaffected by the inability of those kings to improve their lot, simply moved away from those lands controlled by their rulers. When this happened, Maya kings lost their most important resource: people. This is clearly reflected in the almost complete cessation of temple construction at many Maya cities after A.D. 950.

The series of collapses experienced by the Maya, including the most dramatic of them in A.D. 950, may be explained, at least in part, as a result of a subsistence system inadequate to meet the needs of a growing population, accompanying soil depletion, and, finally, bloody conflicts. In previous collapses, the Maya had been able to recover; new cities cropped up, ruled by new kingly lineages who directed new bursts of pyramid and temple construction. Had the Spanish not arrived in the early sixteenth century, it is entirely possible that the Maya would have experienced yet another resurgence with an attendant explosion of new cities, spectacular temples, and graceful pyramids. We will, of course, never know. We can state, however, that the fall of the Maya is no longer a great mystery but a challenging puzzle whose secrets are being revealed through anthropological research.

Stonehenge

In the summer of 1996 I made a pilgrimage, of sorts, returning as an adult to a place that had amazed and inspired me as a teenager. My wife, our two kids, and I spent two weeks in Great Britain, and we made it a point to make the trip from London to Stonehenge.

My family and I were part of a gaggle of tourists from the United States and all over Europe as well who were visiting the ancient monument that day. Reflecting the "world" culture that permeates much of the planet, we were all dressed pretty much alike; most of Stonehenge's visitors were wearing sneakers, jeans, and T-shirts emblazoned with the logos of assorted rock bands, cartoon characters, and software companies. But there alone, amidst the Smashing Pumpkins and Beavis and Butt-head shirts, was a rather striking-looking individual, a woman dressed from head to toe in black. She had on black boots, loosely fitting black pants, a black shirt, and finally was enveloped in a long, rather dramatic, black velvet, hooded cape.

She stood still in her solitude, and I watched as she, almost imperceptibly, began to rock back and forth to some internal, inaudible rhythm, her eyes shut and her lips mouthing a silent mantra. I wondered, in a whisper to no one in particular, who she was. Someone answered: "Oh, she fancies herself the reincarnation of a Druid princess." Of course. It was a peculiar sight, indeed, but we were to see many peculiar sights on our trip.

We visited other "stone circles." Stonehenge is an extreme example of an ancient circle laid out in monumental stone or "megalithic" sentinels, but there are hundreds in Great Britain, so many, in fact, that there is an atlas/tourist guide of them (Burl 1995) and a truly beautiful "gazetteer" of 300 of the most impressive of the sites (Cope 1998). In some we found people meditating in their geometric centers, hoping to focus the ancient and mysterious energy supposedly contained within them. At Avebury, a town encircled by an ancient monument of standing stones, the shelves of the tourist shops were filled with healing crystals, pyramid pendants, and even dowsing rods (pairs of bent brass rods going for five pounds, about $7.50, each) for channeling the "ancient energies" ostensibly focused in the prehistoric monument.

The ancient past of Great Britain has been invaded, or so it seems, by people espousing New Age beliefs (see Chapter 11). Seeking salvation and redemption in the fabric of antiquity, they congregate at the stone circles of Great Britain. In late June on the summer solstice they descend on Stonehenge to practice so-called ancient, pagan rites. Traditionally, a riot ensues as the local police attempt to protect the site from the scores of ecstatic, sometimes naked, latter-day Druids who have, in the past, climbed the ancient stones of the monument. Too often, the modern, reconstructed Druids revert to the historical behavior of the people they base their worldview on and rain violence down on the local constabulary.

What is Stonehenge, really? Is it some great archaeological mystery? Does it vibrate with some ancient and mystical energy? My then 10-year-old son Josh found "awesome" to be the most appropriate word to describe Stonehenge—and who could argue with his use of that term? Awesome it is. About 4,900 years ago an otherwise simple farming people first excavated an almost perfectly circular ditch about 100 meters (300 feet) in diameter. At first, this is all that Stonehenge was. Then, 4,500 years ago, the Stonehenge people transported dozens of volcanic stones (called bluestones for their slightly blue hue) to Stonehenge from the Preseli Mountains in southwest Wales, a distance of about 200 kilometers (125 miles). Each of the bluestones weighed up to 4,000 kilograms (almost 9,000 pounds), and they were arranged in a double half-circle in the center of the circle demarcated by the ditch. Moving stones weighing more than 4 tons more than 100 miles and then erecting them was no mean feat for a people with no mechanical contrivances or draught animals. But even this impressive, early incarnation of Stonehenge was a pale premonition of what it was to become.

Barely a hundred years after building the bluestone semi-circle, major construction commenced on the Stonehenge we all recognize today. Beginning around 4,400 years ago, the builders of Stonehenge began shaping and transporting thirty upright sarsen stones from Avebury in the north, a distance of about 30 kilometers (18 miles). The sarsens dwarf the bluestones and are hard as iron; each was over 3 meters (10 feet) tall and weighed an astonishing 25,000 kilograms (55,000 pounds). The thirty sarsens were erected in a circle within and concentric with the older ditch, 30 meters (100 feet) across (Figure 12.6; Ruggles 1996).

Thirty *lintels*, each weighing about 5,500 kilograms (6 tons), were perched in a continuous ring atop the sarsens. Each lintel was connected to two adjacent sarsens using mortise-and-tenon joinery. The tops of the sarsens were shaped to produce two nobs (tenons), and two hollows (mortises) were sculpted on the bottom of each lintel. Further, each lintel was shaped precisely, curved on the exterior and interior to match the arc of the circle of the sarsens. What resulted was a smooth circle of stones, precisely positioned and joined together. "Awesome" truly is the only word to describe it (Figure 12.7), and there is more.

Figure 12.6 Even in ruin, Stonehenge is an evocative monument, reflecting the remarkable abilities of its ancient builders. (K. L. Feder)

Figure 12.7 Depiction of an intact Stonehenge upon completion 4,000 years ago. Note the precision with which the enormous sarsens and trilithon uprights were connected to each other by their associated lintels.

Five sets of three stones known as the *trilithons* were erected within the sarsen circle. Arranged in a giant horseshoe shape, the trilithon uprights were the largest stones erected by the builders of Stonehenge. Each trilithon upright stands about 8 meters (24 feet) above the surface, with an additional 2 meters (6 feet) of stone buried in the chalky ground underlying the monument. The largest of the trilithon uprights weighs 45,000 kilograms (50 tons), and the associated lintel weighs 9,000 kilograms (10 tons); and remember,

Figure 12.8 Four examples of the megalithic monuments of Great Britain: the Swinside (above) and Castlerigg (opposite, bottom) stone circles located in England; Long Meg, a huge upright stone (near right) also located in England; and the Stones of Stenness (opposite, top) in the Orkney Islands, Scotland. Swinside consists of more than fifty stones and Castlerigg has thirty-eight stones, set in circles nearly 100 feet across. Long Meg is part of an enormous set of originally about seventy stones called "her daughters." The tallest of the Stenness stones looms more than 30 feet above the surrounding surface. (K. L. Feder)

each of these 10-ton blocks had to be raised up to the top of its 24-foot-high trilithon upright pair (for the facts and figures behind Stonehenge see Chippindale 1983 and Wernick et al. 1973).

Other concentric rings of smaller stones were at one time contained within the sarsen circle. Other uprights were placed outside the sarsens, including the so-called heelstone—a 73,000-kilogram (80-ton) stone located about 80 meters (240 feet) northeast of the center of the sarsen circle.

Explaining Stonehenge

Stonehenge has justifiably generated a prodigious amount of interest. How did an ancient and presumably simple farming people construct the monument? How did they quarry the stones? How did they move them? How could they have planned and designed the monument? How did they erect the huge stones? And finally, perhaps the greatest mystery, why did they do it?

Some of the mystery of Stonehenge is a result of our own temporal bias. We find it hard to conceive of ancient people as being inventive, ingenious, or clever. Certainly, it took ingenuity and not just a little hard work to produce Stonehenge and the thousands of other megalithic monuments that are found in Europe (Figure 12.8). If we can leave our temporal preconceptions behind, we can clearly see that the archaeological record of the human past shows that people, including those from 5,000 years ago, are capable of

Figure 12.9   Artist's conception of the raising of the lintels at Stonehenge. Through construction of a series of wooden platforms, the heavy stone lintels could have been levered up to their places atop the sarsens and trilithons. (From C. Chippindale, *Stonehenge Complete,* London: Routledge)

ingenuity and hard work. We need not fall back on lost continents or ancient astronauts to explain the accomplishments of the megalith builders or any other ancient human group.

How was Stonehenge built? The stone likely was quarried by taking advantage of natural breaks in the bedrock and using fire, cold water, and persistent hammering to split the stones into the desired shapes. The stones could have been moved on wooden sledges pulled by rope, perhaps using log rollers to quicken the pace. In an episode of the science series *Nova* (Secrets of Lost Empires 1997), replicative experiments were conducted in an attempt to discover how Stonehenge might have been built. Two parallel sets of squared-off log beams were placed in the ground, producing a wooden track. An upright trilithon-size cement block weighing 50 tons was attached to a wooden sled that fit onto the long trackway. The crew of fewer than two hundred volunteers certainly pulled some muscles and worked up a sweat, but once the trackway was greased, they were able to move the enormously heavy replica relatively easily.

The upright stones were likely erected using levers, and the lintels raised by a combination of levering and the construction of wooden staging around the uprights (Figure 12.9). The accomplishment was—and is—truly remarkable but, echoing a theme presented previously in this book (Chapter 9, for example), certainly within the capabilities of a large number of dedicated people working diligently toward a desired goal.

Figure 12.10   An enormous, beautiful, and elaborate pattern made by flattening a crop in a cornfield in Wiltshire, England, in July 1990. As the "crop circles" became more intricate through time, it became increasingly obvious to many that they were the result of pranksters (some of whom later confessed) and not extraterrestrial aliens. (© Fortean Picture Library)

That leaves unanswered the question of why the enormous task of Stonehenge's construction was undertaken, and numerous suggestions have been made (Chippindale 1983).

Circular Reasoning About Stonehenge

Among the more bizarre hypotheses proposed for Stonehenge is one that explains its appearance as a Neolithic artistic representation of a *crop circle*. The modern crop circle phenomenon peaked in the 1980s and was centered in England, though circles and myriad other, sometimes quite beautiful and complex patterns of flattened wheat and other crops were reported for Canada, the United States, Australia, and elsewhere (Figure 12.10; see Jim Schnabel's 1994 book, *Round in Circles*, for an in-depth look at the phenomenon).

The mysterious patterns of flattened crops were ascribed to whirlwinds, little understood earth energy vortexes, and even the mating patterns of oversexed hedgehogs. A favorite explanation of the circle watchers concerned UFOs; they believed that extraterrestrial spacecraft hovering over wheat fields induced the patterns through energy emanations from beneath the spacecraft. Because Stonehenge was built in a pattern of concentric circles, some of the crop circle afficionados saw a connection and suggested that ancient British farmers found crop circles in their own fields, realized they were caused by mysterious floating objects, and then proceeded to replicate the phenomenon in stone by constructing Stonehenge and other circular megalithic monuments.

There were more than a few problems with this explanation. It quickly became obvious that the circles were not the product of an extraterrestrial version of "prop-wash." Throughout the 1980s, the patterns became increasingly complex and playful; alongside one particularly interesting design was a message produced in flattened wheat reading "We Are Not Alone." When two locals, Dave Chorley and Doug Bower, confessed to the hoax in September 1991, the circle phenomenon petered out at least for a while. Chorley and Bower showed how they had produced the circles, always staying one step ahead of those who sought to explain them. They made their first circles with a steel bar that Bower used to secure the door to his picture framing shop. They hauled the bar out into a field in the middle of the night, set one end of the bar into the ground, and then by swinging the bar around that end they flattened a circular path, whose radius was the length of the bar, in the wheat (or whatever the crop). Next, they moved out to the edge of the circle, following its circumference and using the bar to flatten an additional ring around the original circle. Continuing this process, Chorley and Bower estimated that they could flatten a 30-foot-diameter circle in about thirty minutes (Schnabel 1994:268).

Later, they used an approach that employed 4-foot wooden planks. They threaded rope through the ends of the boards. Holding onto the ropes with both hands, they then balanced one foot on the board and, while applying a bit of pressure by pulling on the board, simply walked over the crop, leaving flattened patterns in their wake. For a time, they even used a sighting device attached to a baseball cap to ensure that their lines were straight, their circles round, and their other patterns geometrically accurate.

The biggest blow to those who hypothesized that the entire phenomenon was related to UFOs or mysterious earth energies occurred when Chorley and Bower, in cahoots with a television producer, secretly made a flattened crop pattern in front of television cameras. A number of crop circle experts, unaware of the conspiracy, were invited to examine the circle. They declared it genuine, beyond the capabilities of any mere human hoaxer. Needless to say, their credibility, along with the credibility of their esoteric explanations for the crop patterns, suffered tremendously. It seems that we can safely rule out crop circles as an explanation for Stonehenge.

An Ancient Astronomy?

Perhaps the most interesting theory proposed to explain Stonehenge has been that proposed by astronomer Gerald Hawkins (1965) suggesting that Stonehenge was, in effect, an astronomical computer designed to keep track of the sun's position on the horizon at sunrise and sunset, as well as the moon's position on the horizon at "moonrise" and "moonset." He went on to suggest that Stonehenge was even used as an eclipse predictor.

In essence, Hawkins sees Stonehenge as an enormous sighting device. From the center, one's view of the surrounding horizon is limited; one is not afforded a 360-degree vista, since much of the horizon is blocked by sarsens or trilithons. Hawkins hypothesizes (and tests his hypothesis, using a computer to check all of the possible horizon sighting points) that those points on the horizon that one can see from the center of Stonehenge and that appear to be marked by additional stones outside of the sarsen circle are all significant astronomically. Most obvious is the sighting from the center of Stonehenge to the northeast. Hawkins relates this orientation to the rising of the sun.

The sun does not "rise in the east and set in the west" as many think. In fact, the sun's position on the horizon at sunrise and sunset moves slightly from day to day during the course of a year. In the Northern Hemisphere, the sun's position at sunrise moves a little bit north along the horizon each day in the spring until it reaches its northernmost point on the first day of summer—the specific *azimuth,* or angle, differs depending on one's latitude.

After its northernmost rising, the sun appears to rise a little farther south each day. On the first day of fall, the *autumnal equinox,* it rises due east. It then continues to rise farther south until it rises at its southernmost position on the first day of winter, the *winter solstice.* The sun then appears to change direction and rise a little farther north each day, rising due east again on the first day of spring, the *vernal equinox.* Continuing its apparent motion north, it again reaches its northernmost rising point exactly one year since it previously rose in that spot.

At any given location in the Northern Hemisphere, the sun rises at its farthest northern point on the horizon on the longest day of the year, the *summer solstice.* For the latitude of Stonehenge, the compass direction of that farthest northern point is 51 degrees (remember, of course, that north is located at zero degrees and due east would be 90 degrees). Standing in the center of Stonehenge, the compass direction of the heelstone is that very same 51 degrees. In other words, upon sunrise on the summer solstice at the precise latitude of Stonehenge, one can look toward the compass direction of 51 degrees and see the sun rise directly over the heelstone.

Is this coincidental? As long ago as the early eighteenth century, Stonehenge investigator William Stukeley recognized the orientation of Stonehenge toward the summer sunrise. Hawkins maintains that this orientation of Stonehenge is no coincidence and that many of the possible solar and lunar sighting points at Stonehenge relate to significant points like the sunrise at the solstice.

Hawkins proposed that Stonehenge began as a simple, though large-scale, calendar for keeping track of the seasons—a valuable thing for people dependent on farming for their subsistence—and evolved over some 2,000 years into the impressive monument we see today. Others, however, have questioned Hawkins, particularly in his more extreme and speculative claims concerning eclipse prediction (Atkinson 1966).

Why Was Stonehenge Built?

Most writers about Stonehenge recognize that there is no great mystery surrounding how the monument was built. We have a pretty good idea of how the megalith builders moved the stones, how they shaped them, how they erected the uprights, and even how they raised the lintels to the top of the sarsens and trilithons. But *why* did the builders of Stonehenge go to such an incredible amount of trouble? To many writers, this is the great unsolved mystery of Stonehenge.

The construction of Stonehenge is no mystery at all, however, if we but look at ourselves. As human beings we revel in the construction of great public edifices. The builders of Stonehenge were no different. Generation after generation, they contributed to a monument whose destiny lay deep in a distant future. There is no mystery in that but only surprise born of an intellectual and temporal conceit on our part. We look back four or five thousand years and see nothing but primitive and alien strangers—this is our fundamental mistake—and from this we contrive a mystery. When we look back at the builders of Stonehenge and the painters of Paleolithic masterpieces and the creators of the civilization of the Maya, what is it that surprises us? Their familiarity! We recognize ourselves in the care, effort, time, and skill reflected in these ancient accomplishments.

We continue to be awed by the monument today, even building replicas—from the reverential full-size model in poured concrete located in Maryhill, Washington, about a hundred miles east of Portland, Oregon, to the hilarious Carhenge in Alliance, Nebraska, a model faithful to the appearance of the real ruin, except that instead of being constructed of large stone monoliths, it is made entirely of old automobiles!

Stonehenge is a great cathedral, a colosseum, an impressive temple, a skyscraper. It is a reflection of what humans are capable of. It is a manifestation of our unique understanding that though we are individually ephemeral, our works can be eternal. In this, the builders of Stonehenge were remarkably successful. Stonehenge commands our attention. Millions of tourists, scholars, myth-makers, and fools alike are drawn to this monument. The builders of Stonehenge have attained that which they could have secured in no other way—they have achieved immortality. There is no mystery to this quest, only a remarkable continuity between the past and the present.

Conclusion: A Past We Deserve

Obviously, the past no longer exists. It is gone, whether we are contemplating human evolution, the earliest settlement of the Americas, the origins of civilization, the veracity of biblical stories, or any of the past times and events discussed in this book. In this sense, all of us are forced always to invent or construct an image of the past in the present.

Nevertheless, scientists and historians hope to construct a past that is veritable, that is accurate in terms of actual past events. We believe we can do this because, though the past is gone, it has left its mark in the present. But the data of antiquity are often vague, ambiguous, and difficult to interpret. Therefore, many different possible pasts can be constructed. All scientists, in whatever field, who consider the past history of the universe, the planet, life, or humanity recognize this. The message of this book has been that, although there are many different possibilities, not all of these constructed pasts—not all of the possibilities—are equally plausible.

Ultimately, then, we get the past we deserve. In every generation, thinkers, writers, scholars, charlatans, and kooks (these are not necessarily mutually exclusive categories) attempt to cast the past in an image either they or the public desire or find comforting. Biblical giants—some, apparently, walking their pet dinosaurs—large-brained, ape-jawed ancestors, lost tribes, lost continents, mysterious races, and ancient astronauts have all been a part of their concocted fantasies.

But I believe, and have tried to show in this book, that we deserve better—and we can do better. We deserve a veritable past, a real past constructed from the sturdy fabric of geology, paleontology, archaeology, and history, woven on the loom of science. We deserve better and can do better than weave a past from the whole cloth of fantasy and fiction. Finally, I hope I have shown in this book that the veritable past is every bit as interesting as those pasts constructed by the fantasy weavers of frauds, myths, and mysteries.

◈ ◈ ◈   FREQUENTLY ASKED QUESTIONS   ◈ ◈ ◈

1. How could ancient people have been so advanced as to have built places like Stonehenge and the cities of the Maya?

Based on the size and shape of the brain, human beings have had the same essential intellectual capacity for the last 195,000 years or so. Cultures all over the world and at various times have developed remarkable civilizations. Though twenty-first-century Western culture is the most sophisticated technological civilization the world has seen, we are no smarter than the ancient people of the Salisbury Plain or the tropical lowlands of Mesoamerica. It really should be no surprise that human beings of long ago developed technologically impressive cultures.

2. *When the questions raised about the cave painters of Europe, the Maya, and Stonehenge are answered, does archaeology run out of mysteries?*

Of course not. Human antiquity is a dynamic field of study. We learn more about the history of our species every day. As old questions are answered, new ones are raised: What is the significance of the recently recovered Neandertal mitochondrial DNA? What is the meaning of newly discovered evidence of widespread warfare and cannibalism in the American Southwest? How far back can we trace the first Native Americans—and how did they come to the New World? There will always be questions; there will always be mysteries. With the use of new methods of analysis and the application of new perspectives, we will continue our largely successful attempt to answer and solve them.

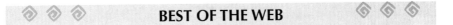

BEST OF THE WEB

CAVE PAINTERS

http://www.culture.gouv.fr/culture/arcnat/chauvet/en/
Official Web page of the French Ministry of Culture focusing on Chauvet Cave. The site includes a photo album, map, history, and links to Web sites devoted to other Upper Paleolithic painted caves.

http://www.culture.fr/culture/arcnat/lascaux/en/
Splendid Web site devoted to Lascaux Cave. Take a virtual walk through the cave and gaze upon most of the major works of art.

MAYA

http://www.d.umn.edu/cla/faculty/troufs/anth3618/mamaya.html
Web site with many links to Web pages that discuss the culture of the Maya people, both ancient and modern.

http://www.halfmoon.org/
Wide range of material related to the Maya.

http://www.mesoweb.com/

A Web site focusing on all things Mesoamerican. Links to articles, Web sites, news, excavations, and just about anything else you might want to know about Mesoamerica.

STONEHENGE/STONE CIRCLES

http://www.stonepages.com/home.html

If you want a virtual visit to almost any megalithic site in England, Scotland, Ireland, Wales, France, or Italy, go to this Web site. Lots of photographs and detailed information.

http://easyweb.easynet.co.uk/~aburnham/eng/index.htm

A photo guide to the megalithic monuments of England. May be the best place on the Web for photographs of megalithic sites, aerial shots, and even audio tours.

◈ ◈ ◈ CRITICAL THINKING EXERCISE ◈ ◈ ◈

Using the deductive approach outlined in Chapter 2, how would you test these hypotheses? In each case, what archaeological data must you find to conclude that the hypothetical statement is an accurate assertion, that it describes what actually happened in the ancient human past?

- The cave paintings of the Upper Paleolithic in Europe served a magical function. Rendering the animals on cave walls represented a spiritual "capturing" of food animals that the ancient artists hoped literally to capture in the hunt.
- The collapse of the ancient Maya civilization was caused by an invasion of outsiders from the Valley of Mexico.
- The function of Stonehenge was as a giant solar calendar.

References

Achenbach, J. 1999. *Captured by Aliens: The Search for Life and Truth in a Very Large Universe.* New York: Simon and Schuster.

Adovasio, J. M., J. Donahue, and R. Stuckenrath. 1990. The Meadowcroft Rockshelter radiocarbon chronology—1975–1990. *American Antiquity* 55:348–353.

Aitken, M. J. 1959. Test for correlation between dowsing response and magnetic disturbance. *Archaeometry* 2:58–59.

———. 1970. Magnetic location. In *Science in Archaeology,* ed. D. Brothwell and E. Higgs, pp. 681–694. New York: Praeger.

Aksu, A. E., P. J. Mudie, A. Rochon, M. A. Kaminski, T. Abrajano, and D. Yasar. 2002. Persistent Holocene outflow from the Black Sea to the Eastern Mediterranean contradicts Noah's Flood hypothesis. *GSA Today* 12(5):4–10.

Albers, A. 1999. Mystical Journeys: Sedona Special Places, Palatki Ruins. http://www. visionsofheaven.com/journeys-sedonadocs/sedPalatki.html.

Allen, J. M. 1999. *Atlantis: The Andes Solution.* New York: St. Martin's Press.

Altman, R. I. 2004. First, . . . recognize that it's a penny: Report on the "Newark" Ritual Artifacts. The Bible and Interpretation. http://www.bibleinterp.com/articles/Altman_Newark.htm.

Applebaum, E. 1996. Holy stones. *Jewish News.* August 23:47–51.

Arnold, B. 1992. The past as propaganda. *Archaeology* 45(4):30–37.

Arnold, D. 1991. *Building in Egypt: Pharaonic Stone Masonry.* Oxford: Oxford University Press.

Arsuaga, J. L. 2002. *The Neanderthal's Necklace: In Search of the First Thinkers.* New York: Four Walls Eight Windows Press.

Arthur, J. 1996. Creationism: Bad science or immoral pseudoscience. *Skeptic* 4(4): 88–93.

Ashe, G. 1971. Analysis of the legends. In *Quest for America,* ed. G. Ash, pp. 15–52. New York: Praeger.

Atkinson, R. J. C. 1966. Moonshine on Stonehenge. *Antiquity* 40:262–274.

Atwater, C. 1820. *Description of the Antiquities Discovered in the State of Ohio and Other Western States.* Transactions and Collections of the American Antiquarian Society. New York: AMS Press (reprinted in 1973 for the Peabody Museum of Ethnology and Archaeology, Harvard University).

Bailey, R. 1983. Divining edge: Dowsing for medieval churches. *Popular Archaeology,* Feb.:5.

Bailey, R. N., E. Cambridge, and H. D. Briggs. 1988. *Dowsing and Church Archaeology.* Wimborne: Intercept.

Bakeless, J. 1964. *The Journals of Lewis and Clark.* New York: Mentor Books.

Ballard and the Black Sea: The Search for Noah's Flood. 1999. http://www. nationalgeographic.com/blacksea/.

Barrett, T. H. 2002. *1421: The Year China Discovered the World* by Gavin Menzies: A Review. http://www.kenspy.com/Menzies/review2.html.

Barton, B. S. 1787. *Observations on Some Parts of Natural History.* London.

Bartram, W. 1791. *The Travels of William Bartram.* 1928 reprint. New York: Dover.

Baugh, C. 1987. *Dinosaur.* Orange, Calif.: Promise Publishing.

Bellantoni, N. 2002. The Pachaug Forest artifact hoax.*Connecticut Preservation News* 25(5):3.

Berlitz, C. 1984. *Atlantis: The Eighth Continent.* New York: Fawcett Crest.

Bermúdez de Castro, J. M., J. L. Arsuaga, E. Carboneli, A. Rosas, I. Matinez, and M. Mosquera. 1997. A hominid from the Lower Pleistocene of Atapuerca, Spain: Possible ancestor to Neandertals and modern humans. *Science* 276: 1392–1395.

Bird, R. T. 1939. Thunder in his footsteps. *Natural History* 43(5):254–261, 302.

Bird, S. E. 1992. *For Enquiring Minds: A Cultural Study of Supermarket Tabloids.* Knoxville: University of Kentucky Press.

Bjornstad, T. 1998. Sinking Viking ship. *Archaeology* 51(1):25.

Blavatsky, H. P. 1888–1938. *The Secret Doctrine.* Wheaton, Ill.: Theosophical Publishing House (6 volumes).

Blinderman, C. 1986. *The Piltdown Inquest.* Buffalo: Prometheus Books.

Bond, F. B. 1918. *The Gate of Remembrance.* Oxford: Blackwell.

Bortolini, M.-C., et al. Y-chromosome evidence for differing ancient demographic histories in the Americas. *American Journal of Human Genetics* 73:524–539.

Bower, B. 1990. Minoan culture survived volcanic eruption. *Science News* 137:22.

Bresee, R., and E. Craig. 1994. Image formation and the Shroud of Turin. *Journal of Imaging Science and Technology* 34:59–67.

Breuil, H. 1952. *Four Hundred Years of Cave Art.* Montignac, France: Centre d'Études et de Documentation Prehistorique.

Brewer, D. J., and E. Teeter. 1999. *Egypt and the Egyptians.* Cambridge: Cambridge University Press.

Briuer, F., J. Simms, and L. Smith. 1997. Site Mapping, Geophysical Investigation, and Geomorphic Reconnaissance at Site 9 ME 395 Upatio Town, Fort Benning, Georgia. *U.S. Army Corps of Engineers, Miscellaneous Paper* EL-97-3.

Brown, D. 1970. *Bury My Heart at Wounded Knee.* New York: Bantam.

Bruhns, K. O. 1994. *Ancient South America.* Cambridge World Archaeology. Cambridge: Cambridge University Press.

Buckley, T. 1976. The discovery of Tutankhamun's tomb. In *The Treasures of Tutankhamun,* edited by K. S. Gilbert, J. K. Holt, and S. Hudson, pp. 9–18. New York: The Metropolitan Museum of Art.

Burdick, C. 1950. When GIANTS roamed the earth: Their fossil footprints still visible. *Signs of the Times,* July 25:6, 9.

Burl, A. 1995. *A Guide to the Stone Circles of Britain, Ireland, and Brittany.* New Haven: Yale University Press.

Butzer, K. 1976. *Early Hydraulic Civilization of Egypt: A Study in Cultural Ecology.* Chicago: University of Chicago Press.

Byrne, M. St. Clere (ed.). 1979. *The Elizabethan Zoo: A Book of Beasts Fabulous and Authentic* (selected from Philemon Holland's 1601 translation of Pliny and Edward Topsell's 1607 *Historie of Foure-Footed Beastes* and his 1608 *Historie of Serpents*). Boston: Nonpareil Press.

Cahill, T. 1987. The Vinland map revisited: New compositional evidence on its inks and parchment. *Analytical Chemistry* 59:829–833.

Cardiff Giant, The. 1869. *Harper's Weekly,* p. 776.

Cardiff Giant, The. 1898. *Ithaca Daily Journal,* Jan. 4. Ithaca, N.Y.

Carlin, G. 1997. *Brain Droppings.* New York: Hyperion.

Carroll, R. T. 2003. *The Skeptic's Dictionary: A Collection of Strange Beliefs, Amusing Deceptions, and Dangerous Delusions.* Hoboken, N.J.: John Wiley.

Case of the Ancient Astronauts (television program). 1978. *Nova*. Boston: WGBH.

Castleden, R. 1998. *Atlantis Destroyed*. London: Routledge.

Cayce, E. 1968. *Edgar Cayce on Atlantis*. New York: Hawthorn Books.

Chambers, H. 1969. *Dowsing, Divining Rods, and Water Witches for the Millions*. Los Angeles: Sherbourne Press.

Chang, J., L. D. Elam-Evans, C. J. Berg, J. Herndon, L. Flowers, K. A. Seed, and C. J. Syverson. 2003. Pregnancy-related mortality surveillance—United States, 1991–1999. *Morbidity and Mortality Weekly Report* 52(SS-2):1–8.

Charpak, G., and H. Broch. 2004. *Debunked: ESP, Telekinesis, and Other Pseudoscience*. Baltimore: Johns Hopkins.

Chauvet, J.-M., É. B. Deschamps, and C. Hillaire. 1996. *Dawn of Art: The Chauvet Cave*. New York: Abrams.

Chippindale, C. 1983. *Stonehenge Complete*. Ithaca: Cornell University Press.

———. 1990. Piltdown: Whodunit? Who cares? *Science* 250:1162–1163.

Clark, A. 1970. Resistivity surveying. In *Science in Archaeology*, ed. D. Brothwell and E. Higgs, pp. 695–707. New York: Praeger.

Clark, R. J. H., and K. L. Brown. 2004. The Vinland Map: Still a 20th-century forgery. *Analytical Chemistry* 76(8):2423.

Clarke, D. 1978. *Analytical Archaeology*. New York: Columbia University Press.

Clayton, P. A. 1994. *Chronicle of the Pharaohs: The Reign-by-Reign Record of the Rulers and Dynasties of Ancient Egypt*. London: Thames and Hudson.

Clottes, J., and J. Courtin. 1996. *The Cave Beneath the Sea: Paleolithic Images at Cosquer*. New York: Abrams.

Clottes, J., and D. Lewis-Williams. 1998. *The Shamans of Prehistory: Trance and Magic in the Painted Caves*. New York: Abrams.

Coe, M. D. 1992. *Breaking the Maya Code*. London: Thames and Hudson.

Cohen, D. 1969. *Mysterious Places*. New York: Dodd, Mead.

Cohn, N. 1996. *Noah's Flood: The Genesis Story in Western Thought*. New Haven: Yale University Press.

Cole, J. R. 1979. Inscriptionmania, hyperdiffusionism, and the public: Fallout from a 1977 meeting. *Man in the Northeast* 17:27–53.

———. 1982. Western Massachusetts "Monk's caves": 1979 University of Massachusetts field research. *Man in the Northeast* 24:37–70.

Cole, J. R., L. Godfrey, and S. Schafersman. 1985. Mantracks: The fossils say no! *Creation/Evolution* 5(1):37–45.

Collina-Girard, J. 2001. L'Atlantide devant le detroit de Gibralter? Myth et geologie. *Comptes Rendus de l'Academie des Sciences (2a)* 333:233–240.

Collins, A. 2002. *Gateway to Atlantis*. New York: Carroll and Graff.

Conkey, M. 1980. The identification of prehistoric hunter-gatherer aggregation sites: The case of Altamira. *Current Anthropology* 21(5):609–639.

———. 1987. New approaches in the search for meaning? A review of research in "Paleolithic art." *Journal of Field Archaeology* 14:413–430.

Conyers, L. B. 2003. Ground Penetrating Radar in Archaeology. http://www.du.edu/~lconyer/graves.htm.

———. 2004. *Ground Penetrating Radar for Archaeology*. Walnut Creek, Calif.: AltaMira Press.

Conyers, L. B., and D. Goodman. 1997. *Ground Penetrating Radar: An Introduction for Archaeologists*. Walnut Creek, Calif.: AltaMira Press.

Cope, J. 1998. *The Modern Antiquarian: A Pre-Millennial Odyssey Through Megalithic Great Britain*. London: Thorsons.

Cowen, R. 1995. After the fall. *Science News* 148:248–249.

Crawford, G. W. 1992. Prehistoric plant domestication in East Asia. In *The Origins of Agriculture: An International Perspective*, ed. C. W. Cowan and P. J. Watson, pp. 7–38. Washington, D.C.: Smithsonian Institution Press.

Cremo, M. A., and R. L. Thompson. 1993. *Forbidden Archaeology: The Hidden History of the Human Race*. San Diego: Govardhan Hill.

———. 1994. *The Hidden History of the Human Race*. San Diego: Govardhan Hill.

Daegling, D. J. 2004. *Bigfoot Exposed: An Anthropologist Examines America's Enduring Legend*. Walnut Creek, Calif.: AltaMira Press.

Dall, W. H. 1877. On succession of shell heaps of the Aleutian Islands. In *Contributions to American Ethnology*, Volume 1:41–91. Washington, D.C.: U.S. Department of the Interior.

Damon, P. E. 1989. Radiocarbon dating of the Shroud of Turin. *Nature* 337:611–615.

Daniel, G. 1977. Review of *America B.C.* by Barry Fell. *New York Times Book Review Section*, March 13:8ff.

Danin, A., and U. Baruch. 1998. Floristic indicators for the origin of the Shroud of Turin. Retrieved from the World Wide Web: http://www.shroud.com/papers.htm.

Darwin, C. 1859. *On the Origin of Species by Means of Natural Selection*. 1898 reprint. New York: Appleton.

———. 1871. *The Descent of Man*. 1930 reprint. London: C. C. Watts.

Darwin Theory Is Proved True. 1912. *New York Times*, Dec. 22.

Dawson, C., and A. S. Woodward. 1913. On the discovery of a Paleolithic human skull and mandible in a flint bearing gravel overlying the Wealden (Hastings Beds) at Piltdown, Fletching (Sussex). *Quarterly Journal of the Geological Society* LXIX:117–151.

Deacon, R. 1966. *Madoc and the Discovery of America*. New York: Braziller.

Deagan, K., and J. M. Cruxent. 1997. Medieval foothold in the Americas. *Archaeology* 50(4):54–59.

———. 2002. *Archaeology at La Isabela: America's First European Town*. New Haven: Yale University Press.

de Camp, L. S. 1970. *Lost Continents: The Atlantis Theme in History, Science, and Literature*. New York: Dover.

Deloria Jr., V. 1995. *Red Earth, White Lies: Native Americans and the Myth of Scientific Fact*. New York: Scribner's.

Dembski, W. A. 1999. *Intelligent Design: The Bridge Between Science and Theology*. Downer's Grove, Ill.: Intrauniversity Press.

Derenko, M. V., T. Grzybowski, B. A. Malyarchuk, J. Czarny, D. Miscicka-Sliwka, and I. A. Zakharov. 2001. The presence of mitochondrial haplogroup X in Altaians from south Siberia. *American Journal of Human Genetics* 69:237–241.

de Tapia, E. M. 1992. The origins of agriculture in Mesoamerica and South America. In *The Origins of Agriculture: An International Perspective*, ed. C. W. Cowan and P. J. Watson, pp. 143–171. Washington, D.C.: Smithsonian Institution Press.

Dillehay, T. D. 1989. *Monte Verde: A Late Pleistocene Settlement in Chile, Vol. 1: Paleoenvironment and Site Context*. Washington, D.C.: Smithsonian Institution Press.

———. 1997. The Battle of Monte Verde. *Sciences*. Jan./Feb.: 28–33.

———. 2000. *The Settlement of the Americas: A New Prehistory*. New York: Basic Books.

Dillehay, T. D., and M. B. Collins. 1988. Early cultural evidence from Monte Verde in Chile. *Nature* 332:150–152.

Dincauze, D. 1982. Monk's caves and short memories. *Quarterly Review of Archaeology* 3(4):1, 10–11.

DiPietro, V., and G. Molenaar. 1982. *Unusual Martian Surface Features*. Glen Dale, Md.: Mars Research.

Dirty-digger scandal spreads to 42 sites nationwide. 2001. *Mainichi Shimbun*, October 7, 2001.

Dixon, E. J. 1999. *Bones, Boats, and Bison: Archaeology and the First Colonization of Western North America*. Albuquerque: University of New Mexico Press.

Dolnick, E. 1989. Panda paradox. *Discover*, Sept.:71–76.

Donnelly, I. 1882. *Atlantis, the Antediluvian World*. 1971 reprint. New York: Harper.

Donohue, D. J., J. S. Olin, and G. Harbottle. 2002. Determination of the radiocarbon age of parchment of the Vinland Map. *Radiocarbon* 44(1):45–52.

dos Santos, A. N. 1997. Atlantis: The Lost Continent Finally Found. http://www.atlan.org/.

Downey, R. 2000. *Riddle of the Bones: Politics, Science, Race, and the Story of Kennewick Man*. New York: Springer-Verlag.

Doyle, A. C. 1891–1902. *The Celebrated Cases of Sherlock Holmes*. 1981 reprint. London: Octopus Books.

Drawhorn, G. 1994. *Piltdown: Evidence of Smith-Woodward's Complicity*. Paper presented at the annual meeting of the American Association of Physical Anthropologists.

Du Pratz, L. P. 1774. *History of Louisiana*. London: Printed for T. Becket.

Dutch, S. 2003. The Piri Reis Map. http://www.uwgb.edu/dutchs/PSEUDOSC/PiriRies.HTM.

Eaton, R. 1978. The evolution of trophy hunting. *Carnivore* 1(1):110–121.

Edwords, F. 1983. Creation/evolution update: Footprints in the mind. *Humanist* 43(2):31.

Eggert, G. 1996. The enigmatic "Battery of Baghdad." *Skeptical Inquirer* 20(3):31–34.

Elvas, Gentleman of. 1611. *The Discovery and Conquest of Terra Florida by Don Ferdinando de Soto and Six Hundred Spaniards, His Followers*. The Hakluyt Society. 1907 reprint. New York: Burt Franklin.

Fagan, B. M. 1977. Who were the Mound Builders? In *Mysteries of the Past*, ed. J. J. Thorndike Jr., pp. 118–135. New York: American Heritage Press.

———. 2000. *In the Beginning: An Introduction to Archaeology*, 8th ed. New York: Prentice-Hall.

Faulkner, C. 1971. *The Old Stone Fort*. Knoxville: University of Tennessee Press.

Fears, J. Rufus. 1978. Atlantis and the Minoan Thalassocracy: A study in modern mythopoeism. In *Atlantis: Fact or Fiction*, ed. E. S. Ramage, pp. 103–134. Bloomington: Indiana University Press.

Feder, K. L. 1980a. Foolsgold of the gods. *The Humanist*, Jan./Feb.:20–23.

———. 1980b. Psychic archaeology: The anatomy of irrationalist prehistoric studies. *Skeptical Inquirer* 4(4):32–43.

———. 1981. Waste not, want not: Differential lithic utilization and efficiency of use. *North American Archaeologist* 2(3):193–205.

———. 1984. Irrationality and archaeology. *American Antiquity* 49(3):525–541.

———. 1987. Cult archaeology and creationism: A coordinated research project. In *Cult Archaeology and Creationism: Understanding Pseudoscientific Beliefs About the Past*, ed. F. Harrold and R. Eve, pp. 34–48. Iowa City: University of Iowa Press.

———. 1990. Piltdown, paradigms, and the paranormal. *Skeptical Inquirer* 14(4):397–402.

———. 1994a. Review of *Forbidden Archaeology: The Hidden History of the Human Race* by Richard A. Cremo and Richard L. Thompson. *Geoarchaeology* 9(4):337–340.

———. 1994b. The Spanish *entrada:* A model for assessing claims of pre-Columbian contact between the Old and New Worlds. *North American Archaeologist* 15:147–166.

———. 1995a. Archaeology and the paranormal. In *Encyclopedia of the Paranormal,* ed. G. Steiner. Buffalo: Prometheus Books.

———. 1995b. Ten years after: Surveying misconceptions about the human past. *CRM (Cultural Resource Management)* 18(3):10–14.

———. 1997. Indians and archaeologists: Conflicting views of myth and science. *Skeptic* 5(3):74–80.

———. 1998. Perceptions of the past: Survey results—how students perceive the past. *General Anthropology* 4(2):1, 8–12.

———. 1998–99. Archaeology and Afrocentrism: An attempt to set the record straight. *A Current Bibliography on African Affairs* 29(3):199–210.

———. 2004. *Linking to the Past: A Brief Introduction to Archaeology.* New York: Oxford University Press.

———. 2005. Skeptics, fence-sitters, and true believers: Student acceptance of an improbable prehistory. In *Archaeological Fantasies: How Pseudoarchaeology Misrepresents the Past and Misleads the Public,* ed. G. Fagan. Oxford: Routledge.

Feder, K. L., and M. A. Park. 2001. *Human Antiquity: An Introduction to Physical Anthropology and Archaeology,* 4th ed. Mountain View, Calif.: Mayfield.

Feldman, M. 1977. *The Mystery Hill Story.* North Salem, N.H.: Mystery Hill.

Fell, B. 1976. *America B.C.: Ancient Settlers in the New World.* New York: Demeter Press.

———. 1980. *Saga America.* New York: Times Books.

———. 1982. *Bronze Age America.* New York: Times Books.

Fernandez-Armesto, F. 1974. *Columbus and the Conquest of the Impossible.* New York: Saturday Review Press.

Fiedel, S. J. 1999. Artifact provenience at Monte Verde: Confusion and contradictions. *Discovering Archaeology* 6(Nov./Dec.):1–12.

Fitzhugh, W. 1972. *Environmental Archaeology and Cultural Systems in Hamilton Inlet, Labrador: A Survey of the Central Labrador Coast from 3000 B.C. to the Present.* Smithsonian Contributions to Anthropology, No. 16. Washington, D.C.: Smithsonian Institution Press.

Flem-Ath, R., and R. Flem-Ath. 1995. *When the Sky Fell: In Search of Atlantis.* New York: St. Martin's Press.

Forrest, B. C., and P. R. Gross. 2003. *Creationism's Trojan Horse: The Wedge of Intelligent Design.* New York: Oxford University Press.

Foster, J. W. 1873. *Prehistoric Races of the United States of America.* Chicago: S. C. Griggs.

Fowler, M. 1974. *Cahokia: Ancient Capital of the Midwest.* Addison-Wesley Module No. 48. Menlo Park, Calif.: Cummings.

———. 1975. A Precolumbian urban center on the Mississippi. *Scientific American* 233(2):92–101.

———. 1989. *The Cahokia Atlas: A Historical Atlas of Cahokia Archaeology.* Studies in Illinois Archaeology 6. Springfield, Ill.: Illinois Historic Preservation Agency.

Franco, B. 1969. *The Cardiff Giant: A Hundred Year Old Hoax.* Cooperstown, N.Y.: New York State Historical Association.

Friedlander, P. 1969. *Plato: The Dialogues,* volume 3. Princeton: Princeton University Press.

Frodsham, J. D. 1989. The enigmatic shroud. *The World & I,* June:320–329.

Frost, F. 1982. The Palos Verdes Chinese anchor mystery. *Archaeology*, Jan./Feb.:23–27.

Fuson, R. 1987. *The Log of Christopher Columbus*. Camden, Maine: International Marine.

Galanopoulos, A. G., and E. Bacon. 1969. *Atlantis: The Truth Behind the Legend*. Indianapolis: Bobbs-Merrill.

Gallup Jr., G. H., and F. Newport. 1991. Belief in paranormal phenomena among adult Americans. *Skeptical Inquirer* 15:137–146.

Gantz, T. 1993. *Early Greek Myth*. 2 vols. Baltimore: Johns Hopkins.

Gardner, M. 1985. Notes of a psi-watcher: The great stone face and other nonmysteries. *Skeptical Inquirer* 10(1):14–18.

Garvin, J. 2001. The "Face on Mars" trail map. http://science.nasa.gov/headlines/y2001/ast24may_1.htm?list540155.

Gee, H. 1996. Box of bones "clinches" identity of Piltdown paleontology hoaxer. *Nature* 381:261–262.

Gibbons, A. 1996. The peopling of the Americas. *Science* 274:31–33.

Gibson, J. 2000. *The Ancient Mounds of Poverty Point*. Gainesville: University of Florida Press.

Gilovich, T. 1991. *How We Know What Isn't So*. New York: Free Press.

Gish, D. 1973. *Evolution? The Fossils Say No*. San Diego: Creation Life.

Goddard, I., and W. Fitzhugh. 1979. A statement concerning America B.C. *Man in the Northeast* 17:166–172.

Godfrey, L. 1985. Footnotes of an anatomist. *Creation/Evolution* 5(1):16–36.

Godfrey, W. 1951. The archaeology of the Old Stone Mill in Newport, Rhode Island. *American Antiquity* 17:120–129.

Goodman, J. 1977. *Psychic Archaeology: Time Machine to the Past*. New York: Berkley.

———. 1981. *American Genesis*. New York: Berkley.

Goodwin, W. 1946. *The Ruins of Great Ireland in New England*. Boston: Meader.

Goodyear, Albert C. 1999. Results of the 1999 Allendale Paleoindian expedition. *Legacy* 4(1–3):8–13.

Gottfried, K., and K. G. Wilson. 1997. Science as a cultural construct. *Nature* 386: 545–547.

Gould, S. J. 1980. The Piltdown conspiracy. *Natural History*, Aug.:8–28.

———. 1981. A visit to Dayton. *Natural History*, Nov.:8ff.

———. 1982. Moon, Mann, and Otto. *Natural History*, Jan.:4–10.

Gove, H. E. 1996. *Relic, Icon or Hoax? Carbon Dating the Turin Shroud*. Philadelphia: Institute of Physics.

Gradie, R. F. 1981. Irish immigration to 18th century New England and the stone chamber controversy. *Bulletin of the Archaeological Society of Connecticut* 44:30–39.

Greene, J. 1959. *The Death of Adam: Evolution and Its Impact on Western Thought*. Ames, Iowa: Iowa State University Press.

Gross, P. R., and N. Levitt. 1994. *Higher Superstition: The Academic Left and Its Quarrel with Science*. Baltimore: Johns Hopkins.

Haas, J. 1982. *The Evolution of the Prehistoric State*. New York: New York University Press.

Halverson, J. 1987. Art for art's sake in the Paleolithic. *Current Anthropology* 28:63–71.

Hamilton, R. A. 2004. CGA instructor believes Atlantis is no longer lost. *New London Day* (Connecticut), Nov. 19, 2004.

Hancock, G. 1995. *Fingerprints of the Gods*. New York: Three Rivers Press.

———. 2003. *Underworld: The Mysterious Origins of Civilization*. New York: Three Rivers Press.

Hanke, L. 1937. Pope Paul III and the American Indians. *Harvard Theological Review* 30:65–102.

Harlan, J. 1992. Indigenous African agriculture. In *The Origins of Agriculture: An International Perspective*, ed. C. W. Cowan and P. J. Watson, pp. 59–70. Washington, D.C.: Smithsonian Institution Press.

Harris, M. 1968. *The Rise of Anthropological Theory*. New York: Crowell.

Harrison, W. 1971. Atlantis undiscovered—Bimini, Bahamas. *Nature* 230:287–289.

Hattendorf, I. 1997. From the collection: William S. Godfrey's Old Stone Mill archaeological collection. *Newport History* 68(2):109–111.

Hawkins, G. 1965. *Stonehenge Decoded*. New York: Dell.

Haynes, C. V. 1988. Geofacts and fancy. *Natural History*, Feb.:4–12.

Hearn, Lafcadio. 1876. The Mound Builders. In *The Commercial*, Cincinnati, Ohio.

Hempel, C. G. 1966. *Philosophy of Natural Science*. Englewood Cliffs, N.J.: Prentice-Hall.

Henningsmoen, K. 1977. Pollen-analytical investigations in the L'Anse aux Meadows area, Newfoundland. In *The Discovery of a Norse Settlement in America*, ed. A. S. Ingstad, pp. 289–340. Oslo, Norway: Universitetsforlaget.

Henry, D. O. 1989. *From Foraging to Agriculture: The Levant at the End of the Ice Age*. Philadelphia: University of Pennsylvania Press.

Hertz, J. 1997. Round church or windmill? New light on the Newport Tower. *Newport History* 68(2):55–91.

Heyerdahl, T. 1958. *Aku-Aku*. New York: Rand McNally.

Hoagland, R. C. 1987. *The Monuments of Mars: A City on the Edge of Forever*. Berkeley: North Atlantic Books.

Hoffman, C. 1987. The Long Bay Site, San Salvador. *American Archaeology* 6(2):96–101.

Hoffman, M. 1979. *Egypt Before the Pharaohs*. New York: Knopf.

———. 1983. Where nations began. *Science 83* 4(8):42–51.

Hoggart, S., and M. Hutchinson. 1995. *Bizarre Beliefs*. London: Richard Cohen Books.

Holden, C. 2002a. Darwin retains seat in Ohio. *Science* 298:739.

———. 2002b. Ohio the next Kansas? *Science* 295:963.

———. 2003. Structural failure. *Science* 290:1083.

Hole, F. 1981. *Saga America*: Book review. *Bulletin of the Archaeological Society of Connecticut* 44:81–83.

Hole, F., K. Flannery, and J. A. Neely. 1969. *Prehistory and Human Ecology of the Deh Luran Plain: An Early Village Sequence from Khuzistan, Iran*. Ann Arbor: University of Michigan Press.

Holzer, H. 1969. *Window to the Past*. Garden City: Doubleday.

Hopkin, M. 2004. Return of the mummy: An ancient Egyptian has a virtual life at London's British Museum. *Nature* 430:406.

Howard, R. W. 1975. *The Dawn Seekers*. New York: Harcourt Brace Jovanovich.

Huddleston, L. 1967. *Origins of the American Indians: European Concepts, 1492–1729*. Austin: University of Texas Press.

Hughes, R. 1995. Behold the Stone Age. *Time* 145(6):52ff.

Hutchins, R. M. (ed.). 1952. *The Dialogues of Plato*, trans. B. Jowett. Chicago: William Benton/Encyclopaedia Britannica.

Incredible Discovery of Noah's Ark, The. 1993. Sun International Pictures.

Ingstad, A. S. 1977. *The Discovery of a Norse Settlement in America*. Oslo, Norway: Universitetsforlaget.

———. 1982. The Norse settlement of L'Anse aux Meadows, Newfoundland. In *Vikings in the West*, ed. E. Guralnick, pp. 31–37. Chicago: Archaeological Institute of America.

Ingstad, H. 1964. Viking ruins prove Vikings found the New World. *National Geographic* 126(5):708–734.

———. 1971. Norse site at L'Anse aux Meadows. In *The Quest for America*, ed. G. Ashe, pp. 175–198. New York: Praeger.

———. 1982. The discovery of a Norse settlement in America: In *Vikings in the West*, ed. E. Guralnick, pp. 24–30. Chicago: Archaeological Institute of America.

Ingstad, H., and A. S. Ingstad. 2000. *The Viking Discovery of America: The Excavation of a Norse Settlement in L'Anse aux Meadows, Newfoundland*. St. John's, Newfoundland: Breakwater Books.

Irwin, G. 1993. *The Prehistoric Exploration and Colonisation of the Pacific*. Cambridge: Cambridge University Press.

Isaak, M. 1998. Problems with a Global Flood. http://www.talkorigins.org/faqs/faq-noahs-ark.html.

Iseminger, W. R. 1996. Mighty Cahokia. *Archaeology* 49(3):30–37.

Ives, R. 1956. An early speculation concerning the Asiatic origin of the American Indians. *American Antiquity* 21:420–421.

Jackson, K., and J. Stamp. 2003. *Building the Great Pyramid* Buffalo: Firefly Books.

Jackson, N. F., G. Jackson, and W. Linke Jr. 1981. The "trench ruin" of Gungywamp, Groton, Connecticut. *Bulletin of the Archaeological Society of Connecticut* 44:20–29.

Jacobs, A. 2004. Georgia takes on "evolution." *New York Times,* January 30, 2004.

Jacobsen, T. W. 1976. 17,000 years of Greek prehistory. *Scientific American* 234(6):76–87.

James, G. G. M. 1954. *The Stolen Legacy.* New York: Philosophical Library.

James, P. 1998. *The Sunken Kingdom: The Atlantis Mystery Solved.* London: Ramboro Books.

Jaroff, L. 1993. Phony arkaeology. *Time,* July 5, p. 51.

Jochim, M. 1983. Paleolithic cave art in ecological perspective. In *Hunter-Gatherer Economy in Prehistory: A European Perspective*, ed. G. Bailey, pp. 211–219. Cambridge: Cambridge University Press.

Johanson, D., and M. Edey. 1982. *Lucy: The Beginnings of Humankind.* New York: Warner Books.

Johnson, E. B. 1994. Not all tabloids are created equal, but they sure sell. *National Forum* 74(4):26–29.

Jones, D. 1979. *Visions of Time: Experiments in Psychic Archaeology.* Wheaton, Ill.: Theosophical Publishing House.

Jones, G. 1982. Historical evidence for Viking voyages to the New World. In *Vikings in the West*, ed. E. Guralnick, pp. 1–12. Chicago: Archaeological Institute of America.

———. 1986. *The Norse Atlantic Saga.* New York: Oxford University Press.

Jordan, P. 2001. *Neanderthal.* London: Sutton.

Josenhans, H., D. Fedje, R. Pienitz, and J. Southon. 1997. Early humans and rapidly changing Holocene sea levels in the Queen Charlotte Islands–Hectate Strait, British Columbia, Canada. *Science* 277:71–74.

Josselyn, J. 1674. *An Account of Two Voyages to New England Made During the Years 1638, 1663.* 1865 reprint. Boston: W. Veazie.

Kaminer, W. 1999. *Sleeping with Extraterrestrials.* New York: Pantheon.

Kehoe, A. B. 1989. *The Ghost Dance: Ethnohistory and Revitalization.* New York: Holt, Rinehart, and Winston.

———. 2005. *The Kensington Runestone: Approaching a Research Question Holistically.* Long Grove, Ill.: Waveland Press.

Keith, A. 1913. The Piltdown skull and brain cast. *Nature* 92:197–199.

Kemp, B. J. 1991. *Ancient Egypt: Anatomy of a Civilization*. New York: Routledge.

Kennedy, K. A. R. 1975. *Neanderthal Man*. Minneapolis: Burgess Press.

King, M. R., and G. M. Cooper. 2004. *Who Killed King Tut? Using Modern Forensics to Solve a 3,300-Year-Old Mystery*. Buffalo: Prometheus Books.

Koch, D. 2003. Rewriting history with a grand theory. *Skeptical Inquirer* 27(6):57–58.

König, R., J. Moll, and A. Sarma. 1996. The Kassel dowsing test. *Swift* 1(1):3–8.

Kopper, P. 1986. *The Smithsonian Book of North American Indians Before the Coming of the Europeans*. Washington, D.C.: Smithsonian Books.

Kosok, P., and M. Reiche. 1949. Ancient drawings on the desert of Peru. *Archaeology* 2(4):206–215.

Kossy, D. 2001. *Strange Creations: Aberrant Ideas of Human Origins from Ancient Astronauts to Aquatic Apes*. Los Angeles: Feral House.

Krings, M. A., A. Stone, R. W. Schmitz, H. Krainitzki, M. Stoneking, and S. Pääbo. 1997. Neandertal DNA sequences and the origin of modern humans. *Cell* 90(1):19–30.

Kuban, G. 1989a. Retracking those incredible mantracks. *National Center for Science Education Reports* 94(4):13–16.

———. 1989b. Elongate dinosaur tracks. In *Dinosaur Tracks and Traces*, ed. D. D. Gillette and M. G. Lockley, pp. 57–72. New York: Cambridge University Press.

Kuhn, T. 1970. *The Structure of Scientific Revolutions*. Chicago: University of Chicago Press.

Kühne, R. W. 2004. A location for "Atlantis"? *Antiquity* 78(300).

Kusche, L. 1995. *The Bermuda Triangle Mystery Solved*. Buffalo: Prometheus Books.

Kvamme, K. L. 2003. Geophysical surveys as landscape archaeology. *American Antiquity* 68:435–457.

Lafayette wonder, The. 1869. *Syracuse Daily Journal*, Oct. 20. Syracuse, N.Y.

Lamberg-Karlovsky, C. C., and J. A. Sabloff. 1995. *Ancient Civilizations: The Near East and Mesoamerica*. Prospect Heights, Ill.: Waveland Press.

Larson, E. J., and L. Witham. 1997. Scientists are still keeping the faith. *Nature* 386:435–436.

Lee, D. 1965. Appendix on Atlantis. In *Plato*, pp. 146–167. New York: Penguin.

Lefkowitz, M. 1996. *Not Out of Africa*. New York: Basic Books.

LeHaye, T., and J. Morris. 1976. *The Ark on Ararat*. San Diego: Creation Life.

Lehner, M. 1997. *The Complete Pyramids: Solving the Ancient Mysteries*. London: Thames and Hudson.

Lepper, B. T. 1992. Just how holy are the Newark "Holy Stones?" In *Vanishing Heritage: Notes and Queries About the Archaeology and Culture History of Licking County, Ohio*, ed. P. E. Hooge and B. T. Lepper, pp. 58–64. Newark, Ohio: Licking County Archaeology and Landmarks Society.

———. 1995a. Hidden history, hidden agenda. *Skeptic* 4(1):98–100.

———. 1995b. *People of the Mounds: Ohio's Hopewell Culture*. Hopewell, Ohio: Hopewell Culture National Historical Park.

———. 1995c. Tracking Ohio's Great Hopewell Road. *Archaeology* 48(6):52–56.

———. 1998a. Ancient astronomers of the Ohio Valley. *Timeline* 15(1):2–11.

———. 1998b. Great Serpent. *Timeline* 15(5):30–45.

———. 2001. Paleolithic archaeological frauds. *Current Research in the Pleistocene* 18:vii–ix.

———. 2002. *The Newark Earthworks: A Wonder of the Ancient World*. Columbus: Ohio Historical Society.

————. 2005. *Ohio Archaeology: An Illustrated Chronicle of Ohio's Ancient American Indian*. Wilmington, Ohio: Orange Frazer Press.

Lepper, B. T., and J. Gill. 2000. The Newark Holy Stones. *Timeline* 17(3):16–25.

Leroi-Gourhan, A. 1968. The evolution of Paleolithic art. *Scientific American* 209(2):58–74.

Lewis-Williams, J. D., and T. A. Dowson. 1988. The signs of all times. *Current Anthropology* 29(2):201–217.

Lieberman, L., and R. C. Kirk. 1996. The trial is over: Religious voices for evolution and the "fairness" doctrine. *Creation/Evolution* 16(2):1–9.

Lippard, J. 1994. Sun goes down in flames: The Jammal ark hoax. *Skeptic* 2(3):22–33.

Lippert, D. 1997. In front of the mirror: Native Americans and academic archaeology. In *Native Americans and Archaeologists: Stepping Stones to Common Ground*, ed. N. Swindler, K. E. Dongoske, R. Anyon, and A. S. Downer, pp. 120–127. Walnut Creek, Calif.: AltaMira Press.

Long, G. 2004. *The Making of Bigfoot*. Buffalo: Prometheus Books.

Lovgren, S. 2004. Masks, Other Finds Suggest Early Maya Flourished. National Geographic News. http://news.nationalgeographic.com/news/2004/05/0504_040505_mayamasks.html.

Luce, J. V. 1969. *Lost Atlantis: New Light on an Old Legend*. New York: McGraw-Hill.

MacCurdy, G. 1914. The man of Piltdown. *Science* 40:158–160.

MacNeish, R. S. 1967. An interdisciplinary approach to an archaeological problem. In *The Prehistory of the Tehuacan Valley: Volume 1—Environment and Subsistence*, ed. D. Byers, pp. 14–23. Austin: University of Texas Press.

Magnusson, M., and H. Paulsson (trans.). 1965. *The Vinland Sagas*. New York: Penguin.

Malin, M. 1995. The "Face on Mars." http://barsoom.msss.com/education/facepage/face.html.

Manifort Jr., R. C., and M. L. Kwas. 2004. The Bat Creek Stone revisited. *American Antiquity* 69:761–769.

Marden, L. 1986. The first land fall of Columbus. *National Geographic* 170(5):572–577.

Marinatos, S. 1972. Thera: Key to the riddle of Minos. *National Geographic* 141:702–726.

Marshack, A. 1972. *The Roots of Civilization*. New York: McGraw-Hill.

Martin, M. 1983–84. A new controlled dowsing experiment. *Skeptical Inquirer* 8(2):138–142.

Matthews, L. H. 1981a. Piltdown Man: The missing links. *New Scientist* 90:280ff.

————. 1981b. Piltdown Man: The missing links. *New Scientist* 91:26–28.

McCrone, W. C. 1976. Authenticity of medieval document tested by small particle analysis. *Analytical Chemistry* 48(8):676A–679A.

————. 1982. Shroud image is the work of an artist. *Skeptical Inquirer* 6(3):35–36.

————. 1988. The Vinland map. *Analytical Chemistry* 60:1009–1018.

————. 1990. The Shroud of Turin: Blood or artist's pigment? *Accounts of Chemical Research* 23:77–83.

————. 1996. *Judgement Day for the Turin Shroud*. Chelsea, Mich.: McCrone Research Institute.

————. 1997. Letter dated Sept. 10.

————. 2000. The shroud image. *Microscope* 48(2):79–85.

McDougall, I., F. H. Brown, and J. G. Fleagle. 2005. Stratigraphic placement and age of modern humans from Kibish, Ethiopia. *Nature* 433:733–736.

McGhee, R. 1984. Contact between native North Americans and the medieval Norse: A review of the evidence. *American Antiquity* 49:4–26.

———. 2000. A new view of the Norse in the New World. *Discovering Archaeology* 2(4):54–61.

McGovern, T. 1980–81. The Vinland adventure: A North Atlantic perspective. *North American Archaeologist* 2(4):285–308.

———. 1982. The lost Norse colony of Greenland. In *Vikings in the West*, ed. E. Guralnick, pp. 13–23. Chicago: Archaeological Institute of America.

McGowan, C. 1984. *In the Beginning . . . A Scientist Shows Why the Creationists Are Wrong.* Buffalo: Prometheus Books.

McIntosh, G. C. 2000. *The Piri Reis Map of 1513.* Athens: University of Georgia Press.

McIntyre, I. 1975. Mystery of the ancient Nazca lines. *National Geographic* 147(5):716–728.

McKillop, H. 1994. Ancient Maya tree-cropping. *Ancient Mesoamerica* 5:129–140.

McKown, D. B. 1993. *The Mythmakers Magic: Behind the Illusion of "Creation Science."* Amherst, N. Y.: Prometheus Books.

McKusick, M. 1976. Contemporary American folklore about antiquity. *Bulletin of the Philadelphia Anthropological Society* 28:1–23.

———. 1979. Some historical implications of the Norse penny from Maine. *Norwegian Numismatic Journal* 3:20–23.

———. 1982. Psychic archaeology: Theory, method, and mythology. *Journal of Field Archaeology* 9:99–118.

———. 1984. Psychic archaeology from Atlantis to Oz. *Archaeology* Sept./Oct.:48–52.

———. 1991. *The Davenport Conspiracy Revisited.* Ames: Iowa State University Press.

McKusick, M., and E. Shinn. 1981. Bahamian Atlantis reconsidered. *Nature* 287:11–12.

McNaughton, D. 2000. A world in transition: Early cartography of the North Atlantic. In *Vikings: The North Atlantic Saga*, ed. W. W. Fitzhugh and E. I. Ward, pp. 257–269. Washington, D.C.: Smithsonian Institution Press.

Meltzer, D. J. 1993a. Pleistocene peopling of the Americas. *Evolutionary Anthropology*, pp. 157–169.

———. 1993b. *Search for the First Americans.* Smithsonian: Exploring the Ancient World. Washington, D.C.: Smithsonian Books.

———. 1997. Monte Verde and the Pleistocene peopling of the Americas. *Science* 276:754–755.

Menzies, G. 2002. *1421: The Year China Discovered America.* New York: Perennial.

Michigan Historical Museum. 2004. Digging Up Controversy: The Michigan Relics. http://www.sos.state.mi.us/history/michrelics/index.html.

Millar, R. 1972. *The Piltdown Men.* New York: Ballantine Books.

Miller Jr., G. S. 1915. The jaw of Piltdown man. *Smithsonian Miscellaneous Collections* 65:1–31.

Milner, G. R. 2004. *The Moundbuilders: Ancient Peoples of Eastern North America.* London: Thames and Hudson.

Mitchell, J. S. 2002. The truth behind Noah's Flood. *Scientific American Frontiers.* http://www.pbs.org/saf/1207/features/noah.htm.

Montague, A. 1960. Artificial thickening of bone and the Piltdown skull. *Nature* 187:174.

Montgomery, J. 2002. *How to Read Maya Hieroglyphs.* New York: Hippocrene Books.

Mooney, J. 1892–93. *The Ghost-Dance Religion and the Sioux Outbreak of 1890.* 1965 reprint. Chicago: University of Chicago Press.

Moore, R. A. 1983. The impossible voyage of Noah's ark. *Creation/Evolution* XI:1–43.

Morris, H. 1974. *The Troubled Waters of Evolution.* San Diego: Creation Life.

———. 1977. *The Scientific Case for Creation.* San Diego: Creation Life.

———. 1986. The Paluxy River Mystery. *Impact* No. 151. El Cajon, Calif.: Creation Research Institute.

Morris, J. 1980. *Tracking Those Incredible Dinosaurs and the People Who Knew Them.* San Diego: Creation Life.

Mueller, M. 1982. The Shroud of Turin: A critical approach. *Skeptical Inquirer* 6(3):15–34.

Nantambu, Kwame. 1996–97. Egypt and European supremacy. *A Current Bibliography on African Affairs* 28(4):357–379.

NASA. 2001. Unmasking the "Face on Mars." http://science.nasa.gov/headlines/y2001/ast24may_1.htm?list540155.

Nelson, M. R. 2002. The mummy's curse: Historical cohort study. *British Medical Journal* 325:1482–1484.

Neudorfer, G. 1980. *Vermont Stone Chambers: An Inquiry into Their Past.* Montpelier: Vermont Historical Society.

Newport, F. 1997. What if government really listened to the people. The Gallup Organization. Retrieved from the World Wide Web: http://www.gallup.com/poll/fromtheed/ed9710.asp

News. 1912. *Nature* 92:390.

Nickell, J. 1983. The Nazca drawings revisited. *Skeptical Inquirer* 7(3):36–44.

———. 1987. *Inquest on the Shroud of Turin,* 2nd ed. Buffalo: Prometheus Books.

———. 1989. Unshrouding a mystery: Science, pseudoscience and the cloth of Turin. *Skeptical Inquirer* 13(3):296–299.

Nisbet, M. 1999. New poll points to increasing paranormal belief. Retrieved from the World Wide Web: http://www.csicop.org/articles/poll/index.html.

Noël Hume, I. 1974. *Historical Archaeology.* New York: Knopf.

Noorbergen, R. 1982. *Treasures of the Lost Races.* New York: Bobbs-Merrill.

Normile, D. 2001. Japanese fraud highlights media-driven research ethic. *Science* 291:34–35.

———. 2001. Questions arise over second Japanese site. *Science* 294:1634.

Nuland, S. B. 2003. *The Doctors' Plague: Genes, Childbed Fever, and the Strange Story of Ignac Semmelweis.* New York: Norton.

Oakley, K. P. 1976. The Piltdown problem reconsidered. *Antiquity* 50 (March):9–13.

Oakley, K. P., and J. S. Weiner. 1955. Piltdown Man. *American Scientist* 43:573–583.

O'Connor, D. 2003. Origins of the pyramids. In *The Seventy Great Mysteries of Ancient Egypt,* ed. B. Manley, pp. 45–49. London: Thames and Hudson.

Odess, D., S. Loring, and W. W. Fitzhugh. 2000. Skraeling: First peoples of Helluland, Markland, and Vinland. In *Vikings: The North Atlantic Saga,* ed. W. W. Fitzhugh and E. I. Ward, pp. 193–205. Washington, D.C.: Smithsonian Institution Press.

Oestreicher, D. M. 1996. Unraveling the *Walam Olum. Natural History* 105(10):14–21.

O Hehir, B. 1990. *Barry Fell's West Virginia Fraud.* Unpublished manuscript.

Oldest boat of pharaohs found. October 31, 2000. Retrieved from the World Wide Web: http://www.discovery.com/news/briefs/20001031/hi_royalboat.html.

Omohundro, J. T. 1976. Von Däniken's chariots: A primer in the art of crooked science. *Zetetic* 1(1):58–67.

Ortiz de Montellano, B. 1991. Multicultural pseudoscience: Spreading scientific illiteracy among minorities: Part I. *Skeptical Inquirer* 16(1):46–50.

———. 1992. Magic melanin: Spreading scientific illiteracy among minorities: Part II. *Skeptical Inquirer* 16(2):162–166.

Ortiz de Montellano, B., G. Haslip-Viera, and Warren Barbour. 1997a. Robbing Native American cultures: Van Sertima and the Olmecs. *Current Anthropology* 38:419–441.

———. 1997b. They were not here before Columbus: Afrocentric diffusionism in the 1990s. *Ethnohistory* 44:199–234.

Orton, C. 2000. *Sampling in Archaeology.* Cambridge: Cambridge University Press.

Osborn, H. F. 1921. The Dawn Man of Piltdown, Sussex. *Natural History* 21:577–590.

Ovchinnikov, I., A. Götherström, G. Romanova, V. Kharitonov, K. Lidén, and W. Goodwin. 2000. Molecular analysis of Neanderthal DNA from the northern Caucasus. *Nature* 404:490–492.

Paleolithic Man. 1912. *Nature* 92:438.

Paleolithic skull is missing link. 1912. *New York Times,* Dec. 19.

Pauketat, T. R. 1994. *The Ascent of Chiefs: Cahokia and Mississippian Politics in Native America.* Tuscaloosa: University of Alabama Press.

Pauwels, L., and J. Bergier. 1960. *The Morning of the Magicians.* 1964 reprint. New York: Stein and Day.

Pearsall, D. 1992. The origins of plant cultivation in South America. In *The Origins of Agriculture: An International Perspective,* ed. C. W. Cowan and P. J. Watson, pp. 173–205. Washington, D.C.: Smithsonian Institution Press.

Pellegrino, C. 1991. *Unearthing Atlantis: An Archaeological Odyssey.* New York: Random House.

Perez-Accino, J.-R. 2003a. The Great Pyramid. In *The Seventy Great Mysteries of Ancient Egypt,* ed. B. Manley, pp. 61–66. London: Thames and Hudson.

———. 2003b. The multiple pyramids of Snofru. In *The Seventy Great Mysteries of Ancient Egypt,* ed. B. Manley, pp. 57–60. London: Thames and Hudson.

———. 2003c. Were the pyramids built by slaves? In *The Seventy Great Mysteries of Ancient Egypt,* ed. B. Manley, pp. 54–56. London: Thames and Hudson.

Peterson, M. A. 1991. Aliens, ape men, and whacky savages. *Anthropology Today* 7(5):4–7.

Phillipson, D. W. 1993. *African Archaeology,* 2nd ed. Cambridge: Cambridge University Press.

Plait, P. 2002. *Bad Astronomy.* New York: John Wiley.

Poundstone, W. 1999. *Carl Sagan: A Life in the Cosmos.* New York: Henry Holt.

Powell, E. 2004. Theme park of the Gods? *Archaeology* 57(1):62–67.

Powell, J. F., and J. C. Rose. 1999. Report on the osteological assessment of the "Kennewick Man" skeleton. National Park Service. Retrieved from the World Wide Web: http://www.cr.nps.gov/aad/Kennewick/powell_rose.htm.

Pringle, H. 1997. Death in Norse Greenland. *Science* 275:924–926.

Putnam, C. E. 1886. The Davenport Tablets. *Science* 7(157):119–120.

Quinn, D. B. (ed.). 1979. *New American World: A Documentary History of North America to 1612.* New York: Arno Press.

Raloff, J. 1995. Dowsing expectations: New reports reawaken scientific controversy over water witching. *Science News* 148:90–91.

Ramenofsky, A. F. 1987. *Vectors of Death.* Albuquerque: University of New Mexico Press.

Randi, J. 1975. *The Magic of Uri Geller.* New York: Ballantine Books.

———. 1979. A controlled test of dowsing abilities. *Skeptical Inquirer* 4(1):16–20.

————. 1981. Atlantean road: The Bimini beach-rock. *Skeptical Inquirer* 5(3):42–43.

————. 1984. The great $110,000 dowsing challenge. *Skeptical Inquirer* 8(4):329–333.

————. 1993. *The Mask of Nostradamus.* Buffalo: Prometheus Books.

Reiche, M. 1978. *Mystery on the Desert.* Stuttgart: Heinrich Fink.

Rice, P., and A. Paterson. 1985. Cave art and bones: Exploring the interrelationships. *American Anthropologist* 87:94–100.

————. 1986. Validating the cave art-archaeofaunal relationship in Cantabrian Spain. *American Anthropologist* 88:658–667.

Richardson, S. 2000. Vanished Vikings. *Discover* 21(3):64–69.

Richardson, S. C. 1999. *A Study of Student Beliefs in Popular Archaeological Claims.* Southampton, England: University of Southampton.

Roach, J. 1999. Everest climbs to new heights. National Geographic Society. Retrieved from the World Wide Web: http://www.ngnews.com/news/1999/11/111299/everest_7303.asp.

Robertson, M. G. 1974. *Primera Mesa Redonda de Palenque.* Pebble Beach, Calif.: Robert Louis Stevenson School.

Romancito, R. 1993. American Indians and the New Age: Subtle racism at work. *Skeptical Inquirer* 18:97–98.

Rose, C., and G. Wright. 2004. Inscribed matter as an energy-efficient means of communication with an extraterrestrial civilization. *Nature* 431:47–49.

Ross, A., and P. Reynolds. 1978. "Ancient Vermont." *Antiquity* 52:100–107.

Rowe, J. H. 1966. Diffusionism and archaeology. *American Antiquity* 31:334–337.

Ruggles, C. 1996. Stonehenge for the 1990s. *Nature* 381:278–279.

Ruspoli, M. 1986. *The Cave of Lascaux: The Final Photographs.* New York: Abrams.

Russell, M. 2003. *Piltdown Man: The Secret Life of Charles Dawson & the World's Greatest Archaeological Hoax.* Gloucestershire: Tempus.

Russians seek Atlantis off Cornwall. 1997. BBC News. http://news.bbc.co.uk/2/hi/uk_news/43172.stm.

Ryan, W., and W. Pitman. 1998. *Noah's Flood: The New Scientific Discoveries About the Event That Changed History.* New York: Touchstone.

Sabloff, J. 1989. *The Cities of Ancient Mexico: Reconstructing a Lost World.* New York: Thames and Hudson.

————. 1994. *The New Archaeology and the Ancient Maya.* New York: Scientific American Library.

Sagan, C. 1963. Direct contact among galactic civilizations by relativistic interstellar spaceflight. *Planetary Space Science* 11:485–498.

————. 1996. *The Demon-Haunted World: Science as a Candle in the Dark.* New York: Random House.

Sallee, R. 1983. The search for Noah's Ark continues. *Houston Chronicle,* Aug. 20, Section 6:1–2.

Sanford, R., D. Huffer, and N. Huffer. 1995. *Stonewalls and Cellarholes: A Guide for Landowners on Historic Features and Landscapes in Vermont's Forests.* Waterbury, Vt.: Vermont Agency of Natural Resources.

Saunders, J. W., R. D. Mandel, R. T. Saucier, E. T. Allen, C. T. Hallmark, J. K. Johnson, E. H. Jackson, C. M. Allen, G. L. Stringer, D. S. Frink, J. K. Feathers, S. Williams, K. J. Gremillion, M. F. Vidrine, and R. Jones. 1997. A mound complex in Louisiana at 5400–5000 years before the present. *Science* 277:1796–1799.

Saura Ramos, P. A. 1998. *The Cave of Altamira.* New York: Abrams.

Schele, L., and D. Freidel. 1990. *A Forest of Kings.* New York: William Morrow.

Schick Jr., T., and L. Vaughn. 1999. *How to Think About Weird Things: Critical Thinking in the New Age,* 2nd ed. Mountain View, Calif.: Mayfield.

Schiermeier, Q. 2004. Noah's flood. *Nature* 430:718–719.

Schledermann, P. 1981. Eskimo and Viking finds in the High Arctic. *National Geographic* 159(5):575–601.

———. 2000. Ellesmere: Vikings in the far north. In *Vikings: The North Atlantic Saga,* ed. W. W. Fitzhugh and E. I. Ward, pp. 248–256. Washington, D.C.: Smithsonian Institution Press.

Schmidt, K. 1996. Creationists evolve new strategy. *Science* 273:420–422.

Schnabel, J. 1994. *Round in Circles: Poltergeists, Pranksters, and the Secret History of Crop Watchers.* Buffalo: Prometheus Books.

Schneour, E. 1986. Occam's razor. *Skeptical Inquirer* 10(4):310–313.

Scholz, M., L. Bachmann, G. J. Nicholson, J. Bachmann, I. Giddings, B. Rüschoff-Thale, A. Czarnetzki, and C. M. Pusch. 2000. Genomic differentiation of Neanderthals and anatomically modern man allows a fossil DNA–based classification of morphologically indistinguishable hominid bones. *American Journal of Human Genetics* 66:1927–1932.

Schoolcraft, H. R. 1854. *Historical and Statistical Information Regarding the History, Condition, and Prospects of the Indian Tribes of the United States.* Part IV. Philadelphia: Grambo.

Schwartz, S. 1978. *The Secret Vaults of Time: Psychic Archaeology and the Quest for Man's Beginnings.* New York: Grosset and Dunlap.

———. 1983. *The Alexandria Project.* New York: Delacorte Press.

Scott, E. C. 1987. Antievolutionism, scientific creationism, and physical anthropology. *Yearbook of Physical Anthropology* 30:21–39.

Secrets of Lost Empires: Stonehenge (television program). 1997. *Nova.* Boston: WGBH.

Selling it: Monkey business. 2000. *Consumer Reports* 65(9):67.

Severin, T. 1977. The voyages of "Brendan." *National Geographic* 152(6):770–797.

Shafer, H. J. 1997. Research design and sampling technique. In *Field Methods in Archaeology,* ed. T. R. Hester, H. Shafer, and K. L. Feder, pp. 21–40. Mountain View, Calif.: Mayfield Publishing.

Shanks, N. 2004. *God, the Devil, and Darwin.* New York: Oxford University Press.

Shapiro, H. 1974. *Peking Man: The Discovery, Disappearance, and Mystery of a Priceless Scientific Treasure.* New York: Simon and Schuster.

Sharer, R., and W. Ashmore. 2003. *Archaeology: Discovering Our Past.* New York: McGraw-Hill.

Shaw, I. (ed.) 2000. *The Oxford History of Ancient Egypt.* London: Oxford University Press.

Shaw, J. 2003. Who built the pyramids? *Harvard Magazine* July/August: 43–49, 99.

Shermer, M. 1997. *Why People Believe Weird Things.* New York: W. H. Freeman.

Shermer, M., and A. Grobman. 2000. *Denying History: Who Says the Holocaust Never Happened and Why Do They Say It?* Berkeley: University of California Press.

Shorey, P. 1933. *What Plato Said.* Chicago: University of Chicago Press.

Shutler, R., and M. Shutler. 1975. *Oceanic Prehistory.* Menlo Park, Calif.: Cummings.

Silverberg, R. 1989. *The Moundbuilders.* Athens, Ohio: Ohio University Press.

Skelton, R. A., T. Marston, and G. O. Painter. 1995. *The Vinland Map and the Tartar Relation.* New Haven: Yale University Press.

Skidmore, J. 2004. Cival: A Preclassic Maya Site in the News. *MesoWeb.* http://www.mesoweb.com/reports/cival.html#.

Smith, B. D. 1995. *The Emergence of Agriculture.* New York: Scientific American Library.

Smith, G. E. 1927. *Essays on the Evolution of Man.* London: Oxford University Press.

So big: The all time mass market best sellers. 1989. *Publishers Weekly,* May 26:531.

Solheim, W. 1972. An earlier agricultural revolution. *Scientific American* 226(4):34–41.

Spanuth, J. 1979. *Atlantis of the North.* London: Sidgwick and Jackson.

Spence, K. 2003. What is a pyramid for? In *The Seventy Great Mysteries of Ancient Egypt,* ed. B. Manley, pp. 50–53. London: Thames and Hudson.

Spence, L. 1926. *The History of Atlantis.* 1968 reprint. New York: Bell.

Spencer, F. 1984. The Neandertals and their evolutionary significance: A brief history and historical survey. In *The Origins of Modern Humans: A World Survey of the Fossil Evidence,* ed. F. Smith and F. Spencer, pp. 1–50. New York: Alan R. Liss.

———. 1990. *Piltdown: A Scientific Forgery.* Oxford: Oxford University Press.

Spencer, F., and C. Stringer. 1989. Piltdown. In Radiocarbon dates from the Oxford AMS system: Archaeometry Datelist 9, ed. R. E. M. Hedgtes, R. A. Housley, I. A. Law, and C. R. Bronk. *Archaeometry* 31:207–234.

Spennemann, D. 1996. *Current Attitudes of Parks Management and Ecotourism Students II: Popular Opinions About the Past.* Albury, NSW, Australia: Charles Stuart University.

Squier, E. G., and E. H. Davis. 1848. *Ancient Monuments of the Mississippi Valley: Comprising the Results of Extensive Original Surveys and Explorations.* Smithsonian Contributions to Knowledge, Volume 1. New York: AMS Press (reprinted in 1973 for the Peabody Museum of Archaeology and Ethnology, Harvard University).

Stevenson, K. (ed.). 1977. *Proceedings of the 1977 United States Conference of Research on the Shroud of Turin, March 23–24, 1977,* Albuquerque, New Mexico. New York: Holy Shroud Guild, Bronx.

Stevenson, K. E., and G. R. Habermas. 1981a. *Verdict on the Shroud.* Ann Arbor, Mich.: Servant Publications.

———. 1981b. We tested the Shroud. *Catholic Digest,* Nov.:74–78.

Steward, T. D. 1973. *The People of America.* New York: Scribner's.

Stiebing, W. 1984. *Ancient Astronauts, Cosmic Collisions, and Other Popular Theories About Man's Past.* Buffalo: Prometheus Books.

Stokstad, E. 2000. "Pre-Clovis" site fights for recognition. *Science* 288:247.

Stone Giant, The. 1869. *Syracuse Standard,* Nov. 1. Syracuse, N.Y.

Stowe, S. 2001. Archaeological hoax raises query: Why? *New York Times,* March 4, Section 14CN, p. 3.

Strahler, A. N. 1999. *Science and Earth History: The Evolution/Creation Controversy.* Amherst, N. Y.: Prometheus Books.

Stuart, G. 1993. New light on the Olmec. *National Geographic* 184(5):88–115.

Sullivan, W. T. III. 2004. Message in a bottle. *Nature* 431:27–28.

Sutherland, P. D. 2000a. The Norse and Native North Americans. In *Vikings: The North Atlantic Saga,* ed. W. W. Fitzhugh and E. I. Ward, pp. 238–247. Washington, D.C.: Smithsonian Institution Press.

———. 2000b. Scattered signs: The evidence for native/Norse contact in North America. Paper presented at Vikings, The North Atlantic Saga, Washington, D.C.

Swauger, J. L. 1980. Petroglyphs, tar burner rocks, and lye leaching stones. *Pennsylvania Archaeologist* 51(1–2):1–7.

Tarzia, W. 1992. The linguistic behavior of cult archaeologists: Literary approaches to diffusionist texts. Paper delivered at the symposium *Alternative Archaeology: A World of Wonder.* Halifax, Nova Scotia.

Tattersall, I., and J. Schwartz. 2000. *Extinct Humans.* New York: Westview Press.

Taylor, A. E. 1962. *A Commentary on Plato's Timaeus.* Oxford: Clarendon Press.

Taylor, H. 2003. The religious and other beliefs of Americans 2003. *The Harris Poll #11.* http://www.harrisinteractive.com/harris_poll/index.asp?PID=359.

Taylor, P. 1985a. *Young People's Guide to the Bible and the Great Dinosaur Mystery.* Mesa, Ariz.: Films for Christ Association.

———. 1985b. *Notice Regarding the Motion Picture "Footprints in Stone."* Mesa, Ariz.: Films for Christ Association.

Taylor, R. E., and R. Berger. 1980. The date of Noah's Ark. *Antiquity* 44:34–36.

Terrell, J. 1986. *Prehistory in the Pacific Islands.* Cambridge: Cambridge University Press.

This Old Pyramid (television program). 1993. *Nova.* Boston: WGBH.

Thomas, C. 1894. *Report on the Mound Explorations of the Bureau of Ethnology.* Washington, D.C.: BAE (reprinted 1985 by Smithsonian Institution Press).

Thomas, D. H. 1987. The archaeology of Mission Santa Catalina de Guale: Search and discovery. *Anthropological Papers of the American Museum of Natural History* 63(2):47–161.

———. 1999. *Archaeology: Down to Earth,* 2nd ed. New York: Harcourt Brace Jovanovich.

———. 2000. *Skull Wars: Kennewick Man, Archaeology, and the Battle for Native American Identity.* New York: Basic Books.

Tobias, P. V. 1992. Piltdown: An appraisal of the case against Sir Arthur Keith. *Current Anthropology* 33(3):243–260.

Trento, S. 1978. *The Search for Lost America: Mysteries of the Stone Ruins in the United States.* New York: Penguin.

Turner, B. L., and P. Harrison (eds.). 1983. *Pulltrouser Swamp: Ancient Maya Habitat, Agriculture, and Settlement in Northern Belize.* Austin: University of Texas Press.

Turner, C. G. 1987. Telltale teeth. *Natural History,* Jan.:6–10.

van Kampen, H. 1979. The case of the lost panda. *Skeptical Inquirer* 4(1):48–50.

van Leusen, M. 1999. Dowsing and archaeology: Is there something underneath? *Skeptical Inquirer* 23(2):33–41.

Van Sertima, I. 1976. *They Came Before Columbus.* New York: Random House.

Van Tilburg, J. A. 1987. Symbolic archaeology on Easter Island. *Archaeology* 40(2):26–33.

———. 1994. *Easter Island: Archaeology, Ecology, and Culture.* Washington, D.C.: Smithsonian Institution Press.

———. 1995. Moving the Moai: Transporting the megaliths of Easter Island: How did they do it? *Archaeology* 48(1):34–43.

Vaughan, C. 1988. Shroud of Turin is a fake, official confirms. *Science News* 134(15):229.

Vescelius, G. 1956. Excavations at Pattee's Caves. *Bulletin of the Eastern States Archaeological Federation* 15:13–14.

Vespucci, A. 1904. *The Letters of Amerigo Vespucci and Other Documents Illustrative of His Career.* The Hakluyt Society. New York: Burt Franklin.

Vogt, E., and R. Hyman. 1980. *Water Witching U.S.A.* Chicago: University of Chicago Press.

von Däniken, E. 1970. *Chariots of the Gods?* New York: Bantam Books.

———. 1971. *Gods from Outer Space.* New York: Bantam Books.

———. 1973. *Gold of the Gods.* New York: Bantam Books.

———. 1975. *Miracles of the Gods.* New York: Bantam Books.

————. 1982. *Pathways to the Gods*. New York: G. P. Putnam's Sons.

————. 1989. *In Search of the Gods*. New York: Avenel.

————. 1996. *The Eyes of the Sphinx: The Newest Evidence of Extraterrestrial Contact in Ancient Egypt*. New York: Berkley Books.

————. 1997a. *Chariots of the Gods? The Mysteries Continue*. Stamford, Conn.: Capital Cities/ABC Video.

————. 1997b. *The Return of the Gods*. Boston: Element Books.

————. 1998. *Arrival of the Gods: Revealing the Alien Landing Sites of Nazca*. Element Books.

————. 2000. *Odyssey of the Gods: The Alien History of Ancient Greece*. Boston: Element Books.

————. 2002. *The Gods Were Astronauts: Evidence of the True Identities of the Old Gods*. London: Vega Books.

Walker, A., and R. Leakey (eds.). 1993. *The Nariokotome* Homo erectus *Skeleton*. Cambridge, Mass.: Harvard University Press.

Wallace, B. 1982. Viking hoaxes. In *Vikings in the West*, ed. E. Guralnick, pp. 51–76. Chicago: Archaeological Institute of America.

————. 2000. The Viking settlement at L'Anse aux Meadows. In *Vikings: The North Atlantic Saga*, ed. W. W. Fitzhugh and E. I. Ward, pp. 208–215. Washington, D.C.: Smithsonian Institution Press.

Walsh, J. E. 1996. *Unraveling Piltdown: The Science Fraud of the Century and Its Solution*. New York: Random House.

Warner, F. 1981. Stone structures at Gungywamp. *Bulletin of the Archaeological Society of Connecticut* 44:4–19.

Waterston, D. 1913. The Piltdown mandible. *Nature* 92:319.

Weaver, K. 1980. Science seeks to solve the mystery of the Shroud. *National Geographic* 157(4): 730–751.

Webster, D. 2002. *The Fall of the Ancient Maya: Solving the Mystery of the Maya Collapse*. London: Thames and Hudson..

Weidenreich, F. 1943. Piltdown man. *Paleontologica Sinica* 129:273.

Weiner, J. S. 1955. *The Piltdown Forgery*. London: Oxford University Press.

Weir, S. K. 1996. Insight from geometry and physics into the construction of Egyptian Old Kingdom pyramids. *Cambridge Archaeological Journal* 6:150–163.

Wendorf, F., R. Schild, and A. Close. 1982. An ancient harvest on the Nile. *Science 82* 3(9):68–73.

Wernick, R., and the editors of Time-Life Books. 1973. *The Monument Builders*. New York: Time-Life Books.

Weymouth, J. W. 1986. Geophysical methods of archaeological site surveying. In *Advances in Archaeological Method and Theory*, volume 9, ed. M. Schiffer, pp. 311–395. Orlando: Academic Press.

Whitcomb, J. C., and H. Morris. 1961. *The Genesis Flood*. Nutley, N.J.: Presbyterian and Reformed Publishing.

White, R. 1986. *Dark Caves, Bright Visions: Life in Ice Age Europe*. New York: Norton.

White, T. D., and G. Suwa. 1987. Hominid footprints at Laetoli: Facts and interpretations. *American Journal of Physical Anthropology* 72:485–514.

Whittaker, J. C. 1997. Red Power finds creationism. *Skeptical Inquirer* 21(1):47–50.

Wilford, J. N. 2004. The oldest Americans may prove even older. *New York Times*, June 29, Section F, p. 1.

Willey, G., and J. Sabloff. 1993. *A History of American Archaeology*. London: Thames and Hudson.

Williams, S. 1991. *Fantastic Archaeology: The Wild Side of American Prehistory.* Philadelphia: University of Pennsylvania Press.

Wilson, D. 1988. Desert ground drawings in the lower Santa Valley, north coast of Peru. *American Antiquity* 53(4):794–803.

Wilson, I. 1979. *The Shroud of Turin: The Burial Cloth of Jesus Christ?* New York: Image Books.

Woodward, J. 1695. *An Essay Toward a Natural History of the Earth.* London.

Wynn, C. M., and A. W. Wiggins. 2001. *Quantum Leaps in the Wrong Direction.* Washington, D.C.: Joseph Henry Press.

Yokoyama, Y., K. Lambeck, P. De Deckker, P. Johnsston, and L. K. Fifield. 2000. Timing of the last glacial maximum from observed sea-level minima. *Nature* 406:713–716.

Index